THE

Choreography
of Resolution

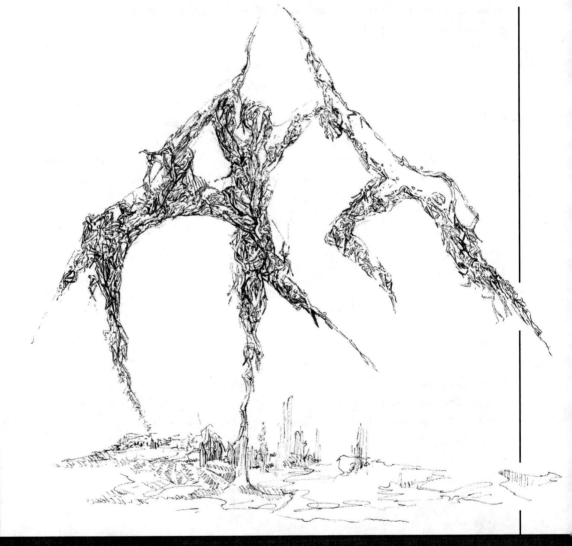

Conflict, Movement, and Neuroscience

Michelle LeBaron, Carrie MacLeod,
and Andrew Floyer Acland, *EDITORS*

AMERICAN BAR ASSOCIATION
Section of
Dispute Resolution

Cover and book design by Monica Alejo/ABA Publishing. Illustration by Roksan Kohen.

Printed in the United States of America.

17 16 15 14 13   5 4 3 2 1

Library of Congress Cataloging-in-Publication Data

ISBN 978-1-62722-137-5

Discounts are available for books ordered in bulk. Special consideration is given to state bars, CLE programs, and other bar-related organizations. Inquire at Book Publishing, ABA Publishing, American Bar Association, 321 N. Clark Street, Chicago, Illinois 60654-7598.

www.ShopABA.org

The stories in this book belong to real people whose lives have been affected and, in some cases, devastated by conflict. This book is dedicated to them. May we find new dances with one another as a human family that do not clash but harmonize across the differences and histories that divide us.

Contents

Acknowledgments

No book is written in solitude, and this one benefited from contributions from an extraordinary group of scholar-practitioners who pushed past the discomfort of reaching beyond their disciplines to explore difficult questions. They all gave enormously of their time and energy, first by coming to the European Graduate School in Switzerland to participate in the Dancing at the Crossroads workshop and then in writing chapters based on their reflections and fields of practice. We thank them for their grace and dedication.

Rick Paszkiet of the American Bar Association and Daniel Bowling of the American Bar Association Publications Committee were quick to grasp the originality of the ideas in the book and to support the book as a useful innovation for the field of conflict resolution. We thank them for their vision, courage, and patience.

Internationally renowned dancer Margie Gillis caught our excitement about the potential of dance-connected work for conflict and inspired us throughout. She came to Switzerland with a myriad of original ideas and worked tirelessly to support everyone in the workshop to explore this new interface. Without her, the project would not have achieved this milestone. Margie is a deeply beloved friend and a dedicated supporter of this work; she has a heart for peace and the passion to inspire others to share it.

We very much appreciate the University of British Columbia Faculty of Law at Allard Hall for their support throughout the project. We especially thank Anna Holeton for invaluable assistance in obtaining the grant that supported the project. Gratitude also goes to Megan Coyle and Andrew Dilts of the Faculty of Law, who worked diligently and long, lending their talents and technical wizardry to the manuscript in ways that saved us hours and helped create a smooth process. Megan, Andrew, and Anna were unfailingly positive and were there when we most needed them. Emily Beausoleil, UBC PhD graduate in political science, and Andrew Dilts offered superb research and editorial assistance. For their hard work, patience, and ingenuity, we thank them very much.

We are also indebted to the European Graduate School. Its visionary leader, Dr. Paolo Knill, and his colleagues Drs. Margo Fuchs Knill and Stephen and Ellen Levine allowed us to use the beautiful Saas-Fee campus for the dance and conflict workshop that formed the basis of this book. Their generosity, creativity, and innovative leadership continue to inspire us and we are endlessly thankful for ongoing opportunities to collaborate.

We also want to acknowledge the support of the staff and newcomers at MOSAIC,[1] the Immigrant Services Society of British Columbia, Kinbrace, and CAUSE Canada who participated in and supported our workshops on arts-based approaches to intercultural conflict.

Thanks to our funders and supporters, the Social Sciences and Humanities Research Council of Canada, the Margie Gillis Dance Foundation, MOSAIC, the University of British

Columbia Hampton Fund, the University of British Columbia Faculty of Law at Allard Hall, and the European Graduate School, for generous assistance throughout the project. Together, they made possible what would otherwise have been impossible.

Our families supplied patience, kindness, and material support throughout the project; for this, our deep thanks.

About the Authors

Andrew Floyer Acland specializes in designing and facilitating dialogue processes in complex, multi-party, multi-issue contexts, often with environmental, social sustainability and scientific dimensions. He has worked nationally and internationally with business, government, non-governmental and civil society organizations on many controversial issues, such as nuclear waste, renewable energy, industrial development in environmentally sensitive areas, climate change, corporate social responsibility and many others. Andrew is regarded as one of the pioneers of ADR and stakeholder dialogue in the United Kingdom, and has written and taught extensively on negotiation, mediation and conflict transformation.

Nadja Alexander is Director of the International Institute of Conflict Engagement and Resolution (IICER) and Professor of Conflict Resolution and Law at Hong Kong Shue Yan University. An accredited mediator in Hong Kong (HKIAC) and Australia, (LEADR) she has extensive experience as a practitioner and consultant in Australia, Asia and Europe. Professor Alexander's areas of practice extend to mediating workplace, intergovernmental, business and cross-cultural disputes. She has extensive experience as a mediation practitioner, trainer, author and consultant internationally. Nadja holds academic qualifications in law and dispute resolution; in addition she has a background in dance, performance and outward bound. She is a multi award-winning teacher known for her creative and experiential style.

Emily Beausoleil is a Lecturer in Politics at Massey University, New Zealand, where she explores the conditions, challenges, and possibilities of democratic engagement in diverse societies with a particular focus on artistic and embodied strategies to facilitate listening in politics. Connecting affect, democratic theory, neuroscience, and the performing arts, Beausoleil's work responds to compelling calls to find new models for coalition and community by asking how we realize these ideals in concrete terms. Her work has received numerous awards and been published in *Constellations* and *Conflict Resolution Quarterly*, as well as various books.

Daniel Bowling is a mediator and mediation trainer in the ADR Program for the US District Court for Northern California in San Francisco. He began mediating in 1986 and has taught mediation throughout the US and internationally. He co-edited/co-authored Bringing Peace into the Room and co-authored The Mediation Process in A Litigator's Guide to Effective Use of ADR in California. Mr. Bowling was Executive Director of the Society of Professionals in Dispute Resolution (SPIDR), guided the merger that created the Association of Conflict Resolution (ACR), and served as ACR's first CEO. He co-founded and served as the president of the first mediation organization in SC. He practiced law and was Public Defender in Charleston, SC and was listed in the National Directory of Criminal Lawyers, as one of the best criminal defense lawyers in the US. He also served on the founding faculty of Antioch

Law School, following his graduation from Harvard Law School. He currently serves as the Chair of the ABA Section of Dispute Resolution Publications Board and as President of the Spirit Rock Insight Meditation Center Board of Directors.

John Burt is co-founder of the non-government support organization, Cambodian Living Arts. Under his leadership, Cambodian Living Arts commissioned and produced the new Cambodian-American rock opera, *Where Elephants Weep*, which had its World Premiere in Phnom Penh, Cambodia in 2008. He currently serves on the CLA board of directors and as chairman of its new initiative, *Season of Cambodia*, a multi-discipline festival of Cambodian arts that premiered New York in the spring of 2013. John Burt has been a theatrical producer and practicing expressive arts therapist and coach for thirty years. He received a Master of Arts in Expressive Art Therapies from Lesley University and is currently a doctoral candidate in Expressive Arts at the European Graduate School, Switzerland. He is president of the Fresh Sound Foundation and is past board member of the Marion Institute, Save the River and the Roberts Foundation.

Geoffrey Corry works as a family mediator with the state run Family Mediation Service in Dublin, Ireland. He has facilitated over 50 political dialogue workshops at the Glencree Centre for Reconciliation, for party activists between the 1994 ceasefires, and for the 2007 agreement within the Irish peace process. He is the founder of three community mediation schemes and has served as a chairperson of the Mediators Institute from 1999-2002. He is a well-known contributor to innovation and reflective practice in peacebuilding and mediation, and has worked in post-conflict zones around the world.

Andrew Dilts has served as a McConnell Research Fellow in Social Innovation, Editor-In-Chief of the UBC Law Review, and has been recognized on multiple occasions for excellence in teaching and leadership. He holds a law degree from the University of British Columbia and a master's degree in management sciences from the University of Waterloo. Leadership, service, inquiry, and compassion are central to his lived philosophy.

Margie Gillis is an internationally acclaimed solo modern dancer/choreographer, Margie Gillis has been creating original works for over forty years. Her repertoire includes more than one hundred dances, her signature solos, as well as duets and group pieces. She also gives lectures on dance and the role of art in society. With her unique approach of "Dancing from the Inside Out", she teaches her art form to professionals and aficionados. She also mentors fellow artists of excellence and new dancers alike. Her numerous awards and distinctions include the Lifetime Artistic Achievement Award from the Governor General's Performing Arts Award Foundation and the Stella Adler Studio of New York first MAD Spirit Award for Exceptional Humanitarian Actions by an Artist. She is Knight of the Ordre national du Québec and Officer of the Order of Canada. (www.margiegillis.org)

Carrie Herbert is the Co-Director of Ragamuffin International Arts Therapy, Training, Supervision and Consultancy Services. Carrie Herbert and Kit Loring founded Ragamuffin in the UK in 1999 and together direct and deliver its International work. Carrie is currently based in Cambodia, where Ragamuffin has been pioneering Creative Arts Therapy training and Services since 2000. As a UK registered Arts Psychotherapist, Trainer, Clinical and

Organizational Supervisor, Carrie has extensive clinical experience in the areas of: mental health, trauma and abuse, post conflict and emergencies, developing therapeutic programs for refugees and asylum seekers, professional development, clinical supervision and de-briefing, organizational supervision and development. Carrie has conducted international consultancy work in India, Singapore, Indonesia, Hong Kong, Peru, Kazakhstan, Mexico and the UK.

Christopher Honeyman is managing partner of Convenor Conflict Management, a consulting firm based in Washington, DC. He is co-editor of The Negotiator's Fieldbook (ABA 2006) and of the four-volume Rethinking Negotiation Teaching series (DRI Press 2009, 2010, 2012, 2013), and author of more than 70 published articles, book chapters and monographs. He has directed a twenty-year series of research-and-development programs in conflict management. He has also served as a consultant to numerous academic and practical conflict resolution programs, and as a mediator, arbitrator or in other neutral capacities in more than 2,000 disputes since the 1970s.

Emmy Humber is employed by the Province of British Columbia where her work focuses on implementing key strategic transformation projects in the health care sector. She works on strategies which leverage evidence-based improvement methodologies to bend the cost curve and ensure efficient and high quality care. Emmy completed a BA in Linguistics with a specialization in Aboriginal Language Revitalization, and is currently completing her Masters in Dispute Resolution at the University of Victoria. Her research interests are centered around how transformative and deliberative principles can strengthen government relationships with citizens.

Charlie Irvine is a Professor at Strathclyde Law School, Glasgow, Scotland, where he teaches a Masters program in Mediation and Conflict Resolution. His research interests include mediation in civil justice and the place of music and the arts in resolving conflict. A former lawyer and professional musician, his mediation practice includes family, employment and commercial disputes. Charlie is also Chairman of the Scottish Mediation Network and Adjunct Professor at John Marshall Law School, Chicago.

Clemens Lang has studied environmental and climate physics at the Universities of Würzburg and Bern/Switzerland. Since 2000, he has worked as a consultant on corporate social responsibility, sustainability management and international development in Switzerland and abroad. Currently he is head of the CSR business unit of Neosys Ltd. consultancy company (www.neosys.ch). After a post diploma study in organizational development and coaching he started to work in these fields, under the label "Phönix" (www.phoenixteam.ch). His intention is to combine business and societal issues with organizational and personal development approaches.

Michelle LeBaron - Professor Michelle LeBaron is a conflict transformation, and scholar/practitioner at the University of British Columbia Faculty of Law. She has done seminal work in many types of conflicts including intercultural, international, family, organizational and commercial. Over the past ten years, she has brought artists and scholars from multiple disciplines into collaboration with community members in exploring how intractable conflict can be addressed using the arts. Professor LeBaron's publications include several monographs and books including Bridging Troubled Waters: Conflict Resolution from the Heart, Bridging Cultural Conflicts: A New Approach for a Changing World and Conflict Across Cultures: A Unique Experience of Bridging Differences.

Carrie MacLeod is the Research Director for the Dancing at the Crossroads conflict transformation and dance project at the University of British Columbia. She has also designed and facilitated arts-based educational programs for refugee communities throughout Vancouver for the past several years. Her continuing involvement in resettlement issues stems from previous peace and reconciliation initiatives in Sierra Leone, West Africa and with social justice projects throughout India and Central America. Carrie MacLeod is on the faculty at the European Graduate School, is the co-founder and Director of ICAP (International Center for Arts in Peacebuilding) Research Institute and facilitates Expressive Arts trainings internationally.

Maureen Maloney is Professor of Public Policy at Simon Fraser University. Previously she was the Lam Chair in Law and Public Policy and Director of the Institute for Dispute Resolution at the University of Victoria. She returned to the University of Victoria following a term as Deputy Minister to the Attorney General (1993 to 2000) and Deputy Attorney General (1997 to 2000) of the Province of British Columbia. Before assuming these positions, Prof. Maloney was the first woman to be a Dean of Law in British Columbia. She has published and lectured extensively. Her current teaching and research interests relate to justice systems, international human rights, and conflict management/resolution. Professor Maloney is and has been actively involved in international governance, dispute resolution and human rights projects in South-East Asia, Iraq, China, Brazil, Guatemala and South Africa. She has also served as a member of the Canadian Human Rights Tribunal based in Ottawa.

Simon J. A. Mason is a senior researcher and head of the Mediation Support Team at the Center for Security Studies (CSS), ETH Zurich. He holds a doctorate in environmental science and is a trained mediator. His main research interests lie in the use of mediation in peace processes and the use of mediation in conflicts with religious and cultural dimensions.

Mark McCrea supervises alternative dispute resolution services for the Workers' Compensation Division of the Minnesota Department of Labor and Industry. He provides dispute resolution services for a number of state and national alternative dispute resolution panels. Over the past three decades, he has mediated or arbitrated hundreds of employment, organizational and public policy conflicts. Mark has conducted advanced mediation, negotiation and conflict management skills courses in several states, as well as Canada. He has assisted numerous organizations and individuals in managing intractable conflict involving workplace practices and dynamics. Mark has a MS in Vocational Rehabilitation Counseling and BS in Urban Studies from Minnesota State University at Mankato.

Susan Allen Nan serves as Associate Professor of Conflict Analysis and Resolution at the School for Conflict Analysis and Resolution at George Mason University, where she directs the Center for Peacemaking Practice. She is currently engaged in peacemaking in the South Caucasus and evaluating conflict resolution programs. Previously, Dr. Nan taught at American University, and practiced conflict resolution at The Carter Center and the Alliance for

Conflict Transformation. She holds an M.S. and Ph.D. from George Mason University in Conflict Analysis and Resolution, and a BA in Political and Social Thought from the University of Virginia. She has authored multiple publications on evaluation, practice, networks, and coordination in conflict resolution, and is the co-editor of Peacemaking: From Practice to Theory.

Tara Ney holds a doctorate in clinical psychology and is a Professor at the University of Victoria. Prior to her faculty appointment at the School of Public Administration, Tara worked in government, non-profit, and private sectors as a clinical and forensic psychologist, and has extensive experience in community development, both locally (restorative justice programming) and internationally (post-conflict zones). Her current research focuses on exploring more inclusive but effective ways to do our policy arguments. She is the author of over 40 journal articles and reports, as well as two edited volumes. In 2008 she was elected to political office as a municipal councillor in Oak Bay.

Rachel Parish is the Artistic Director of Firehouse Creative Productions and works regularly as a freelance theatre director, community organizer, academic author, conference contributor, and artist in residence. Her work has taken place in the UK, Ireland, Beijing, Switzerland, the USA, and Gabon, with support from organizations including Arts Council England and the AHRC. Recent academic posts include lecturing, workshops and performances at University of Georgia, Macon State University, and Georgia College and State University and at the Crossroads Writers Conference at Mercer University. Rachel trained in London at the Royal National Theatre Studio and the Royal Central School of Speech and Drama and in the states at the University of Georgia.

Toni Shapiro-Phim is a cultural anthropologist with specializations in the performing arts, migration and social justice. She received her Ph.D. from Cornell University, writing about the relationship between war, dance and music in Cambodia, and has held research and teaching positions at the University of California, Berkeley, Yale University and, currently, at Bryn Mawr College. Co-editor of *Dance, Human Rights and Social Justice: Dignity in Motion* (2008), her writing has also appeared in *Annihilating Difference: the Anthropology of Genocide* (2002), the *Oxford Encyclopedia of Theatre and Performance* (2001), and other books, magazines and journals. Between 2008 and 2010 she founded and developed a dance archive at the Khmer Arts Theatre in Cambodia. She is Director of Programs at the Philadelphia Folklore Project, overseeing arts and social change initiatives.

Virginie van de Loe - After studying Interior Architecture, Virginie moved abroad with her young family to Australia, Bahrain, Taiwan and the UAE. As an artist and life coach currently working in France, Virginie combines a variety of healing modalities with dance and movement approaches to foster inner and outer health and wellbeing. Her work accents intuition, translating the unseen into visibility where it can be understood and blocks can be shifted.

Foreword

What James Joyce said of Mr. Duffy, that he "lived a short distance from his body," can be said of many of us involved in conflict resolution. We are heads walking around, unfortunately, at great distances from our bodies, especially whenever we are caught in our own conflict or are working with others' conflicts. We have forgotten the ancient teachings of Socrates to Plato that our minds need close connection with our bodies in order to think clearly and especially to understand and generate true dialogue with and among others. The mind-body connection is apparently so obvious that its very obviousness makes us oblivious to it. Unaware that physical and verbal expressions are ancient relatives, located in the same region of our brains, we become lost in the ozone of our minds. We lose all contact and connection with our bodies. As a result, we lose awareness of the simple, relaxing quality of breathing mindfully, of the open, receptive state that arises when we shift our awareness from our constantly perseverating minds to the open clarity of our bodies and allow that connection to quiet our minds and nurture our beings. We have inured ourselves to the devastating consequences of this disconnection, leaving us striving to *do* conflict resolution, rather than relaxing into the natural, fundamental mind-body connection that allows us to *be* conflict resolution.

Participants in the *Dancing at the Crossroads Project*, a four-year exploration of new directions in conflict theory and practice, wrote this ground-breaking, marvelously creative book. Conflict resolution scholars Michelle LeBaron and Carrie MacLeod facilitated the project, along with renowned Canadian dancer and dance instructor—Margie Gillis. The project included a gathering of experienced conflict resolution scholar/practitioners at the European Graduate School in Saas Fee, Switzerland. The project's dual purposes were: (1) to highlight our bodies as paramount in both the origin and transformation of all conflict, and (2) to make the case for including those same bodies in our conflict resolution work, through invigorating conflict theory and practice with a physical vocabulary. The project was premised on the fundamental belief that human *being* needs to be featured in conflict resolution work as consciously as human *doing*.

When I am personally caught in conflict, I feel heavy, weary, and dull, if I pay any attention to my body at all. I am stuck inside my mind, which is either racing between disconnected thoughts and exaggerated fears, down familiar neuronal grooves of negativity and separation, or is numb and lifeless, unable to focus, even though I know that the simplest physical movement, such as taking a walk outdoors, will begin to soothe and focus my mind to deal more skillfully with that conflict. Yet how often do any of us think of this distinction when we find ourselves caught in our own personal conflict or facilitating a tense, seemingly intractable conflict among others? Anywhere we look in our world, we see my individual pattern repeated in our politics, in our business and personal relationships, in our sectarian divisions, and, above all, in our treatment of the Earth.

Consider, for a moment, your own body in conflict. What are your habitual, unconscious patterns? Does your stomach become queasy? Do you clench your hands or your jaw? Do you toss and turn, unable to sleep? Do you eat compulsively or lose your appetite? Also, think of your most recent conflict resolution experience. Recall the tension and stress you felt in your own body exuding from the participants as they entered the room. Recall the manner in which they moved around the room or gathered in safe groupings. Recall their lack of eye contact or acknowledgement of the other side.

I was quite fortunate, as a young public defender in Charleston, South Carolina to have a book on yoga literally fall into my hands as I walked through a bookstore one Saturday morning. While learning yoga from a book was not the best way to begin, it awakened my awareness of my breath and body and began my personal journey of bringing my own mind-body connection into my work. One day in the courtroom, I noticed another attorney stiffly reading his closing argument to a jury, totally disconnected from his body, and I watched the bored and sleepy jury, totally disconnected from what he was saying. That lesson ultimately led me to the discovery that if I listened to witnesses, not just with my mind, but with my body, I could reliably feel or sense when they were lying, almost always about some irrelevant, tangential issue. Nevertheless, like a cat with a mouse, I had them, no matter whether their lie was relevant to the facts of the case. When I challenged their lie, they would immediately get stuck in their heads, conveying their physical discomfort to the jury, opening the door for me to convince the jury that all their testimony was false.

Until the *Dancing at the Crossroads Project* and this book you are holding, the literature and pedagogy of the conflict resolution field have generally ignored my yoga-derived courtroom learning. They have failed to focus on the nexus of conflict and the bodies that contain conflict to inform and deepen our understanding or generate new questions and insights about conflict resolution, despite the fact that research has demonstrated that a high percentage of our communication is nonverbal. While many of us are already deeply aware of the positive shifts that occur in our overall sense of inner health and wellbeing after some physical movement or exertion, we likely struggle or fail to bring that same awareness into our work, often because we simply do not know the distinctions necessary to bridge this gap. This courageous, revolutionary book invigorates this fundamental but oft-forgotten connection between mind and body. Reading it will provide new insights that will reshape your approach to conflict.

Far too many conflict resolvers are stuck in being technicians, following a one-size fits all, repetitive approach no matter the conflict. For example, the legal Alternative Dispute Resolution field has virtually been stripped of its intellectual capital and is dominated more and more by retired judges who conduct stripped-down, no-joint-session, traditional labor-style bargaining—essentially settlement conferences masquerading as mediations. The contributors to this book repeatedly remind us that such cookie-cutter approaches are rigid and fragile, lacking in imagination, curiosity, relationality, flexibility, creativity, or emotionality. Learning to focus on our bodies, on the other hand, calls forth these qualities in us as well as in the conflicting parties, enabling us to meet the greatest challenge in conflict resolution—seeing the essence or heart of the stuck places in and between the minds of the parties. Seeing this essence can only be achieved through ways of knowing that include the whole in addition to the parts, through developing capacities and pathways that rely on intuition as well as cognition and, therefore, must rely on a connected mind and body.

One of the contributors quotes a beautiful, poetic description of a conflict resolver's work, written by T.S. Eliot in his immortal *Four Quartets*:

> "At the still point of the turning world. Neither flesh nor fleshless;
> Neither from nor towards; at the still point, there the dance is,
> But neither arrest nor movement, And do not call it fixity,
> Where past and future are gathered. Neither movement from nor towards,
> Neither ascent nor decline. Except for the point, the still point,
> There would be no dance, and there is only the dance.
> I can only say, there we have been: but I cannot say where.
> And I cannot say, how long, for that is to place it in time."

A young Russian woman helped me begin to understand the meaning of these words and the importance of developing awareness of my own mind-body connection, as well as that of the conflicting parties, while I was engaged in a conflict facilitation/team-building session years ago for the international staff of a large health and wellness retreat in the Berkshire Mountains of Massachusetts. The young woman remained silent and withdrawn from everyone else in her department, refusing to participate in any of the exercises or to speak a word during the first four days of the facilitation. I never observed her interacting with anyone, including during the breaks or at the beginning and ending of each day. The night before the final day, some of the staff played music while the guests at the retreat center enjoyed a festive dance. I watched as the young woman played a huge bongo drum with great skill and complete abandon, totally opposite from her withdrawn presence in the facilitation.

Without a clue as to what I was going to do or say to her, the next morning I walked to the corner of the room where she was sitting, wrapped in a blanket, almost hidden from view. Watching my own breathing and recognizing I could not "think" my way through how to work skillfully with her, I softly invited her to talk with me about her experience of working at the retreat center and in this department. She remained silent, buried in her blanket. I surprised myself by describing watching her playing the drums the night before, how beautiful it was to see the skill and enthusiasm with which she played and drove the rhythm of the music. I asked, "Do you endeavor to bring that same skill and enthusiasm to your work on this team?" More silence, but she did allow the blanket to slide off her. I waited, completely stumped.

Then I heard and felt the music from the previous night begin to run through my body. Without taking my eyes off her slumped form, I said to the group, "Please begin to drum together with your hands on the tables or your chairs or however you wish." They began, stiffly and uncertainly, but they soon found a rhythm that slowly built momentum. As I felt her body begin to respond, I waited until I sensed the drumming more fully engage her. Then, I reached out my hand and said, "Will you move around the room with me to greet your team-mates?" When she finally took my hand, I gently pulled her up, and we began to move slowly around the room to the rhythm of the now thunderous drumming, but her eyes remained downcast. She made no eye contact with me or any of her teammates, until I said, "I sense a great deal of love and appreciation for you and your courage in the room right now. Would you like to look around and see it?" When she did, she saw many broad smiles and tears, yet I noticed she only quickly glanced up and looked indirectly at a few of her teammates.

After we completed our impromptu dance around the room, I waved the drumming to a stop and asked her to look at me. She met my gaze with great difficulty through her own tears. I asked her to tell me the story that was running in her head at that moment. She replied, "In my native Russia, we never, ever made eye contact with anyone. We never knew who would report us to the KGB for any reason, or no reason, so wherever we went, we never met any-one's gaze."

I allowed the power of her story and what it revealed about her inability to connect with her teammates to penetrate the room before I spoke quietly. "Well, you are no longer in Rus-sia, dear friend. You are safe now. Please look at your teammates and experience for yourself, your new freedom and safety." She did, and a shy smile spread across her face. There were no dry eyes, including my own.

This memory arose as I read the varied descriptions by the scholar/practitioner partic-ipants in the *Dancing at the Crossroads Project* of their experiences with spontaneous and improvised movement, followed by periods of critical reflection that opened pathways of mindful awareness to their own deeply ingrained, habitual thought patterns, biases, and feelings. As you read, you may have similar memories of instances in which you intuitively allowed your body-mind connection to guide you, rather than staying locked in your head. The contributors explain how focusing on physical movement pushed to the surface flawed assumptions underlying their habitual thought patterns, thereby creating dissonance and new openings to experience a more balanced, body-mind integrated self-understanding, both personally and professionally—just as physical movement did for the young Russian woman, her teammates, and me.

The contributors describe how physical movement enables more holistic access to decod-ing emotions that are invariably physiological, containing both mental and embodied nuances. The body and mind are in constant conversation. Emotions begin with physical sensations, and the neurological processing that gives meaning to these sensations is unconscious. The contributors remind us that when energy is blocked by conflict arising from aggression and fear, the related (and mostly unconscious) muscle contractions actually block further move-ment of energy, constrict breathing, and limit our capacity to think clearly. We thus lose our ability to find and stand on our own ground as we struggle with anticipatory, fear-driven reac-tions that blunt our awareness of whatever is being revealed in the moment. No wonder con-flict resolution is so challenging! The contributors also underscore the importance of, and present many creative ideas for, including physical movement in conflict resolution training. If, like me, you were trained to mediate from the neck up, you, too, will appreciate the ways in which the contributors illuminate the physical, emotional, and relational intelligences that relate to conflict resolution

This book takes us on an exploratory journey through the body as the fundamental place to which we must return with full awareness amidst the shifting ground and upheaval of conflict, reminding us how a closed body leads inevitably to a closed mind. The contributors advise us that the forward-thinking necessary for conflicting parties to escape conflict, and for conflict resolvers to support their process, calls on all these intelligences, not just mental, to cross the bridge from the known to the unknown, from the surface to the hidden. One contributor acquaints us with Albert Einstein's observation: "The intuitive mind is a sacred gift, while the rational mind is only its faithful servant . . . but our society honors the servant and has forgotten the gift."

Like most of you, I was originally taught mediation from an interest-based perspective and that work definitely marked a major, positive shift in conflict resolution theory. Several contributors teach us that interest-based negotiation is grounded firmly in our highly individualistic Western culture. It often lacks cultural and ethical sensitivity and places no emphasis on intelligences other than mental. It also fails to emphasize essential conflict resolution capacities, such as creativity, perspective-taking, and fluidity—capacities, that the contributors inform us, are particularly critical to effective conflict resolution, citing contemporary research on negotiation and peace-building training and processes.

Interest-based approaches arose prior to the recent breakthroughs in neuroscience that are revealing the profound effects of neuroplasticity, mirror neurons, and related brain capacities on conflict resolution. This book explores these exciting neuroscience breakthroughs from multiple perspectives. One contributor points out that neuroscience is now proving what dancers have known for centuries—that emotion, cognition, memory, communication, and empathy are all embodied processes. Our bodies contain the answers to the ever-changing unconscious factors that shape what we believe we know, as well as our perceptions and behavior. We all have well-worn neuronal pathways—literally grooves in our brains—that are created from habitual behavior and thinking, such as resistance to the very idea that movement can contribute to conflict resolution.

The new research is disproving our previous notions that the brain stays the way it was formed in our childhood. In fact, we can grow and develop our brain, especially if we consciously choose to train ourselves in new ways of acting, thinking, and perceiving that include the mind-body connection. For example, researchers taught a simple mindfulness meditation technique to individuals who agreed to practice for 15 minutes a day for eight weeks. When measured against a control group, the pre-frontal cortex—the youngest region of our brain that controls higher functions such as empathy, relationality, and insight—had grown significantly in each meditator. The contributors point to research that is also demonstrating that linear and verbal approaches to conflict address only one-half of any conflict story. Physical movement can and does activate and shift our concepts, emotions, and perspectives. As we open to the power of a more balanced, embodied approach, we gain access to many skills and deeper wisdom than is contained in interest-based thinking.

This book will begin a journey for you, a journey toward reshaping and developing your own mind, as well as your approach to conflict resolution. That journey will lead you inevitably to Eliot's "still point," the vast territory of the paradox where what we know is what we do not know and where we are is where we are not, to the place where we begin to understand the spaces in Japanese gardens described eloquently by one contributor as "the pauses between things that allow each to stand out from the mass" that "are not empty but lend feeling and texture to the whole as well as enjoying their own kind of fullness." These are the "spaces" arising through the mind-body connection, in which the source and meaning of conflict moves from the known to the unknown that is deeply, intuitively grasped, the "spaces" we experience when practicing mindfulness in which our empathy and relationship with ourselves and others expand and develop, the "spaces" in which authentic, lasting conflict resolution and transformation occur. I commend this ground-breaking work to you, confident that by opening yourself to the creativity it contains, you will traverse a great deal of territory on your journey to *being* a conflict resolver.

G. Daniel Bowling, JD
Program Staff Attorney and Mediator
Alternative Dispute Resolution Program
U.S. District Court for Northern California
San Francisco, California

Introduction

Let's Dance

MICHELLE LeBARON AND CARRIE MacLEOD

> *In the myth of Persephone and Demeter, the arts are stolen from the earth while Persephone is in the underworld. The dark frozenness that ensues is thawed only by Persephone's return, bringing dance and stories back to life. Like the land, people in the winter of conflict can be renewed by the creative arts.*

Without physical bodies, there would be no conflict or resolution. There would be no human-created art or imaginative expression as a catalyst for resilience and reconciliation. This book aims to do two things: to foreground the body as essential in the genesis and the transformation of conflict and to make a case for the inclusion of an aesthetic, physical vocabulary in conflict theory and practice. To this end, a wide range of talented authors powerfully highlight dance and movement as key approaches through which the mysteries of conflict can be understood, engaged, shifted, and transformed in new ways.

The authors are a part of the Dancing at the Crossroads project, a four-year exploration of new directions in conflict theory and practice. Many people have asked how we came to examine these directions. The answer is simple: through partnership and dialogue with many inspiring people whose work shows the way to resilience in the face of wrongs that cannot be righted, to hope in the midst of unspeakable pain, and to mobility in frozen or rigid contexts. After decades as scholar-practitioners seeking to help others navigate challenging conflicts, we searched for what was missing from our canon and why conflicts had not more successfully shifted in local and global settings. We came to believe that, in worldview and intractable conflicts, cognitive methods drawing on so-called rational processes have limited applicability unless they are accompanied by tools that access the less-obvious aspects of conflict as it lives in our bodies and affects our ability to relate with others. As we reflected further on our work in dialogue and mediation, we realized that a much wider range of conflicts could benefit from embodied praxis.

Much is not understood about even personal conflict behavior. People surprise themselves with the intensity of responses or when something they had not anticipated would deeply affect them carries a strong charge. Dance, the art in which the body is the canvas, offers ways to access and affect perception as well foster shifts and transformations in conflict. As documented in this book, developments in neuroscience reinforce the legitimacy of this research direction, as do conflict intervention field reports from around the globe.

Some of the initial questions that guided this inquiry include the following:

- How does conflict live in our bodies and how can we embody it safely? What does this show us about how we can experience conflict safely in ways that promote health?
- How do we embody our roles as catalysts for change in a healthy way? What can this teach about how we can support others in conflict?
- How do we embody strong emotions? How is flexibility a part of our practice and experience? How can body-based praxis open awareness, generating new nuances and suppleness in expressiveness and communication?
- How can bodies, central to relationality, teach us about ways to move through conflict?
- How do body-based methods implicate creativity and satisfy our thirst for beauty in the midst of destructive conflict?

Why Is the Physical Realm So Important?

Conflict arises over ideas and ideologies, how we share and occupy territory, how we manage our needs in the face of competing values, and over identities—how who we are is acknowledged, respected, and accommodated physically and relationally. Even the ways we speak about handling conflict are in corporeal terms, such as

- I sidestepped that issue.
- I am not going there!
- I'm feeling off center.
- This is weighing me down.
- Can we create a little more room for discussion?
- Let's take a breather and come back to this later; you've given me nowhere to go on this issue.
- The solution is just beyond our grasp.
- I wish he'd just get out of the way and let me do it.

Turning points and shifts in conflict are also replete with physical references, such as

- I felt a load off my shoulders when he said that.
- Something inside me dissolved when the papers were signed.
- I could breathe more easily once we had talked about it.

Yet even as these descriptions of conflict are everywhere in colloquial and artistic expression, they have been largely missing from scholarly and practice literature about conflict analysis and transformation. Intellectual biases overwhelmingly prevail in our work, evincing a preoccupation with logic, reason-based problem solving, and reductionist analysis. While these approaches are important, they are not sufficient for addressing real human problems in all their complexity, cultural diversity, intractability, and unpredictability. Thus seasoned scholars Bernie Mayer and John Paul Lederach (and others) have alternately called for awareness of human systems and emotional intelligence in *Beyond Neutrality*[1] and for the use of embodied arts in *The Moral Imagination: The Art and Soul of Building Peace.*[2]

Human *being* needs to be on the map of conflict resolution as much as human *doing*. Conflict scholars have done a good job of coming up with processes, actions, and strategies but a less less-thorough job of shining light on states of being, diverse ways of perceiving, dynamics of identity, and the making of meanings—all related to embodied functioning. Along with colleagues in many parts of the academy, we have ignored the body, treating it as more of an also-ran than as the integral and essential sensing wonder that it is.

This neglect of the body as a site and resource in conflict is changing through two important influences. First, artists are increasingly involved in peace-building processes around the world,[3] and arts-based methodologies are being developed and applied in multiple contexts.[4] Second, recent neuroscientific findings revealing the astonishing effects of neuroplasticity, mirror neurons, and other phenomena have aroused new interest in approaches to conflict that tap these capacities. Arts-based tools are very promising in this regard because they engage our whole beings in powerful ways. Led by artists and scientists, conflict scholars and practitioners are focusing more and more on physical resources for everything from professional development to conflict intervention and peace building.

In the aftermath of violent or intractable conflicts, physical and emotional safety must be secured and the imagination reignited. For this, the body is key. Physical safety can be arranged through peace agreements and careful boundary observance and enforcement. But the need to reknit communities and restore a sense of individual and collective coherence can be met only with tools expansive enough to hold contradiction and complexity. Dance and other physically based arts-inspired forms summon the necessary imagination for finding ways forward. This has been known and practiced around the world in cultures since time immemorial as rituals of dance, song, and feasting mark transitions through conflict.

Physical bodies are sites of trauma, anchors of pain, and divisions between one group and another. They are also vessels of possibility, vehicles of change, and places of healing. When we bring a difficult conflict into our awareness, our tissues feel heavy with its emotional weight and our minds can fall into well-traveled pathways of negativity. Yet bodies are also the places where we experience the relief of letting go, the relaxation of resolution, and the glimmer of possible futures into which we may walk. Experienced mediators and facilitators report that their bodies gift them with cues about how processes are working, when shifts or breaks are needed, and when something is out of alignment in a process.

Intercultural aspects of conflict also point unfailingly to the body as a common denominator. When language and translation barely stretch across divides, when people share a common language and look beyond words for cues, and when people realize the limitations of words in communicating symbolic aspects of conflict, including identity and meaning—the body is put into use. Nonverbal communication is well known to be powerful in ways that spoken or written language is not. Indeed, Mark Patrick Hederman has written that before he learned to read or write, he was more in touch with imaginative possibilities arising from nature through physical exploration and adventuring.[5] Because people in conflict need to find ways to access imagination and intuition and to move beyond the frames that keep them stuck and confined, physical attunement and engagement are essential.

The work of Dancing at the Crossroads was born from these realizations. We sought ways that body awareness could help people in conflict and help those who assist them access and make generative choices about largely unconscious identity influences, essential narratives, cultural norms, and worldviews that shape perceptions and escalate conflict. We invited a group of experienced scholar-practitioners to a beautiful, purpose-built location at the European Graduate School in Saas-Fee, Switzerland, to explore movement and dialogue as they inform conflict dynamics and interventions. The results are chronicled in this book by those who attended the weeklong session. At the session and afterward, we explored a number of questions, first about movement and then dialogue, including:

- What insights and understandings of conflict complexities can be generated from body-based modes of inquiry?
- How can a body-based vocabulary and sensibility inform intervention and transformation of actual conflicts?
- What practical and theoretical links exist among dance, movement, and conflict transformation, and what research questions arise from these links?
- How might interdisciplinary research on dance and kinesthetic learning inform effective strategies for pedagogy and practice in intercultural conflict transformation?

In short, we wondered what dance and dancers could teach mediators and dialogue facilitators that they did not know through other avenues of learning. We also wondered what alchemy could arise in communing with one another and a master dancer: would old questions reform themselves or would new insights be revealed?

What Did We Learn?

First, we realized that those traditionally outside the field of conflict intervention have a lot to share with those who work within it. Artists, community and international development workers, and others who respond to calls to forgotten or conflict-ravaged places know well the terrain of the body. They know it as the site of deprivation, contest, and battleground; they have also witnessed it as a place of healing. These people have given their time and energy to help, often at great personal cost. Their work has taken them to postgenocide Cambodia and war-ravaged Sierra Leone; it has also taken them to boardrooms where corporate and labor leaders, community members, and activists work with the help of conflict practitioners to handle difficult situations closer to home. We asked how work with a physical focus could be helpful in communities whose members seek outside accompaniment. This book contains the answers, inklings, and emerging possibilities that arose.

Second, we observed that scholar-practitioners in a range of practice contexts—from family to commercial to environmental/public policy to international—have the body in common. All of us are blessed with unique, finely tuned physical instruments that guide, nudge, filter, and shape our attempts at resolution. All of us have physical habits—ways of paying attention—that influence points of view, perceptions of self and others, and reflexive responses to conflict dynamics. These are shaped by personal and cultural experiences; they are part of the reason different people can see the same scene and experience it differently. Physical habits of attention, when understood by counterparts in conflict, can help normalize differences, taking the focus away from enmities and putting it on the unchecked perceptions and assumptions that can divide people and escalate conflict. In the workshops, we found physical commonalities and shared experiences that gave us a way to exchange ideas and discover resonances far below the skin—deeper than if we had convened a series of "from the neck up" panel discussions.

Third, we saw that learning via the body yielded new vocabularies, awareness of nuances, and unnoticed intersections within and between us. Conflict at its most difficult is a series of knots, a complex interweaving of bodies needing locations that can support their weight in healthy and respectful ways. As Fisher, Ury, and Patton encouraged generating integrative interpersonal possibilities years ago in *Getting to Yes*,[6] now body-based work turns our attention to worlds within and how developing new neural pathways and physical habits can be useful in shifting conflicts. Engaging paradox and enacting transformative possibilities are both assisted by body-based work. Psychotherapists have long known this; when a therapist's clients are unable to make a desired change in their lives, the therapist may encourage them to "act as if" they can do it. When we act in new ways, feelings can shift and possibilities emerge, facilitating the formation of new habits.

Here is a simple way to explore this. Choose someone about whom you may have had negative thoughts or judgments. Start treating the person with curiosity and kindness. Approach this individual with an open body posture, inviting his or her perspectives and ideas. Share your own. This is not to suggest acting in insincere or disingenuous ways; rather, let the thoughts or judgments that were present hang suspended for a time. After a short while, check in again with your feelings. To the extent you have been successful in following the tributaries of curiosity to the stream of another's life, you will almost certainly have experienced—and expressed—empathy. It is much harder to maintain a negative emotional stance toward another once empathy is present. At the least, your perception of the person may have become more complex and more attuned to his or her humanity—and your own.

This has obvious implications for conflict. Emotions are impulses to act, but they may be braided with feelings of anger, revenge, or frustration. Engaging in actions that express curiosity and openness can create a range of possible responses to these impulses. No one feels secure all the time. We sometimes act from small, frightened, or threatened places. As we cultivate awareness from the inside out, the body becomes a reliable way to access feelings of security. Paradoxically, feelings of safety arise from our willingness to be vulnerable and to act from what we *do not* know about another. This is hugely important in conflict and goes directly against legal training that advises avoiding asking a question to which the answer is not already known.

Finally, we learned that dance and movement are very promising tools for intercultural conflict transformation. Veronique Schoeffel, one of the Saas-Fee participants and a leader in international development work from Switzerland, observes that "intercultural communication is about learning to dance to new music, or learning a new dance. Each of the dancers takes his or her dance for granted, knows it so well, and does it automatically. When we dance that well- known dance, the steps flow from the music, no conscious thinking act is needed, just the wonderful feeling in the body, the heart, and the soul. This experience of ease and of perfection gets disturbed if the partner dances a different dance."

Partners always do different dances, often without awareness of the extent of value and worldview diversity that separates them from others. As Schoeffel reminds us, intercultural conflict transformation requires that we try "to understand each other across cultures, taking into account the visible and invisible parts of the cultures, as well as the context, the situation, and the personality of all actors."

The Dancing at the Crossroads gathering gave us a safe space to experience the power of enacting positive change in physical and other ways. So many rich ideas emerged connecting practice theory and research that we committed to produce this book to share, broaden, and expand the conversation. Together, the authors show us how we can literally find new stances in conflicts as parties or third parties. Their work is critical yet inspiring; provocative and prospective. It covers multiple worlds, as is evident from the overview below.

Overview

The perspectives and themes explored in this book illuminate how modes of engagement in conflict are filtered through complex systems of somatically braided cognition. As the authors transit the boundaries of diverse cultures and disciplines, they acknowledge and examine the body as a key resource for conflict transformation. They consider the role of movement in conflict dynamics, expose the limitations of omitting the body from understandings of conflict, explore ethical dimensions of embodied approaches, and propose key strategies for conflict intervention. The authors explore the genesis, generation, and escalation of conflict through physical geographies, asking who we are and how our physical selves participate as blocks and resources in shifting what is stuck. These interdisciplinary accounts capture the centrality of corporeal sensibilities in addressing challenging relational dynamics. The contributors have woven theory and practice from multiple disciplines, yielding a range of strategies to handle conflict as it gets "under our skin." Theoretical frameworks, case studies, and hands-on interventions are offered for those working and living in complex conflict terrains.

This work invigorates connections between somatic knowledge and conflict transformation. Taken together, the chapters address this question: How does the nexus of movement and conflict inform and deepen understandings and generate new questions and insights about conflict geography and the choreography of resolution? Juxtaposing autobiographical and practice experiences with diverse cultural, historical, and social realities highlights both challenges and breakthroughs in this burgeoning area.

The chapters also reveal the importance of symbolic and nonliteral language in expressing and addressing the true toll of trauma on an individual or a community. Metaphor and ritual situate and reposition possibilities for exchange beyond fixed grids of bounded relations. Because webs of conflict always exist within multiple meaning and identity structures, they cannot be easily reduced to a formulaic analysis. Rather, many subaltern identities determine the routes conflict takes, and reconciliation may be contingent on how plural identities are accounted for and acknowledged. Perceptual, imaginative, and symbolic frameworks are needed for conveying intricacies of meaning and identity in conflict, and these necessarily rely on the body.

Several of the chapters refer specifically to the Dancing at the Crossroads studio sessions with the Canadian dancer Margie Gillis. These sessions sparked conversations about the body as a reflexive instrument in conflict and negotiation. Without even realizing it, we approach problems by repositioning ourselves or unconsciously shifting our stance in relation to a particular dynamic. We may clench our hands, tighten our jaws, or feel uneasiness in our stomachs as people "overstep our boundaries." Since our bodies are vehicles for enactment and change and receptacles of lived experience, our somatic sensibilities attune us to feeling "off center" or "off-kilter." One of the realizations arising from Saas-Fee was the pervasive influence of movement metaphors related to conflict.

Readers are accompanied down this less-trodden path with provocative insights that arose from the authors' experiences at Saas-Fee of inhabiting the "space in between" and exploring shared spaces that were *not* contested. The authors examine how physical vocabularies offer currencies of meaning when verbal communication breaks down, generating real and imagined gaps.

In the first section of the book, Why Dance?, the authors examine neuroscientific and other theoretical underpinnings for this work. Beausoleil distills recent work on the brain with a bearing on conflict and movement. Ney and Humber explore the powerful roles of metaphors in shaping our perceptions, expectations, and behaviors in conflict, concluding that dance has heuristic, aesthetic, empirical, and moral value as a metaphor for conflict. Gillis shares contextual information and examples from her work and how it came to be related to conflict.

In the second section, How Dance?, the authors make links between field experiences and choreography. MacLeod describes work with former child combatants in Sierra Leone, and Honeyman and Parish analyze movement in theater-based work, connecting it to the broader theme. Acland reflects on the Saas-Fee workshop and the changes it brought to his thinking about dialogue and mediation.

The third section, Teaching Dance, features contributions by Alexander and LeBaron and Irvine about how movement and other experiential methodologies can be integrated into curriculum design and teaching and learning. Mason, Nan, and van de Loe examine how this work relates to helping conflict workers deepen intuition. Gillis then provides a series of somatic approaches that can be applied in a range of conflict dynamics. Following this, the section titled Dance and Resilience: Select International Examples includes chapters by

Maloney and Corry on work from Ireland and by Shapiro-Phim, Burt and Dilts, and Herbert on Cambodian applications. Organizational contexts are considered in Organizations: Finding Coherence, where McCrea and Lang offer examples of how movement-based work informs their thinking about practice. Finally, a conclusion by Carrie MacLeod presents concluding thoughts, ethical questions, and avenues for future inquiry.

Throughout the book, we emphasize the accessibility and practicality of embodied interventions. Conflict will always be understood through traces of bodily inscriptions, and dance offers a nuanced approach for the translation of these markings. We hope that the book is a trail of bread crumbs that will lead conflict scholars and practitioners to build on it by examining physical and aesthetic dimensions of conflict with curiosity while acknowledging and respecting the potency of the body as a partner in change.

Why Dance?

*T*his first section introduces the three themes that dominate the whole book and provide its raison d'être. It also sets the scene for subsequent sections in which the authors explore these themes from their respective areas of experience and expertise.

So why dance? For Emily Beausoleil, a Canadian political scientist and dancer with a particular interest in neuroscience, the answer is obvious: by leaving our bodies out of the dispute-resolution equation, we also neglect a whole realm of experience and perception, without which our understanding of what is going on whenever people meet can never be complete. "We are what we eat," according to the old adage; we are also how we move, says Emily, and we should never forget it.

Meanwhile, Tara Ney, a psychologist and practitioner in dispute resolution, and Emmy Humber, a conflict-resolution scholar, look at how our understandings of conflict depend heavily on the metaphors we use to describe it. They examine why dance is a particularly vivid metaphor for the ebbs and flows of conflict, not least because it is a metaphor that we can actually climb into and *do*. So, they argue, by leaving words behind, if only for a moment, and physically becoming in dance the emotions and attitudes we feel, we can add a whole new dimension to our understanding of what we and others experience in conflict.

Are they really suggesting that middle-aged diplomats and expensively accoutred lawyers exchange their dark suits for dancing shoes? Perhaps. But if renowned Canadian dancer Margie Gillis's contribution is anything to go by, they could do a lot worse. Margie talks us through the logic of the work she has done teaching movement to people working with conflict in many contexts around the world. Suddenly the idea of bringing her immense knowledge and experience into new professional fields seems no more preposterous than the idea that the language of movement should be excluded from the process of helping people to handle conflict.

Indeed, if the experience of the participants in the Dancing at the Crossroads workshop in Switzerland that provoked these essays is anything to go by, we can look forward—if not to dancing lawyers and diplomats—at least to lawyers and diplomats who have an understanding of why movement matters in their repertoire of skills.

1

Dance and Neuroscience
Implications for Conflict Transformation
EMILY BEAUSOLEIL

Introduction

This chapter makes the case for dance as an aid and resource for legal practitioners in the field of conflict transformation—certainly in their training and in contributing to the personal resilience that enables them to work in situations of sustained stress and complexity and perhaps also, in the right circumstances, in their practice. Other chapters make the same case from a range of viewpoints and mainly on the basis of personal experience. This one underpins such experience by exploring the implications of compelling discoveries within the field of neuroscience.

In recent years neuroscientists have begun to explore the physiology of emotion, communication, receptivity, attunement, empathy, and creative thinking, all of which are important in transforming conflict. In a relatively short time, they have demonstrated the intimate and complex relationship between cognitive and "embodied" states, expanding vocabularies for understanding how movement affects patterns of thought and interaction—the patterns that either make change possible or render it impossible. This work reveals new possibilities for the value of dance in training third parties and in helping to shape the nature of interventions.

I will begin by describing what I see as the key neuroscientific insights that support the idea that movement and dance may offer creative tools for use in our approaches to conflict. I will then set out the implications for practitioners, how the experience of dance in particular can provide additional insights into human interactions in conflict, and how it can sharpen practitioners' responses to the situations and behaviors they confront. The arguments here are all based on evidence drawn from specialist journals and publications. To avoid ending every sentence with a footnote I have referenced only the work directly quoted.

Embodiment: The Mind in the Body, the Body in the Mind

Neuroscientists are not alone in their interest in "embodied knowledge," the notion that knowledge is embodied beyond the limitations of traditional mind-body dualism; this has become a key focus in a range of fields from linguistics and artificial intelligence to psychology, memory research, and political theory. Neuroscience has, however, made a singular contribution in revealing just how truly connected the body and mind are. A whole psychosomatic network of neurological, hormonal, gastrointestinal, and immune systems keep the entire body in constant communication, a network so well integrated that the neuroscientist Candace Pert has referred to it as the mobile mind.[1] Cognition, attitudes, and emotions are all grounded in the physical cues from this elaborate body-wide network. The following five aspects of human functioning are particularly significant and relevant here.

1. Perception

Our perceptions of ourselves and of the world emerge through this complex system, connecting bodily sensations and feelings with conscious awareness. Three forms of perception have been studied by neuroscientists for their dynamics and interrelations. They are

- interoception—the body's sense of internal stimuli such as pain, temperature, itch, and touch;
- exteroception—the body's sense of the external world; and
- proprioception—the body's sense of its own location in space.

Together, these forms of perception provide the brain with a complete map of the body, from which we construct a sense of ourselves and of our ability to be effective in the world. As Robert Baruch Bush and Joseph Folger famously say in *The Promise of Mediation*[2], the combination of self-awareness and a sense of personal agency are essential aspects of empowerment, which in turn is recognized as an important element in transforming conflict. So a process such as dance, which cultivates our physical awareness of the links between our internal and external worlds, will therefore hone the skills and heighten the capacities we need to be effective parties or to intervene effectively as third-party mediators or facilitators.

2. Memory and Receptivity

Our perceptions are not solely determined by immediate physical cues in our surroundings; our bodies also store and process memories, which shape and limit our perceptions and responses. Memories from childhood, and those with a more recent emotional charge, are carried in the body even though they may be outside conscious recollection, having bypassed the hippocampus (which deals with conscious memory) for processing by the amygdala (which shapes and processes our emotions). These unconscious impressions shape how and when our sympathetic and parasympathetic systems are activated, and these in turn regulate whether we feel calmness, tension, openness, fear, or a host of other emotions that may affect our responses in situations of conflict. Such bodily memories can create structural changes in the limbic and autonomic nervous systems in the right brain that affect what we perceive, how we interpret what we perceive, and how we behave in response to those interpretations.

The influence of memories does not stop there. Under stress, threat, or shame, our autonomic nervous systems are unconsciously triggered to increase the body's production of adrenaline and cortisol, which then limit blood flow to the frontal lobes of the brain. When this happens, our thinking is affected: it becomes more difficult to be receptive to unfamiliar people or ideas or to respond other than habitually to conflict because our brain is, *quite literally*, short-circuited. Conversely, when we feel safe, the autonomic nervous system supports the state of open receptiveness that has been found essential for learning and integrating new information, as well as preventing retraumatization when we remember past experiences.

The implications of this last point for practicing mediators, for example, are clear: people need to be in this state of open receptiveness when reviewing the past; otherwise they are liable to be sucked back into it with all the negative consequences that may result. If a mediator pursues negotiation and compromise without an awareness of the physical dynamics that may block or severely truncate progress, the likelihood is that his or her clients will feel more threatened and the conflict may escalate. Increasing awareness of unconscious physical regulation systems is thus essential for third parties and arguably useful for the conflicting parties as part of their preparation for processes such as mediation, which may involve revisiting events that carry unpleasant memories.

3. Emotional State: How We Feel

The body shapes our perceptions and responses in other ways in addition to the role it plays in emotional processing. Physical sensation is not only the expression but also the *source* of emotion: the limbic system interprets sensory cues, assigning them affective significance when the anterior insular and anterior cingulate cortices are activated. These brain components form an emotional network, with the insular cortex generating conscious feelings and the cingulate cortex stimulating how we behave in response to them. In turn, the limbic system connects with the cortical process areas that determine the relevance of this information.

What this means is that emotions are physiologically based, arising from the brain's subjective interpretation of "somatic markers" such as hormonal levels, blood flow, digestive activity, neurotransmitters, and other dimensions of the metabolism. As a result of complex neural interactions, the brain assigns meaning to the physical sensations we experience. Indeed, even before the brain has assigned meaning, we understand sensations such as chest tightness, agitation, shivering, trembling, increased blood flow, nausea, or energy moving through the body as emotional responses even before we identify the feelings that caused them. The body and brain are in constant conversation—each system producing, in the words of neuroscientist Candace Pert, "a specific tone, humming a signature tune, rising and falling, waxing and waning, binding and unbinding, and if we could hear this body music with our ears, then the sum of these sounds would be the music that we call the emotion."[3] In summary, emotions begin with bodily sensations, and the neurological processing that gives these sensations meanings for us occurs beneath the level of consciousness.

Just as our emotions are based on bodily sensations, so too can subtle changes in our physical state incite profound changes in our emotions. For instance, someone who takes the sort of physical posture that we associate with fear, anger, or sadness will have measurably higher levels of these emotions. A person slouching is likely to show less confidence, feel less pride when praised, and give up more quickly when trying to solve a problem than someone who stands upright. Similarly, our body postures and facial expressions affect how we feel. For instance, someone gripping a pen between his or her teeth is more likely to feel happy than a person gripping one between the lips, because the first engages the musculature of a smile and the second that of a frown. Botox, meanwhile, which reduces facial mobility, has been shown to dampen experiences of intense emotions.

There are profound implications in the realization that physical sensations and slight changes to stance, gesture, or movement can affect the emotional state of people in conflict. One implication, for example, is that interventions designed around changing physical states, such as asking people to stand up and move around or even to take a walk, are more likely to be effective than attempting to shift people's emotions through a purely verbal exploration of what is causing them. This possibility is even more compelling when we understand that the early stages of emotional processing sidestep the conscious mind altogether and thus are not amenable to conscious verbal approaches drawing on reason. Learning about emotions and the physical processes associated with them will help practitioners and parties alike be better able to manage and respond to the emotions that arise in conflict.

4. Cognition

The physical body does not merely store and process perception, emotion, and memory; it is also the site of cognitive functioning. Posture and gestures influence decision making, movement patterns reliably predict how people approach making decisions—and so serve as indicators of outcomes of decision-making processes. This is similar to the way we use gestures to help us to retrieve words, convey ideas, and even solve problems: we are noticeably less capable of tasks like these when our physical movements are inhibited. The way we move shapes and even limits how we think, because our perceptions, feelings, and even our ability to understand language are grounded in the sensorimotor systems we use to interact with the world. Therefore, the subtlest of shifts in our posture, movement, or gestures may shift our thought processes and facilitate our insight, thereby increasing our ability to solve problems or make decisions. As we learn more about how gesture, posture, and cognition interact, we will likely also learn more about using different types of movement when we intervene in conflict, or at least learn how to combine types of movement with the reason and talk that we currently use when trying to shift attitudes and behaviors.

Physical activity in general has been shown to improve brain functioning and facilitate learning by stimulating the growth and repair of neurons and intersynaptic connections. Moving regularly improves our mood, energy level, motivation, and capacity to focus, and such changes happen relatively quickly—several days or weeks of activity can yield substantial results. Cognitive processes change in the course of movement, and movement itself has been shown to enhance overall cognitive capacity. Heightened body awareness develops a sense of agency, which has both physical and cognitive effects: the mobile person feels more able to do a wider range of things. For people in conflict, the effect of increased mobility may be to make accessible a broader range of possible behaviors to address the issues they face.

5. Communication

A final aspect of research into the mind-body connection that holds promise for conflict transformation is the relation between physical movement and communication. A substantial portion of our communication is achieved nonverbally, and physical and verbal expression are ancient relatives, located in the same region of the brain. Broca's area in the right hemisphere of the brain is activated during both speech production and expressive movement. In fact, the brain's pathways for speech seem to be overlaid on the areas that do sensorimotor work, suggesting that the neural processes for verbal language are relatively recent specializations, with movement a form of pre-linguistic communication. Movement is more than an alternative and instinctual mode of expression; for some forms of communication, and in some situations, it may be more effective than verbal language. When the language center of the brain is temporarily deactivated, individuals often exhibit savant-like mental capacities, including improved artistic, mathematic, and proofreading abilities. If movement is the historical precedent to speech and continues to play such a significant role in present day communications, it is arguable that movement may have a role in conflict transformation in ways we have yet to explore.

Emotionally charged conflicts involve our whole bodies, whether through our physical responses or the filtering of events through the memories we store. Given that these processes occur largely beneath the level of consciousness, the body may be a key ally in increasing our awareness of new possibilities. Likewise, if physical posture, gesture, and movement are integral to cognitive functioning, problem solving, attention, and emotional states, then the body must be a rich resource on which to call when progress through conflict becomes difficult. Given that movement is intimately linked to communication and language, nonverbal processes may offer a means to reach new understandings when verbal communication cannot.

The Plastic Brain

This line of inquiry hinges, of course, on the notion that it is actually possible to change the patterns of thought, action, and relationship that are essential to conflict transformation. Fortunately neuroscience is revealing that the brain is much more malleable than originally thought; the discovery of "neuroplasticity" offers new hope, for example, for conditions previously thought to be permanent, such as obsessive-compulsive disorder, phantom-limb syndrome, stroke, depression, and cerebral palsy. The basic law of neuroplasticity is, in the words of some poetically inclined neuroscientists, that "neurons that fire together, wire together, and those that fire apart, wire apart," implying that the brain is akin to other muscles of the body, constantly rewiring itself in response to external influences.[4] These changes can occur relatively quickly. We are not infinitely malleable: the very flexibility of neural wiring creates pathways in the brain that, when reinforced over time, become neural "superhighways" that make the roads less traveled difficult to access. But there is great practical hope for the field of conflict transformation in the idea that we can identify how to access and engage entrenched patterns of thought and behavior and effectively "rewire" patterns we previously thought unalterable.

In the pressure and threat of conflict, we not only fall back on familiar patterns of thought, reasoning, and behavior but also have greater difficulty in perceiving alternatives. We may, as the mediator Alan Tidwell has said, "through [our] own training, become blind to alternatives … [relying instead on cognitive pathways that have] become so habituated to one set of behaviors that no others seem possible."[5] We get "locked in" to perceptions, behaviors, and dynamics, despite their limitations and the likelihood that they will create impasses. Yet the same plasticity that enabled the formation of those patterns also offers the possibility of change.

In the following sections, we look at three ways in which movement and dance can be used to unlock aspects of our functioning that will help us resolve and transform conflict. First, we consider dance as a means of bringing more than just our minds and words to the conflict arena; next, we look at dance as a means of developing much greater degrees of empathy with others, and particularly with those we find challenging; and finally, we see dance as a means of bringing both halves of the brain to bear on conflict problems. None of this suggests, I should add, that I expect dance *per se* to be used anytime soon in many of the situations where it would in theory be most effective; the challenge is to find a means to translate the lessons and benefits of dance to contexts where dance itself is unlikely.

Embodied Awareness: Bringing Our Bodies to the Table

The starting point here is that dance can help us develop our own neuroplasticity, which, at its simplest, will heighten our capacity for proprioception, interoception, and exteroception. Linked as these three capacities are to self-perception and agency, increased neuroplasticity will expand our self-awareness and ability to create change in the contexts where change is needed.

Enhancing physical awareness through dance can also facilitate greater understanding of the often unconscious physical sensations and processes that inform emotions, perceptions, and behaviors. With its unique emphasis on creativity, nuance, and intention, dance combines affective and expressive elements in a process that expands awareness: it can express the aspects of experience, belief, and emotion that we hold most dear yet sometimes find hardest to communicate. Working at the largely unconscious level, dance can potentially reveal dimensions of identity, experience, and value that often remain elusive when confined to verbal, linear discourse. Similarly it can offer a window into others' bodily cues, displaying subtle mental or emotional shifts related to opportunities or obstacles. It can also heighten the cultural fluency so valued by cross-cultural conflict scholars and practitioners, potentially helping to prevent many of the "missed signals" and misunderstandings that can fuel conflict.

Because dance engages the physiological processes associated with emotion, belief, and experience, it is also a way into diffuse aspects of conflict, such as identity, meaning making, and perception. It can bring affective dimensions underlying perceptions to consciousness opening new possibilities for change. By engaging emotions as they emerge through the subtle and often unconscious sensory cues of the body, practitioners can enhance their somatic and kinetic awareness and benefit from the sense of agency this yields.

This is something that dance therapists have explored and from which they have been able to demonstrate significant positive outcomes. The therapist Kalila Homann, for example, confirms that "[m]oving actively, with full effort, can allow strong feelings, such as anger, rage, or joy, to be more consciously experienced and expressed, making them more available for verbal processing."[6] As physical sensations, emotions, and memories are activated and expressed, people find the language also to express previously inaccessible or inexpressible memories or experiences, which can then be consciously integrated into their personal stories. Sometimes simply doing a body scan—going through the body and "listening" to what each part has to "say"—can release traumatic memories and the physical pain associated with them.

Practice in movement can also enhance openness to others, given that when we are physically in a state of openness, we are better able to hear and integrate new information. Because dance focuses attention on internal and external physical sensations, it has positive effects on the neurophysiological regulation systems that enable receptiveness, both enhancing a feeling of relaxation and safety and providing a way to rework habitual responses. Music can be used in concert with dance to affect the autonomic nervous system that regulates emotions, with pulse rate, skin response, and blood pressure changing as the body matches tempo. Some conflict practitioners have already used music to transform negative emotions, such as unacknowledged shame and anxiety, into more positive and potentially creative emotions. It seems likely that combining music with dance, in appropriate situations, could offer similarly potent results.

As mentioned earlier, we know that creative movement—especially complex physical movements requiring high coordination—can enhance cognitive capacities such as problem solving and decision making. It is therefore hardly surprising that dance, one of the most complex physical activities, has particular potential to improve brain functioning and facilitate shifts in affective states important to transforming conflict. Dance is adaptable, accessible, and powerful in elevating mood, energy levels, and motivation; its results are faster and have fewer side effects than medication.

The actual physical nature of dance contributes to its ability to shift us beyond the familiar. It jolts our perceptions, physically shakes us up, and, as important, because when we dance we resonate with others physically and emotionally, it creates new bridges of connection. As Michelle LeBaron and Venashri Pillay say in *Conflict across Cultures*, dance "open[s] hearts and bring[s] people together" and is able to "[shift] the way we have organized our thinking and our perception of others."[7] Following from this, dance provides us with a way to explore, metaphorically or literally, physical space, awareness of positions, contested territory, and perhaps even cultural differences affecting understandings of personal space. Koshland and Wittaker, among others, have shown that dance enables children from diverse cultural backgrounds to work through conflict together.[8] It seems possible that adults, too, in appropriate situations, could gain something from such experience.

Embodied Empathy: Sensing the Actions, Intentions, and Feelings of Others

A second major intersection between dance and conflict informed by neuroscience is the study of empathy. The ability to read and imitate the actions of others appears at birth in the mirroring gaze between parent and infant and subsequently plays a crucial role in the development of language and behavior. This capacity for empathy is central to what Frith and Frith call "the social brain."[9]

We achieve empathic understanding of others primarily through physical cues: the subtlest changes in posture, muscles, movements, and gestures inform our perceptions of others' emotional states even when we cannot read their facial expressions. In fact, there is some evidence that we pay more attention to bodily cues than to facial expressions, perhaps in part because the physical dimensions of empathy can be easily observed. Studies have shown that we become "entrained," or synchronized, when we interact, mimicking one another's gestures, posture, speech patterns, and facial expressions.[10] Besides inciting similar bodily states in the observer, mirroring others' postures also improves accuracy in reading their emotions. But it does not stop there: watching another person being touched can produce a similar emotional state in the observer. Research has shown that thinking of an elderly person or a slow animal results in the thinker moving more slowly; exposure to happy or angry facial expressions has resulted in research subjects drinking significantly more or less. Our ability to *feel* with others seems intimately connected to our ability to *move* with others, and our bodies, in turn, move in response to such feelings.

This innate capacity to sense and match the actions, intentions, and states of others is explained by the presence of "mirror neurons." Giacomo Rizzolatti and his team first discovered a cluster of neurons in the premotor cortex in monkeys that were active both when observing and performing a similar action.[11] Sparked by this discovery, Marco Iacobini found that the human capacity to imitate is impaired when the Broca's area of the brain, associated with language and communication, is disrupted. It seems that humans, too, possess a comparable network of mirror neurons for perceiving and imitating the actions of others.[12] When we observe, imagine, or plan actions, the same motor neurons and muscle groups become activated as when the action is being performed. In fact, it is only the suppression of a motor command that distinguishes these conceptual processes from the actual ones. The connections among imagination, observation, and action are so strong that it can potentially take as long to imagine walking somewhere as actually walking—and even longer when one imagines carrying a heavy object, breathing more rapidly, and running!

This ability to understand and imitate the actions of others is directly connected to kinesthetic empathy, also called embodied identification. The firing of identical motor neurons when observing others gives us what is effectively a firsthand experience from which to understand and empathize with them. It turns out that neurons respond to context, demonstrating that our brains track the inner states of those whose actions are being observed. Because mirror neuron impulses are interpreted by the same limbic system that processes our physical sensations as emotions, we are able to understand and feel the intentions and emotions of others. Therefore, when witnessing pain or fear in others, for example, the area of the brain associated with painful emotions is activated in the observer. Likewise, when people watch others move, or move together, their brains are essentially practicing ways of relating to one another and sharing embodied neural information. In one striking example of this, when caregivers intentionally mirrored the actions of autistic children, the children demonstrated more-socialized behavior and engaged in more-reciprocal play. This suggests that mirroring is integral to empathy.

Vittorio Gallese and others argue that mirror neurons provide the neurophysiological foundation for empathy, bonding, and human interaction: we are neurologically wired for mutual understanding and feeling, and this human capacity to imitate, learn, and connect with others arises from and through the body.[13] While more work needs to be done to refine understandings of this phenomenon, a growing convergence of scientific opinion supports the theory.

Dance as Embodied Empathy: Implications for Conflict Practitioners

We have seen how embodied practices can help cultivate empathy and awareness of emotional states, memories, and agency—both our own and others'—because of the way they trigger mirror neurons. Dance, as one of the most synchronized activities people perform, is particularly well suited to this purpose. In fact, the AVPR1a gene, which has been associated with both dancing and social bonding, may indicate that dancing and social bonding have a common genetic origin.

This should not be surprising. Techniques such as embodied attunement, echoing, mirroring, and rhythmic synchrony have been used by dance and movement therapists for decades to help people connect. Likewise, taking on another person's stance or gestures can increase our knowledge and understanding of that person: it is a shortcut to empathy. Actions such as this stimulate the limbic system, which in turn improves our ability to read facial expressions and to better appreciate how others are feeling.

Learning a specific dance also creates neurological connections between dancers. We perceive movement differently, depending on our previous experience. The more familiar we are with the movement we observe, the more our motor-neuron system is activated. The more familiar we are with any action, the stronger the internal stimulation; more regions of our brain that concern episodic memory light up with activity. ("Expert" brains—or those of people who have previous knowledge of the movements they observe—also respond in the ventromedial frontal cortex, the area activated in emotion processing, social judgment, and the regulation of social behavior.) But it is not just our familiarity with the movement we observe that stimulates our brains: the movement carries with it a whole world of meaning and associated value systems. When we learn dance movements with other people, we are not only learning a different way of relating and communicating but also developing a shared framework of meaning and values that underpins the mutual understanding that comes with moving together.

What is even more encouraging is how quickly such bonds can form. Cross, Hamilton, and Grafton have demonstrated that complex motor resonance can be developed for a new movement after only five weeks.[14] This has practical implications for conflict resolution. As we learn new ways of moving, we simultaneously rewire our brains to establish shared conceptual, emotional, and experiential ground. Like mirroring, sharing such experiences can help foster empathy and open up new ways of relating. Dance, which, as Steven Brown and Lawrence Parsons argue in *The Neuroscience of Dance*, "demands a type of interpersonal coordination in space and time that is almost nonexistent in other social contexts," would, in the appropriate circumstances, offer opportunities for interaction that would quickly and deeply forge unexpected bonds and establish shared understanding.[15] Even in situations where dance as such is clearly never going to happen, building shared experiences through other forms of creative movement would allow participants to discover connections and establish commonalities, which would in turn foster receptive and empathetic listening and a sense of shared ownership of a conflict.

Conflict scholars, such as Bush and Folger in *The Promise of Mediation*[16] and Kenneth Cloke in *Mediating Dangerously*[17], have argued that receptivity, empathy, and responsiveness are vital in transforming conflict. In addition, (re)discovering connections with others can help transform the very terms of and possibilities for conflict. The tendency as conflict unfolds is, as Lee Ross argues, for communication to "narrow and coarsen"—communication channels are shut down, and information that contradicts positions and perspectives about the other party and the issues tends to be ignored or devalued, decreasing listening.[18] Engaging the whole body can counteract these tendencies, and the right kind of shared movement can reveal surprising resonances and connections, build capacities for meaningful relationships, and establish the necessary ground for constructive resolution or transformation.

Right-and-Left-Brain Integration

The differences between left- and right-brain functioning are probably the aspects of neuroscience most familiar to non-specialists in the subject, and many practitioners in the conflict world have long been familiar with the basics, even if they are less familiar with the underlying science and evidence or unsure how to take advantage of the information in practice.

While conventional approaches to conflict often engage the left brain by focusing on linear, verbal, and conscious processes, the right brain is where relationships live and is essential to interpersonal communication and interaction. Many of the right brain's processes occur beneath the level of consciousness, as it interprets bodily signals and filters experience through body-based memories and meaning systems. The right brain determines the emotional tones of interactions and the associated resonances and degrees of attachment. Considerable neurological research has linked the right brain to autobiographical memory, perception of one's body, self-awareness, and identification with and empathy for others.

The right brain works holistically, through whole-body sensation, emotion, image, and metaphor, perceiving a world of interconnections and creative possibilities. It apprehends nuance and complex contingencies and fosters presence that leaves us open to the unfamiliar and unexpected. Improvisation and associated new thoughts and behaviors are governed by the right brain, and the right hemisphere is also where the present moment lives; after experiencing a massive left hemisphere stroke, the neuroanatomist Jill Bolte Taylor was amazed by the euphoric sense of being dominated, even for only a few hours, by the right hemisphere. Between moments of left-brain lucidity that insisted, in its analytical and rational way, that there was a problem to solve, Taylor found herself completely immersed in the sensory experience of the present moment. She was unable to distinguish between where her own body stopped and the rest of the world began, seeing only interconnection and expansiveness in what she calls a state of "nirvana."[19] By contrast, the left brain perceives absolutes: something *is* true or correct; the world simply *is* this way. In seeking control and certainty, the left brain can arguably contribute to the escalation of conflict.

Scholars inspired by neuroscientific findings have promoted mindfulness practices to quiet the constant chatter of the left brain and activate the parasympathetic nervous system that reduces stress and increases calmness and happiness. The quality of presence associated with the right brain also spawns innovation and expression. Neuroscientists and jazz musicians Charles Limb and Allen Braun write that the region of the brain that controls self-expression becomes activated in improvisation and the region that controls self-scrutiny switches off. Creativity seems to require dissociation in the frontal lobe with its control functions so that people are willing to make mistakes, risk the unfamiliar, and explore generative impulses.[20] The significance for conflict resolution is that entrenched patterns for thought and action, particularly in response to threat, are obstacles to the discovery of possible ways forward.

Dancing with the Whole Brain: Implications for Conflict Resolution

As we have seen, dance engages right-brain processes and states via nonverbal, visual, spatial, expressive, emotional, embodied, and metaphoric modalities, so it offers direct access to implicit processing, emotional states, and creative thinking. These right-brain engagements cultivate experiences in which parties are primed to see connections and nuances that the left brain would not—a generous and curious state that moves through connection rather than distinction, perceiving collaborative, open-ended, and spacious contexts for innovation rather than zero-sum or bartering frames. This is what Johan Galtung means when he writes that "life unites what concepts and dualisms keep apart. And art, like peace, has to overcome false dichotomies by speaking both to the heart and to the brain, to the compassion of the heart and the constructions of the brain."[21] Creative inquiry that engages the right brain through imagery, metaphor, emotion, and the body thus allows the mind to relax so that new information can be synthesized, insights can emerge, and new patterns and interconnections can arise.

Dance facilitates heightened perception by focusing observers and dancers on the present moment. Even in watching dance, the novelty of movement stimulates awareness. It can seam together past and present understandings, transcending whatever habits of memory or perception normally limit the individual's response. Creative movement that at any moment can, as Ivar Hagendoorn puts it in *The Dancing Brain*, "stop, expand, contract, or continue in any other direction" elicits "an agility of perception equal to the agility of the dancer."[22] As a result of attending to the novelty of a dance, observers are acutely present, unaware of other stimuli and thoughts. In summary, both observing and participating in movement quiet the left brain and its tendencies to self-scrutiny, absolutes, and divisions. In its place, the expressive, creative, and holistic dimensions of the right brain are given free rein, allowing the unexpected, unfamiliar, and unknown to emerge and be perceived in new and creative ways.

When creative movement elicits imagination, the hold of habitual patterns and perceptions is loosened and parties can begin to experiment with "rechoreographing" in conceptual, emotional, and behavioral terms. In this way, the tendency described by Dennis Sandole of old patterns of behavior remaining robust as "a response to yesterday's [behavior] by the adversary" is superseded by possibilities for change.[23]

Conclusion

Neuroscience is proving what dancers have known for years—that emotion, cognition, memory, communication, and empathy are all embodied processes. The body holds the key to shifting unconscious factors that shape perception and behavior into conscious, flexible ones. In this way, physical movement can lead to conceptual, emotional, and interpersonal shifts. Research shows that linear and verbal approaches to conflict speak to only one half of a conflict story, overlooking an entire hemisphere that holds vast potential for cultivating the very conditions of receptiveness and creative thinking that resolving and transforming conflict require. As we acknowledge the centrality of the body to conflict, dance, the "most highly complex and codified of kinesthetic practices," according to the anthropologist Jane Desmond, presents a key context through which to critically engage the dimensions of conflict that are most elusive to conventional approaches.[24]

Little wonder, then, that dance is being explored as a training tool for third parties and, in some situations, as an actual tool for addressing conflict. In south central Los Angeles, Northern Ireland, Bosnia and Herzegovina, and South Africa, for example, dance has been used to galvanize marginalized communities, to help assert agency and dignity, and to foster communication in seemingly insurmountable conflicts.[25] At the present time, dance is most commonly found in grassroots, communal contexts rather than being accepted into the canon of traditional Western ways of handling conflict. This is not surprising—it is hard to imagine middle-aged attorneys or insurance adjusters shedding their suits in favor of leotards—but the objections go much deeper than the sartorial. Since Descartes, Western thought has discounted, dismissed, and overridden the very body that dance brings to the fore, despite its being, as neuroscience is revealing, a potent vehicle for thought, communication, and action.

The challenge is to find ways that enable conflict practitioners to take more account of the body's importance and, consequently, through greater awareness of the role movement plays, to make better use of its resources. Dance practice is one of these ways, and there must surely be others that can be used in contexts where dance, as currently and conventionally understood, is unlikely to be an option.

Dance as Metaphor

The Metaphor of Dance and Peace Building
TARA NEY AND EMMY HUMBER

"The shape of our futures may depend on the metaphors we now choose to guide us."[1]
Daniel Rigney

Introduction

This chapter explores ways that the metaphor of dance can contribute to our current understandings of conflict theory. Over the past fifty years, numerous conflict theories have been developed in Western academic thought, extending also to negotiation and peace-building practices.[2] Since about 1980, a surge of rationalistic decision-making models have arisen from Fisher and Ury's *Getting to Yes*[3] and the Harvard Negotiation Project. These first-generation approaches, also called "interest based," give disputing parties an opportunity to participate in the decisions that affect their lives and offer a constructive alternative to adversarial modes of engagement. Interest-based models have had a vast impact on Western practices of responding to disputes in business,[4] organizations,[5] criminal and civil law,[6] public policy,[7] urban planning,[8] and international relations.[9]

Critiques have emerged about the underlying assumptions and resulting practices of first-generation approaches. Steeped in the values and principles of Enlightenment thinking, interest-based work is firmly oriented to the grander project of individualism. The critiques include concerns about ethical incoherence, cultural insensitivity, and a lack of emphasis on relationality, emotionality, physicality, and tacit experiences. In addition, essential capacities such as creativity, perspective taking, and fluidity are typically not incorporated into interest-based modes of engagement.[10] Significantly, contemporary research on negotiation and peace-building training suggests that these capacities in particular are critical to effective conflict processing.[11]

In response to these critiques, Folger and Bush and others[12] have advocated for more-transformative approaches to conflict resolution. Like Mary Parker Follett before them, they suggest approaches that are process oriented, privilege relationality and emotionality, and explicitly value collaboration, inclusivity, and participation.[13] Unfortunately, transformative practices (including restorative practices, participatory deliberations, and family-group conferences) have had a sporadic uptake compared with interest-based models. This trend has frustrated so-called second-generation negotiation researchers and advocates, who continue to publish, present, and educate, convinced that second-generation values and practices are worth using and developing.[14] These scholars and practitioners have expressed their bewilderment at the lack of infusion of second-generation principles into existing training, policies, and practices. For example, LeBaron and Patera, recognizing the "cultural deficit" in first-generation conflict training, ponder why "the ideas elaborated [in second-generation approaches] seem not to have penetrated first generation approaches to negotiation training."[15] Roberto Chene, concerned about how cultural deficits contribute to inequities and unfairness for many, observes that "a monocultural dynamic has set in [that] has contributed to the domination of narrowly construed understandings of both practice and theory."[16]

It is worth reminding ourselves that the discipline of "conflict studies" is newly invented and is necessarily interdisciplinary: political science, law, sociology, psychology, humanities, and, more recently, neurobiology are actively informing the field. Yet its fledgling and interdisciplinary nature makes the slow uptake of advances that are observed in other fields particularly puzzling. In this chapter, we investigate the phenomenon with a spirit of inquiry, arguing that physical wisdom contained in the metaphor of dance is an essential element missing from conflict theory and practice.

One explanation for the failure to incorporate these critical dimensions is the possibility that they have become dominated and subsumed by more-powerful but invisible discourses that influence law and politics, such as neoliberalism, bureaucratization, and institutionalism, which value rationality, efficiency, and outcome.[17] As a result, first-generation practices, which are consistent with these values, prevail, while second-generation approaches have yet to make sustained inroads in training and the "real world" of law, politics, and public policy. There seems to be a gap between knowing and doing: knowing about deficits does not necessarily ensure changes in doing the work. How can this gap between first- and second-generation theory and practice in negotiation and peace building be bridged?

Other chapters in this book address the gap by bringing attention to different meanings and uses of dance across cultures and how they can deepen our understanding of conflict theory and practice. This chapter takes a different turn: we will use metaphors to enrich and vitalize the infusion of second-generation ideas into negotiation and peace-building practices. First, we will describe what we mean by metaphors—and dance metaphors specifically—as they pertain to conflict work. Then we will situate and critically spotlight the central tenets of two grand theorists with very different approaches to conflict—Machiavelli and Gandhi. Our analysis will confirm the powerful way in which metaphors shape our perspective and show the direct relationship between what we think and how we respond to conflict. We will apply Rigney's methodology for metaphor analysis to show how dance metaphors can reshape conflict theory and practice in ways that promote social justice. Our goal is to encourage both practitioners and theorists to be more conscious about the metaphors they choose to live and work by and how those metaphors shape, limit, or broaden the range of possibilities within conflict work.[18]

Metaphor

Daniel Rigney says a metaphor is "a mode of thought wherein we interpret one domain of experience through the language of another."[19] The language of metaphor works through a fusion of associations between two domains of experience. But metaphor is much more than a linguistic device. Lakoff and Johnson famously asserted that we not only speak in metaphors but "live by metaphors."[20] This notion is profound: it means that metaphor is not just language—it shapes thought and action, literally creating our realities.[21] Thus we take a "constructivist" approach here, arguing that metaphors are derived from and shape the ways we think, see, and enact our social world; of course they also create expectations about how we engage in conflicts.

Several scholars have already recognized the utility of the concept of metaphor in negotiation and peace-building work.[22] For example, John Paul Lederach writes that for peace builders, "metaphors are like a living museum of conflict resources."[23] Similarly, Schneider and Honeyman conclude that "identifying and understanding the metaphors used by the disputants is the single most important step we can take toward helping the disputants," but they also point to the paradox that metaphor "can be the key to a solution, as well as the central problem."[24] It is important to acknowledge that the meanings and directionality of metaphors shift over time. For instance, if we map war onto an argument, we are linking the two fields of meaning. But there may be movement in the opposite direction as well. An argument may escalate until we find that we *are* at war. Thus metaphor has a dynamic relationship with our social environment that shapes our thoughts, feelings, and actions, and it can feed back into the social context from which it emerged—it is reflexive. Therefore we need to become conscious of how social metaphors shape our thinking and actions and how they function to reveal new possibilities and insights. In the next section, we demonstrate the potency of metaphors in shaping understandings of conflict by examining the discourses of Niccolò Machiavelli and Mohandas Gandhi.

Two Grand Conflict Theorists

At first glance, the theories of Niccolò Machiavelli and Mohandas Gandhi may appear so different that they barely warrant comparison. Yet in spite of their utterly dissimilar philosophical and moral premises for addressing conflict, both men had their work taken up by those who sought to overcome conflict. Our analysis of Machiavelli and Gandhi reveals the strength and salience of metaphor in conflict theories and the ways that historical and social contexts influence conflict theorists.

Machiavelli lived in turbulent times where social and political conflict was a central feature of everyday life. Bloody, warring city-states in southern Europe prevailed; unstable governments, violence, and danger were the norm. Machiavelli saw life as a "brutal struggle for survival driven by natural human passions for the accumulation of wealth, power, and glory."[25] For him, human nature was selfish and politics was the art of warfare, a battle in which each person was out for his or her own self-interest. Machiavelli cautions that "a man who strives after goodness in all his acts is sure to come to ruin, since there are so many men who are not good."[26] Then he steers us to the darker, more sinister side of human nature, where "cruel deeds" are permitted as long as they are committed "well" and not "badly."[27] To transcend violent conflict and achieve political control, Machiavelli counsels state authorities to be suspicious, clever, and conniving—likening them to "powerful lions" and "cunning foxes" who strive for survival in a dog-eat-dog world. Power is equated with political control, and strategies of maligning, fearmongering, and even warfare are fair game. Practical success is privileged above upholding traditional moral values. Machiavelli advocates power over others, paradoxically, to foster stability and social peace.

Gandhi's social world also featured injustices and oppression in the colonial environments of South Africa and India at the time. His religious upbringing oriented him toward service to others who were less fortunate, valuing selflessness to overcome injustice and untruth. Gandhi developed a strategy called *satyagraha*, based on Hindu and Christian teachings. Roughly translated, *satyagraha* instructs that the oppressor can be converted (and social justice achieved) through the practice of love and self-suffering.[28] Gandhi's metaphor of the seed and the tree is relevant here: "The means may be likened to a seed, the end to a tree; and there is just the same inviolable connection between the means and ends as there is between seed and tree."[29] Here, violence is not justified as a means to an end, as it was for Machiavelli, because the means are as important as the ends. For Gandhi, violence cannot be justified "because when it appears to do good, the good is only temporary; the evil it does is permanent."[30] In other words, good means realize good ends, and bad means necessarily yield bad ends.

Gandhi's early experiences in colonial South Africa and India shaped his conceptions of power as residing within the self. To him, power imbalances are therefore best addressed by recognizing and mobilizing personal and collective action. In contrast to Machiavelli, who focused on retaining and exploiting power, Gandhi rejected the use of violence and class oppression to retain power. Above all, he valued truth and love as organic ways to transform oppression and violence.

This brief comparison of Machiavelli and Gandhi illustrates how these political activists' methods of pursuing "social peace" were quite different: Machiavelli advocated political conniving and warfare to maintain order; Gandhi sought social justice through nonviolent engagement. In political conflict, Machiavelli's stealth strategies were contained in battle metaphors focused on wresting away power from his opponents; Gandhi's growth metaphor informed acts of nonviolent civil disobedience to reorient power and mobilize individuals to collective action to cultivate a higher morality.

By contrasting the root metaphors of Machiavelli and Gandhi, we have revealed similarities and implicit differences between their conflict theories. The analyses show how metaphors reflect and shape conflict thought and behavior and powerfully influence social perceptions and actions. Further, metaphor can be used as a tool to reveal assumptions about knowledge, values, and practice that have become invisible and buried within our tacit cultural consciousness. What are the contemporary metaphors of conflict that shape our conduct, and what can we learn from the metaphor of dance?

Dance and Metaphor

Not all metaphors are created equal. Some have more utility or resonate better with common values. How might the metaphor of dance deepen our understandings of conflict processes? Perhaps dance can expose certain limitations of first-generation negotiation and conflict-resolution theory and offer insights into better possibilities. It may also facilitate the realignment of conflict-resolution practice with culturally sensitive and sustainable values. We will now explore how defining features within the metaphor of dance—such as flexibility, attunement, improvisation, relational movement and identity, shifting constellations, shared ground, and being in the moment—may be useful for understanding and responding to conflicts.

To approach this possibility, consider these examples about how someone might argue: "She *attacked* my position and I *defended* myself." "I tried a different *strategy* but was *shot down.*" "The criticisms were on *target.*" "I intend to *win* this argument." Here, argument is characterized by a war metaphor. Notice how the talk becomes the reality: points of view are not listened to and understood—they are attacked and defended; issues are not discussed— they are won or lost; dialogues become arguments; and listening is replaced with strategizing. Thus the metaphor of war shapes and justifies how we think about, talk about, and enact our differences, affirming the power of metaphors to structure thought and action.

Imagine this alternative: a context where a difference of opinion is understood through the metaphor of dance, where differences are opportunities to create relational connection, synchronicity is a skill that is valued, and the task is to stay in step. Dancers focus on listening, understanding, and then responding, while embracing emotional expression. A dance metaphor is more likely to elicit a dialogue, a quest for balance, or a collective choreography than an argument.

The difference between these two metaphors is fundamental. Through the war image, existence of conflict is destructive: parties to the disagreement are good or bad, and each side tries to reduce the conflict through attrition, taking whatever it can until the other side has as little as it will settle for. The dance metaphor envisions interdependence; within it, the fullness of human experience can be expressed, and common understandings may be shared. As a dancer, existing conflict (whether intrapersonal or interpersonal) is explored for emotional and relational dimensions, and connections become opportunities for integrating multiple voices and visions into a common reality and future.

Of course, dance does not necessarily mean cohesion or erasure of conflict. The metaphor makes room for, and values, tension, contradiction, and differences that may contribute to an emergent outcome. For example, the dance image can bring attention to *rhythm* in conflict where participants may move at different paces or alternate between movement and stillness—or among center stage, the wings, and supporting roles. It may also evoke a range of *directions*, as participants pursue different trajectories to express concerns, desires, and possible solutions. Dance may reveal various ways of perceiving *space* where participants can be in proximity to or distant from one another as needed—creating moments of coalition or yielding to solitude. Dance also evokes co-creating rather than contesting—bringing attention to a sense of collective responsibility and the importance of *how* things are said as much as *what* is said. The two orientations are so intrinsically different that the practice of conflict through the metaphor of war or dance would shape fundamentally different engagements.

Of course, the metaphor of dance can conjure other images as well. For example, dance is used in performance ritual, where dancers reenact cultural myths, histories, and conflict stories. Some dances, like the ballet *Swan Lake*, express the complications of passion and love while revealing incredibly repressive gender codes. In traditional contexts, war dances may be used to prepare for fighting. What is common to all dance metaphors is that the body and all of its expressive capacities are used to connect—to tell a story about the way things are at a particular time and place. Dance metaphors are spacious enough to allow expression of personal and cultural experiences.

Metaphor Analysis

Rigney warns that if we are "[t]o guard against provincial and imperial claims to final truth about human societies in all of their variety and mercurial complexity, it is essential that we sharpen our powers of metaphorical analysis, learning to recognize both the strengths and the limitations of metaphorical models in the social sciences and cultural studies."[31] Here, we build on these observations, using a rigorous and systematic analytic approach to examine existing modes of thought and practice to deepen contextual understandings of conflict, negotiation, and peace building. This methodology draws on four criteria of judgment—heuristic, aesthetic, scientific, and ethical—to assess dance metaphors in relation to conflict.[32]

1. Heuristic Potential

Does the dance metaphor have heuristic value? Does it render insights and strategies that can assist in providing useful answers to specific questions or issues? At first glance, the metaphor of dance may seem far-fetched for negotiation and peace building in settings dominated by expectations of efficiency, rationality, and certainty. But its value arises from its dissimilarity to more common images of negotiation. Consider the meanings and images that are conjured with the notion of the "science of negotiation" (objectivity, rationality, rigor, logic) versus the "art of dance" (subjectivity, emotionality, grace, soulfulness). For example, imagine a court proceeding where the "science of decision making" is administered by rules, evidence, and objective arguments; in contrast, envision a restorative conference characterized by a dance metaphor, which is likely to provide space for the (emotional) expression of individual perspectives, perhaps by including a ceremony to share food and ending with a soulful prayer. Metaphors arising from science or art implicate imagination in very distinct ways. As Rigney tells us, it is not the sameness of metaphors but their contrast that provides "the capacity to surprise us with a fresh view of a familiar subject, to suggest fruitful new concepts, and to generate novel lines of inquiry."[33]

The metaphor of dance immediately brings attention to movement, artistry, and soul. Consider this observation by Martha Graham, one of American dance's most prominent artists and theorists:

I am absorbed in the magic of movement and light. Movement never lies. It is the magic of what I call the outer space of the imagination. There is a great deal of outer space, distant from our daily lives, where I feel our imagination wanders sometimes. It will find a planet or it will not find a planet, and that is what a dancer does.[34]

Graham brings explicit attention to the many layers of metaphor as she describes the magic of movement, outer space, imagination that wanders, and finding a planet. These metaphors point to serendipity and uncertainty, the unexplored, and the inexplicable, which in turn invoke capacities such as intuition, curiosity, and soulfulness. Consistent with Graham, the humanist philosophers Douglass and Moustakas confirm that "imagination, intuition, self-reflection, and the tacit dimension" are critical heuristic devices to advance knowledge and understanding of particular domains.[35] The emphasis on informal, tacit knowledge that may not be verbalized and of which people may not even be aware points to the significance of the dance metaphor for conflict.[36]

John Paul Lederach, a renowned conflict scholar and practitioner, observes that conflict specialists have become "more technicians than artists," who implement cookie-cutter approaches that are both rigid and fragile.[37] In contrast, the capacities embodied by dancers have also been advocated in the second-generation negotiation literature: imagination,[38] curiosity,[39] relationality,[40] flexibility,[41] rhythm,[42] creativity,[43] emotionality,[44] and bodily tacit knowledge.[45]

Second-generation theorists pose the common scenario of an impasse in conflict that became unstuck not by a better argument, but by an unanticipated gesture—a hug or touch, a story or song. The dance metaphor has significant heuristic potential because it brings to the surface approaches arising from humanist philosophical traditions suggested by second-generation conflict specialists.

2. Aesthetic Value

Is the dance metaphor particularly creative, elegant, or poetically insightful? The heuristic criterion described above spotlights experience-based capacities invoked by dance. Here, we consider aesthetic criteria, neglected in most practices and theories of conflict. The following observations explain how the metaphor of dance resides within the domain of the aesthetic: Ted Shawn tells us that "[d]ance is the only art of which we ourselves are the stuff of which it is made."[46] Shanna LaFleur reminds us that "[i]t takes an athlete to dance, but an artist to be a dancer."[47]

What does this metaphor reveal about the aesthetic dimensions of negotiation and peace building?

Lederach has much to say. Negotiation and peace building, whether in relation to individual or social change, *require* creative acts to build and sustain adaptive and responsive processes. Lederach insists that an "aesthetic of life," more than cognitive technique and skill, creates constructive change. He is firm that peace builders and negotiators need to "envision [themselves] as artists [and] . . . return to aesthetics."[48]

In his book *The Moral Imagination*, Lederach observes that "the hardest challenge of peacebuilding is to see the *essence*" and that seeing the essence is achieved "through aesthetics and ways of knowing that see the whole rather than the parts, a capacity and pathway that rely on intuition more than cognition."[49] In this sense, the aesthetic value *is* a heuristic value as discussed in the previous section. Lederach's main premise, developed during his work in peace building, highlights aesthetic vision and intuition as essential core capacities for making lasting and sustainable transformation. He affirms that a conflict specialist who is unable to exercise these capacities will "miss the flow." The metaphor of dance is aligned with Lederach's discussion of haiku—the mastery of which requires intuition, creativity, and mindfulness. Negotiators are advised to embrace the complexity of situations through aesthetic simplicity, which Lederach labels a core requirement of effective peace building. "If you do nothing else, take time to get a picture, an image. When you see the picture better, you will have achieved a synthesis. The key to complexity is finding the elegant beauty of simplicity."[50] Lederach draws from famous poets who have also understood this artistic capacity, as when Ezra Pound concluded, "image is that which presents an intellectual and emotional complex in an instant of time."[51]

According to Lederach, the field of peace building has been slow to embrace these capacities. He concludes that "[k]nowing and understanding conflict does not take place exclusively, nor perhaps primarily, through processes of cognitive analysis, the breaking down of complexity into manageable pieces."[52] As peace builders and negotiators, we must reach into the domain of the aesthetic, learning to open ourselves to intuition and creativity, so we can connect with the essence of the conflict. The following narrative demonstrates how the capacity of intuition—the art of listening and connecting to find the essence—can play a significant role in the midst of the messiness of a real-life high-stakes conflict.

In 1978, Jimmy Carter, then president of the United States, brokered a treaty between President Anwar Sadat of Egypt and Menachem Begin, the prime minister of Israel, which is now famously known as the Camp David Accords. But before the signing, the talks had broken down, and Sadat and Begin were ready to return home with no peace between them. In Carter's book *Keeping Faith*, he describes the moment of breakthrough:

> Earlier, my secretary, Susan Clough, had brought me some photographs of Begin, Sadat, and me. They had already been signed by President Sadat, and Prime Minister Begin had requested that I autograph them for his grandchildren . . . I . . . walked over to Begin's cabin with them. He was sitting on the front porch, very distraught and nervous because the talks had finally broken down at the last minute.
>
> I handed him the photographs. He took them and thanked me. Then he happened to look down and saw that his granddaughter's name was on the top one. He spoke it aloud, and then looked at each photograph individually, repeating the name of the grandchild I had written on it. His lips trembled, and tears welled up in his eyes. He told me a little about each child, and especially about the one

who seemed to be his favorite. We were both emotional as we talked quietly for a few minutes about grandchildren and about war.[53]

Following this encounter, Prime Minister Begin returned to his cabin and reemerged after five minutes, asking to look at the peace proposal once again. How do we explain what happened in that pivotal moment? Carter says it was about "faith"; Yeats might explain that the "heart's core" was invoked;[54] Mills refers to the "moral imagination."[55] The moment summoned the essence of intuition: all the complicated, technical details of the treaty were set aside while Carter and Sadat considered the future they would leave for their grandchildren, evoked by the children's names on some photos. Those visual images communicated the essential importance of the talks.

This story is an example of how the aesthetic dimension is important in complicated conflict. Carter "changed the steps of the choreography" by addressing each picture to a particular grandchild. In deciding to "move a little differently," he prioritized intuition and heart over tradition, protocol, and formality. He relied on his own sense of choreography, eliciting a new dance from the parties. Lederach reiterates: "[W]e have overemphasized the technical aspects and political content to the detriment of the art of giving birth to and keeping a process creatively alive."[56] His appeal that "we need to envision ourselves as artists" is similar to Agnes de Mille's observation that "[t]o dance is to be out of yourself. Larger, more beautiful, more powerful."[57] The lines between where metaphor begins and practice ends become blurred. But Lederach knows that negotiators use intuitive capacities, and de Mille knows that dance fosters intuition. Using aesthetic criteria to gauge the value of a dance metaphor, we ask: If dancers and audiences can learn the art of intuition through dance, how might the metaphor of dance help peace builders and negotiators?

3. Empirical Legitimacy

This criterion derives from the positivist tradition and the quest for theoretical reliability. The legitimacy of artful activities has historically been left for the scholars of humanities, who have attended to how artisitc expressions resonate with the senses and authenticity. Good poetry evokes imagery that takes us into deep thought, good music excites our passion, and good dance is tacitly soulful. Still, we examine how the dance metaphor may lend itself to explanatory power and predictability.

a. *Adequacy of explication. Is the dance metaphor able to contribute to explaining or developing our notions of conflict?* A metaphor is valuable when it reveals resemblances that would otherwise be left implicit—connecting two separate domains of our experience.[58] When we examine commonalities between dance and conflict, what do we find? Consider the following quote from Doris Humphrey, a famous dancer and author of *The Art of Making Dances*, which includes her theories on dance and composition. She contemplates:

> The Dancer believes that his art has something to say which cannot be expressed in words or in any other way than by dancing . . . there are times when the simple dignity of movement can fulfill the function of a volume of words. There are movements which impinge upon the nerves with a strength that is incomparable, for movement has power to stir the senses and emotions, unique in itself. This is the dancer's justification for being, and his reason for searching further for deeper aspects of his art.[59]

From Humphrey's observations about movement, we can ask a number of questions in relation to negotiation and peace building: How is the dancer like a negotiator or person in conflict? How can movement fulfill or extend verbal expression and serve as a powerful source of communication during conflict? Are there commonalities among movement, dance, and the process of conflict transformation? How is the relationship between dancer and movement like the relationship between conflicting parties? What are the similarities between dance and conflict, and what are the implications for the negotiator's role in the conflict? Mapping Humphrey's language about movement onto negotiation and peace building yields some useful notions to consider. For example, movement

- fulfills and supersedes the function of words,
- stirs the senses and emotions,
- is dignified, and
- impinges upon the nerves.

Taking the metaphor of movement seriously may inform and enrich conflict practice. We can also generate a glossary of key dance terms and expressions that relate to conflict and negotiation. The following links become possible: dance and conflict are both performance and artful communicative processes that connect with the soul; parties in conflict dance expected, rehearsed, and improvised routines/steps as they sense, intuit, and respond to verbal and physical cues; and power (im)balances are always in operation when they are performed physically and through narrative.

How do these insights inform understandings of conflict? Imagine a divorce, where each party engages in a "performance" for his or her side, the movements choreographed from familial, social, and cultural scripts. The "battle" may be transformed into a more restorative process through a subtle gesture or kind word that "changes the choreography," helping the parties improvise new rhythms together after years of entrenched patterns. Or perhaps one person deviates from the expected "dance structure" (missteps by giving in prematurely or behaving badly in some way) and that person's counterpart swirls about in an effort to move back to an accepted norm for "dancing divorce." The performance plays out on the stages of family meetings, divorce courts, counseling offices, and other venues. The children dance their parts, and audiences of family and friends cheer or jeer. There are often victims, heroes, and dragons in this narrative, and these roles may shift or change. A dance metaphor raises questions about how a practitioner can "get inside the performance" and contribute to the choreography or how the performers themselves can influence the story differently.

b. *Explanatory power. Can the metaphor of dance and accompanying analogies lead to the discovery of general explanatory principles applicable to negotiation and peace building?* The previous discussion demonstrates the explanatory value of dance metaphors for conflict. Now we examine whether dance metaphors can enhance conflict theories, elucidate underlying principles, and yield more-nuanced knowledge of the capacities required to successfully process conflict.

We need to first assess what dance can teach us about conflict, and then we can venture a general theory of "conflict movement," inspired by dance. Ideally, the theory will transcend the metaphor so that dance and conflict are no longer seen as *like* movement but *as* movement—particular instances of bodily expressions and motion, shaped by a unified set of principles. For example, much of negotiation is about sorting through multiple truths and perspectives. Martha Graham observes that truth resides in the body: "[T]he body says what words cannot . . . the body never lies."[60] As conflict specialists, we can give serious recognition to the "voice" of bodily expressions and use our bodies' wisdom. The dance metaphor encourages attention to alignment and congruence of the body, both of which can shed light on the truth or veracity of behavior.

The dance metaphor opens further possibilities in this regard as we think *about* it and not just *within* it. For instance, much of conflict work is based on the assumption of a separation between self and other; interdependence (at least within the individualistic paradigm) is somewhat counterintuitive. The dance metaphor puts the self and other back together again. As Graham and neuroscientists remind us, keeping our attention on the primacy of bodily experience connects us to the kinesthetic basis of empathy, social cognition, and even morality.[61] Neuroscience research reveals that many phenomena can be understood by the way neurons mirror environments and subsequently shape behaviors and ethical choices. It is now clear that humans process experiences physically and relationally, not just cognitively and intellectually.

Neuroscience also demonstrates that the environment (the setting, for example) has a tremendous impact on bodily and neuronal experiences. For example, if there is a weapon present in a setting, conflict is more likely to escalate to violence than if no weapon is visible.[62] In contrast, LeBaron has documented examples of negotiations that shifted over a casual lunch or a bus outing—when people were in less-formal physical environments.[63] Bodies respond to these "naturalized" conflict settings in more open ways as the context influences people to be more sociable and less hostile in their interactions. Shifting the setting of negotiations can therefore be seen as a form of "stagecraft," where the dance is changed by using a different backdrop and props. Thus the dance metaphor highlights the primacy of the body and its significance in relation to social, relational, and spatial dynamics with far-reaching consequences.

c. *Predictive power. Does the metaphor of dance generate testable hypotheses or predictions that may be relevant to negotiation and peace building?* Consider this accepted dance tenet: "Great dancers are not great because of their technique. They are great because of their passion."[64] This leads us to consider that emotion may be as important as (if not more important than) technique; it inevitably directs attention toward soulful expression featuring creativity and intuition. Other key dimensions of dance involve space, time, and energy in relation to cadence, rhythm, and flexibility. For example, we can predict that conflict is better addressed if attention is paid to pace. Sometimes, allowing for a rest period and easing the pace with gentler "stretches" or maneuvering may be productive. Other times, it is better to act with speed, zeroing in on a problem that might otherwise become entrenched and intractable. Can we be time sensitive in our engagement, intuitive during the process, flexible in our approach, creative in finding solutions, and fluid in our agreements? Taking language from artistry and dance, we ask: Might this lead to more successful and long-lasting agreements? Here are some additional questions for future research:

- Do conflict processes that use dance language and sensibilities result more often in durable agreements, transformed relationships, or unexpected and creative solutions compared with those that use a battle or science metaphor?
- Can negotiators and peace builders refine their capacities for intuition, creativity, imagination, self-reflection, and understanding of the tacit dimension through training in physical discernment and wisdom? If so, what training is most useful?
- How can physical training be delivered in academic and professional settings without being co-opted by dominant discourses or watered down by existing pedagogy?
- Which cultural and situational contexts will be most receptive or will benefit most from these approaches? Are there contexts where it would not be effective or appropriate to use them?

We hypothesize that the dance metaphor can enhance understanding of conflict dynamics, perceptions, and approaches to ameliorate conflict. There is mounting evidence that we *should* give these capacities more weight. For example, disputes that result in the highest satisfaction are not necessarily those that have an ideal outcome. Instead, people report that most positive experiences occur when more is achieved than expected; when solutions *never* thought of before emerge due to innovation, flexibility, and collaboration; and when they feel they are seen and heard.[65] There is also evidence that justice, fairness, and satisfaction tend to be obtained through strategies, goals, and dynamics that resonate better with a dance metaphor than with a battle metaphor.[66] Based on this research and our experience, we believe that dance metaphors inform practices that yield more-engaged and more-collaborative processes and outcomes.

4. Moral and Ideological Value

Given that conflict processes always have moral and ideological dimensions, whose interest does the dance metaphor serve, and which kinds of outcomes might it elicit? Our discussion of explanatory and predictive elements was derived from a positivist, empirical perspective. Ethical and ideological dimensions are also important and cannot be approached solely through empiricism. Of course, metaphors are not ideologically neutral. They shape and reflect what we value and how we act in the world.

The fundamental difference between the two conflict metaphors described earlier (war and growth) becomes apparent when we consider the practical and political ramifications of each. Metaphors are always contextual, evoking meanings and bodies of knowledge that have particular ethical, social, and political consequences. It is important to remember that the knowledge associated with a given metaphor has power but only for those who have access to that knowledge.[67] Thus, by imagining a metaphor in conflict situations, we can determine which values are being favored, whose interests may be served, and which values or interests may be overlooked. These determinations are significant because metaphors exert power by creating fields of meaning that shape communication and ideas of relevance, usefulness, and possible solutions.

Imagine a circumstance of intractable conflict, such as the chaotic time in which Machiavelli lived. Could Machiavelli's model "fix" the conflict? His model, centered on war, creates and perpetuates "command and control," leading to tactics including violence, deceit, and marginalization to increase power and win. This orientation re-creates the outcomes it attempts to change. It leaves decision making to the elite and removes opportunities for collective participation in decisions, continuing the need for realpolitik strategies and elite power struggles; there is no way out of the cycle. Values of care, inclusivity, integrity, and transparency are sidelined.

By conceiving conflict through the lens of warfare, Machiavelli's model overlooks the dimension of "overcoming" conflict that Gandhi's growth metaphor necessarily entails. Gandhi's theory, centered in compassion and love, prompts equality, dignity, self-determination, and participation. Here conflict is overcome. Peace is not achieved through competition for power; it is a natural outgrowth of love and compassion.

What are the moral and ideological dimensions of the dance metaphor, with its focus on relationality? Dancers express their needs and desires, pain and pleasure, joy and sorrow, clarity and confusion. As they do so, they connect and attend to the space around them, other dancers, and the audience; their dance demonstrates and inspires human connectivity and empathy.

Seeing conflict through the metaphor of dance focuses attention on the ethical significance of reciprocity and feelings. As Buber observed, "[t]he interwoven nature of our existence requires an ethic of responsibility and care for others."[68] Relationality highlights positive, productive relationships between individuals and within society. It inspires an ethic of care and responsibility that leads to positive social and cultural relations. Actions that could be destructive to relationships are suppressed. The dance metaphor attunes us to the social world, and this is a chief aspect of its ethical value.

When we value relationship in conflict, we are less likely to value time, money, and victory, which tend to be accentuated in first-generation conflict-resolution strategies. Consider the metaphor of conflict as a marketplace, which evokes profit-related images like expediency, efficiency, competition, and optimal outcomes. This metaphor elicits behavior oriented to "maximiz[ing] individual gains and . . . joint gains if [peoples'] own interests are not compromised."[69] Who is served by negotiation practices that privilege efficiency over relationality, competition over cooperation, and outcome over process? Some possible answers are institutions, business, and administration, and those within them who have positional, social, economic, and political power. Negotiation and peace-building processes informed by a marketplace metaphor do not necessarily provide space for simultaneous expressions of reason and reciprocity[70] and can produce substantive and procedural inequalities.[71] We cannot assume that negotiation processes in marketplace economies offer equal and fair processes for all, particularly not for those who are socially and politically marginalized.

Lederach suggests that "[b]eing moral is the substance of seeing oneself in the bigger picture of relationship and of keeping people, not humanly created structures, at the center of public life."[72] The metaphor of dance conjures principles and practices that can address power inequities by engendering more-inclusive, more-authentic engagement. We believe that the dance metaphor is a promising way to foster accessible, fair, and empowering processes for all involved in a conflict.

Conclusion

As we enter a new era of conflict theorizing, we have an opportunity to reflect on our existing conflict metaphors and mindfully engage in creating a social world that is more coherent with our values. Rigney's observation that "[t]he shape of our futures may depend on the metaphors we now choose to guide us"[73] frames our inquiry: What metaphors will we choose going forward? Because theories and practices of conflict are always socially and historically located, the metaphors we choose to live by will be powerful tools in shaping and transforming our lives. Both Machiavelli's and Gandhi's philosophies were shaped by their time and context. Each man chose to amplify certain ways of seeing and being in the world. These examples show how imperative it is for conflict specialists to be radically intentional about the metaphors they choose to shape thought and actions. Machiavelli's war image creates self-interest and perpetuation of conflict; Gandhi's organic-growth metaphor constellates empowerment and cooperation via recognition, transformation, and reconciliation.

In conclusion, we consider how a dance metaphor can constructively shape conflict practice. It is a legitimate tool that creates a fresh space in which to examine habitual assumptions about and responses to conflict with both heuristic worth and aesthetic resonance. It is theoretically, empirically, and practically rigorous. Most important, many of its defining features (for example, relationality, reciprocity, and positive emotionality) can reinvigorate an ethic coherent with generative approaches to conflict. The dance metaphor orients and attunes us to possibilities not previously accentuated in conflict studies—the primacy of tacit or bodily knowledge, the importance of timing and rhythm, the necessity of creativity and intuition, and the need for practitioners to display artistry as well as technical expertise. These capacities are key to creating pivotal moments in times of true crisis. They are also important in addressing power inequities that otherwise supplant fairness and equality.[74] Chene encourages us to "uproot [the] comfortable, anachronistic model in order to grow into a more workable one."[75] The dance metaphor can contribute to this project, yielding more-workable practices and more-ethical and more-sustainable solutions to our many differences.

Dance as Praxis

MARGIE GILLIS

> *"Bless the continual stutter of the word being made into flesh."*
> *The Window*, Leonard Cohen

Introduction

Conflict is with us for our whole lives as individuals and communities, yet we are often stymied by it, unable to make the shifts necessary to resolution. One of the elements missing in many approaches to resolving conflict is the body. It is the movement of our bodies that allows the blood to flow, our elimination systems to function, and detoxification to take place, supplying fresh blood to the brain and renewed clarity of thought. For this reason, dance and movement offer a surprisingly solid, simple, experiential way to engage and transform conflicts, because dance itself is living change, problem solving in motion, and when the body and conflict are seen as elements of the same continuum, change can happen more rapidly and with greater awareness.

The experience of motion and transformation also informs us about our own healing processes and our bodies' conditions. Health encompasses both balance and counterbalance. Cultivating stability in motion—one of the essences of dance—is a way to experience health from an embodied perspective, just as learning how to find areas of stability within the tension of opposing forces is essential for conflict prevention and transformation. Once we are sensitive to such parallels, we can begin to ask ourselves the questions that translate from one to the other and back: What shifts need to occur to find health in motion with one another? What is inertia, and in what situations might immobility be necessary and important? How can we find ways to occupy the same space, yet each have autonomy and belonging? These and many other questions can be fruitfully explored using dance and movement.

Dancing from the Inside Out

Dancing from the inside out is a way I have begun to examine these questions. It both describes and names my working process with dance. It is an artistic approach that seeks to reconnect with and work through the most central, if often most dismissed or neglected, dimension of human experience—the physical body—as the means to develop and deepen one's inner and outer relationships in the world. This kinesthetic process focuses on and facilitates the experience of how movement manifests from our inner landscape. Our thoughts, emotions, spirituality, images, sensations—the cinema of who we are—all become electricity traveling the body, touching the muscles, and connecting to create physical expression and resonant metaphor. These inner impulses and processes run the path of the nerves, stimulate the various muscles, and cause an orchestra of contractions and releases. This reaction, response, and connection can be sensed under the skin as "feelings" or can be given full expression in both pedestrian movement and dance. In and with this experiential wisdom, we come to a place of profound instinct, intuition, and transformation.

It is from these resulting kinesthetic sensibilities that we can truly initiate and make profound shifts in life. We can experience changes in long-standing and immobile attitudes, increasing our facility to move from rigid ideas to curiosity. In cultivating an awareness of this potential, we can begin to have the capacity to shift from aggression to contemplation. Over time, it becomes more possible to experience, expand, and renew our sense of safety. We are able to move into ways of finding alternative capacities for creative solutions that were previously unavailable or elusive. Opening ourselves to this new realm of experience is also a way to counter the sad truth that many of us have become so disconnected from and disrespectful of our own natures and, indeed, of nature itself—that the planet's health and human survival are now precarious. To me, this seems to be a symptom of distance from our fully embodied selves, and I believe we need to reconnect our intellect and spirituality to our bodies and to our personal natures, which are part of the larger world and universe.

As a methodology, dancing from the inside out is an ever-expanding group of dances, exercises, and mudras. Some are of my own creation and imagination, some modified from various dance and theater forms, and some inspired by yoga, gymnastics, or sport fitness. They are designed to help dancers and nondancers alike explore, create, and transform who they are in motion—posing, clarifying, and exploring questions about themselves and their relationships with others and the world. This embodiment engages experiential wisdom and creativity to see more clearly who we are; to witness and support mutual transformation; and to explore, understand, and shift perspectives. A myriad of questions can be put into motion, and the corresponding momentum can begin to illuminate new answers and new states of being.

Exploring the Methodology and Its Applications

The initial development of this multisensory approach was to support dancers in performance technique, exploring ways of creating and developing artistry and quality of movement. From these beginnings, dancing from the inside out developed further into ways that could facilitate improvements in individuals' health, celebrate life in general, and help people find creative solutions in the midst of conflict or tension.

As well as guiding workshops and classes for professional dancers of various disciplines (ballet, modern, jazz, flamenco, Indian, butoh, etc.), I have introduced this work to people of many ages, abilities, needs, interests, and disciplines. I have worked in diverse settings with elite athletes and sport psychologists; with actors, sculptors, fine artists, educators, and writers; with children, the elderly, and AIDS patients; with those who have emotional and social challenges; and with those who have physical disabilities, such as impaired vision. Recently, I have offered this work to mediators and conflict practitioners.

It is the breadth of the work that enables it to address and inspire participants to find their own abilities and creative solutions for a wide spectrum of specific challenges and goals. It achieves this by focusing on problem solving in motion, tapping into body wisdom, and encouraging a safe and expansive exploration through an attentiveness to the nature of play, curiosity, discernment, and, perhaps most of all, to the many meanings of health.

It is always asking, directly and indirectly: What is health? How do we get there? How do we maintain a relationship with health? Why is health paramount for those working in conflict? How do we move toward greater personal and collective health? What are the diverse worldviews associated with concepts of health? How can divergent perspectives on health influence relational patterns in communities? One's overall attitudes toward health are often contingent on culture and context and vary according to age and mental, emotional, and physical states. I see health as the ability to embrace opposites, to have a supple strength, and to be able to move flexibly and freely in a range of situations and challenges. However varied and complicated the definitions of health in different cultures, primary notions of health can be explored, discovered, and redefined through embodied explorations. Dance is a fertile way to begin to understand and come into relationship with what health is uniquely for ourselves and in relation to others.

In exploring aspects of health through the body, we experience the mind as demanding answers. The body in motion and dance tempers this insistence and can offer a more-complete answer: one that is experiential, embracing intellect and mystery while moving us to deeper problem solving. I believe that as the body moves toward health and healing, this process assists the mind and psyche to a parallel opening and shift toward health. In fact, within the last few years, the medical community has confirmed what many have known to be a deep truth for their artistic lives: that the neuromuscular system of each audience member and of the performer connect and mirror through the performance ritual and, in essence, all experience and share the same dance. For people in the audience, the effects of this mirroring are happening under the skin; for the dancer, this relationship is manifested in full in the physical working of his or her body. Whether you are observing or participating in dance, dancing from the inside out can enhance awareness, fulfill potential, and nurture discovery in both an artistic and a therapeutic sense.

So what does this mean for the practitioner interested in the health of a community or society affected by conflict? How can dance be used to support the process of finding creative solutions for a wide spectrum of unique situations? The answer is that dance can offer vivid and surprising insights into the creative resources that are present and available amid shifting and uncertain conflict dynamics. In the next section I will explain how I approach this work, and later I will offer an illustration of what it can teach in practice.

The Workshop Process

Developing a framework is essential for establishing both safety and continuity for participants. To begin each workshop or class, I choose from a series of exercises designed to focus the participant/mover/dancer. These can be applied in diverse contexts—from formal conference rooms to dance studios. They are intended to be nonthreatening, intellectually stimulating, and are designed to engage participants from a range of backgrounds. Each exercise is intended to bring needed oxygen into the body and at the same time clear out stale energy that may be contributing to impasse.

Music is not often integrated into the exercises at the outset. To cultivate focus, guidance begins with the simplicity of the spoken word. As I talk participants through the exercises, I am putting forward ideas and images as a form of "music" to guide and support their movement. While facilitating, I look for visible health traits, points of resilience, resources, blocks, resistance, and weaknesses, both collectively and individually. I use my kinesthetic knowledge to perceive (not "name" since we are still in the initial "feeling out" stage) where impasses may be preventing people from recognizing their resources, and I highlight basic aspects of physical and physiological alignment and balance. Depending on the nature of the class, the way into, or the way to become open to, this exploration may be anywhere in the spectrum from descriptive words coupled with gentler movement to rigorous movement coupled with sparse or abstract dialogue. Once the group has experienced small, clear movement exercises to establish physically safe parameters and I have witnessed the participants' level of comfort, health, and concentration, we collectively move forward to more in-depth exploration. The next level of engagement that builds on the initial warm-up period is a dance exercise called Inventory.

Inventory is a guided movement scan of the sensations inside the body and a "touching in" on how and where you are in the room and in relation to others. "Let it be there, let it change'" is the repeated direction. Each person is asked to move in accordance with a directed focus on various body parts, observing the sensations that arise from each part. I encourage participants to see also how sensations from different areas can link and form lines of motion through and out of the body, and I ask them to give these physical interior impressions expression or release while observing the quality of the movement. I ask participants to observe areas of immobility due to scar tissue or injury, lack of use, or discomfort and to explore ways to be at ease with and incorporate these areas into movement. Inventory is also an opportunity to explore various relationships to injury and healing. I encourage participants to listen to the uniqueness of what their body requires for optimum health, and I invite them to fulfill this in motion. In the momentum, their consciousness remains in the "observer position," and from this vantage point they can begin to witness how their experiences are manifested physically. Body wisdom becomes actively engaged here. The diverse and changing needs of each person are approached with delicate care; in this shifting kinesthetic frame, dancers are guided gently to become their own intuitive healers.

With breath as our focus, we begin the exploration of our current state and ourselves in motion, keeping in mind this question: What is generative for the health of my body? I pose this as an open-ended question so that the dancers can allow their own specific meanings of health to rise. I alter or refine the emerging meaning if I perceive movements to be nonorganic or to be moving away from individual or collective health. This exercise focuses on how to facilitate the bodily tendency that moves naturally toward the search for health. Such studio work asks us to literally get out of our own way and let the body tell us where to go, what to do, and how to navigate through new terrain. This is a revealing, an opening up, and the resulting vulnerability is facilitated with kind encouragement and care. The word *possibility* is often in my vocabulary here.

As the dance exercises are put forward and explored by the participants, I am able to observe and discern where there is engagement and health and where support is needed. I know that a subtle physical change can correspond to an enormous change of perspective. This knowledge comes from years of keen observation and verification, as the work arrives in very subtle ways and can be similar to intuition. How does the body reveal the soul, intellect, emotion, and desire of each of us? I keep these questions in mind and in my skin, as my skin allows me to see insights through another lens. I keep all intellect embodied as I draw from new repertoires that respond to needs and desires that arise in the group. In response to what arises, I will slow down or speed up; I will change perspective, change level of difficulty, or add or take away music or speech.

Subtle shifts support nuance and curiosity and create ease with the challenges that are faced moment by moment. Alternative or quick shifts in the quality of approach can alter the dynamics in the room. If necessary, more-radical changes are introduced to clear the air or to support dexterous, creative minds and catalyze a further opening to new ideas. The main goals are explorations that illuminate, transform, heal, inspire, and allow participants to engage with their own creativity and inherent wisdom. The starting point is exactly where they are in the present moment. When we achieve a level of nuance and qualitative, not just quantitative, experience, we are more able to tease out large problems and address multiple levels of complexity without being overwhelmed. As one's curiosity engages in the nuances of movement, it becomes possible to move toward states of possibility, imagination, and creative problem solving. New issues, desires, and questions arise as one moves, breathes, and is able to be more physically present in the space. Here we begin to hold a place of possibility for ourselves and for others. In the subtlety of movement, it is possible to shift toward curiosity, and by doing so, we begin to cultivate creative negotiations with our perceptions and inner narratives. In the process, we become open and available to new solutions.

Transforming Conflict: The Crack Opens

The artistry and humanitarian focus of my work, in combination with being a solo performer, has granted me the opportunity to tour many places in the world that could not support a full dance company. As I have developed and taught dancing from the inside out, it has taken me into a progressively wider range of diverse communities and has allowed me to explore questions far beyond those of conventional artistic practice. One experience in particular helped to reframe the potential applications of this work in the context of conflict transformation and reconciliation.

I was teaching a dance class of secondary-school boys and girls in a working-class community in Quebec fifteen years ago and was struck by the contrast between the energy and physicality of the boys and that of the girls. This reality became clearer and clearer as the class progressed. There was imbalance, tension, and a strong sense of a lack of safety within the group. The boys—volatile, scared, and awkward with their young, strong, and powerful bodies—seemed as if they were desperately trying to control and underplay their own vital yet potentially explosive energy. The girls appeared frightened and were physically wary of the strength of these young men, particularly, it seemed, in light of their own comparatively diminutive size and burgeoning delicacy and femininity.

This growing tension and emotional charge began to culminate as I initiated an exercise called Third Person. Leading into Third Person, I had the class first engage in losing and catching their balance to explore how they initiated fall and recovery and where their consciousness was in the play of balance/off balance. As they became comfortable with fall and recovery in their own bodies, we moved on to the next "dance." Third Person is done in partners (and can optionally be explored in groups later). The instructions are that the dance that emerges is not about you or the other person but rather about the energy between you—an imagined third person. The partners are to sense this third presence and move in relationship to it. (There are further parameters of engagement to enhance and foster health, safety, and respect.) To start, the partners need to feel safe with taking turns initiating small changes that push each other off balance. The recipient of the push experiments with the safe ways of losing and catching his or her balance in response.

The class understood the rules, but they were reluctant and frightened to engage. The boys began to bully one another while the girls began to move toward the edge of the room and seemed to be trying to disappear. I took the hand of one of the boys at random and asked him to push me. Everyone stopped as the boy looked at me with apprehension. Again I said clearly, "Push me." I pushed his shoulder gently, with about a third of the level of strength I wanted him to use on me. He finally complied and pushed my shoulder. I took the trajectory of his push and allowed my body to flow into an open circle until the energy of the push was dissipated. I asked him to push again. He pushed my arm, and I allowed the movement to roll and unravel down the arm. I asked him to push harder, and he did, this time with a downward thrust on my shoulder. I rolled with the motion, unraveling this forceful energy until it dissipated. We began pushing each other and dissipating the volumes of energy. We escalated and de-escalated the power of the pushes. Suddenly the delight of discovery of nuance became accessible and available to all of us, and we began to dialogue about the joy of force and its appropriately nuanced use.

We returned to the Third Person exercise, starting with the boys eagerly engaging with one another, laughing and playing with volumes of energy. In doing so, they were learning how to shift, to move negative and "stuck" energy, and be safe while doing it. The girls began to join in, dancing together, and gradually the boys and girls began to develop trust and dance with one another. The boys were able to use the full strength of their bodies while the girls used their size and relative strength in the same nuanced way. Relatively quickly, the previous impasse was overcome, and everyone began to feel more safe, curious, and engaged. The "elephant in the room" became a playmate; volatile, explosive energy was harnessed and experienced as a useful tool of engagement. The class and I were deeply changed in our awareness that it can be safe to be centered in motion with others of lesser or greater physical strength. We could own this "living safety" for ourselves and for others through direct experience. The school administration recognized the powerful results from that class, and the creation of a dance department was the tangible response. This department still has full attendance and is supported by the government.

For me as a teacher, this was a pivotal class: it gave me the courage to explore and understand conflict and deepen my understanding of volatile energy. It first showed me how I could help others shift from a place of being fearful and overwhelmed into a place of exploration and connection. The deliberate engagement with nuance allowed the volume in the room to be safely explored. Since the class, I have continued to explore ways in which seemingly intractable conflicts can be transformed into positive outcomes. Third Person is a valuable tool in allowing people to feel the energy between them without it becoming too personal. Through this approach, participants can learn to sense, fulfill, test, and change their collective dynamic. It also becomes possible to cultivate somatic knowledge around how other elements, such as beliefs, community, or ancestors, play into the dynamics of a conflict.

We may be dancing for ourselves, and we might also be dancing with a large communal history in us. The engagement of the "third" can be abstract and involves an attentive posture of "listening" with all the senses and even the skin. The dance between us can then become personified, and dialogue remains in a neutral focus: it is neither you nor I, but what is between us, a separate yet connected sense of reality. This spacious area can offer many subtle insights. The third-person perspective can often break down rigid, preconceived notions of "other," offering surprises, clues, and solutions to problems. It creates new starting points for people who are wary of one another and need an alternative way to engage safely and easily. This emergent space facilitates an experiential transformation brought about by curiosity and nuance as the body arrives at solutions of which the brain can then become aware.

Such workshops, or "collective investigations through dance," have been part of my ongoing work with diverse communities around the world. I have moved increasingly from working with dancers to applying these ideas with people who have a wide range of physical awareness and abilities. Across this demographic range, the connecting thread always comes back to the power of a body-based inquiry. This dynamic form of knowledge creation heightens self-awareness, reveals new connections and ideas, and develops personal and collective capacities that will enrich and deepen any investigation of any situation in which human beings are in tension with one another.

The Saas-Fee Workshop: Dance as a Means to Understand Conflict

For five days, participants from around the world gathered in Saas-Fee, Switzerland, to explore the convergence of movement and conflict resolution. Each brought diverse cultural and professional experience to the workshop, as acclaimed scholar-practitioners, mediators, conflict-resolution practitioners, arbitrators, counselors, trainers, psychotherapists, expressive-art therapists, diplomats, and peace builders participated in the sessions. Each day was framed around a guiding question to focus the exploration on issues of embodied conflict and emotions, safety and change, flexibility and inflexibility, and practical applications for the field of conflict analysis and intervention. On each day I led participants—some for the first time—in two dance/movement sessions and assisted with the facilitation of two daily dialogues where insights and potential applications from the movement sessions were discussed. The themes of conflict transformation have emerged within my work over the years and have often shaped my classes and workshops. This weeklong event in Saas-Fee, however, was one of the first projects where conflict and reconciliation were intentionally placed at center stage.

I began the Saas-Fee workshop with a strong sense that health plays a crucial role in generative approaches to conflict. With that as the foundation, I initiated exercises that explored the multiple facets of health, because I believe that resolving conflict in our own bodies helps to illuminate the essential mechanics required to transform conflicts with others and for others.

From my previous work with Michelle LeBaron and Carrie MacLeod, I imagined that the participants themselves would need to experience and embody their own transformations to know their habitual patterns in conflict and understand their range of possibilities for solutions. This was indeed the case. It became apparent that some had experienced various levels of burnout with their demanding workloads, and all were welcoming the opportunity to experience renewal and play. By play, I mean relaxed and unfocused movement layered with increments of risk taking. Introducing elements of intentional play with this group created frameworks for engagement that were both stimulating and calming. The sessions began to have a tide-like rhythm that supported streams of action and reflection.

The participants expressed a collective need for both renewal and rigor, and dance was able to address this through the convergence of mental and physical stimuli. It was a challenging delight to be of service to those who are dedicated to easing suffering and transforming conflict in complex situations. Witnessing and supporting participants as they discovered how to navigate through conflict with a newfound physical language was an extraordinary privilege. As the days progressed, the physical and mental shifts became more apparent as new insights and possibilities for conflict interventions emerged. This week served as a significant catalyst for the overall direction of the Dancing at the Crossroads research initiative, as participants set out to apply the tangible and experiential lessons to their own contexts.

The insights gathered from my diverse teaching experiences provided fertile ground to explore a new crossroad in Saas-Fee. I was able to build on earlier sessions related to conflict used with advanced dancers in my workshops for Springboard, a summer intensive in Montreal for gifted young professional dancers primarily from the Julliard School for the Arts in New York. We had modeled situations arising in conflict and I had developed "dances" that teased out, illuminated, and transformed problems. I had also previously done some work on movement applicable to negotiating for those with limited mobility. The Saas-Fee project furthered my understanding of how to engage with active contemplation and offer what I had discovered.

De-escalation, Crisis Conflict, and Reconciliation: Reflections

Along with support and renewal for conflict-transformation practitioners, I see the possibility of three different areas of focus for applying the work: de-escalation, crisis conflict, and reconciliation. I am exploring health models of movement for minor-to-moderate injury and imbalance (de-escalation and return to health), traumatic injury with a minimum of motion (crisis conflict and survival), and rehabilitation from physical injury (reconciliation).

These parallels are more than metaphors. I see direct crossovers between these shifting states of being and the correlating physicality of problem-solving capacities that emerge through dance. I have seen, for example, how those in crisis can develop a range of solutions to particular problems through their innate somatic intelligence and tangibly enact those solutions in the world. Similarly, exploring the momentum of conflict through spatial negotiations can be very revealing: it can be hard for people to turn their back on their enemies or stand next to those with whom they are in conflict. Retaining a sense of fluidity in motion helps participants feel the energy and tension surrounding the conflict without being stuck in the center of it. Movement can create invitations for comfort and coexistence, as discovery can take place from multiple points. Seemingly abstract patterns of movement can generate new patterns of thought.

Dance can also help people locked in conflict in very personal ways. It can help us discover how to engage with our intuition from different perspectives, and our kinesthetic sensibilities can provide relational cues in ways that verbal communication cannot. Dance can move us toward a deepened sense of curiosity and respect and allow us to be literally more in touch with ourselves and with others. Intentional movement can release and shift trauma that lies in the muscle memory. We can learn how to feel for the flow and take care of the breaks in fluidity that often arise from legacies of scar tissue or other physical limitations. Dancing new ideas into the body serves to ground experience through the senses, bringing us into the immediacy of the present moment. An idea that lives in the body as a total experience creates a meaning system of its own in the present; it is not something that is simply relegated to a hypothetical reality. Abstractions that may seem to be formless can be put into concrete terms. It becomes possible to witness and experience how embodiment transforms old architectures of meaning into new forms.

I encourage groups to start where they are and to think subtly, not become lost in the gross volume of trying to change or accomplish too much. If we can engage a newfound sense of curiosity in the smallest gestures, we can begin to soften immobility, ease and respect the shroud of seriousness and of being overwhelmed, and use this curiosity and the desire emanating from dance to override debilitating fears. Cultivating a sense of wonder in combination with a safe and playful space enables extensive exploration and allows people to view, discard, or revisit possible solutions from a variety of vantage points. Solutions become more accessible when mobility and fluidity are present.

Dance is likewise able to hold a deep respect for the interwoven complexity of questions surrounding issues of survival, history, gender, land, community, and health. Issues that normally don't surface in dialogue can be addressed and "teased out" through embodied encounters.

With dance, "the problem can hold the solution" and can reveal where the locus of transformation can take place. Through the multiple languages within dance, these shifts can become more visible. In this sense, dance enables us to not only work toward an issue but also *through* complex challenges with a heightened sense of safety, artistry, and a nuanced awareness.

Sometimes it is necessary to create a physical architecture to see and sense where the essential health could be and what the next step is or should be. There are times when the solution is very apparent at the outset, but in some circumstances it remains hidden for longer periods of time. For the solution to be felt, seen, perceived, or known, moving through levels of abstraction is often a necessary first step.

Dance is a rigorous testing area for these discoveries, but they are just the beginnings. Certainly not everything has been discovered yet, since there are as many dances as there are people in this world.

How to Teach the Work and Things to Keep in Mind

Teaching embodied approaches in diverse settings and across cultural divides involves creating a safe space that will allow participants to find solutions and revelations from their own somatic starting points. Two people exemplified this for me.

Daniel Jackson was my artistic adviser for many years, and his invaluable lesson to me as a creator was simple and clear. He would enter a room believing actively that discovery, risk, and genius could arrive and be with us at any time. He did so with an extensive knowledge of art and dance but kept that information at quiet service. If the risk and genius did not arrive, he actively waited for the next day, and the next. He always believed they would come, and when they did, he would deliberately acknowledge what happened and when and how. Indeed, they did always arrive. Michelle LeBaron also holds the space for possibility, respect, and imagination. She waits in active faith for imaginative solutions to arise through arts-based conflict interventions. Both of these people know how to engender trust and carefully hold vulnerability from the dynamic position of the witness. In order to discover, one must enter an area where one does not know, and this can be a seemingly impossible challenge for someone in conflict.

To create safety is one element; to embrace possibility and solution is challenging and requires active engagement. Issues arise as we dance and invite flexibility and fluidity to facilitate transformation. I hear Carrie MacLeod's words in my ear: "the hint of a possibility." A little revelation, a small adjustment, a hint of transformation; these can often open the floodgates to greater possibilities. One has to support and encourage, entering gently and carefully, because of the depth and the intimacy of the work. Accompanying threads of discernment and compassion are also needed. Letting participants know aspects of what you are seeing, even as a "seed," or observing something that is just arising can help them recognize needed ingredients for change within themselves. A little shift can start a river of possibilities, and the emergence of possibility is the precursor to problem solving. When this happens, there is no limit to what can be revealed and achieved.

I hope that this book can be used to help lawyers explore, transform, and heal on multiple levels. Working with a human being in this way encourages a deep experiential understanding and transformation. Spurs on neuromuscular pathways can be dissolved, facilitating creative problem solving and ultimately changing who we are. Working in this way makes it possible to double-check the validity of intuition from multiple viewpoints. Sensing and seeing. Sensing and seeing. Our bodies can always live into the questions: Where is the source, the healing, the compassion, the transformative energy, the clear communication, the deep dance of nature, and a felt sense of nurture and possibility? I am excited by the possibility of further developing movement-based interventions that carefully transform complex problems into creative solutions. The compelling beauty of embodied inquiry leads us down generative pathways. Through dance, we can become attentive to how such dynamic modes of inquiry holistically engage the heart, mind, soul, and body.

Summary and Conclusion

Looking back over this work, I feel hopeful. My hopes arise from conceiving, initiating, and witnessing the potential of human transformation. I have seen how this work offers support and renewal for conflict-resolution practitioners. Dance is a tool that helps explore nuance and subtlety in communication patterns, always relevant to conflict. Dance is not always expansive movement or major shifts. It can be adapted to a range of capacities for movement and flexibility. Indeed, the smallest shifts in gestures can offer expansive possibilities as people become aligned with new starting points. For instance, focusing on negotiations at tables as dances offers a currency of comfort for those who may not be familiar with full physical expression. This work can allow the "dance under the skin" to become easier to perceive and thus offers more transparency and flexibility in terms of conceivable responses.

Participants will often modify the volume and range of their needs as they intuitively learn how to attend to themselves with a health-centered focus. As this momentum grows, a new language for problem solving emerges. By physically modeling states of being, we find our inner worlds begin to surface and become more conscious. In moving through kinetic worlds, new relational possibilities find focus and form; obstacles disappear or change shape, and we experience unanticipated shifts and openings. In short, our capacities to receive inspiration and find new ways forward increase as our range of motion expands.

How Dance?

*T*his section focuses on some practical ways our bodies, move and how we choose to move them, and how our bodies can affect the processes of communication, negotiation, and resolution.

It begins with Canadian scholar and practitioner Carrie MacLeod's reflections on how the body is used as a vehicle for the expressions of grievance or ambition that underlie conflict. Think, for example, how mass amputation has been a weapon of civil war in Sierra Leone and, equally, how dance has been used there and elsewhere as an antidote to the psychic traumas of dismemberment. This is the first introduction to dance and movement as conflict intervention in the aftermath of civil war—a theme that emerges in several contributions to this book.

In contrast, the British scholar-practitioner Andrew Floyer Acland relates how his initial skepticism about dance and his struggle to find relevance in the project at Saas-Fee was gradually replaced with a growing understanding of what the experience could teach him about responding to the everyday challenges of his work. He takes us from his new appreciation of how the spaces between people need to be managed through a more-profound appreciation of nonverbal communication to how his enhanced perception of movement has helped him to discern the flow of energy among participants in partnership disputes and difficult public meetings.

Conflict-resolution practitioners Chris Honeyman, American negotiation expert and managing partner of Convenor Conflict Management, and Rachel Parish, the British American artistic director of Firehouse Creative Productions, begin with the argument that all collaboration involves unconscious skills akin to those used by dancers. They illustrate this with a striking photograph of a team of glaziers at work and then go on to explore the three types of movement—mental/creative, sociocontextual, and individual/embodied—that are essential in any shared endeavor. They conclude that dance is applied kinesthetic intelligence that can equally be called coordination or even logistics and that it offers a way into the creativity and flexibility required of negotiators and mediators.

Choreography of Conflict

Refinding Home
CARRIE MACLEOD

Conflict is no longer just about striving for physical territory or for the triumph of certain ideas. Violence to the human body has become an end in itself, often designed to prevent people from pursuing their political or cultural identities through physical expression. I will support this claim with examples of two different sociocultural contexts where the body has been at the center of conflict dynamics. The first example describes postconflict reconciliation programs in Sierra Leone, and the second focuses on immigration tensions within refugee communities in Canada. The scenarios from these conflicts may not initially appear to apply to other contexts. However, the following accounts demonstrate how kinesthetic sensibilities can help catalyze peaceful coexistence in a range of intercultural conflicts when identities are threatened.

Dehumanization begins and ends with the body. With corporeal terrain at the forefront of divisive conflict, the proliferation of peace-building and reconciliation initiatives cannot be fully comprehended unless the body is recognized as a primary site of violence, resilience, and renewal. As crucibles of social and cultural meaning, our physical selves are particularly vulnerable to exploitation embedded within conflict tactics. Therefore, returning to the body to find a semblance of meaning and mobility may be the most-crucial starting point for engaging with conflict. In this chapter, I will explore how somatic intelligence offers a poignant compass for navigating through conflict dynamics across borders and diverse fields of knowledge.

The Body as a Site of Violence and Renewal

The breaching of physical boundaries can have global implications. While working in the context of arts-based peace-building and resettlement initiatives after the eleven-year civil war in Sierra Leone, I witnessed firsthand the ramifications of fractured social systems. Years of mass terrorization led communities to a seemingly impossible question: How can one make sense of an imposed reality when primary senses are missing because of amputation of a limb? As Myriam Denov says in *Child Soldiers: Sierra Leone's Revolutionary United Front*, "In response to the 1996 Sierra Leonean presidential election campaign, and particularly the campaign slogan of 'The Future is in Your Hands', the RUF (Rebel United Front) embarked on mass amputations to terrorize the population and to punish and prevent them from voting."[1] For those who endured brutal amputations, conflict remained alive "under the skin" in the postconflict environment. Seemingly unresolvable conflict dynamics could not be comprehended solely through cognitive means and yet remained as stories inhabited in the body. Extreme episodes of personal, communal, and political upheaval also evaded linear conceptions of memory re-call. Delving into the past became a formidable challenge as specific memories became an-nihilated in the ongoing terror. Alternative modes of translation were needed to dismantle hierarchies of power that continued to disrupt local leadership structures. As bodies became symbolic sites of occupation during the war, the renegotiation of meaning systems needed to begin with reconfiguring human relations and accompanying societal structures that marked the legacies of the war.

The enormity of unsettled injustices that coincided with the displacement of over two mil-lion people in Sierra Leone necessitated the formation of community-led transitional justice mechanisms. Localized frameworks set apart from national truth and reconciliation initia-tives aimed to strengthen collective accountability while illuminating how conflicts are not only "behind" but also living corporeal entities in the present. These interventions moved beyond testimonial truth telling and focused more broadly on exposing the underlying and intersecting truths in national and international peace-building discourses. Before people could tell the truth, they were first compelled to move *through* the truth.

As amputees and ex-combatants lived in close proximity to one another during the re-settlement period, dance became a way to depersonalize entrenched patterns of blame and/or shame. By using the body as the primary translator between the past, present, and future, declared impasses began to shift through the self-organization that could be generated only from literally moving with one another. Amputee and war-wounded dance ensembles con-currently took up the challenge of inverting official accounts of archived history. Creating a sense of mobility in contested spaces made it possible to carve out room for a local recov-ery strategy. Recontextualized dance traditions became social movements that surpassed the oversimplified "forgive and forget" slogans that were pasted on billboards throughout Free-town, the capital city. In the center of some of the world's most-haunting absences, the weight of forgiveness could only be expressed through the sinews of the body.

The National Commission for Social Action fueled this momentum through its aim to re-store cultural dignity in forty Sierra Leonean chiefdoms through symbolic reparations.[2] Com-munity-led initiatives for transitional and restorative justice focused on the interdependence of perceived victims, perpetrators, and stakeholders in the surrounding regions. The Limba, Kuranko, Mandingo, Yalunka, Fula, and Susu ethnic groups explored avenues for peaceful coexistence through performances that combined oral storytelling with dance. This became a precursor for broader community-outreach strategies. There was an intrinsic understanding that intersections between truth and memory could not be understood through a disembod-ied analysis. A sensory vocabulary offered more than one homogenized version of history, and what was forgotten in the mind could be reassembled in the body.

In the collectivist society of West Africa, the emphasis on maintaining community cohe-sion takes precedence over the preservation of individual autonomy. Rebuilding relational webs became crucial amid identity friction that reinforced silos during the war. Varied reparations were granted to those labeled "war wounded," "amputees," "rebel wives," and/or "child soldiers," and such labels became points of contention, fraught with competition. These distinctions had a purpose in helping with funding allocations for aid organizations, but sociocultural stigmas were often magnified from associative meanings attached to these labels. A living system of justice that could focus on the shifting local, regional, global, and cultural influences was needed to address the limited perceptions of static identities. The perceived boundaries of implication needed to be expanded.

To reestablish bonds of social trust in this context, peace processes needed to account for the underlying values of social inclusion. Without pressuring people to disclose the intimate details of personal and political testimonies, dance created a ritual framework that fostered its own choreography of community accountability. Re-storying identities through the symbolic realm became a priority for redressing harms. Metaphors expressed through the body could touch on the enormity of loss, grief, and anger among survivors more effectively than a play-by-play verbal account of the "facts." Some people were convinced that it would be too dangerous to talk about the past and feared further retribution; others believed that overtly referring to past evils could actually disrupt a spirit realm that should not be tampered with. Many thought that recounting specific details would open old wounds and ultimately retraumatize individuals and communities. Apologies needed to be iterated and encountered in a culturally congruent manner. The dignity of dance created a physical grid to begin mapping the unspeakable and unknowable.

Creating momentum for peaceful coexistence was a formidable challenge after the war. Acts of dismemberment had left entire communities immobilized with amputations. Although the mind of conflict was physically branded on young skin with permanent inscriptions from the Rebel United Front, deeper sensibilities of resilience could not be destroyed. As movement patterns naturally filtered into the cultural milieu of the camps of the wounded and amputees, silenced stories of forced conscription became visible through embodied politics. Corporeal contracts began to replace wartime contracts of resentment and retaliation, and dance ensembles momentarily "stepped back" to reimagine conflict dynamics through the literal repatterning of relationships. The nonsensical aspects of war could be revisited first through the senses.

Transforming war-ravaged nonplaces into mobile cultural spaces ignited a sense of communal agency. Polarized victim/perpetrator dichotomies were gradually dismantled through new social contracts that were both dynamic and dialectical. Coexistence in the postwar climate depended on cultivating an ongoing exchange that would generate continued human connection. Such collaborations with trained and untrained dancers reconfigured previous victim narratives of exclusion. This communal choreography encoded new identities into old roles, making it possible to carve out culturally fluent strategies for peaceful relations. Embracing the realities of unsettlement provided the necessary choreography for settlement.

When the flurry of international aid began to dissipate, dancers from various chiefdoms, of their own volition, began to contest narratives of forced coercion. Local performances created a semblance of form for unformulated histories. In *All the Missing Souls: A Personal History of the War Crimes Tribunals*, David Scheffer describes Sierra Leone's underlying pattern of "tribunal fatigue and passing the buck to experts who would take their time making reports and recommendations . . ."[3] Local civilians were often impatient with imposed confessional processes that dismissed the importance of upholding cultural continuity. Some communities held coordinated responses to official juridical frameworks through the staging of unofficial truths that had never been spoken but were intrinsically known. Aesthetic, social, and political realms all contributed to the rebuilding of a cultural order that could provide a framework for memorialization, remembrance, and eventual reconciliation.

Most of the testimonies from remote regions in Sierra Leone have never made it to evidentiary contexts like the Truth and Reconciliation Commission, but many have been actively witnessed as truth-seeking bodies at the ground level. The truncated time frame of formalized systems could not possibly address all of the war narratives that changed the face of Sierra Leone. Even though traditional peace processes were not always included in "national" decision making, vignettes of cultural wisdom publicly acknowledged the disappeared and dispossessed. Unearthing these harbored truths from the tyranny of the past will likely take generations. However, if such time lines are solely dependent on a commission of outside experts, transitional justice will not reach its full potential.

There is much to learn from these culturally determined indicators of resilience that embraced the incomplete nature of peace processes. After the Lomé Peace Accord was signed in 1999, the outcomes took time to be fully realized in all levels of society. The guarantors of the agreement were faced with the dilemma of how to ensure equitable participation in all regions, as marginalized sectors outside of the capital city were often excluded in centralized peace processes. Commemorative dance rituals enabled civilians to find their rightful space amid the chaos of displacement. Interventions involving the nexus of arts, culture, and peace building brought performers and audiences closer to challenging issues without enforcing premature resolutions.

The velocity of tensions that are built up over time in a postconflict environment can lead to the breakdown of cultural traditions that are usually passed down between generations. Intergenerational tensions are referred to in other chapters of this book as well, because social bonds and kinship ties often crumble under the grinding weight of conflict. In Sierra Leone, generational pressures emanating from the conflict took time to unravel and could not be exiled prematurely from the nation's memory.

Prolonged states of political uncertainty created incongruous value gaps between elders and youths that became delicate junctures to move through. Returning to the traditional dances that had been passed down through successive generations prior to the war became a welcome starting point for intergenerational dialogue. Youths chose to combine versions of modern dance with traditional choreography to relay nonverbal narratives of Sierra Leonean history through the ages. Despite the new hybrid dance forms that emerged, the young people's interest in revitalizing dance pleased the elders greatly. This collective reclamation of the body offered a level ground for mutual connection in the midst of instability.

As dancers took up the challenge to rearrange social location (and dislocation) through new spatial grids, productive friction between bodies in motion created alternative reference points for both humility and humor. From new entry points of awareness, youths and elders alike could recover muted histories from the past, restructure the present, and reimagine the future. Stephen K. Levine recognizes this in *Trauma, Tragedy, Therapy: The Arts and Human Suffering*, stating that "[t]o be in time means to be embodied."[4] A rewriting of history involves perspective taking as well as ways of generating new perspectives. As the body stretches beyond the familiarity of pedestrian movement patterns, perceptual fields shift and the relationship to history is altered.

This is touched upon further by John Paul Lederach and Angela Jill Lederach, writing in *When Blood and Bones Cry Out: Journeys through the Soundscape of Healing and Reconciliation*. They gesture toward the momentum that unravels from using movement-based strategies: "Here we must envision elements of movement metaphors—for example, repetitiousness or circularity—as contributive and positive components of change, rather than as negative components that are stagnating, reactive or detrimental."[5] From these shifting angles, "senseless" acts of injustice and inexplicable absences may be inherently known, or sensed, even though they cannot be explained in a rational manner. In many instances, an end to hostilities does not ensure that consensus or peace will ultimately be reached. Learning how to engage with conflict relies on reauthoring the given narratives of contestation. If people do not engage physically, ambivalence can prevail as they literally and figuratively lose touch with one another. The artistry of reconciliation arises from the palette of the senses.

As demonstrated in the context of Sierra Leone, conflict dynamics are not necessarily resolved solely through written peace agreements. Sustained social cohesion could not thrive apart from the cultural constructs that influenced social interactions. Peace building relied on creating affective communication between all levels of society and governing elites. Movement scores revealed emerging leadership patterns and showed how decision-making processes actually fell into certain hands or on other shoulders. In Sierra Leone, a place marked by the absence of limbs, dance served as a multifold peace monitor and prosthesis of choice from which to realign corporeal absences with a strengthened political and cultural presence.

Mobilizing Identities

In some instances, dance may distinctively act as a mobile mediator, revealing how we are obliged to others through subtle or overt contracts. Amid the climate of globalization, we find ourselves literally and metaphorically in the hands of one another. Dance reveals that our lives are in constant motion as a woven choreography of interdependence. More than ever, it is important to ask where and how contested borderlands influence identity and conflict. Physical and metaphorical positioning will influence who handles the politics of forced migration across borders. In an era of uprooted lives, we need to discern how we position ourselves alongside those seeking refuge. We can begin to orient our individual and collective positions around these questions: Do we receive strangers with hostility or hospitality? Do we assume postures of welcome or suspicion for newcomers? How does our political stance reflect our embodied stance?

Catherine Dauvergne humanizes the issue of forced migration through tracing the physical and legal routes that "make people illegal,"[6] casting them as insiders or outsiders. In *Making People Illegal: What Globalization Means for Migration and Law*, she poignantly describes these repercussions of immigration regulations: "Migration laws make national borders meaningful for people, determining who can enter and who must be turned away. Through this process such laws constitute the community of insiders, and also spell out degrees of belonging and entitlement through the hierarchical systems they establish."[7] Amid the politics of dislocation, the body pivots to find new systems of belonging and social contracts in response to contested identities. We are not passive observers in this dance but actually become pivotal points of exchange as we choose to participate in acts of exclusion or inclusion. As composite forces that hold infinite potential to make and unmake identities, our bodies can be prime conduits for the proliferation of violence or peace building. Can a society ever collectively embark on the "unmaking"[8] of a child soldier? Some violent acts can never be unmade but can still be shaped.

While initiating arts-based refugee-settlement programs for youths and women throughout Vancouver, Canada, in the context of the CRANE[9] and Dancing at the Crossroads[10] projects, tensions among those with the abridged labels of "refugee," "immigrant," "newcomer," and "permanent resident" became apparent and—for some—could be fully narrated only through the body. For those who had fled war, persecution, or natural disaster, the gravity of loss and ensuing isolation was largely inexpressible. The haunting sense of arriving somewhere but belonging nowhere overshadowed their lives as they stood between gestures of welcome and fearful gazes of suspicion.

Creating living laboratories of dance and music became an ongoing source of "place making" for refugee youths who continually moved from one transitional housing complex to the next. Dance has provided a humane counterbalance to inhumane metaphors that have permeated media headlines for the past decade. Denigrating terms such as "human cargo" and "illegals" have objectified refugees—dislocating them with antagonistic language and tagging them as inhuman objects. The youths were sensitive to this imbalanced tension between hypervisibility and social invisibility and wanted to transpose these public anxieties into movement scores. It became apparent in the early stages of the project that they longed to be known first for *who they were*, not solely as passive and victimized refugees in need of care.

Although the segregated media language was a source of aggravation, the words ironically served as a catalyst for the creation of a dance piece titled *When Words Fall Apart*. Original choreographies provocatively revealed how the "other" is located just outside of visible sight lines, with something or someone always standing in the way. The youths were determined to overcome acts of dismissal and move together into a place of being seen and known. Their dance piece confronted the core meanings of citizenship and served as a performed critique of the ideological underpinnings in the media. Even beyond identification with the other, dance offered a superordinate springboard from which to confront, construct, and create new frames for a contextually sensitive social choreography. Ironically, in moving awkwardly with one another into the unknown, it became possible to become more meaningfully known.

In tracking the pacing, tempo, and levels of connectivity of the dance ensembles, the evolving nature of both in-group and intergroup relations became tangible as interweaving patterns of dissonance arose in the evolving choreography. When dancers were challenged to combine divergent ideas into one choreographic score, opposing tensions served as catalysts for creative solutions. As Robin Grove and colleagues indicate in *Thinking in Four Dimensions: Creativity and Cognition in Contemporary Dance,* it became apparent that "the search for meaning is often resolved when the right form is found."[11] How the youths reconfigured themselves with one another influenced how the production was created. Clear breakthroughs occurred as youths formed new affiliations and improbable relationships between "strangers." They were literally within reach of new understandings. These encounters revealed that *home* is not merely a noun but is also a verb to be actively inhabited with all of the senses.

The stressors of resettlement affected the youths in very specific ways. Some perceived their forced displacement to be amorphous, curved or circular, without any particular anchor points; others could recall the minute details of border crossings from more-linear accounts. Dance created an abridged form for the range of unsettled exchanges that encompassed the multiple departures and arrivals. In the final phases of the project, the newcomers were the primary choreographers and took the initiative to invite youths from the surrounding host communities to join in. This invitation provided an opportunity for those from host cultures to reframe their perceptions of the newcomers as they found their place in the already-established choreography. This inverted space was not based on ideals of assimilation but on visions of how differences could be recognized, embraced, and honored. The culminating original dance piece was performed in several locations for the neighborhood and ended with a series of postperformance dialogues between the dancers and the audience. Social patterns became transparent as the youths had to negotiate varying levels of inclusion while maintaining distinct identities. The performance unmasked what was previously hidden. The dynamic points of reference created through dance made it possible for displaced youths to transition from a crisis model of survival to a creative model of resilience.

The Geography of Embodiment: Foundations for Communication

A sensory vocabulary is essential for moving through conflict dynamics in a variety of contexts. For instance, cultivating a sensory acuity in family mediation will make it easier to recognize the physiological shifts and impulses that arise from deeply entrenched patterns. One family member may claim to never feel "seen" by others, but this perception likely extends into a more-encompassing sense of feeling unacknowledged. Finding modes of mutual exchange that do not spiral into degenerative patterns of blaming and judging can be challenging. In contexts like this, a tactile inquiry into underlying commitments and assumed obligations can be insightful. A heightened awareness can arise as family members are invited to move into spatial configurations that convey their instinctive affiliations. The person who feels unseen may move into closer physical alignment with certain family members. Working with spatial proximities in certain scenarios can reveal interrelated motives and expectations that stem from deeply seated family patterns. If bodies remain closed or "shut down," it may be challenging to shift positions and untangle certain loyalties. A closed body leads to a closed mind over time. An embodied framework like this can be very helpful in exposing how systems of belonging are instinctually choreographed.

As the example suggests, a vast world of insight lives beyond familiar dominant frames of reference if we can extricate ourselves from our usual habits of attention and perception. Venashri Pillay reiterates the necessity of seeing through wide-angle lenses to view the full horizon of conflicts. In her essay "Culture: Exploring the River," she reminds us that "contexts and experiences vary and cultures are never static, so there is always the possibility of changing frames, making adjustments, or adding new lenses to our repertoire."[12] Pillay goes on to underline the importance of proactively developing cultural fluency. She writes: "Given that differences can be construed in damaging ways, we should not wait for the actual moment of interaction with someone different to gain awareness of our own lenses and our repertoire of other cultural lenses."[13] In practicing relational dances with others in a safe environment, we can learn how to respond supply when conflict actually does arise.

Our positioning in conflict is consciously or unconsciously mediated through the body. Even without overtly naming what needs to be addressed, subtle resolutions may emerge unbidden in corporeal terrain. If we loosen our grip on agenda-driven approaches, there can be room to expand shortsighted views. A crisis or an impasse does not necessarily mean that all sensory capacities are blocked; our kinesthetic intelligence can be rerouted into choices that are generative and life giving.

A Third Space for Contact

Deteriorating patterns of retaliation accompany narrow-mindedness and hurtful dominance. Dance holds the potential to override a narrowed gaze through offering multiple pathways for exchange at every turn. Preconceived agendas can be temporarily suspended to make room for what is arising in the moment. Overcoming tunnel vision calls for an expansive choreography of linguistic, symbolic, and conceptual explorations. In a collaborative task where we can become resensitized to affective relations, a "third"[14] space can emerge. New vantage points can be leveraged and attended to in this "arriving third,"[15] creating opportunities to transform confrontational stances into fluid positions. This spaciousness allows for literal breathing room. In "Another view of 'we': Majority and minority group perspectives on a common ingroup identity," John Dovidio and colleagues further articulate the potential of this overarching third space for mediating in-group and out-group relations, claiming that "if people continue to regard themselves as members of different groups but at the same time part of the same superordinate entity, intergroup relationships between subgroups will be more positive."[16]

With the opportunity to extend beyond mere contact,[17] working on an original dance piece can create shared experiences that transcend the limitations of existing commonalities and differences. In an exploration of contact hypothesis, scholars Dixon, Durrheim and Tredoux argue that interaction between members of different groups reduces intergroup prejudice if—and only if—certain optimal conditions are present.[18] The two groups need to be of equal status at the time of contact, and individual interactions need to occur among the members of the two groups. Further, it is suggested that the two groups should have a common goal that can be reached through cooperation.[19] This is not always possible, especially with groups that have deep lines of enmity constructed between them. A dance ensemble offers an alternative frame for intergroup contact and opens up new possibilities for textured collaborations that reflect larger cultural imperatives. Valuable lessons can be gleaned from this process because the challenge of creating a cohesive choreographic score mirrors the challenge of communicating across worldview differences. Turning focus away from the perceived problem and turning to the body for solutions opens up space to move beyond a scarcity mentality. Channeling energy away from antagonistic positions diffuses the literal weight of a conflict. This provides the necessary "leg room" in places where binding logic may be hindering spacious and animated responses. As Michelle LeBaron suggests in *Bridging Cultural Conflicts*, "[s]hifts happen throughout dynamic engagement,"[20] and if we have even a hint of mobility within our reach, we can begin to imagine the world anew.

Movement patterns tend to find their own resolutions, just as chords tend to resolve in music; in this way, movement becomes a vital source of information for understanding intergroup dynamics. The point is not to strive toward unification as an end product but rather to trust that incremental agreements will emerge through the dance itself. When movement coalesces and becomes crystallized[21] into an original composite form, new insights can inform the process of creative negotiation. Dance reveals how entry and exit points are chosen, how unanticipated intersections are addressed, and whether habits of attention can be shifted when multiple agendas converge. Dance can support the suspension of judgment while new relational reference points are being discovered through the body moment by moment.

Mapping Lived Experience

Because bodies are carriers of culture, our physical schemata determine how we position ourselves in relation to conflict. A sense of cultural cohesion is often compromised in the midst of conflict. Creating culturally fluent interventions that are transparent is therefore particularly important, as cultural codes are tacitly contained and communicated via physical encounters. Kinesthetic patterns can expose how we strategically and intuitively occupy space when conflicts become heightened. In some cultures, there may be a magnetic pull toward gathering collective strength; in other cultures, the first response may be to rely solely on oneself.

The body is a primary translator for cultural practices of meaning making. Cultural conditioning is inscribed on our bones, and our kinesthetic responses communicate far more than we realize. Our ingrained habits can inevitably affect the transmission of messages. In high-context cultures, implied meanings arise from the physical setting, relational cues, or shared understandings. In such settings, a simple gesture or slight shift in gaze may open up possibilities for subtle breakthroughs in negotiations. In low-context cultures, where physicality may be overtly embedded in communication patterns, a more-direct approach might be more acceptable. Anxieties around movement-based approaches may limit the potential of this work in some cultural contexts.

From physical descriptions throughout this book, we learn that conflict is not stagnant but exists largely within a web of moving fissures and fault lines. Knowledge that is mapped within our sensorimotor system offers tactile wisdom that truly makes "sense," creating new avenues for mobility beyond the impasse of polarized thinking. The body's task is to follow through with choices that originate in the neuromuscular system. We may be able to move beyond dissensus by grasping new perspectives if we maneuver fluidly and approach conflict with open hands.

Literal and figurative elements constantly inform one another through gestural cross-overs in dance. This interchange creates spaces for receptivity and openness. Cognitive and kinesthetic channels are always part of symbiotic loops because, as the Lederachs put it, "[m]ovement material that is created, performed or observed engages motor and kinesthetic processes and leads to cognitive and affective reactions. Rich in gesture, expression and affect, contemporary dance is a heightened form of nonverbal communication."[22] Therefore, "choreographic cognition"[23] directly influences the choreography of conflict.

Re-embodying Conflict Theory

Ironically, the body is often conspicuously absent in dominant discourses on peace building and conflict transformation. Although passivity and physical withdrawal often lead to impasse in conflict, many interventions fail to honor the body's place in catalyzing cognitive mobility. Is this a form of censorship in conflict discourse? Absence of the body may mean that we have withdrawn our essential selves from conflict interventions and theories of practice. Narratives of reconciliation cannot be dissected apart from the body. However, there is a disquieting risk in exposing our sensory selves to one another. Understanding the limitations of context-specific interventions is essential for ethical practice.

Constantly defaulting to verbal communication overlooks social referents that emerge from the messages that stem from our musculature. Dance offers a corporeal map for conscious and unconscious patterns that exist between and within bodies in motion. In *Creativity and Conflict Resolution: Alternative Pathways to Peace*, Tatsushi Arai digs down further into shifting tectonic layers of meaning to seek out the source of value judgments and discovers that "they are shaped and reshaped not only through cognitive and emotive processes at the conscious level, but also through meaning-making processes that take place beneath the conscious, namely, the preconscious."[24] Through embodying the physical and emotional substrata that shape the very nature of our identities, we are relearning how to craft new inner and outer relational comfort zones.

Another challenge lies in connecting conflict theory with the body so that the intrinsic value of kinesthetic intelligence can be leveraged with more credibility across disciplines and spheres of discourse. The body is often met with suspicion and distrust; social, historical, or cultural constraints may compound this reality and limit the scope for embodied engagement. A commitment to creating culturally fluent interventions will uphold the power of social bonds that are often lost in the midst of conflict. In Arai's words: "Cultural fluency asks us to remember that culture is a set of internalized understandings and ways of interacting with the world."[25] Productive mediation and negotiation begin with multiple intelligences that can physically stretch across both internal and external lines of enmity. Michelle LeBaron clearly confirms this in *Bridging Cultural Conflicts* when she states that cultural "[f]luency involves sense-making."[26] Cultivating proprioceptive sensibilities inverts conflict interventions from a top-down analysis to a multisensory synthesis. An embodied inquiry into the subtle intricacies of nonverbal language can begin to reveal points of unease. Forward thinking relies on all of the senses.

Through a proprioceptive lens, our perspectives expand to include what the neuroscientist Ian McClosky describes as "the sensory processes responsible for the conscious appreciation of posture and movement, and also the many sensory inputs involved in unconscious, reflex adjustments of balance."[27] These active adjustments are always happening in dance, with the reliance on proprioceptive sensibilities to get an overall sense of how and where the body can move. According to Imogen Walker's analysis, this ability has been deemed "the fastest internal feedback system" and is often referred to as our "sixth sense."[28] It is available to us at all times and can help us understand the underlying "cultural logic"[29] that may not be easily discernible through verbal language.

Activating this sixth sense has the potential to crack limited assumptions that we have about the other. Through these emergent openings, dance harnesses the potential of sociocultural proprioception. New or reorganized systems of meaning can arise from choices that are collectively made through the wider sensory radius that dance is able to cultivate. Recent dance and neuroscience research by Jola, Davis and Haggard affirms the "outstanding proprioceptive ability"[30] of dancers and recognizes that in relation to other artistic and athletic disciplines the "proprioceptive aesthetic sensibility of the dancer is most pronounced."[31] With this somatic intelligence in mind, a comprehensive understanding of conflict depends on a coherent understanding of the body as a whole. Bodies bear the schema of conflict in both explicit and implicit ways, and dance compositions can illuminate the interrelatedness of both.

Spatial and temporal elements are often manipulated to confine, isolate, or segregate individuals or groups in the midst of conflict. The capacity for movement and choice is limited in the presence of coercion. Unscripted responses and imperceptible interests may be suppressed, yet they live on in the body. As identities become subsumed and divided in webs of conflict, movement traces the lines and sources of distinctive behaviors that may otherwise evade acknowledgment. With sensations serving as a starting point, mobilization of the body becomes a vehicle for fluidity and receptivity.

We can aptly apply Pruitt's readiness theory[32] to an embodied approach in negotiation. In this theory, set out in "Readiness Theory and the Northern Ireland Conflict," an active stance of "readiness" is required to address the "two [necessary] variables of motivation and optimism"[33] when a negotiation begins. This heightened sense is a precondition for creating momentum and finding the support to move through conflict. Readiness is not a unilateral state of mind but a multilateral approach that is embodied. As impulses accompany thoughts, tacit knowledge directs how we literally and symbolically move toward or away from one another. Conciliatory or nonconciliatory gestures reveal a readiness for engagement as levels of commitment are exposed through embodied dispositions. Danielle Goldman points us in this direction in *I Want to Be Ready: Improvised Dance as a Practice of Freedom*, with an exploration of "improvised dance as a vital technology of the self—an ongoing critical, physical and anticipatory readiness that, while grounded in the individual, is necessary for a vibrant sociality and vital civil society."[34]

As unexpected stimuli come to us, readiness also involves self-care. Through an active stance, we are available to "catch" ourselves if we become overloaded, overstimulated, or off balance. In physically listening to others, we in turn become attuned to the tone and cadence of conflict patterns within ourselves. Contact improvisation dancers rely on this keen level of attunement, says Danielle Goldman, as they seek ways "to improvise in the midst of unfamiliar falls" and "to make choices and maintain safety in moments of physical duress."[35] The common sentiment "I've got your back" needs to find truth first in our own dexterity, balance, and sense of alignment. Protracted conflict remains static and suspended if inflexibility persists. As we stand in relation to the commitments and contracts we have made with one another, our skeletal systems can serve to support a greater sense of congruence and flexibility. This active receptivity requires an element of risk as we engage the ambiguities that surround us. Dance does not promise neat outcomes but does offer enlivened responses that can dissolve apathy or indifference.

Navigating Spatial and Temporal Terrain

There is a visceral, bodily tension that often lingers in the lives of those who have been displaced by upheaval. Social pressures of acculturation can lead people to be unseen, unheard, and untouched within the realms of the dominant culture. How we perceive and receive one another is traceable through the body, and dance exposes visible reference points that reveal implicit modes of communication. Dance calls us to share encounters rather than merely speaking at one another.

With the capacity to hold possibility and contradiction, dance can suspend assumptions until movement finds its own solutions. If we become aware of how physical habits of attention orient us in space, we will be more aware of how much room we have to accommodate the other. Stagnant positions may prevent us from literally reaching out to others or touching on what is essential. New solutions arise through the body as physical shifts remove old patterns.

Embodying a New Grid for Coexistence

From these overlapping fields of inquiry, we have seen that somatic interventions have a central role to play in reconciliation and resettlement processes. For those who have endured years of suffering through perpetual upheaval, a symbolic and literal return to the body can restore aspects of truth telling that have previously been denied. Relational grids find new intersections through movement, creating space for grievances to be publicly acknowledged. Former antagonists can also face one another in a ritualized framework and begin to mend disjointed relations through a physical vocabulary. In contested spaces across literal and symbolic borderlands, the starting point for opening oneself to the other begins with an embodied consensus.

Unlearning habitual responses and resetting the internal and external compasses of conflict orientation became part of this intricate dance in Sierra Leone and Canada. The "third space" of dance made it possible to step beyond the categories of "us" and "them" and negotiate terms of coexistence with dominant and minority groups in diverse societies. In the chasms between irresolvable differences, the return to an embodied praxis has reframed how conscious and unconscious metaphors can be mined. These new choreographies have boldly reclaimed space—one gesture at a time.

This sensory grounding is the bedrock of effective conflict transformation and peace building. Through body language we can begin to move toward one another with a sense of tactile recognition and step aside from habitual responses that may undermine effective communication. Past identities can become repositioned through the immediacy of the senses. In the new relations born of these interactions, the phoenix can indeed rise from the ashes of conflict.

Choreography of Space
Transforming Conflict through Movement
ANDREW FLOYER ACLAND

Introduction

It was on the second or third day that something clicked for me. Margie Gillis lined us up on one side of the room and said we should work with another person and be everywhere that person was not.

So a partner was chosen by an inclination of the head and a reciprocal smile. I found myself trying very hard indeed not to be where she was. At first we moved slowly, getting used to the shape and pace of each other's steps and dips. She was clearly a dancer, her graceful bends and lifts putting to shame my clumsy attempts to take over the places she had been or thrust my awkward feet into the space where her small and neat ones might otherwise be.

Suddenly we seemed to find a rhythm. We began to anticipate more fluently where the other was not going to be and find ourselves there and then away again. We passed each other faster and closer, arms and legs almost meeting but missing, bodies angled in, then away, then in again, as if twined by an elastic that allowed so much but no more. We reached closer to the floor, higher toward the ceiling, lost in the shuffle and pad of our feet, breath coming harder, bodies more fluid, limbs curling and curving, intertwined yet independent, the connection with and awareness of the other made more acute by the need to not intrude or collide.

Then it was over. We subsided onto a bench, flushed, slightly triumphant. We had crossed a room without crossing each other, and we had created a space between us that was empty and full at the same time. It lasted only a few minutes but added a whole new dimension to my quarter century of experience in mediation and conflict resolution.

The temptation in writing this chapter was to follow habit and rush into a cerebral analysis of the lessons that dance can offer, but I decided to pursue the process that those moments of dance revealed to me, allowing ideas and realizations to flow from the experience and leaving summary and analysis until later. I would use my visual and kinesthetic memories to shape my writing in the same way that they had transformed my understanding of this alien world of art and dance.

History and Context

The previous week, it would have been hard to believe I would have such an epiphany halfway up a Swiss mountain. I had spent one day locked in negotiation over the program for a three-day meeting intended to bring together people from all over the world to discuss sustainable development. The organizers, realizing rather late that some of their sessions were likely to be impassioned, had invited me and a colleague to design and facilitate the program. Another long day had been devoted to a complex dialogue among scientists, policy makers, and various pressure groups about the ethics and economics of government policy on the genetic modification of crops. I had also spent a day in court as a justice of the peace, dealing with some of the myriad criminal cases that the United Kingdom's lower courts, staffed by volunteers like me, cope with every year.

Two of these roles—process designer and mediator/facilitator of dialogue—are complementary and reflect the bulk of my work in many different contexts over the past twenty-five years. The anchor word is *dialogue*, regardless of whether I am working with politicians and diplomats, environmentalists and civil society campaigners, or corporate strategists and consultation managers. Dialogue—real, deep, exploratory, messy dialogue—is what builds relationships and resolves conflict. I find the tension—dialogue—between these two types of roles a way to sharpen my understanding of both. My other role as a magistrate, imposing life-changing judgments on others, is in deliberate counterpoint to the rest of my professional life.

These are all word-heavy roles, however, and as I performed them I was already both excited and daunted by the prospect of word-light dance looming over my schedule. It meant leaving a safe and familiar world and doing something utterly unsafe and unfamiliar. As the time to catch my plane and train to Saas-Fee drew closer, increasingly I looked for some dialogue between these two worlds, some link between the two ways of being that were about to converge.

The epiphany was a long time coming, and I had been everywhere that everyone else was not before the link appeared and things began to click.

Space and Absence

The first lesson was that empty space can be full of where we are not. This realization brought to mind a long-ago holiday that I had devoted to learning to draw, taking with me a miraculous book called *Drawing on the Right Side of the Brain*[1] and discovering from it that one of the problems for tyro artists is the tendency to draw things not as they are but as our memory and experience tell us that they should be.

Drawing negative spaces—what is not there—is a way to reach beyond the tyranny of habit and established knowledge into the immediacy of present vision. One exercise to reveal the value of this, for example, involves copying from an upside-down drawing or photograph. Because the picture is upside down, you do not as readily recognize what you are drawing, so you give equal attention to positive and negative shapes. Distracting the part of the brain that rationalizes perception results in a drawing that reflects more accurately what is actually in sight.

I have used this idea in training mediators and facilitators. It is easy to talk about mediation and conflict resolution as creative processes: the importance of generating options that encourage people to come out of the corners into which they have painted themselves or of expanding the pie before dividing it. But creativity is one of the first casualties of conflict. The instinct is to hunker down in one's own trench and avoid the risks that creativity can entail. Helping people see that the negative has a shadow, shape, and substance can be a more-constructive way of pointing out that doing nothing also has costs.

The same point is made more broadly by Alan Fletcher when he discusses the importance of understanding space as a substance:

> Space is substance. Cézanne painted and modelled space. Giacometti sculpted by *"taking the fat off space."* Mallarmé conceived poems with absences as well as words. Ralph Richardson asserted that acting lay in pauses . . . Isaac Stern described music as *"that little bit between each note—silences which give the form."* The Japanese have a word (*ma*) for this interval which gives shape to the whole. In the West we have neither word nor term. A serious omission.[2]

Stumbling across this was also helpful. I remembered gardens I had seen in Kyoto, with their entrancing swirls of sand and gravel around rocks, the single plants amid layers of moss, the use of understated suggestion. This had perfectly reflected my clients' reluctance to commit to any solutions to their problems, their preference for vague hints, and their comfort with ambiguity and reticence, quite alien to Western corporate thinking. Some of my colleagues found this approach maddening, both in work and gardening. They looked in vain for more evidence of hard decision making and planting as well as space, since in the modern world we tend to fill our waking moments with perpetual noise. The spaces in Japanese gardens are about the rhythm of shapes, the pauses between things that allow each to stand out from the mass; similar to retreat houses, I imagine, where each thought has time to crystallize and mature. Such spaces are not empty but lend feeling and texture to the whole as well as enjoying their own kind of fullness.

Fletcher illustrates the point with the poem *The Uses of Not*, by the Taoist philosopher Lao Tse:

> Thirty spokes meet in the hub,
> but the empty space between them
> is the essence of the wheel.
> Pots are formed from clay,
> but the empty space between it
> is the essence of the pot.
> Walls with windows and doors form the house,
> but the empty space within it
> is the essence of the house.[3]

Making these preliminary connections started to transform dance for me. It went from something done for artistic expression, which I found hard to appreciate, to something quite different—something that might bridge the gap between reason and the point in conflict work where reason is not enough. I realized that dance might also change my understanding of dialogue and my role as a mediator and facilitator in the everyday world.

Movement and Shape

My new acquaintance with dance led me to see that it is about turning movement into art, and as with all art, to this nonartist at least, there is a division into what is seen and what is felt. The seeing part is relatively easy: posture, gesture, and positioning. Presumably the equivalent of negative space for the dancer is not just the space between the dancer and others but the space that is created by nonmovement.

In terms of what is felt, nonmovement, with its expectations that the moment will pass and movement will resume, brings with it a certain tension. There is the anticipation of what will happen next but also an awareness of the relationship between the dancers. What does that space feel like for them? What is it like to be still with someone, in the aftermath of movement, and in the expectation of more?

Without movement there is space for other things, such as the feel of connection with the other person. Perhaps you notice the person's breathing, which normally would be swallowed up and out of perception. Such a space also means that anything you do, such as a tiny movement, a change of breathing, the flexing of a muscle, or the slight inclination of a limb or the head, must have a magnified meaning for the other person because he or she is free to notice it.

The parallels with dialogue and conflict work are obvious. People bring their relationships with one another, and with themselves, into the dialogue. They come with their personal histories, their past experience of one another, and their current and future expectations. These all converge into a tangle of threads and knots that somehow have to be untangled and woven into the rope that carries people across the chasm from where they are to where they want to be.

If dance expresses itself through nonverbal communication, then presumably its steps and gestures, its postures and movements, are the equivalents of the words and grammar in dialogue; and these are the individual strands that must be woven into the rope across the chasm. Trying to understand more about this idea of dance as a means of nonverbal communication, I asked Margie Gillis if she could always understand what a dancer was trying to express. No, she said, not always. One might get a feeling for what a dancer is trying to convey, but it is usually unclear, shrouded in uncertainty, somewhat mysterious.

Since writing this, I have had colleagues point me to some of the literature on the subject. Judith Hanna's work on dance and its meanings at different times and in different cultures, for example, includes a profound study of the parallels and differences between dance and verbal communication. "Dance," she says, "is a physical instrument or symbol for feeling and/or thought and is sometimes a more effective medium than verbal language in revealing needs and desires or masking true intent."[4] For me there is warning here as well as revelation. The cursory mentions of nonverbal communication that often accompany mediation training sometimes teach that nonverbal communication can be more revealing than the words a person uses: it is commonplace to be told that how people arrange their physiology in a meeting reveals more about what they really think than anything they may say. Hanna's work is a useful counterpoint to this naive belief that the body cannot deceive as fluently as the mouth. If, as she says, "dance is human thought and behavior performed by the human body for human purposes," then the body will deceive as fluently as the mouth if that is the purpose to be served.

There is an obvious parallel here with fencing, which is as much art as sport. Success depends on using physical communication to deceive an opponent into parrying in the wrong direction while one thrusts in another and likewise to not be deceived by an opponent into defending the wrong part of the body. Sometimes it is no more than the fractional movement of the sword point or the slight change of weight from one foot to another that indicates an intention. In the days when the swords were sharp and the masks and padding absent, such attunement to physical cues could, of course, have meant the difference between life and death.

Poetry and Prose

Margie's reply also introduced the next stage in my journey of understanding. It made me think that perhaps dancers communicate in the *poetry* of movement rather than in the *prose* of movement employed by athletes (other than fencers). I remembered how much I had enjoyed poetry at university thirty-odd years before. I wondered whether mediation and dialogue appeal to me because they are more like poetry than prose, and mediators more like poets than the stern essayists who might appeal to the lawyers and policy makers with whom I work.

If this is the case, what makes my work more like poetry than prose? I can think of two immediate answers: the narrative, storytelling element and the elusive, allusive hints and subtleties that alert a mediator's intuition to what is *not* being said because it is too painful, too clouded, too little understood by the persons themselves. Mediation is also, like poetry, the art of posing the right questions, in just the right words, to the right people at the right moments; and it is those "rights" that make mediation more art than science and a process resting on unconscious intuition as much as on deliberate and conscious judgment. In this it resembles fencing, where action and reaction need to be faster than conscious thought can ever be.

I felt I was getting somewhere, especially when these thoughts combined with the idea of negative space between dancers. They awoke a half-remembered notion of "negative capability," tracked down to the poet John Keats, who described it as the state of being "in uncertainties, mysteries, doubts, without any irritable reaching after fact and reason."[5] It seemed to me that the negative spaces of art and dance might be kin to this sense of potential untrammeled by too much reason and analysis in the same way that mediators are drawn to what is unvoiced as both a source of conflict and a possible resolution or transformation. Is it the role of artists, poets, and dancers—and mediators—to act as a bridge between the known and the unknown, between the surface and the hidden?

Intrigued by this train of thought, I was reminded of another poet I loved, Gerard Manley Hopkins, and his concepts of "inscape" and "instress."[6] Hopkins describes inscape as the particular features of something, usually a natural object or phenomenon, that render it unique and special, different from any other; he saw instress as the experience of inscape and how it is received into the sight, memory, and imagination of the perceiver. The appreciation of uniqueness is something else that artists and mediators share: one of my first lessons was that every conflict situation, however much it may resemble another, is always unique to those enmeshed in it. It is why case histories are of limited value in training mediators and why I despair of those who would reduce mediation training to the formulaic. I have too often seen or heard mediation taught as a series of moves akin to those in a courtroom: first one side makes a statement, then the other side; then you separate them for caucuses, and you shuffle between them until one side or the other comes up with an offer that you can turn into a deal. This is mediation as prose.

Mediation as poetry enables people to escape the constraints of the purely rational and enter the real world, which, if it were run entirely on reason, would not need the services of mediators in the first place. Mediation as poetry involves, first of all, teaching people to listen to one another and then to understand what they are hearing in the way that it is intended; to understand what is being said but also what is not being said; to appreciate fully what is rational and what is less rational but equally significant; to see into others' hearts and souls as well as their minds. Most of all, it involves understanding and responding to each individual and each situation as unique, even when you have been through a thousand similar encounters.

Focus and Energy

This latter realization made another link for me. If we should teach mediators about poetic concepts such as instress and inscape as vehicles for seeing more deeply into the souls of others, then maybe we should teach mediators to dance as another way to feel and recognize the essence and uniqueness of others. Dancing with someone, I suddenly realized, had given me a vivid sense of her inscape, and it was the instress of her, the impression of her, that had flowed through the space between us. This had shaped the space and given it a kinetic energy as we soared and plunged across the floor.

How can space have kinetic energy? The remnants of my school physics told me it was impossible; my experience in Saas-Fee contradicted this and suggested that understanding the energy in the space between people might be something that mediators need to be aware of when facing the silence and the space between those in conflict.

What else might be learned from dance that would help us sense, measure, and understand such spaces? Those few minutes on the dance floor had inspired in me a passionate hunt for links, analogies, and ideas that could shed light on one of the most difficult aspects of intervening in conflict. Many of us find ourselves wondering what to do in the times and places when nothing seems to be happening or when the vacuum of inaction is so begging to be filled that some ill-considered action seems preferable to no action at all. It is similar to the vacuum caused by uncertainty, a frequently overlooked cause of conflict that locks people into a cycle of fear in response to it, hostility in response to that fear, conflict as a consequence of the hostility, and further uncertainty as a result of conflict.

With the associations flowing, I finally accepted the idea that mediators and artists of all sorts might have more in common than I would previously have thought. I started looking for more parallels between mediation and dance and the only art form at which I have ever demonstrated any ability: sculpture. Sculpting is about finding something alive within materials that seem dead—releasing something that is already there. The process begins with becoming open to the shape and spirit of ordinary objects and materials, learning to appreciate them in their smallest particulars of weight, shape, color, and texture. This is the start of a strange alchemy: if you come to appreciate the individuality of something, even a random piece of wood or a stone, it becomes special, it loses its randomness, and you start a dialogue with it that begins to draw out its essence and what other life it contains. The sculpting process is also the beginning of appreciating things for their own sake. A stone has no objective value; it is just one stone among many. But once you have selected it, carried it, and picked it up to feel it and rub it a few times, it is no longer just any stone. It has an intrinsic value based on your relationship with it and the significance it carries for you, and it acquires a new energy that others recognize when they see or feel it. Dance, I realized, is doing sculpture where the sculptor and the material become one: you sculpt, and you are what is sculpted.

The more I danced, the more I realized that the medium of movement enables people to bring into the open capacities that are otherwise locked within them, just as the work of the chisel elicits a form of life from a block of stone or wood. These are both mediating processes that allow something inherent to be released into the light of day, and in the same way, the mediator creates opportunities for people in conflict to release the human urge to have resolution. Mediators do not resolve conflict; our job is to help people free themselves from whatever it is that prevents them finding their own way to resolution. We bring the energy they may need to find the insights or the empathy or the understanding that will transform the situation and their approach to it.

I finally understood that this is why mediators need to be artists as much as they need to be lawyers or psychologists or management consultants, because it is the job of artists to discern hidden possibilities, cultivate new tones and tempos, explore nuances of shade or meaning, and bring to life what is inherent. This is what artists do, whether poets, sculptors, designers, or dancers. Of all these, though, perhaps dancers have the most to teach mediators because of the awareness dance brings of presence, movement, and the uses of space—and, of course, because dance involves creating with human beings rather than nonhuman materials. The resolutions we help people find may be already embryonic within them, but they are born, take shape, and evolve in the spaces between people. We need to ensure that these spaces are suitably welcoming and nurturing.

Beginning to Translate

Dance still seemed a world away from my daily work, but between sessions on the dance floor I was fielding emails about an upcoming mediation for a county council, and it began to feel like a test case: Could my experience with dance translate into lessons or insights that would help me resolve that situation?

The word I kept coming back to was still *space*: what fills it and how it feels; how space can be inhabited in a way that welcomes others into it and perhaps encourages them to share it in a way that is freeing rather than inhibiting. I could not forget the freedom I had felt in trying to be where my fellow dancer was not, and I was curious to better understand how that space between us had changed from being a source of tension and embarrassment to one of energy and enjoyment. Was it something we did, or, in our efforts to be everywhere the other was not, was it perhaps more what we did *not* do?

I began to see the upcoming mediation as a way to anchor these gossamer ideas and turn them into something that I could explain to hardheaded colleagues and fellow practitioners. If I were them, I thought, I would want to know what dance could teach me about filling spaces. I would want a process, a technique, or at least a set of steps that would bring something new to our labors in the corporate and municipal bunkers of modern Britain.

The meeting took place in the medieval guildhall of a market town. Beneath the portraits of long-dead kings and an eighteenth-century sign exhorting the justices of a bygone age to "Be Just and Fear Not," I worked hard to repair and rebuild a damaged partnership between the county council and its subordinate districts. The tension between them dated back many years, and the poor relations among them now threatened their ability to work together in the service of their electors. The tides of the meeting flowed back and forth across the wooden floor, and the feelings in the room rose and subsided as we discussed old grievances, refuse collection, local taxes, and the challenges involved in increasing recycling rates. This is the bread and butter of the jobbing mediator: helping sturdy burghers bury rusty hatchets and make difficult decisions. Of what conceivable relevance could dance be?

In retrospect it was obvious: a mediation such as this *is* a dance. The participants had been dancing with one another around issues too sensitive to confront directly, forming temporary alliances to pursue a particular point, and finding areas of consensus where all could come together as a momentary relief from the pressures of not agreeing about other things. The stolid characters in sober suits could have been dressed in the same velvet and lace as the kings in the portraits; the women could have been ladies of the royal court, resplendent in silks and shawls, flirting behind their fans as they formed lines and circles around the room. Those formal courtly dances were designed, in obedience to the mores of the time, to keep people where their partners were not, just as our dance did in the workshop.

Seeing the meeting as a dance helped me notice the flow of energy within and between the participants. It helped me know when to intervene by asking a question and when to intervene by saying nothing but using my arms and body to query what was being said or to indicate that we needed to hear more from one person rather than another. It also helped with the pacing: the perpetual dilemma facing all mediators is when to speed up to maintain momentum and when to slow down to give people time to find their own way. The differences in my behavior were probably not huge—I have done such things many times before—but they were probably significant in that the meeting ran more smoothly and effectively than I would have expected.

Since then I have looked for opportunities to test further this idea of conflict as a dance, and I have found during a number of meetings and situations buzzing with tension that looking at people in conflict as if they are dancers means paying attention to things that previously I might not have noticed. Using dance as a lens has been useful on several levels. On a purely practical level, it has helped focus my attention on not just individual gestures or nonverbal signals but on the whole flow, pace, and shape of words and movement among and between people. It has also worked as a living metaphor: I have found that if I perceive participants in meetings as dancers as well as lawyers or businesspeople or bureaucrats, then I can discern more of what they are thinking and feeling. Perhaps this comes from removing labels and seeing people more as individuals than as holders of positions; perhaps it is simply an acuter awareness of the spaces between them, of how they open and close with their unconscious movements; or perhaps it is listening differently: hearing lines of poetry with meanings shrouded and taking time to absorb them rather than merely hearing official positions being stated and opposed.

There is another aspect of translating dance whose implications I am still considering: the difference between *reacting* and *responding*. This, again, is nothing new to a properly trained mediator, but the experience of dance has brought its significance home to me as an example of something that is best learned physically and viscerally. Reacting is finite; it conveys the message that there is no more to be done, no move that can take the process anywhere else, and, crucially, it places responsibility for this on the other person and so justifies blaming that person and indulging in some self-righteous anger, grief, and fear. Responding, on the other hand, means taking responsibility on oneself by acknowledging what has happened and one's own role in it, coupled with an invitation to explore further.

Being able to respond rather than react is a marker of emotional maturity. It is a way to ensure that the decisions we make and the behaviors we use take emotion into account without being dominated by it. This is an important counterpoint to the stance of many people, not least those embroiled in corporate and legal disputes, who prefer to believe that reason and emotion inhabit separate realms. We know from the work of neuroscientists such as Antonio Damasio[7] that all decisions involve emotion, and one of the roles of mediators is to teach our clients how to recognize and manage the emotional dimensions of the situations in which they find themselves. The final gift of dance to me has been learning more about how to manage the emotion contained in the body, to feel more of what I am feeling, and to use this new awareness to develop mature responses and thereby avoid the temptation to simply react.

Applications to Practice

I returned home from Saas-Fee with the conviction that I had experienced things that would be of value to fellow practitioners but with little idea of how to convince them of this. It took a while to realize that the significance of dance lies in what it can teach us about perceiving the real nature and character of the multiple dances, internal and external, that we and other people are doing during the process of mediation. Rather to my surprise, the lessons I have ultimately taken from dance have less to do with the use of movement and space—where I first began to look for insight—and more to do with the amplification of existing skills. The experience of dance does not so much bring new muscles into play as add strength and depth to existing ones.

To demonstrate this, I have decided to focus here on three areas of my current practice where I need to enhance my skills: the use of intuition, particularly in the management of large multiparty situations; the handling of interpersonal conflict; and the evolution of partnerships across cultural divides.

1. Intuition

Many mediators say that amid the rush and pressure of the immediate, the ability to say or do things quickly and intuitively becomes as important as careful and rational judgment and decision making, for which there is no time. It was the same in the "be where your partner is not" exercise, which was driven not by calculations of time and space but by responses to a partner too rapid to be anything but intuitive. Michelle LeBaron has described intuition as "the art of perception through the mind."[8] My week in Saas-Fee persuaded me that intuition can also be the art of perception through the body.

Dancing in a room full of people develops intuition in two directions at once. It increases your awareness of mood and movement in the group as a whole, and it forces you to develop your sensory appreciation of what is particular in every individual with whom you dance. Following on from this, I would argue that there are two more directions.

First, the more intuition develops, the less "nonrational" it becomes and more a skill like any other. Dance helps this process by making greater use of otherwise-underused senses. Perhaps intuition is not so magical but more about making conscious what is normally unconscious. This alone should put dance onto training curricula for mediators, particularly for those intending to work in very busy multiparty environments where there is simply no time to engage only one's rational processes. Dance is a shortcut to behavioral fluency in that it can help us choose the behavior we need at the moment we need it, in the same way that being fluent in a foreign language means that we can choose the right words when we need them. As a simple example, managing conflict in a large meeting means using your body to reassure people that the space is safe for them to express powerful emotions. If you stand too far from the participants, they may feel that you are frightened of what is happening; if you stand too close, they may feel that you are trying to restrict or control what is being said. Your posture can likewise convey similar messages. Dance has increased my ability to judge such distances and to notice any responses that suggest I need to change positions or posture.

The second direction will be more controversial. In a room of interacting people, every individual becomes a part of the dance. Can the mediator really stand *outside* the dance and still be intermediary, catalyst, neutral? I have no answer, but my small experience of dance leads me to see my own role in conflict somewhat differently. In future I may try harder to *join* the dance rather than standing outside it—providing I can do so in a way welcome to those with whom I share the space—and try to bring the group into working intuitively as well as rationally.

2. Interpersonal conflict

If one of the main lessons of dance concerns the increase of sensitivity to nonrational stimuli, it certainly applies to interpersonal conflict. This is a subject that people new to conflict resolution often find the most problematic: What exactly do you do when people are divided by personal animosities? All too often the temptation is to sidestep the issue: "They are just so different;" "It's a personality clash;" "You can't force people to like each other;" and so on. How can dance offer a new perspective on such apparently irreconcilable problems? Let's go back to being everywhere the other person is not. How exactly did we manage to move so fast and so close without colliding? I think the answer lies in three mutual understandings with the other person.

The first step is understanding the other person's *intent*. In the case of the dance, the shared intent was to travel across the room rapidly and closely but without colliding. This required both partners to make every effort, to strain every sense and sinew, to avoid collision. In the case of interpersonal conflict, there is often little understanding of the other person's intent, or that intent is misinterpreted, usually negatively; it is projected from one person onto the other, with the other reacting accordingly; or it is actively contrary. So the first step in resolving interpersonal conflict is for each person to understand more thoroughly the intentions of the other. This may reveal misunderstanding or misinterpretation, in which case a small dose of accurate communication will probably be helpful. If it reveals genuine and intended hostility, then the next steps come into play.

The second step is to explore needs, fears, interests, values, and identities, both shared and not shared. We dancers were fortunate in that while we were very different in many ways, we had enough prior knowledge to realize that the intention not to collide was underpinned by similar approaches to the dance, to each other, and to the context in which we were to perform our dance. Our differences—age, gender, nationality, and interests—were more than balanced by a common determination to avoid the embarrassment of falling over.

This is not true for much interpersonal conflict, which is usually based on actual, perceived, or assumed divergences of needs, fears, interests, values, and identities. And as with others' intent, the vacuum is filled with assumptions and interpretations. Knowing and understanding more about others tends to reduce hostility, but as important as this is, the appreciation of where boundaries lie can sometimes be even more valuable, because once we know that, we can know when we are crossing them and intruding on another's territory. To use the example of the dance again, the only way to avoid stomping on the other person's feet is to be intensely aware of not only where they are now but where they will be in the next moment, the moment after that, and so on.

The third step is to know when your actions are going to trigger problems with another person or when an individual will trigger a reaction (rather than a response) from you that similarly hinders rather than helps the relationship. In both cases the avoidance of triggers comes from first being aware of what the triggers are (such as both dancers heading for the same space in the case of dance or someone behaving in a particular way or using a certain tone of voice in the case of a difficult relationship) and then forming a conscious determination to do something different.

Appreciating the importance of these three steps—to understand another's intent and share it where possible; to understand interests, concerns, and boundaries; and to avoid triggers—is for me a lesson from dance directly transferable to intervention in conflict, perhaps because it goes beyond awareness and metaphor to provide a concrete, physical parallel between these two worlds.

3. Partnerships

The experience of dance is also relevant to partnerships across cultural divides. I am thinking here of personal partnerships and partnerships between organizations operating in different sectors with very different values and priorities. This interest stems from my work with the Partnership Brokering Project,[9] which brokers and supports partnerships among corporations, governments, and civil society organizations, mainly in developing countries and focused on sustainable development. It is a remarkable and pioneering initiative that has done much good and provided valuable training for many people and has also explored and developed the whole process of building partnerships among sometimes unlikely collaborators. Thinking back to the "be where your partner is not" exercise, I see that partnership as not unlike some of those I have studied through PBP: middle-aged, flabby, awkward nondancing male partnered with young, slim, graceful dancing female. What can dance teach about building unlikely partnerships?

First, unlikely partnerships are perfectly possible, providing that they are approached systematically and with the wholehearted consent of the partners. I have to admit, for example, that my choice of dancing partner was not random. I had been struggling with the whole idea of dancing, so I deliberately picked someone I knew a little and who knew of my reservations but still seemed happy to work with me. Despite our physical differences, we had things in common: she was of similar height to me and at least as strong, so that if I fell over or trod on her toes, which was likely, she would not be crippled and I would not be too embarrassed. This is what constitutes a systematic approach when it comes to choosing a dance partner.

Organizational partnering requires a similar approach, starting with identifying possible partners and eliminating those that for whatever reasons—size, organizational culture, budget, personnel—are unlikely to lead to a happy relationship. Then, when a possible partner is chosen, one continues through careful planning, building, managing, and resourcing of the relationship to reviewing, revising, and institutionalizing it. It is similar to the process many people go through in finding and creating partnerships in their personal lives, albeit done less consciously and usually less cold-bloodedly. Organizational partnering is more akin to an arranged marriage than to spontaneously falling in love. The experience of dance, though, has made me think that the organizational equivalent of falling in love is perhaps not to be dismissed so easily, and in the future I will be looking for that intuitive sense of what makes for good chemistry between partners.

Coming Full Circle

At this point we have come full circle: What does dance offer that more-traditional learning processes do not? The final answer for me, beyond all that has been said already, is that dance reaches into and touches parts of us that more-intellectual and less-visceral approaches cannot. It seems a cliché, but the reality is that partnerships and conflict-resolution processes ultimately rest on the willingness of those involved to make themselves a little vulnerable, risk some generosity beyond that required by interests, obligations, or responsibilities, and act with the heart and spirit as well as the head and wallet.

Dance forces you out of the hard, protective shell of intellect. It makes you interact with others in ways wholly unfamiliar to most and probably uncomfortable for more than a few. It takes a couple of days to shed the reluctance to look foolish, a couple more to understand that there is a kind of holy foolishness about dancing, and the rest of a lifetime to understand this new language and way of being. In this, dance and conflict resolution are alike, and perhaps that is the best reason for encouraging others to risk feeling foolish, bearing the unfamiliar, and coping with the uncomfortable.

Choreography of Negotiation

Movement in Three Acts

CHRISTOPHER HONEYMAN AND RACHEL PARISH

Introduction

"We gotta do a dance." For many years, Chris has heard this as the opening line of a phone call from some desperate negotiator. The invitation has nothing to do with dance as choreographed or artistic movement. It signifies instead that the negotiator has overextended himself. "The troops" are not following along, and the negotiator is now about to be cut off at the knees and requires a mediator's assistance. The "dance" is designed to demonstrate the rightness of a certain concession and involves complex ritual rather than performance.

Within Western culture, there is still a general sense of separation between what is seen as cultural (in the sense of *hochkultur*) and what is seen as practical—a consequence of the

Industrial Revolution that we have not yet outgrown. The notion that dance might have some more-literal application to everyday negotiation or to other "nonartistic" work is at odds with this perception. Yet situations often require that, at least on an unconscious level, the skills and habits of dance *must* be employed if a group is to do some very practical thing. We offer as illustration an image of a group of London glaziers at work.

If Chris had approached one of these construction workers and ventured the observation that they were dancing, he would have been lucky to get off with an odd look. Yet if they were *not* dancing, disaster could be predicted. Coordinated, even graceful, movement is essential to their trade. Whether or not the group has ever articulated it, the fact that the glass is intact is evidence that they share an understanding of the need to move *together*.

London construction workers are not the only people who are liable to be put off if told that what they are really doing is dancing. Yet even in mundane negotiations, where dance may be rare, gesture, its close cousin, is routine. Negotiators and mediators often use gesture consciously to express emotion—indeed, it is essential to communicate appreciation, understanding, frustration, or even fury without saying that which cannot be unsaid. Practitioners recognize this: at least one benchmark of mediation skills includes it as an explicit element.[1]

Returning to our desperate negotiator: What if everyone involved was missing something obvious all along? What if this linguistic choice points toward a more complex interpretation, that using a widened problem-solving tool kit in negotiation can help move past a seemingly impassable blockage? The negotiator clearly already knows one such change; that is, bringing in another person to shift the dynamics. Perhaps a case could be made for going further, consciously using *multiple intelligences* in negotiation. Could it be that physical movement, as a case in point, might unlock more flexibility in the "troops" or more intellectual nimbleness on the negotiator's part?

The Obtuse and the Flexible

Some negotiators and mediators—perhaps other contributors in this book—may have deliberately used physical movement all along. But in hundreds of cases in which Chris, as a mediator, was expected to be creative and encourage flexibility, it had simply not occurred to him that some part of his rumored creativity might be enhanced by the fact that he was literally in almost constant motion—back and forth between the parties' separate caucuses and typically on his feet even within a side meeting, moving about and gesticulating. Similarly, it had not occurred to him that some portion of the participants' recalcitrance might be exacerbated by the fact that each party, once an opening joint session was over, tended to stay in its chosen caucus room, settling all too comfortably into its position, in both meanings. And if many among Chris's large acquaintance of practitioner colleagues had been consciously behaving very differently in this area, it seems likely he would have heard of it.

Meanwhile, the field of negotiation and conflict management has long given lip service to the concept of multiple intelligences. Indeed, the originator of the concept, Howard Gardner, was invited to give the keynote speech at a meeting of negotiation scholars some years ago. Gardner has experimented with different formulations over the years. His most recent formal list includes his original seven types (linguistic, logical-mathematical, musical, bodily-kinesthetic, spatial, interpersonal, and intrapersonal) and adds *naturalist*. We are focusing on linguistic intelligence here for simplicity, though of course at least some of the other intelligences are routinely used in schools and in negotiation.[2] But this field has yet to take up Gardner's challenge in general, probably because of the overwhelming dominance of "word people" among its scholars and teachers.[3]

We are interested in *all* the intelligences. We think it's likely that each form of intelligence has something to contribute to our understanding and practice of negotiation and conflict management and that once our field begins to explore them, as-yet-undiscussed *combinations* of nonverbal intelligences will become part of the agenda. For instance, a small but telling application of spatial intelligence was applied by a mediator colleague of Chris. While reviewing the plans for their agency's new offices, he recognized that two critical walls of one particular office he might pick were not load-bearing—so the contractor would probably not care, and perhaps not even notice, if he quietly *erased* those walls and redrew them with the door around the corner. This safely removed his door from the view of the agency's irascible chairman.

As supposedly creative types, negotiators and mediators might be open to looking at the experiences of some rather different but also creative professionals. Working concurrently with all of the multiple intelligences is, as it happens, at the heart of many creative processes in dance, theater, and artistic collaboration. In collaborative ensemble practice in particular—Rachel's specialty—artists communicate with and apply knowledge from the multiple intelligences in order to create a production.

Ensembles are diverse. They are typically made up of individuals with widely varying strengths among the intelligences. At the same time, each individual shares responsibility for achieving a single cohesive product. The ensemble members must find a way to communicate and collaborate. They must create a new and articulate microcosm for the creative process itself as well as for the final production. To achieve collaboration, *negotiations* are held at the intersections of the members' banks of knowledge and modes of communication. There is rich material for future exploration of still other intelligences in this crossroads of physical movement and conflict resolution.[4]

As a practical start to a huge topic, however, in this chapter we will focus on a limited set: the idea of *movement* in three forms. In particular, we will examine how these forms relate to the use of multiple intelligences in collaborative problem solving. We hope to show connections among all three types of movement. Perhaps mental flexibility in relation to conflict might be helped not only through exercising physical flexibility but also through what we will call sociocontextual displacement.

How many varieties of movement might be helpful, or even essential, in a complex consensus process? At one level, we think it's far too soon to say. But we can now examine three types of movement across two domains that are very different from most points of view but which share one strong need: to create true collaboration on difficult material. Deconstructing a recent theater project suggests some possibilities; analyzing a series of academic conferences suggests some of the same possibilities. We will alternate between the two as we consider three concepts of movement.

Three Types of Movement

The mental movement/creative thinking already noted is one of our three types. It is closely associated with linguistic intelligence, if only because a common goal in negotiation is to create solutions that are expressed in writing or speech. But because that is a key objective of not only many legal and business negotiations but also international and even interpersonal ones, we will consider this form as an objective of the other two and will reserve its discussion for last. The others, in turn, can be viewed as drawing heavily on bodily-kinesthetic, spatial, and interpersonal intelligence.

Thus the second type of movement, which we are calling sociocontextual, has a physical element, including movement from one locale to another. But it also contains the idea of *moving between cultures* and exhibits the use of both spatial and interpersonal intelligences. Mark Twain's "The Innocents Abroad," for example, shows why spatial movement alone is not enough: most members of the tourist groups he described traveled to a succession of exotic locales while learning, essentially, nothing.[5] In the next section, we will discuss what that might involve. We will examine how mental shifts came about in a theater-making troupe and look at two instances where a similar shift occurred for a group of professors compared with other instances where it did not.

We will then consider the third type of movement, which we are calling *individual/embodied*. This involves an individual body's physical movement, a concept that includes dance and other types of overt physical motion but logically also includes the subtler physical expressions known as nonverbal communication. (We will not, however, delve into the unconscious movements characteristic of "microexpressions," as analyzed by Paul Ekman[6]. Even though these certainly carry some of the freight of nonverbal communication, they are not intentional and therefore by definition not strategic in negotiation—except, of course, when someone tries to *hide* an indicator of an emotion or of lying.)

The individual/embodied form of movement is allied with Gardner's concept of kinesthetic intelligence. We will consider how physical shifts (applied consciously or unconsciously) can trigger mental ones (whether obvious or unconscious) to get a job done that can only be accomplished through consensus. But first, a bit of background on our chosen settings.

Background to the Theater Story

Firehouse Creative Productions, Rachel's theater company, is unusually consensus based; each collaborator on the team has a particular background, a set of skills, and a vision for both specific aspects and the overall production. The work of the team demonstrates a dynamic process of creation, rife with points of conflict, which results in situations where physical movement, sociocontextual displacement, and multiparty negotiations can all be closely observed.

To mount a reinterpretation of *Stella*, a Goethe play, Rachel began by breaking down the text into its basic plot dynamics, removing specific details such as gender, time, and place. Based on this breakdown, she identified major dilemmas and challenges for each character. She then generated a list of "provocations" relating to these dilemmas, which people today could answer with stories from their own lives. She set up these provocations in conjunction with StoryStation,[7] a dramatic device of her own invention, and then gathered stories from members of the public in London and in Macon, Georgia, over a period of five months. Firehouse cast and workshopped the play in London, developing an outline. Then the company went to Macon, Georgia, in February 2010, and spent five weeks creating a new version of the drama through a deeply collaborative process. The team of five improvised, rehearsed, and wrote the new play; developed the production; and performed it at two locations in Georgia. They then took the production back to London and performed it for a week at the Southwark Playhouse. The work of rewriting and putting on the play involved almost continuous negotiation.

Background to the Conference Story

We have one role in common, that of impresario. Chris's version takes place mainly in academic settings. Over more than a decade, he has organized a series of multidisciplinary, multiday conferences, with a variety of specific goals and a matching variety of academic partners, in Boston; New York; Albuquerque; Carlisle, Pennsylvania; Milwaukee; Rome; Istanbul; and Beijing. These have produced a great deal of new writing,[8] some elements of which now seem particularly relevant.

What all of this spatial movement lacked was a guiding theory. At the time, it was essentially intuitive, with the significant drawback of being potentially sui generis, or difficult to duplicate by others. But the process of thinking through this chapter has now produced at least the beginnings of such a theory. Space here does not permit a thorough analysis of the role of movement in discussions that have drawn from more than thirty different disciplines and practice specialties, and produced five books and eight special issues of academic or professional journals to date. But a brief comparison of just three recent discussions may be illustrative.

For the first meeting of the Rethinking Negotiation Teaching project in Rome in 2008, Chris and his codirectors brought together about fifty scholars from around the world, with plenty to think about and no shortage of resulting output. In retrospect, however, it is notable that not one of over thirty resulting writings drew much, if any, inspiration *from* Rome as the setting of the meeting. We now realize that the team did not really take advantage of an extraordinary setting to create *social* displacement. *Contextual* displacement may well have contributed to the undoubted creativity of much of the writing; but it is inarguable that the academic hothouse the team created had one thing in common with the famous Japanese tour bus: social engagement was almost entirely *within* the group.

Not so the next year, in Istanbul. There, without yet using the terms we are drawn to here, the managing team set out deliberately to require scholars to negotiate not only with one another but also with Istanbul's merchants and other locals. Later we will explore what happened. But first, we will return to our theater story.

Sociocontextual Movement (Rachel)

Rachel grew up in Macon, Georgia, moved to London in 2003, and has been working in the UK theater industry since then. There is a rich history of theater in London, and this is palpable both in the consciousness of the general public and in the creative approach of people within the industry. For a person working in theater in London, the embedded knowledge of other professionals and the audiences provides a wealth of resources—and also a series of constraints. Rachel became interested in seeing if she could circumnavigate some aspects of the latter.

When the creative process for *Stella* moved to Macon, a new population was introduced to a collaborative process to which they had never before had access. The very making of the work in that location therefore contributed some new cultural knowledge to the community. This contextual shift also sharpened the artists' perceptions, as discussed below. But in addition, these shifts created new negotiation environments in which new approaches to problem solving had to be developed. Three influential impacts of going to Macon were that the performers entered an environment that contained no professional peer group, they lived together, and they found social interactions in central Georgia very different from London. Based on the way that people in Georgia related to them, the actors felt that they were truly valued additions to the community, almost as honored artists in residence. At the same time, when social norms are different between two places, outsiders have to learn how to adjust in social situations and are at risk of doing something off-putting to local sensibilities. Living together, meanwhile, meant that members of the troupe were away from home and the comforts and the requirements of everyday life. This triggered a number of positive and negative responses. Most important for the group's negotiations, it meant that they had to rely on one another for emotional as well as practical support—while doing work that classically elicits strong emotions. Being in new interpersonal and spatial contexts forced the troupe to actively use a variety of forms of intelligence in the collaborative creative process, as discussed later in the chapter.

Sociocontextual Movement (Chris)

Despite a significant number of errors in the mechanics of the Istanbul meeting (for instance, a promised debriefing session collapsed when the many small teams, dispatched all over the city with "adventure learning" instructions to negotiate, returned at widely varying times), a sharp difference from the post-Rome book is visible in the post-Istanbul book: at least sixteen of the twenty-seven chapters drew heavily from the actual experience of social as well as contextual movement. Different writing teams focused on different experiences, but many wrote in one way or another about their assigned negotiations in the Grand Bazaar and the Spice Bazaar—fabled environments for what most of them had assumed would be hard bargaining, focused on price. But the book is not simply replete with stories of small negotiations with Istanbul bazaar merchants; an air of surprise prevails. For instance, the scholars discovered that their common assumption that the bazaar was a place of "one-shot" transactions, with all the cutthroat behavior that implies, was far from the merchants' own assumption. More than a few of the sellers, instead, were interested in becoming the buyer's supplier of rugs (or whatever) for life—and the supplier for their families and friends as well. A whole series of typical bargaining assumptions clearly needed some rethinking as a result.

The same meeting, significantly, showed a sharp increase in a second indicator of negotiation effectiveness or creativity: the willingness to put in the extra effort to *write* with people whose backgrounds and disciplinary traditions are very different. The project's final meeting, in Beijing in 2011, had a more refined adventure-learning component—and did even better on this score. (See Table 1.)

A hallmark of Chris's work has been a focus on getting scholars and practitioners of different kinds to work together, developing new thinking in cross-disciplinary teams. This approach was rapidly accepted beginning in the late 1990s, at least among the field's "early adopters" and for purposes of tightly defined and time-limited encounters, such as joint conference presentations. For the deeper and more extended collaboration required for multidisciplinary *writing for publication*, however, progress was notably slower. In effect, these seasoned scholars and practitioners, despite their conspicuous interest, were avoiding the more-difficult negotiation that cross-disciplinary writing almost invariably requires.

The writing has been published in a variety of venues. A tally of the contributions to each multiauthor work can be expressed in terms of the percentage of articles or chapters in each that consisted of cross-disciplinary writing. In date order of the most relevant special journal issues and books, they are as follows:

Table 1

Publication	Cross-disciplinary teams' percentage of writing total
Negotiation Journal vols. 18/4 and 19/1 (2002 and 2003)	6%
Conflict Resolution Quarterly vol. 20/4 (2003)	25%
Penn State Law Review vol. 108/1 (2003)	0%
Marquette Law Review vol. 87/4 (2004)	16%
Rethinking Negotiation Teaching (2009) *and Negotiation Journal* vol. 25/2 (2009)	23%
Venturing Beyond the Classroom (2010)	42%
Educating Negotiators for a Connected World (2013)	67%

The last two of these show a sudden jump. They represent key products of the Istanbul and Beijing meetings, respectively.[9] We recognize, of course, that it is a long path from such preliminary results to proof of causation. For example, the definition of "different field" we used in calculating this table is open to challenge—though we have used the same definition throughout the calculations. Only time and experimentation will clarify whether this was a flash in the pan or a reliable technique in the making.

But since the Istanbul meeting was the first in the series to use both individual/embodied movement *and* sociocontextual displacement conscientiously, the fact that it generated so much greater results in a critical aspect of negotiation creativity and flexibility at least suggests that more experimentation would be warranted. The further increase following the Beijing meeting, with its more sophisticated adventure-learning design, supports this.

Individual/Embodied Movement in Daily Rehearsals (Rachel)

As postulated above, the field of negotiation and conflict management has long honored the concept of multiple intelligences more "in the breach" than in reality. In the theater, however, there is no avoiding multiple intelligences if intelligent work is to be produced. With any craft and art, there are numerous ways for an artist to work: to be primarily intuitive (responsive and going with the gut instinct), intellectual (rationally processing choices before actively applying them), technical (knowing and manipulating the tools of the trade), or kinesthetic (focusing on physical, embodied communication and exploration). In creating the new version of *Stella*, a very interesting situation arose. Each performer collaborating on this new piece had a different "default" starting point. One performer relied first on intuition, one on intellect, one had very strong technique, and the fourth performer was highly kinesthetic. Ultimately, this translated as a combination that would provide a robust stage language. But it also offered many opportunities for conflict. Since the individuals in the company each had different "default" ways of creating, the group had to find many means of bridging communication gaps. Conflict is routine in theater making (as many comedies over the years attest); in this instance, the collaborative ethic of the company meant that a workable production was possible only through honoring all of these approaches—each of which, of course, is associated with one or more forms of intelligence.

Rachel's company used physical movement to broaden the range of resources, bridge communication gaps, and innovate solutions with a number of traditional and nontraditional techniques in the rehearsal process, including warm-ups, table work vs. "on your feet," site-specific rehearsals, dancing the scene, and movement as a stage language.

Warm-ups: The group started every morning (six days a week) with an hour of physical warm-ups, including various forms of choreographed and free dance. This process was more intense than usual because they were living and working together to create a new production from the ground up in a relatively short period of time. By starting each day with physical exercise and letting different members of the group lead the warm-ups, everyone was able to benefit from the diverse skill sets within the group. Taking turns in exerting leadership was also key for the collaborative process to work.

Table work vs. on your feet: The group improvised and rewrote the play using many different source materials. These included the original Goethe script, the scene-by-scene breakdown, and the many stories collected from the public in five months of StoryStation installations. This in turn meant there was a great deal of "table work" to do: reading, writing, listening, transcribing, and more. Since time was short, the group needed to create scenes from the play physically at the same time, figuring out relationships and story "on their feet." Creating work on your feet means getting up and acting out the scene without understanding it logically beforehand. To do this, you must take the risk of putting aside intellectual or rational analysis of a scene. Actors find ways of letting words, actions, choices, and decisions come out of the embodied situation. This often leads to clear and simple discoveries of relationships, situation, character, and more that may have been opaque when sitting at the table, relying predominantly on words and vision. This approach, of course, relies strongly on using combined multiple intelligences. When creating scenes on their feet, the group had to find ways *as* a group—without allowing any individual, even the director, to dominate—of generating new ideas and communicating them. At times, this meant that they had to create the scene multiple times and through multiple modes of communication.

Site-specific rehearsals: In addition to alternating between table work and work on their feet in the rehearsal room, the company also engaged in site-specific rehearsals. Initially, when trying to come to a shared understanding of what the settings for the play looked and felt like, they began by trying to draw maps and create spatial representations of places, as one often does in traditional rehearsal techniques. After a while, however, the group hit an impasse over one particular scene. The problem arose when two characters, Sam and Ray, met for the first time outside Sam's house.

Everyone in the company had very different ideas about how this logistically could have happened. It was integral to most of the aspects of the play that this be concretely decided, since it had a direct impact on the relationship of the characters. Thus everyone had strong opinions. Each individual offered many options to the group, but no two members were "on the same page." So Rachel moved the whole company outside to look at real houses and streets and to discuss and determine, "on their feet," what types of locations would satisfy everyone. When these problems were worked out in an embodied approach, obstacles to certain choices were apparent to everyone, and when a place was finally found that was workable, everyone was able to recognize it because it made sense *physically* for all the characters and relationships.

Thus moving the company to "on-location" rehearsal began as a form of conflict management: the need was to find a setting in real life for that one scene when the group could not find the necessary shared understanding in a rehearsal room. Moving spatially, literally transporting their bodies, their attention, and their collaboration into a fresh and relevant context, solved the immediate issue. But this episode then led further, to a working method: by going out as a company to find other locations they wanted to set a scene in, the group found they could add another dimension to the process. This went well beyond typical location scouting; the company actually rehearsed parts of the relevant scenes on the spot in each case.

Dancing the scene: As Keith Johnstone (1979) points out, when a collaborative theater company devises a new production, each actor has to take on responsibility for leading part of the action of the scene and for responding when another is leading. This becomes a recognizable kind of negotiation: through improvisation, one actor makes "offers" to the others, which open routes for the scene's progression. These offers can be made through both verbal and nonverbal communication. However, at times, one can dominate to an undesirable degree if collaborators have different levels of facility with one mode or the other. "Some people avoid getting involved in action. . . . it's a good idea to start such people off inside a womb, or on another planet, or being hunted for murder. . . ."[10] In improvisation, as Johnstone says, if someone isn't able to actively lead the action, for whatever reason, you have to create a new circumstance for the improvisor to begin creating action. For example, the *Stella* group was devising a scene in which three men play several drunken card games. Each has to extract certain information out of the others for them to realize that they are actually connected to one another in a strange way. As this scene was taking shape, the actor who had the strongest facility with verbal offers was dictating most of its direction. This led to an imbalanced dramaturgical structure. To rebalance the scene, Rachel took the actor with the strongest sense of kinesthetic/physical communication and asked him to *dance* the scene. He created a choreography, which the others could refer to while he danced it.

The process allowed all the actors to identify offers that their characters could make, which were then interspersed throughout offers that the verbal communicator had set up. Thus they created a more-balanced and more-collaborative dynamic in the scene's progression. This has potential resonance in the conflict-management field, in which (for instance) attention—so far—is barely given to the needs of disabled persons, let alone to what additional strengths they may have learned and could contribute (see below).

Movement as a stage language: The experience with dance in rehearsal led to a further use. In the end, the company used choreographed dance as a *stage language* to express moments of extreme emotion. In trying to rewrite these moments or to stage them naturalistically, they repeatedly hit roadblocks with words. They simply could not find ways of adequately expressing the incomprehensible joy or unbearable grief that were part of the play's narrative journey. As they worked through different possible ways of developing a scene, they found themselves using fewer words in their own communication and more body language and gestures. This began as a kind of unspoken shorthand, initially interpretable only by the group and because of the shared experience of the "hothouse" living and working environment over weeks. But it led to the idea of using dance consciously as a stage language to express what the creative collaborators found inexpressible with words. Johnstone again: "Content lies in the structure, in what happens, not in what the characters say."[11]

A central moment for this technique was the consequence of a decision made early in the adaptation of the play to invert the gender roles from the original. This decision worked well for the most part, but one key scene proved problematic. In the original play, this scene, with intense emotional expression, was dealt with explicitly through words. In Firehouse's adaptation, a new solution had to be developed in a way that felt consistent with a contemporary young man's character; yet the group simply could not find words that would encompass the emotions and still "fit in the character's mouth." So they turned away from words altogether and began to create the "spirit" of the young man's emotions in a way more related to sculpture, as described by Constantin Brancusi:

> When you see a fish you do not think of its scales, do you? You think of its speed, its floating, flashing body seen through the water . . . If I made fins and eyes and scales, I would arrest its movement and hold you by a pattern, or a shape of reality. I want just the flash of its spirit.[12]

The group felt that using dance to convey the reality of this character's emotions did better justice to the situation than using words. This demonstrates how one way of telling a story, or even of communicating and recontextualizing an individual's experience, may need to be translated and reconfigured for another person to understand it. The translation may have to be from language to language and perhaps via a different intelligence for other parties to truly engage with it. In other words, depending on factors including age, cultural experience, and exposure to the field of conflict, words may not be the most-effective way of creating a shared understanding of a lived experience.

Individual/Embodied Movement (Chris)

Beyond the routine usage of gesture, it would be a stretch to find a credible equivalent to Rachel's theater stories in Chris's case-handling experience (even with more than two thousand cases to draw from)—admittedly a sad commentary on a huge gap in creativity. We would postulate, however, a Sherlock Holmes–worthy clue in the offing: one of the "dog that did not bark" variety. Since it is now widely accepted that among the population at large only a minority will be truly skilled with words, the *lack* of examples of other forms of intelligence already being used in the resolution of so many conflicts (assuming other negotiators/mediators have acted similarly) is itself an indication of how much potential creativity and openness to alternatives might be available for future conflict handling. Perhaps this is cause for some optimism.

What forms this might take are as yet unknown, although some other practitioners at the Saas-Fee meeting were palpably more aware of the possibilities in this area than Chris had been, so other chapters in this book might collectively suggest that we may already be across the border of an undiscovered country of ability.

In tapping these skills, one caveat should be noted. Recall the Istanbul and Beijing experiments in adventure learning. For the most part, these seem to have met their goals. Yet with respect to individual/embodied movement, a trenchant critique of the first round of these experiments, David Larson, noted the inaccessibility of some of the key elements to those individuals who were physically disabled.[13] Larson's critique, however, squares with Rachel's experience in another respect. Rachel has noted that a key to working out such radical changes in theater making was the advance agreement of all concerned to make the necessary movements—of all three kinds—collaboratively. Larson's critique includes the point (pages 209–210) that much of the discriminatory force of adventure learning can be forestalled or ameliorated by openly discussing the physical demands sufficiently in advance that disabled persons are forewarned. It is not too hard to imagine that this might lead to a more-collaborative and more-creative relationship in which the disabled are empowered to make alternative "movement offers" of their own.

Conclusion: "Making a Move" in Negotiation

Up to now, we have set aside in this discussion the most obvious negotiation connotation of *move*. Admittedly, it is a presumed necessity of most day-to-day negotiation and conflict management that the parties must "make a move," implying a change in their demands, for any progress to be made. Although this often implies some kind of mental shift in their view, that is far from inevitable. Some parties believe they can "game out" the entire negotiation or conflict in advance, so their moves are preplanned and do not necessarily reflect any learning or change of perspective. The apogee of this may be a story told to Chris by a mediator colleague. He described a large and lengthy negotiation in which one of the parties, every time he came back with a fresh proposal from the other side, would take a long caucus—and then hand him the next document in a thick stack of already-typed proposals. They were even numbered in advance.

At the same time, much of the discourse relating to movement in negotiation and conflict management involves concepts about getting other people to move or whether or not the protagonist is making a move. Taking turns is implicit, if not explicit. What is lacking in this construct is a commitment to moving *with*. A large part of collaborative theater practice involves setting up an environment in which all parties begin a process of negotiation with an understanding that they're going to move together. The parties to such a negotiation often come from diverse backgrounds, with very different needs and skills. When they embark on this process, they do not know what the outcome will be, except that they all intend to end up with a single result, with a show, with a solution. The aftermath will reflect, and reflect upon, all parties involved. Conflict is created in and through this process. But the key to finding a solution lies in the consensus that "we've got to move together" from the outset. (We may tend to think about this in the relatively elevated terms of dance and theater, but many children are already familiar with the concept—in terms of a three-legged race, for example. One player's right leg is tied to another player's left leg, and pairs race one another. If, with your legs joined together, you take turns, with one person choosing when to move both legs, your chances of making it to the finish line are a lot worse than if you genuinely move together.)

In day-to-day conflict management there may, in fact, be a plethora of practical equivalents to Rachel's explicit use of dance and movement. But the most-likely venues in which to find that experience are not in Western cultures. We defer to the appropriate experts. Anecdotally, however, it appears that dance and related nonverbal expression may have substantial roles in the handling of conflict in Native American life and in indigenous groups elsewhere. Indeed, our impression, casual as it may be, is that in some societies, remarking that dance might be helpful in negotiating a solution to a practical problem might well be met with a blank look and the retort, "How else could you do it?"

We should caution that this chapter constitutes tentative theorizing. We make no claim to have performed any rigorous research. Our examples are anecdotal, primarily from our very different life experiences, including conflict within a theater-making environment, which was resolved by taking a creative process and a troupe of actors on the road, and mediation between parties like those noted above, who typically remain physically static. We have also mentioned some recent experiments with groups of scholars and practitioners who are being challenged to rethink some of their core concerns; these and related observations led us to compare notes and reexamine some other situations we have separately encountered. Yet while we humbly acknowledge that we do not have reliable data to offer, in the spirit of "practice to theory"[14] we can offer a hypothesis for possible research by others: *Creativity and flexibility in a group's handling of a negotiation may be enhanced by a combination of physical movement and sociocontextual movement.*

And we believe this is just a threshold of a broader and potentially very rewarding line of inquiry. Dance (as applied kinesthetic intelligence) represents only one of the different intelligences that are currently underutilized in conflict management. Yet conflict managers—all our "word people"—are not good for much if they can't find words that create understanding rather than annoyance, such as the discussion of dance might predictably have drawn from the glaziers pictured at the outset of this chapter. So if *dance* won't cut it in industrial parlance, how about *coordination*? Or, on a larger scale, how about *logistics*?[15] In other words, if we are to interest typical negotiators in using all the skills that the arts, sports, music, and other forms of intelligence offer us, we are going to need all our linguistic facility with translation, rewording, and reframing.

There might be two next steps: first, to start an inventory of equivalent "words that work" to reframe multiple-intelligence concepts that initially seem off-putting to many conflict professionals; second, to ask a question: Now that we have a book that puts kinesthetic intelligence "in play" for our field, how might we better employ some of the other forms of intelligence that have mostly been neglected?

Teaching Dance

*I*f, as the two previous sections have argued, it is as important for practitioners to be physically fluent as it is for them to be dexterous in their use of language to resolve conflict and mitigate its impact, then clearly we need to think about how this new skill area should be taught.

Nadja Alexander, a well-known Australian mediator, trainer, and expert on comparative conflict resolution, and Michelle LeBaron, a Canadian world expert on cross-cultural conflict transformation, set out the groundwork for approaching this new frontier. They begin by challenging customary teaching methods, pointing out that we in the West have fallen behind traditional societies in our appreciation of how kinesthetic approaches can address conflict. At the same time, they note that—in some respects—we have in fact embraced disciplines that nurture the synergy of mind and body. They go on to spell out exactly how conflict-resolution trainers can bring the insights in this book into practitioner-training programs.

Charlie Irvine, a Scottish mediator, lawyer, and musician, uses his experience of dance to focus in detail on the management of emotions in mediation. Like Nadja and Michelle, he laments the way that contemporary culture, for all its supposed sensitivity to dimensions of human experience that previous generations preferred to avoid, still tends to sideline feeling in its preference for thinking. Charlie explores how emotions can wax and wane in the course of a mediation process and the need to integrate feelings and thoughts if we are to achieve breakthroughs. He provides a simple method for tracking and noting what is happening beneath the surface.

If there was one aspect of dance that the Saas-Fee workshop brought to the fore, it was the extent to which deliberate movement requires an intuitive understanding of both oneself and others. Simon Mason, a Swiss international mediator, Susan Allen Nan, an American scholar-practitioner, and Virginie van de Loe, a Dutch visual artist, explore vividly and directly from their experiences in Saas-Fee ways that movement can help practitioners develop the intuitive intelligence that assists the perception and interpretation of thought and action in conflict. They also review the role of dance in the health and healing of those who intervene in conflict, setting out how it can be used for recovery from past stresses as well as inspiration to further effort.

7

Building Kinesthetic Intelligence

Dance in Conflict-Resolution Education

NADJA ALEXANDER AND MICHELLE LEBARON

> *"I would believe only in a God that knows how to Dance."*
> Friedrich Nietzsche

In this chapter, we elaborate on alternatives to standardized approaches to conflict-resolution and negotiation training that are more dynamic and embodied and therefore more likely to yield proficiency in practice. Borrowing from fine arts, neuroscience, and intercultural communication, we explain why dance and movement are the frontier and future essential components of conflict-resolution education. From our own and others' experiences in the field, we examine why practitioners and parties can benefit from the effects of mirror neurons, somatic empathy, and other recently elaborated insights if they step away from their tables and—yes, we mean it—dance! Shall we?

Honeyman, Coben, and de Palo,[1] drawing upon feedback from an international group of negotiation teachers, write that negotiation teachers "1) over-rely on 'canned' material of little relevance to students; and 2) share an unsubstantiated belief that role-plays are the one best way to teach."

Here, we build on this work, exploring embodied pedagogy generally and movement-based approaches specifically. Can we find ways to vary training methodologies that are culturally sensitive, foster creativity, and meaningfully develop third-party capacities for our globalizing world? Can essential elements of embodied practice be identified that apply across training methodologies and cultural contexts? How can we take a giant leap forward and move to multisensory, experiential, and culturally fluent training activities?

In the past few years, significant international attention has been directed to innovative ways of enhancing pedagogical methods with diverse experiential learning approaches. For example, a recent international conference, Rethinking Negotiation Teaching, was shaped around a series of adventure learning activities with a focus on authenticity, real-life engagement, creativity, and the role and value of the emotional experiences.[2]

This chapter, will place the spotlight on experiential learning of a different type. We explore possibilities of using dance and movement-based activities to supplement, complement, inspire, and potentially transform experiential education and take it to a new level of teaching and learning. This includes both somatic and kinesthetic dimensions of such activities—in other words, attention to and experience of the body "from the inside out," as well as of the body in motion, through the complex interplay of sensation, emotion, and cognition.[3] In our experiences as educators and intervenors in diverse contexts—from law firms, corporations, and universities to conflicted communities in first- and third-world regions—we have observed that this is a vital frontier. It is vital because complex issues and identities at stake in today's conflicts call for multiple modalities of intervention. Training must help third parties develop the capacities to work effectively not only in cognitive realms but also in emotional, physical, imaginative, intuitive, and spiritual dimensions.

Our experience has taught us firsthand the importance of a multimodal approach. Working with women, youths, and chiefs from remote villages in the fragile and transitional economies of the Pacific and Africa has opened our eyes to the traditional transformative power of dance in many non-Western cultures. In indigenous settings around the world, people have long used dance, movement, music making, storytelling, mime, theater, and ritual to bring conflict to the surface and address it. In such contexts, kinesthetic elements are understood as integral to resolving conflict, making decisions, and effecting change.

Shifting our attention to modern industrialized societies, we note the mushrooming trend of health and mindfulness retreats that focus variously on achieving balance and perspective through mental relaxation and nurturing the body. There is also a significant increase in the popularity of ancient pilgrim trails: taking a period of days, weeks, or even months apart from fast-paced lives to walk in rhythms that gradually reconnect physical, natural, and spiritual aspects of being.[4] These and other developments indicate an increasing collective questioning of the widespread focus on rationally oriented production and linear achievement in modern Western society.

The artificial and still deeply entrenched separation of mind and body, logos and ethos, and brain and brawn is a legacy of the eighteenth-century Enlightenment, also referred to as the age of reason. To preserve the purity and perceived superiority of intellectual reason, cognitive intelligence was separated from the arts, skills, and other intelligences associated with physicality, creativity, imagination, and emotionality. As a result, the Western intellectual tradition yielded pedagogy in universities and professional training contexts that values rational functioning, often to the exclusion of other senses and intelligences. An approach such as this can be described as *disembodied* because it blocks access to and rejects ways of being and knowing that explicitly engage the body. This intellectual privileging has continued despite recent acknowledgment of the importance of kinesthetic approaches to learning.

The Western philosopher Friedrich Nietzsche recognized the inadequacy of this pedagogy when he turned his back on the academic circles and institutions of the nineteenth century. Nietzsche recognized what neuroscientists are now confirming: that the Cartesian assumption of mind-body splits is unfounded, and sound thinking and decision making involve the synergy of multiple intelligences.[5] In other words, knowledge in the sense of "know-why" is inextricably linked to "know-how" and is optimally situated in bodily experience and somatic memory. Today, fields as diverse as neuroscience,[6] political science,[7] education,[8] dance therapy,[9] and philosophy[10] have begun to explore and attest to the significance of aesthetics, emotional intelligence, and somatics to all areas of human activity.

If conflict-resolution education is to be effective, then we must ask ourselves how concepts and skills integral to resolving conflict can be learned and taught in ways that reconnect them with physical dimensions of emotion, intuition, and imagination. Given that cognition and emotion are braided processes that cannot be separated from the body as an instrument of knowing, training methods that target or isolate the intellect can no longer be seen as defensible. It is time that conflict-resolution pedagogy caught up with these developments. In the next section, we examine why dance and movement are particularly potent tools for training repertoires.

Just as unexplored terrain can seem dangerous to the untraveled mind, so body-based work can feel risky and threatening to people whose attention has been focused on the neck up. Yet working in a universe that tries to match competing rationalities of conflict parties without accessing the richness of physical resources is a bit like passing up a feast in favor of a bowl of watery gruel: it is far less enjoyable and truly unnecessary when abundance is available.

Dance, the Moving Imagination

Dance teachers are fond of saying, "If you can walk, you can dance." We would go one step further and suggest that if you can breathe, you can move, and if you can move, you can dance. Dance is, after all, our moving imagination. It is the kinesthetic manifestation of expression, or "the hidden language of the soul,"[11] as Martha Graham, modern dance pioneer, famously said.

Of course, Graham and her contemporaries were working at a time when an essential "true" and stable core identity was a given. Modern dance was meant to give this core "authentic expression." In the protean world of the twenty-first century, complex dynamics of identity and meaning-making animate conflict. As Lifton[12] has written, solving contemporary conflicts calls for suppleness, creativity, and resilience. Those who would intervene may be less focused on the imprecise terminology of a core and more concerned with helping parties find ways through labyrinths of contested meanings and identity-shaped narratives[13].

Dance and movement help with these challenges because they assist parties in bypassing conscious stories of conflict while summoning creativity as the parties:

- articulate and recognize deeply rooted feelings and needs;
- embrace new ways of knowing through heightened mind-body (somatic) sensations, connections, and awareness;
- develop increased awareness of inner geographies where habitual responses to conflict reside, thus increasing repertoires of possible conflict behaviors; and
- experiment physically with new ways of being for the future.

In the conflict-resolution field, we are witnessing increasing interest in, and applications of, embodied knowledge. Consider the use of meditation principles focused on breath and awareness in the practice of mindful mediation.[14] In constellation work pioneered by Insa Sparrer and others in Germany, participants create physical and emotional maps of conflict that yield insights and possibilities outside the reach of conscious cognitive processes.[15] The use of constellations and other related work offers participants creative opportunities to develop a deep somatic understanding of underlying issues and relationships from a systemic perspective. Likewise, conflict-resolution workshops that integrate elements of meditation and physical self-awareness encourage participants to access their inner dancers as they examine personal relationships to conflict and how they respond to it.

In yet another illustration, Augusto Boal's *Theatre of the Oppressed*—directly influenced by Paulo Freire's *Pedagogy of the Oppressed*[16]—has been used worldwide to engage disadvantaged communities in processes of reflection, innovation, decision making, and collaborative lawmaking (legislative theater). Participatory theater has been used by inmates, trade unionists, and hospital staff; by peasants and workers, students and teachers, artists, social workers, psychotherapists, and members of nonprofit organizations. It has empowered marginalized voices and developed innovative solutions to conflict precisely because it uses the embodied and symbolic language of theater rather than conventional approaches. *Theatre of the Oppressed* and Diamond's *Theatre for Living* have been able to help those living in conflict articulate often-excluded, undervalued, or ineffable realities and find creative practical solutions.[17]

Dance and movement have long enjoyed legitimacy in therapeutic circles. The application of dance-therapy principles to help people deal with the aftermath of violent conflict is yet another area where the mind-body connection is nurtured. Therapeutic use of creative movement has yielded profound effects in accessing and processing traumatic memories and strong emotions stored in the body—making these precious aspects of conflict conscious, less charged, and more accessible.[18]

For some, this discussion may seem to take us far from the everyday understanding of the term *dance* and have little connection with recognized forms of dance such as the fox-trot, hip-hop, jazz, or classical ballet. Let's take a look at a standard dictionary definition. The *New American Dictionary* defines dance as

1. a series of movements that match the speed and rhythm of a piece of music; and
2. a particular sequence of steps and movements constituting a particular form of dancing.

The first definition is much narrower than our understanding of dance. We are not aiming to train participants to move in ways that match pace and rhythm to a particular piece of music. In fact, movements that clash with a given rhythm or defy a prescribed tempo can be just as communicative in revealing undercurrents and group dynamics.

The second definition is broader, referring to a patterned sequence of movements as dancing. But when do emerging forms get recognized as dance? Hip-hop, for example, was not always a recognized form of dance. It grew from expression and commentary on everyday life, yet today it is a dance form with a huge following.[19] In recent years, hip-hop has become an accessible catalyst for conflict transformation in marginalized youth cultures from south central Los Angeles to South Africa. Various other forms of contemporary dance continue to push the envelope and challenge the boundaries of what is recognized as dance and what is not.

Still, many people harbor the illusion that they don't dance, at least not outside specific occasions. Insofar as they *define* dance, these standard explanations effectively *confine* dance, creating a sense that dance is a thing that artists do, not something we all do in our everyday lives. A look at colloquial language tells another story. We say, "I'm afraid I stepped on her toes," or "How can we shift the painful dance between us?"

In conflict, references to dance are frequent. Seeking to identify issues, we urge others to "stop dancing around the topic." When offered an outcome, we may "waltz around the offer," playing for time and looking at the proposal from different angles. In the German language, the phrase "to dance at several weddings" (*auf mehreren Hochzeiten tanzen*) provides an equivalent to the English expression "have your cake and eat it too"—words often uttered in situations involving some level of tension or conflict. Similarly, "to dance on someone's nose" (*jemandem auf der Nase herumtanzen*) means to walk all over someone. Muhammad Ali used dance as a metaphor for boxing when he said, "The fight is won or lost far away from witnesses—behind the lines, in the gym, and out there on the road, long before I dance under those lights."[20] Then there is the ubiquitous "negotiation dance," referring to the sequence of strategies and "moves" negotiators make as they work toward agreement. Mark Young and Erik Schlie, for example, explore the metaphors of the dance of positions, the dance of empathy, and the dance of concessions.[21] Once we begin to notice dance as a powerful metaphor that is well integrated in our everyday communications, conflicts, and resolutions, we realize its potency as a way of understanding situations and offering mobility in stuck places.

In this chapter, we embrace dance and—more broadly—movement as forms of embodied expression not limited to a recognized sequence of motions. Dance is, and should be, available to anyone who wants to explore it, regardless of rhythmic ability and coordination. Dance extends to all forms of movement, whether visible to the human eye or not. Dancing on the inside, beneath your skin, or in your mind's eye can be every bit as expressive, exhilarating, and exhausting as a rigorous jive. Indeed, it is possible to be very calm on the outside and feel vibrant on the inside or to move vigorously on the outside from a deep, calm center. Thinking of dance this way, it becomes inclusive, accessible, and much less threatening to many people who might not feel confident dancing in a public space.

We would go so far as to contend that you cannot *not* dance. What happens if you see a day of your life as a dance? You become aware of your movements: their rhythms, textures, and nuances as they express inner states, as they affect others, and as they influence the relational fields around you. Imagine you are on a crowded subway during morning rush hour. How does your body shift, slide, pause, and adaptively dance around the physicality of others? How do you breathe and situate your kinesthetic awareness in the space? What attitudes are communicated by your dance? What do the textures of your movements say? Do you experience the crowded subway as oppressive and invasive as you press yourself against a wall and close your eyes, feigning sleep? Or does your presence comfortably fill the space in and around your rela-tional field? The frame of dance brings a clear focus on nuances of spatial, place-related influ-ences we navigate every day. Was your day spent at a computer working on a long document? How did your posture shift over time? What were the physical sensations you experienced: heavy/light, tense/relaxed, alert/sleepy, engaged/detached? How did the walk to the refrig-erator whisper relief to your muscles, coaxing your circulation to restoration? When your pet brushed against your leg, did you hug it? When your partner called to check on dinner plans, did your state change? These are the kinds of questions that arise from "thinking dance."

If you still feel resistant to the notion of dance as a staple of conflict-resolution training, please join with us in jettisoning images of mediators switching business suits for tutus. Con-sider times when you have experienced a breakthrough in a problem or received a sudden insight. Movement is often a catalyst, whether in the form of walking in the park or mopping the floor. We will see that there are good neurobiological reasons for this. In addition, con-ceptualizing relations between people in conflict as a dance takes away from binary, zero-sum, simplistic notions that pervade much colloquial conflict language. Dancing, as anyone who has tried ballroom steps with a partner can attest, is complex and requires attunement to the other's intentions and to the environment and sympathetic responses to surprises. Let's ex-plore more of the fruitfulness of this idea in relation to conflict theory and practice.

So What Would Happen If We Dared to Let Go of Words?

Dance and movement can open up and strengthen underused channels of communication, giv-ing us ways to engage with one another at kinesthetic, nonverbal levels. The early twentieth-century dancer and choreographer Doris Humphrey explained, "There are times when the sim-ple dignity of movement can fulfill the function of a volume of words." Human dignity, respect for the other, and gracefulness can go a long way to shifting negative relations in instances of long-standing or intense conflict. These crucial dimensions of conflict transformation are often shifted nonverbally: holding another's hand offered in greeting; leaning forward while listening; the energy that infuses silences; the quality and degree of eye contact; the relaxation of one's posture and gestures. Yet while crucial to changing entrenched dynamics, nonverbal aspects of generative conflict handling are among the least examined within the field.

For those in ongoing interdependent relations, imagining new dances may be a useful met-aphor to inspire new ways forward. Understanding conflict through the metaphor of dance yields key insights about rechoreographing dynamics and improvising approaches. We be-lieve that dance's contribution to the field is far more than metaphorical; it offers concrete, practical tools for engaging these often overlooked but ever-present aspects of conflict.

The immense volume of literature around the notion of body language and nonverbal communication points to the power of kinesthetic communication. Too often, however, the focus has been on translating the language of the body into words rather than encouraging the exploration of communication at a kinesthetic level through breath, body awareness, and movement in relation to others.[22]

Grinder and Bandler[23] remind us that "the map is not the territory." Here they refer to the filters involved in representation and how they potentially transform or dilute meaning. For example, the moment we select and articulate words to represent feelings that we are physiologically experiencing, a number of things happen:

1. We categorize and constrain our feelings according to word choice. For instance, how do we choose among *angry, upset,* and *furious*? And how do we know—especially across cultures—that others share the same meanings of these words as we do? Even within the same cultural context, personal interpretations vary tremendously. In a recent mediation, three women—all native-English-speaking lawyers—were unable to agree on the meaning of the word *upset.* They each held different associations with the word and its relationship to the word *angry.*

2. Our word selection is shaped by language choice and, more deeply, worldview. For example, Hanna explains that "with respect to space, Anglos refer to four directions: East, west, north, and south. Laguna Pueblo indigenous people conceive of seven directions: Up, down, and center, as well as the four Anglo directions," indicating arguably more nuanced and sensitive spatial relationships.[24] Such linguistic parameters work to shape conceptual possibilities. For instance, David Hall and Roger Ames have explored how the contextual meaning—even pronunciation—of concepts and characters in Chinese is linked to developments in Chinese philosophy, which did not share the Western philosophical preoccupation with identifying overarching static truth or principles.[25] Similarly, Lee analyzes Chinese characters relevant to negotiation with a view to drawing attention to the cultural and historical contextual meanings embedded in them.[26] As another example, the German language, which tends to require more words to express an idea than English does, is considered by many to be a more-fecund language than English in terms of expressing emotion. In an Al Jazeera interview, Johan Galtung suggests that European languages such as French and German may be more suitable for conducting mediation processes than English because they are less direct and allow more creative possibilities for participants to move in and around the conflict to explore options for resolution while saving face. Interestingly, he offers the view that the Japanese language is possibly even less suitable for mediation than English, but for a very different reason: it is so indirect and noncommittal that it may be difficult to make any progress toward agreement at all![27]

3. Our word selection is also shaped by our level of linguistic fluency and our emotional-kinesthetic awareness (conscious mind-body connection). Here the notion of multiple intelligences is relevant, discussed further below. Shifting conflict often involves engaging different types of intelligences, such as rational (thought), emotional (felt), spiritual (interconnected), and kinesthetic (sensed, intuited), to bridge gaps between conscious ways of knowing and physiological ways of being. As diverse intelligences are welcomed into conflict-resolution processes, they can dance together into new alchemies not previously imagined.

An example of the importance of nonverbal dimensions comes from a multiparty commercial mediation that took place in Australia a number of years ago. Four institutional parties were represented by thirteen people of Anglo-Australian, upper-middle-class background. Legal advisers were available by telephone. Three days had been set aside for the mediation of this matter, which had been litigated for over ten years. The dispute related to employment; a significant amount of money was at stake as well as symbolic issues. Halfway through the second day, little substantive progress had been made. As lunchtime was approaching, the mediator arranged for the participants to walk together to a restaurant where one table had been reserved. She suggested to the parties that they talk about whatever they liked, but it would be good to have a break from the mediation. This they did.

In the afternoon, the participants were invited into groups with peers from their side and one person from another party in each group. Each group was given a separate and private working area. The mediator hoped that group dynamics would shift with the introduction of others into each group. The groups were asked to collaboratively draw an image of how they imagined each of the other three parties felt at this time in the mediation and to find ways to facilitate participation by every group member. After rejoining the plenary, groups shared and explained their images, and the subjects of the images were invited to change or add to them. The visual qualities of the collaborative images were powerful for all present. This intervention—shifting modes of engagement and pausing the conscious mind—was the turning point of the mediation. The change in atmosphere was palpable. The mediation progressed to a sustainable resolution.

For another illustration, we turn to indigenous settings, where mediations involving land issues are often conducted on-site. It is not uncommon for parties, representatives, and lawyers to spend time walking on the land in question. This collective phenomenological engagement with the soil and its textures, the flora and fauna, the flow and feel of the country, can be harnessed meditatively to help tease out how various parties make meaning of—and place value on—the terrain they traverse. For example, some may value its traditional sacredness, some its meaning as a family property over generations, others its environmental values, and yet others its resource richness or development potential. A skillful mediator can then encourage participants to demonstrate appreciation of the values and needs associated with these different meanings—whether through the vehicles of dialogue, ritual, storytelling, or exchange of maps and other representations of the site in question from multiple cultural perspectives.

Here is one final example of somatic intelligence in practice, this time from the Pacific. During a series of conflict-resolution workshops, a senior Ni-Vanuatu[28] chief once shared the view that his country "has peace but no unity." As he continued, it became clear that he was referring to a disembodied concept of peace—a peace that was not felt or experienced among the diverse tribes making up the still-young postcolonial territory. He explained his desire for unity as the need for all Ni-Vanuatu people to feel part of one country and to experience their national identity in embodied ways as strongly as their tribal sense of self. When asked how he would know that such unity had been achieved, he placed his hand on his chest and spoke of the significance of having one voice despite the more than one hundred different tribal languages. Then he moved his hand to cover his heart as he described a collective feeling of pride and love for all tribes within the country. Unity therefore evoked an embodied state of awareness.

The preceding three examples show the ways that language can be powerfully transcended in conflict processing. Given the limitations of language, what would happen in conflict-resolution training and practice if we dared be less dependent on words?

Expressive arts therapy, in particular dance therapy, has been at the forefront of experimentation with "dance language" grounded in physical experience. In intercultural or postconflict settings, from Iraq to Haiti to Bolivia, from sub-Saharan Africa to Israel to Peru, expressive arts modalities have been applied for decades to address conflict-related trauma. This work has consistently revealed the capacity of expressive embodied practices to shape and reshape identities, understandings, and relations. By engaging the creative and imaginative capacity of individuals in addressing situations of conflict or trauma, these methods have been potent in generating change in both mental and material domains.[29]

One of the concrete reasons that embodied practices prove effective in conflict and postconflict settings is that they can quickly and deeply foster intergroup trust, receptivity, and flexibility when encountering the unfamiliar. This is captured succinctly in the comments of one student from a tango class: "Learning to be a good Argentine Tango follower is about surrender. So in Saturday's 'Followers' Workshop' we practiced exercises in trust (yes, gently tipping to the side or backwards or frontwards with our eyes closed, trusting that someone would break the fall), feeling our partner's weight change and again, with eyes closed, being in tune with and following our partners' movement around the floor. I had to slow down, let go of everything else on my mind, and be totally present in the moment. . . . Leave a desire for control at the door. And take the lesson home."[30] As you read this comment, consider the parallels to conflict-resolution skills. How often do we encourage students to trust the process and surrender to it without worrying about the outcome? And what about the skills of mindfulness, being in the present, and drawing on multiple intelligences? Sound familiar?

The experiential lessons we learn from dance have much to offer students and practitioners of conflict resolution. In the next section, we explore the links between culture, multiple intelligences, and dance and consider some ways to integrate dance into experiential training to support the use of role play.

Dance, Culture, and Intelligence

In the 1980s, Howard Gardner first wrote about the concept of multiple intelligences, including linguistic, logical, musical, bodily-kinesthetic, spatial-visual, interpersonal, intrapersonal, naturalist, spiritual, and existential.[31] Such work effectively demonstrated that conventional conflict approaches—so often linear, verbal, deliberative, and disembodied—are insufficient to address the diversity of human modes of understanding. When we come to see the self as a multifaceted perceptual, expressive, and relational center, engaging multiple intelligences becomes integral to engaging complex and diverse individuals in conflict settings.

Neuroscience has recently explored how many forms of intelligence—cognition, emotion, and attitudes—are embodied. For instance, Antonio Damasio, among others, examines the physicality of emotion and shows us that what we come to experience as emotions are in fact interpretations of physical sensations.[32] Examples of physiological expressions of feelings recognizable to many people include goose bumps, blushing, sweaty palms, shortness of breath, butterflies in the stomach, and other manifestations of energy in the body. Physical sensation not only informs our perception but also structures or limits it. The autonomic nervous system, which controls our ability to access thoughts, discover new ideas, and change our behavior, is shaped by physical contact and rhythm from an early age and influenced by physical cues in later life.[33] Because all perception is filtered through the body with its corporeal memory of experiences, including trauma, the body shapes and limits our understandings of and responses to the world. Much of this is precognitive; therefore, it becomes crucial to directly engage the body to bring perceptions, judgments, and emotions to a conscious level of choice.[34] Seasoned conflict practitioners know the role that intuition or gut feeling can play in reading situations. Increasing body awareness can work to enhance perception of the subtle cues and signals—both internal and external—in which such intuition is grounded.

Just as the body shapes perception, so too can embodied approaches reshape it. Physical practices have been shown to have significant effects on cognition, learning, mood, and motivation. Physical exercise promotes development in these areas and does so relatively quickly.[35] Moreover, embodied practices that emphasize proprioception (awareness of the body in space) and encourage internal attunement have been shown to have beneficial effects on the neurophysiological regulation systems that foster openness to change and receptivity toward others.[36] Thus an emphasis on physical dimensions and engaging these dimensions through movement can lead directly to conceptual, emotional, and behavioral shifts.

In fact, the body has been shown to play a role in mental processes where we least expect it. Research has indicated that mental processes once thought disembodied are, in fact, physical phenomena. Almost 100 years ago, the researcher and philosopher Robert Chenault Givler, drawing on the neuroscience and physical sciences of the time, found that the expression of our physical and bodily experiences influences our understanding of, and the meaning we ascribe to, ethical notions such as the concepts of right and wrong.[37] This line of inquiry continues in the present. For example, in her review of research linking body awareness and movement to decision making, Lenore Hervey highlights Warren Lamb's system of movement-pattern analysis and its application to corporate settings.[38] Essentially, the research confirms that all processes of decision making have observable kinesthetic elements, both shaping and being shaped by relational factors. In other words, our bodies play an integral part in conflict, communication, and making choices.

Understanding the influence of the body in shaping perception, responses, and relations is a complex task. While there is evidence for certain pan-human expressions and gestures, it has also been shown that our bodies interpret and code the world around us in culturally specific ways.[39] The anthropologist Judith Hanna explains that cultural differences are usually reflected in movement and that paying careful attention to the body can therefore reveal pivotal cues about cultural differences, uncovering nuances, textures, and relational habits relevant to conflict. At the same time, she warns that phenomenological experiences and expressions also differ from person to person.[40] This is because relationships between body and self are rooted not only in biology but also deeply in social and cultural forms, including rituals, rites of passage, and festivals. Both collective and individual identities are expressed via movement; it is a language that reveals whole worlds to an attuned observer. Hanna suggests that it also may be a more-accurate, less-filtered, and less-adulterated communication vehicle than verbal language.

Dance also heightens kinesthesia, or awareness of one's own body and others' bodies; in fact, learning about the subtle cues, demands, and tendencies of one's body has been linked to developing empathy, or understanding how other moving bodies might feel.[41] Dance therefore provides an essential avenue to more-accurately perceiving not only our own but also others' personal and cultural positions, in physical as well as conceptual terms.

Recent work in neuroscience has explored empathy as an embodied phenomenon. When people observe or plan actions, motor neurons become activated in the same way that they do when the action is actually being performed.[42] In addition, neuroscientists have found that when subjects witness the pain or fear of others, the area of the brain that is associated with pain and affective experiences is activated.[43] When people watch one another move, their brains are essentially practicing ways of relating to others. The human capacity to imitate, learn, and connect with others is, at base, a kinesthetic experience.[44]

Dance also has been shown to help stimulate new neural pathways and shift cognitive habits. Body awareness and the neuromuscular transformations that accompany movement can offer insight into habitual cultural and social patterning. Moreover, movement has been shown to release emotions and latent memories, uncover new connections between groups, and reveal alternative interpretations and innovations on personal, cultural, and political levels.[45] Out of this kinesthetic intelligence, new vantage points and solutions begin to surface as parties develop awareness of, and explore choices about, what was previously unconscious.[46]

The acknowledgment and incorporation of such dimensions into conflict intervention would maximize the resources available for understanding and transformation across seemingly intractable lines of conflict. For example, imagine that a group is struggling with what appears to be an inextricable, entangled series of issues related to a complex environmental problem. Watching a dance on themes of ecology, diversity, harmony, and balance might thicken the parties' conversations, introducing new vitality, increased nuance, and more-thoughtful texture.

Malvern Lumsden brings it all together when he says, "Our sense of what is real begins with and depends crucially on upon our bodies, especially our sensorimotor apparatus, which enables us to perceive, move, and manipulate, and the detailed structures of our brains, which have been shaped by both evolution and experience."[47] Neuroscience now confirms what conflict intervenors, dancers, and others have known through their own methodologies: all decision making involves rational *and* emotional processes centered in the body, and we cannot observe, think, or respond clearly without our bodies and our feelings. Emotocognitive processes cannot be neatly excised from one another; they occur in concert. The body is an essential channel into understanding and engaging these processes. Thus we can engage our kinesthetic and emotional intelligences to help us move through differences with less resistance than if we were relying on rational thinking alone to find our way out of negative feelings or feel our way into positive thoughts.

For conflict-resolution practitioners and teachers, insights from neuroscience and dance theory and practice are crucial to understanding how people in conflict wrestle with ethical dilemmas and make choices. We cannot ignore them.

Building Dance-Related Intelligence

In dealing with challenging conflict situations, we need diverse inner resources and intelligences. Chief among these is somatic, or movement-based, intelligence. This way of knowing assists us in drawing on physical cues and resources to:

- Sense and shift group, interpersonal, and intrapersonal dynamics;
- Discern physical movements in others that signal internal changes;
- Discern changes in vocal rhythms that may relate to shifts in attitudes, relationships, or perspectives;
- Notice via physical cues when processes are safe or unsafe for others; and
- Learn ways of using breath and movement to promote flexibility rather than rigidity when working with strong emotions.

Here are some suggestions for cultivating somatic intelligence, along with tips on increasing it:

- Notice your physical responses to stress and conflict and learn ways to center and calm yourself, using breath, visualization, or movement.
- Adopt a physical practice in your life: an activity or an art form like dance. Keep a journal as you engage in this practice and write what you learn about your body and its ways of signaling.

In conflict-resolution contexts, you can do the following:

- Incorporate centering techniques when tensions are high. The simple act of breathing deeply or shaking limbs can do wonders in shifting mental and emotional states.
- Pay careful attention to nonverbal cues, devising an internal interpretive map as the process proceeds.
- Respond effectively to spatial, temporal, and kinetic dimensions of negotiation. If dialogue reaches an impasse, suggest changing postures or positions in the room; if empathy proves difficult, incorporate subtle forms of physical or conceptual mirroring; if a direct approach is not shifting dynamics, use a creative or embodied method to help parties "step out" of entrenched antagonistic roles.

- Use physical language to give implicit permission to parties to attend to physical needs and cues. For example: "I need to stretch my back. How about taking a few minutes to get our circulation going?"

In premediation workshops, which may form a part of team or multiparty conflict interventions, invite parties to consider how the ways they hold themselves, their postures toward others, and their respect for personal physical signals are all germane to shifting conflict. Exploration of these and other dimensions can be fruitfully done via workshops where movement-based practices are used to tap the body's wisdom on these points.

As we have described, embodiment exercises have the ability to communicate subtle complexities, which form essential themes for addressing conflict at deeper levels. For example, Hervey describes an activity where she asks participants to move to principles and values that she calls out to the group. As part of debriefing, she, with feedback from members of the group, describes what was noticed about the movements. Hervey points out that principles and values, although often-interpreted and one-dimensional ideals—such as justice and fidelity—may evoke diverse embodied responses from participants.[48] Read together, these embodiments highlight the complexity of living values in the twenty-first century and reveal positive stories but also dark and shadowy sides.

In another example, Janis Sarra, a University of British Columbia business-law professor, recently convened a dance-based workshop on fairness.[49] Collaborating with two professional dancers, academicians worked from movement experiences to examine corporeal aspects of fairness and how somatic intelligence can inform nuanced conversations and subtle dimensions of this contentious concept. Participants reflected that movement not only revealed unthought-of aspects of fairness but also gave them more mobility to further thicken their dialogue.

Do Dance and Movement Methods Fit with Traditional Methods, Including Role Plays?

Now hang on a minute, some of you may be thinking. We have just discussed at length the notion of dance as embodied expression. Isn't that exactly what role plays do? Embody learning by making participants move around and experientially play out a role in a given scenario? So aren't we already "dancing"?

Well, yes and no. Yes, role plays do engage kinesthetic learning styles more than traditional lectures. And it is true that conflict-resolution education has traveled a long way from the hierarchical days of predominantly theory-based, one-way oral communication between professors and students. However, the kinaesthetic learning potential of roleplaying is not acheived just by getting particiapants to physically act out a prescribed role within a thity minute time frame. Kinaesthetic learning is about the deep insights available to teachers and learners from authentic somatic experiences rather than once-removed responses to standardized role-play experiences that are constructed at arm's length from participants' real lives. In this section we bring together the ideas presented in this chapter to suggest how role plays and other experiential methods can be enhanced to heighten the quality of embodied learning.

Prework

As conflict-resolution teachers, we usually emphasize the importance of the negotiation or mediation setting. We explain the importance of establishing a collaborative atmosphere where parties can feel safe to voice their concerns without retribution and to engage creatively in problem solving without being prejudged by others. Why should it be any less relevant for somatically integrated conflict-resolution training?

Lumsden explains the importance of creating a safe space where the rules of the regular classroom are suspended and students can behave and move freely, differently, and authentically. He stresses that the requirement of safety encompasses both physical and emotional elements, so the space should offer participants a link "between the internal and external worlds, facilitating the exploration of new ways of being and emotional expression, and experimenting with new dimensions of existence."[50]

How can this be achieved? Creating an environment that evokes playfulness, creativity, warmth, and isolation from the "outside world" is a good start. In *The King's Speech*, the much-acclaimed 2010 British historical film drama, King George VI works with an Australian speech therapist, Lionel Logue, to overcome his debilitating stammer. In one scene, Logue transforms the cold and impersonal but very stately room from which the king will make his speech into a cozy, inviting, and very safe space, draped with throws, curtains, rugs, and cushions from the rooms in which he and King George VI had trained and rehearsed. The warm and familiar environment has an immediate relaxing effect on the king, both mentally and physiologically, and he goes on to make one of his most powerful wartime speeches. Similarly, in workshop situations we might imagine drama and dance studios scattered with diverse, colorful props and remnants of others' imaginative creations, stories, and explorations.

While most of us do not have ready access to therapists' comfortable rooms or custom-built dance studios, there is much we can do to enhance the somatic possibilities of training spaces. For example, encourage all participants to join you in bringing along soft balls, non-fragile objects, scarves, and other props. If you do not have access to a geographically isolated space, see what can be done to block out the outside world; for example, use old sheets, sofa covers, and blankets as curtains. Bring in inflatable furniture—it is cheap and easy to transport. Consider how to integrate the restroom, kitchen, break-out, or hallway spaces. What else can you do to create a comfortable, informal learning space?

In addition to preparing the physical space, think about how you frame the training in announcements and materials sent to participants. Young and Schlie advocate the use of dance as a metaphor for conflict-resolution and negotiation training on the basis that it "challenges such dichotomous constructs as fight versus flight, harmony versus war, and adversaries versus partners." They posit that "creatively accessing a [dance] metaphor . . . can help us understand more of the varied facets of negotiation and approach the field in a more differentiated way."[51] Using dance as a metaphor from the very start to frame the language of negotiation, mediation, and conflict resolution is a powerful way to invoke safety and spaciousness.

At Work

So how might dance intelligence be able to manifest itself in a conflict-resolution workshop? Here are some ideas you might like to try out in your next workshop or training session. Feel free to vary aspects to suit your training needs. Be creative!

- **Work with peripheral vision.** Before students move into a role play, ask them to form a circle and to fix their eyes on a point on the opposite side of the room. Ask participants what they can see other than that point while keeping their eyes focused on it. For example, can they notice the color and texture of the walls, ceiling, or floor? Can they see any surrounding furniture or objects? How many people in the circle are within their view, and what can they notice about them—clothing, hair, shoes? You can also ask participants to move across the room while keeping their eyes on a certain point, navigating people and objects as they go. In this second activity, movement is added to the use of peripheral vision, thereby heightening focus and self-awareness while expanding the visual horizon. The debriefing discussion that follows can address peripheral vision as a physiological skill for conflict intervenors and a metaphor for how people might experience conflict in a very specific or narrow way and how to help them expand their frame of reference. It may also be a metaphor for the ability to identify resources that may not be obvious to those directly involved in the conflict.

- **Embody excellence in mediation.** Invite participants to find a space of their own and to draw an imaginary circle of excellence in front of them into which they will step during the activity. Ask them to think of someone they consider to be the type of excellent mediator that they themselves would wish to be and to imagine that this person is in the room with them. Now ask participants to notice as many details as they can about the excellent mediators. For example, how do the excellent mediators hold themselves and move and sit? How do they express themselves through facial and bodily gestures? How do their eyes move and "speak"? How do they sound and feel? As participants calibrate these details, they step into their imaginary circle of excellence, close their eyes, and emulate and embody these characteristics. This can be a very powerful and transforming experience for many, especially those who identify well with their person of excellence. Depending on the focus of the workshop, participants might embody excellent negotiators, peacemakers, and so on. This activity is best done immediately prior to a role play and at a stage in the training when participants have a realistic idea of the excellence they wish to emulate in conflict-resolution skills.

- **What's your ginch?** *Ginch* is the Canadian dancer Margie Gillis's term for the embodied equivalent of what conflict intervenors might call tension, impasse, deadlock, or just plain being stuck. We all can identify ginches in our bodies, so this activity draws upon somatic knowledge, inviting analogies between how we address ginches in our bodies and how we deal with ginches in a conflict-resolution context. Invite participants to move around the room freely, loosely, and comfortably, "dancing out" any discomfort or tension. After several minutes, ask them to identify their biggest, ugliest, most persistent ginch, whether it be a sore neck, nagging knee problem, locked jaw, tight back, or some other symptom. As they continue to move around the room, suggest to participants that they create space around their ginch and allow it to move and release itself. In other words, rather than letting a robust masseur or mediator hammer the problem, focus on it and let it breathe; give it the space and time to sort itself out.

- **Moving to which music?** Select a piece of music with some texture and complexity, perhaps from the world-music genre. Ask participants to move around the room and respond to different aspects of the music; for example, sad or melancholy themes, happy or lively themes, high or low notes, percussion, melody, and so on. How does the experience of the music change for participants? Are they "dancing" to the same music each time? How might this translate to their understanding of how different people experience the same conflict?

- **Flowing and frozen embodied scenes.** Body-sculpting activities and other somatic methods of learning engage participants kinesthetically and emotionally to enhance and deepen learning. They can be used in numerous ways to explore conflict-resolution themes. Drawing on the illustration in the previously cited work of Hervey, have participants work individually or in groups to move in a flowing tableau to concepts such as hope, fairness, justice, impasse, resolution, fear, trust, and so on. Other options might include making a body sculpture of the felt sense of your group following the activity, showing in two snapshots the emotional texture of your group before and after the activity, or standing in relation to a partner in a way that conveys your understanding about fairness, justice, or some other concept.

Our experience indicates that integrating these types of activities into training heightens the level of authentic engagement of participants and improves the overall quality of integrative learning. Participants seem to be able to bring more of themselves into the roles they play and are better able to share their personal experiences of conflict resolution with others.

Shall We Dance?

Well, go figure . . . It turns out that dance is not as frightening as I had thought. I started using it as a warm-up in a biweekly class on conflict resolution, and it turned out to be the thing students looked forward to most! Dance and movement, when used as part of training and framed as patterned physical activities, can help participants shift perspectives and increase physical health at the same time. Though academic cultures are notoriously physically phobic, it makes sense for people with physical bodies to use them! And doing so not only brings people into awareness of where they may be holding tension but also allows them to find ways to release it.

Who knew I could dance? One of the unexpected outcomes of using dance and movement in teaching and training contexts is that people who express reluctance are often surprised at its positive impact. In one class, participants found ways to talk about mobility that positively affected their relations with one another following movement exercises that included a wheelchair-bound member of their group. Resistance turned to positive anticipation as they moved beyond stereotypes of dance awkwardness and discovered its capacity to transport them into new, more nuanced conversations.

Underneath the skin . . . It is important to remember that not all dance is visible. We dance within—navigating different sensibilities, influences, and inclinations. We maneuver through inner terrain, endeavoring to stay awake to the braided feelings and thoughts that animate our behavior. This inner dance, too, is worth refining. There are many ways to do so, including tools of mindfulness, meditation, and contemplative prayer. Instruments like the Enneagram assist in helping us pay attention to our habits of perception and patterns of behavior. We are always dancing within as long as we are living; the key is having a way to monitor the dance so that we are able to live with suppleness, flexibility, and grace.

In the subway . . . In the midst of the worlds in which we live, dance is a constant. When next in a public place, notice the different rhythms that animate those around you. Notice your resonance with certain people, your desire for distance from others. What dances of connection or empathy are part of your daily travels? What dances of separation or judgment are part of your repertoire? Conflict intervenors have a responsibility to stay current with these questions. Aspiring to neutrality, we are most helpful to parties when we are aware of our inner and outer dances and how our necessary partiality "dances" with others. Dances are everywhere; noticing rhythm, cadence, symmetries, and asymmetries only makes their complexities more evident and, ultimately, more beautiful.

Without rhythm . . . Have you ever felt you lost your rhythm, weighed down by grief or sadness or an unforeseen setback? What is it like to feel that the dance is going on around you, yet you are not a part of it? Everyone feels excluded sometimes; conflict unaddressed can seriously impair a sense of rhythm and coherence in life. Conflict trainers and intervenors are well advised to cultivate empathy for people in these states. One way of thinking about intervention is that it is an avenue to help people find new rhythms with one another after a rupture or falling out. Dance and movement vocabularies are helpful in encouraging parties to discover new resonances and new ways to move forward jointly and individually.

In a professional conflict-resolution context . . . As conflict intervenors, we ask much of disputing clients. We ask them to reveal themselves to us, trust us, and expose their vulnerability while we hide comfortably behind a shield of professionalism. Similarly, as trainers we may find ourselves slipping into the routine of asking participants to role-play while we safely ensconce ourselves behind the veil of facilitator. Dance intelligence is about using our essential somatic awareness. It helps us to access other ways of knowing and being within ourselves and to recognize this in others. It builds bridges between our inner and outer worlds. Dance intelligence helps us, as conflict intervenors and trainers, to connect with others and build empathy and trust. It enhances our ability to weave fluently in and among cultures and to reach that deep level of human awareness that the Africans call *Ubuntu.*[52] Surely that is what conflict resolution is all about.

Building Emotional Intelligence

A Grid for Practitioners

CHARLIE IRVINE

> *"It is perhaps the quintessential error of the modern Western world view to suppose that thought can occur without feeling."*[1]
> *In Search of Human Nature*, Mary E. Clark

Dancing at the Crossroads was an extravagantly intuitive experiment. It brought together thirty-five people from the worlds of conflict resolution and the arts and invited them to do something novel for a week: lay down their skills and knowledge, their processes and models, even their experience and smartness, and just dance.

Dance is, of course, its own justification. You dance for fun and joy, out of exuberance and energy. People probably always have. However, for many of us at this workshop, professional talkers or writers, the thread tying the week together was the question of what dancing might offer—in the form of theoretical insights and methodological strategies—to the field of conflict resolution. Determination, enthusiasm, and a certain work ethic drove us to discuss, debate, keep journals, and share stories. This chapter attempts to capture one sliver of insight from that week.

I start with a recollection. Much of our dancing was unaccompanied by music, so when Margie Gillis did use music, it had particular power. At the beginning we moved mostly in silence, slowly getting used to our bodies and easing past awkwardness and mortification. We were becoming accustomed, at very different levels of expertise, to expressing something—an idea, a word, a feeling—just by dancing. Quite quickly I noticed talk of emotion: someone felt elated, another stricken with negativity, another just sad.

On the second or third day, we were asked to dance to a piece by Bach: *Air on the G String*. The familiar tune enveloped us. First Margie told us to listen for the bass notes and move with them. We stomped out the descending steps of those famous lines. So far, so familiar, feeling Bach's beat as we might the bass at a club. Next we were asked to move with the melody. This was quicker and lighter, pursuing the intricacies of the notes.

Then Margie took us into unfamiliar territory. We were to find the joyful notes. As we felt for them, there they were, soaring, flitting, gliding, as if we were celebrating, with Bach, all that is best in the universe. By now I had stopped thinking about my body and its self-consciousness.

It had become a vehicle for intuiting and expressing, on "automatic pilot," going where it wanted, carried away. After that, and I should have seen this coming, we were asked to feel for the sad notes. Again, there they were. That genius of a composer had pulled an essence of sadness from the air and revealed it for us all. Even more than the joyful notes, the sad ones seemed to open my insides, exposing that "sediment of sorrow"[2] we accumulate just by living.

Finally Margie invited us to feel for the "spaces between the notes." It sounds implausible and tricky, but I felt weightless as I tried to wriggle in between the lines, to squeeze myself into mystical gaps in the soundscape. I finished exhilarated, buzzing with sensation and flushed with joy. I had the sense of being utterly in the moment but still connected to the sum total of my past.

So why does this matter? Of course it's nice for conflict-resolution professionals to enjoy a dance, but the work ethic dictates that I ask, "What did we learn?" The central lesson is that what I have just described was profoundly affecting. It engaged the complexity of my emotions in a way that many, many hours of conflict-resolution training and teaching rarely have. It revealed the intimate connection between body and emotion, a connection that features little in conflict-resolution literature. The experience—and I see that this was probably Margie's intention—defies rationality.

My contention is that conflict-resolution training, by and large, teaches us to mediate "from the neck up." The topic of the emotions is dealt with superficially, if at all, while the link between emotions and our bodies is almost entirely absent. In spite of the evident importance of our emotions in decision making, we lack useful ways of conceptualizing our emotional state and of implicating it in our work as peacemakers. This chapter explores some honorable exceptions before offering a simple heuristic, or grid, which I hope will provide a useful tool for those dealing with their own or other people's conflict. It is not my intention to review the vast and growing literature on emotions[3] but rather to make a practical offering to assist in developing and maintaining our facility with the emotional realm.

Emotions in Mediation

The modern mediation movement has been ambivalent about emotions. People in conflict experience anger and fear, not to mention surprise, sadness, disgust, and, from time to time, happiness. At the same time, mediation's roots in negotiation and the law render it particularly affected by Enlightenment ideas that oppose emotions in reasonable or rational decision making: "folk wisdom suggests that a negotiator (1) should avoid getting emotional and (2) is a passive recipient of the whims of emotion."[4] Riskin asserts: "Negotiators—especially those trained in law—commonly address this problem by trying to exclude emotions from negotiation and to focus solely on so-called objective, rational factors, such as money."[5] In 2000, Retzinger and Scheff wrote that "the lack of detailed attention to emotions and relationships is the biggest gap in our understanding of conflict."[6] Since then, a great deal of attention has been paid to the subject, some of which is reviewed below. The focus is on three areas:

1. The relationship between cognition and emotion in perception
2. The importance of a range of emotions, starting with anger, in contributing to conflict
3. The potential for emotional self-regulation to be harnessed and supported by mediators

The Relationship between Cognition and Emotion in Perception

How emotions function is the subject of keen debate. One idea is to see them as triggers, the body's "early warning system," designed to respond rapidly to threat or change. Jones describes the sequence as *triggering event* (what the emotion is about) → *appraisal* (our interpretation of the triggering event) → *emotion* (appropriate to that interpretation) → *somatic reactions* (the physiological changes preparing us for the action we need to take) → *action tendencies* (the disposition to behave in keeping with all of the foregoing).[7] Patterson et al. describe this sequence as the Path to Action.[8] In both these schemes, regulation—"the ability to decide whether or not to engage in the action tendencies"[9]—takes on particular importance, as it underlines human agency: we are not driven by our emotions, and the ability to regulate them has been described as the "master aptitude."[10]

A more-organic view is presented by Damasio: "[E]motion is the conclusion of a *mental evaluative process*, simple or complex, with *dispositional responses to that process*, mostly *toward the body proper*, resulting in an emotional body state, but also *toward the brain* itself."[11] Emotions implicate brain and body in a swirl of simultaneous experience. Crucially, for Damasio, both are needed for effective decision making: "Emotion and feeling, along with the covert physiological machinery underlying them, assist us with the daunting task of predicting an uncertain future and planning our actions accordingly."[12] He divides emotions into "primary"—unbidden, gut responses to threat—and "secondary"—those that draw on recollections and categorizations in the higher parts of our brains, elegantly described by William Wordsworth as "those thoughts and feelings which, by [a man's] own choice, or from the structure of his own mind, arise in him without immediate external excitement."[13]

Damasio also distinguishes between feelings and emotions. While all emotions generate feelings in most healthy people, not all feelings relate to emotions. He hypothesizes that the mechanism by which we experience emotions involves comparing some new information with a "background feeling"—our sense of ourselves, or the "image of the body landscape when it is not shaken by emotion."[14] The fact that we feel emotions renders them no less trustworthy than that we think thoughts. Feelings are cognitive, too, and "have a say on how the rest of the brain and cognition go about their business. Their influence is immense."[15] Damasio goes on to elaborate a theory of "somatic markers," whereby our gut feelings act as extraordinarily efficient shortcuts, warning us of potentially hazardous (or felicitous) consequences for our choices and thus saving significant time and processing power. Our evaluations of the world thus rely on a seamless calibration of feelings and thoughts. Body and mind are equally implicated.[16]

Some have questioned the universal application of these ideas. While Ekman is convinced that the basic emotions, having evolved as adaptive responses to our environment, are the same across cultures,[17] others see them as "socially shared scripts that are culturally determined to some extent."[18] For example, cultural variables like "honor values" have been shown to affect people's emotional response to an insult.[19] Augsburger goes further and proposes that "moral/ cultural approval" is one of the components of emotions (along with body arousal and mind appraisal).[20] In this view, culture is inextricably woven into our experience of emotion.

Whichever view is more accurate, our capacity to read our own and others' emotional scripts is a crucial one for operating in human society and relies on mind and body, thoughts and feelings. Those who intervene in other people's conflicts have arguably an even greater need for this capacity, suggesting that mediating from the neck up, while comfortable for many of us, carries risks too. I consider below ways in which mediators might enhance and improve their facility with emotions.

Emotions in Conflict

Emotions are often associated with the onset of conflict, a kind of uncontrollable force propelling people into unwise choices that their cooler, more-rational selves would later regret: "If people could always stay perfectly rational and focused on how to best meet their needs and accommodate those of others . . . then many conflicts would either never arise or would quickly deescalate."[21] In this worldview, the task of the intervenor is to cool the emotions and allow reason to return to its rightful place, governing decision making.

And yet in reality, thoughts and feelings, mind and body, are not so easily disentangled. Because our appraisal of a situation occurs rapidly,[22] before the newer (and slower) parts of our brains have begun to operate, if it is erroneous it can lead us to experience the wrong emotion. Once the emotion is engaged, our action tendencies are difficult to reverse,[23] sometimes with disastrous consequences. For example, when a Boston man heard an unfamiliar noise in the middle of the night, he grabbed his gun and shot the "intruder," only to discover it was his girlfriend, using the bathroom.[24] If I believe you intend to harm me or simply disrespect me, I am liable to interpret even innocuous actions, such as arriving late or failing to maintain eye contact, in a negative light. As Beck puts it: "In general, whether we feel anger, anxiety, sadness, or joy in a particular encounter depends on our interpretation, the *meaning*, we assign to it."[25] Ekman talks of "inappropriate emotions: the right emotion at the wrong intensity, the right emotion but shown the wrong way, and the wrong emotion altogether."[26] (Italics added.) Any of these can lead to conflict, particularly when we take into account the additional complexity of each person's potentially biased attributions.[27]

Jones makes the link more concrete: "Since the triggers of emotion and the triggers of perceived conflict are the same, to recognize that someone is in conflict is to acknowledge that he has been triggered emotionally."[28] This emotional arousal floods our brains with chemicals designed for simple flight-or-fight responses. It is then almost impossible to take a range of perspectives into account. In plain terms, if I am "mad as hell" because I think you have insulted me, I am unlikely to extend you the benefit of the doubt. I may even act punitively, although it harms me too.

Emotional arousal is not exclusively negative. Negative emotions are associated with poor judgment and outcomes, but emotions may just as readily assist with the resolution of conflict—love, happiness, sympathy, sorrow, or even fear may drive solution seeking. Cloke names "forgiveness, open-heartedness, empathy, insight, intuition, learning, wisdom, and willingness to change" as positive counterparts to "hostile gut reactions."[29] Shapiro summarizes research indicating that positive emotions are associated with more-integrative results in negotiation.[30]

All of this suggests that mediating from the neck up is high risk for mediators, potentially neglecting the very sources of resolution that matter most to those with whom we work. My evaluation of dancing to Bach implicated bodily sensations, mental processes, and a quick-fire scan of my entire memory. In the same way, when I make a judgment that conflict is lessening its grip on a room or that something positive or even magical has happened between warring parties, I rely on feelings as much as, if not more than, thoughts. Bush and Folger introduce their "transformative" model[31] to experienced mediators by asking them to describe their most successful mediation sessions—almost always times of breakthrough. Their judgments of success rely on qualities such as atmosphere, bearing, attitude, warmth, and contentedness, all impossible to evaluate simply by attending to words alone. Mediation undeniably requires us to integrate feelings and thoughts.

Emotional Regulation

If emotions are so significant in both creating and resolving conflict, can we do anything about them? A clear idea emerging from the literature is that we have the capacity to appraise[32] and regulate our emotions.[33] People who lack this capacity find it difficult to function in society. Damasio relates the story of Phineas Gage, who suffered damage to a portion of his brain that left him seemingly intellectually intact but lacking in self-control, with disastrous consequences for work and relationships.[34] For the rest of us, self-regulation is a crucial feature of our interaction with others, perhaps contributing to the commonsense idea that reason can triumph over emotion in a mature individual.

The implications for conflict resolution are clear. Emotions both trigger and are triggered by conflict. If we have some say over what we feel, it will help us choose positive, not negative, responses to difficult situations. This has been called "emotion analysis": "a way of clarifying the hurt and locating it within the relational matrix of conflict."[35] Third parties such as mediators can assist with this. If they can "focus participants' attention on the appraisals they are making, the parties have the opportunity to 'see' the conflict differently, resulting in a different emotional experience."[36]

What skills do mediators need to develop to assist the task of emotional appraisal and reappraisal? Jones proposes "elicitive questioning" with two purposes: identifying the emotion and then reappraising the situation.[37] Typical questions focus on goals, attributions of blame, and possible solutions. Jameson et al. set out a typology of "emotion-eliciting" strategies:

1. Grant legitimacy
2. Encourage emotional identification
3. Help the person deny the emotion (for example, to save face)
4. Challenge an emotion label (the way an emotion has been defined within the mediation)
5. Confront emotion avoidance
6. Paraphrase emotion
7. Encourage emotional perspective taking
8. Probe meta-emotions[38]

They found 2 and 7 the most commonly employed, while 3, 4, and 8 were unused. This suggests that mediators are familiar with the potential of emotional appraisal but tend to focus their efforts on the first of Jones's tasks, identifying the emotion, rather than the second, reappraising the situation. However, emotion identification may be beneficial in itself: in one experiment, paying direct attention to emotions (rather than reflecting on the details of the situation) reduced amygdala activity and thus attenuated emotional arousal.[39] Jameson et al. make a practical contribution to the debate about emotions in conflict resolution, suggesting that discussing them "is a facilitator for rather than a barrier to effective communication and conflict transformation."[40] They also propose adapting well-known mediator strategies such as paraphrasing and perspective taking to enable the discussion of emotions.

In a recent article, Riskin draws on Fisher and Shapiro's notion that our emotional responses revolve around five "core concerns" for appreciation, affiliation, autonomy, status, and role.[41] He goes on to suggest that the practice of mindfulness can provide mediators with tools to conduct this emotion work.

To summarize the discussion so far, Dancing at the Crossroads highlighted a problem for many professionals. Our training and traditions downplay the physical and emotional components of perception. This approach risks ignoring or undervaluing physical and emotional information; and when it comes to making good, rational decisions, feelings are as important as thoughts. The study of emotions is a vast and growing area. One key recent focus has been on the link between emotions and perception, with some scholars seeking to overthrow Enlightenment ideas of the superiority of thoughts to feelings. The picture emerging is that accurate perception depends on a continuous integration of body and brain. When it comes to the role of emotions in conflict, the depictions have been largely negative, with considerable attention paid to the role of anger and fear in the escalation of conflict. Less remarked on, but still significant, is the contribution of emotions to the resolution of conflict. Finally, turning to conflict-resolution practice, several writers have drawn attention to the beneficial potential of emotional self-regulation. If people in conflict can articulate what their emotions are telling them, they can learn from and modify those emotions and thus their actions. Mediators can assist with this process.

PRACTICE TIPS

- Don't be afraid to discuss emotion in mediation.
- Use familiar mediation techniques such as paraphrasing and perspective-taking to help parties appraise their emotions.

The Emotional Grid

A great deal of the writing about emotions is devoted to categorizing them.[42] It is not the intention of this chapter to focus on those ideas. We are all conscious of the subtlety of emotions. Just as the primary colors hardly capture the dazzling array of shades and tones in the visual spectrum, so the primary emotions seem to lack the nuances and variations of real-time feelings. I propose the following scheme as a simple model for conflict practitioners, but it is not a substitute for emotional typologies.

It has two purposes. The first is intuitive and experiential. Dancing at the Crossroads reminded us of the vast array of emotional information absorbed by and manifest in our bodies. More than any other group, people in conflict need to make sound decisions based on accurate perceptions. It is surely useful for conflict intervenors to enhance their own emotional fluency to better serve participants and ensure their well-being. The second purpose flows from the scholarship summarized previously: this fluency may be vital for helping those in conflict make the most of their capacity for emotional self-regulation. And this same capacity for self-regulation will be a feature of emotionally intelligent conflict intervenors.

The idea of using a grid to display interacting emotions is not new. In 1952, Schlosberg displayed the range of human facial expressions on a 360-degree circle.[43] Riskin's grid, showing the dimensions of mediation, is a staple of training.[44] The "emotional grid" captures a simple idea that emerged from discussions during Dancing at the Crossroads: the volume of an emotion (or a set of emotions) is not necessarily related to the intensity with which the emotion is felt.

For example, if I bang my toe on a table leg, I tend to shout out (to the alarm of my family). This is a high-volume emotion, but gone in a flash. Others witnessing it would waste effort if they confused noisiness with importance. It belongs in the top left corner of the grid.

In contrast, I regularly work with people who are experiencing severe loss. That emotion can color every aspect of the person's life, from relationships to appetite. Sometimes it is volubly expressed, but on other occasions the signs of loss are subtle and low volume: a certain held-in look or a fragile tone of voice. This type of emotion is in the bottom right corner of the grid.

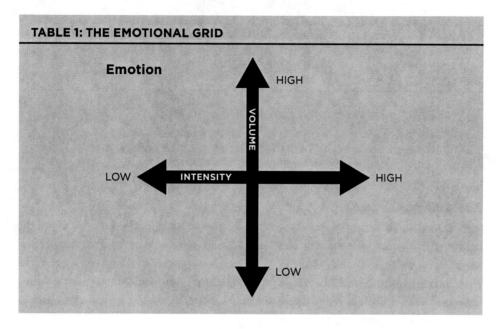

TABLE 1: THE EMOTIONAL GRID

Other clients seem to live in the bottom left quadrant. Little is expressed, and if asked what they think or how they feel, their answers are low-key: "fine," "OK," or the Scottish favorite, "not bad."

And finally there are those who seem to occupy the top right quadrant: emotions are deeply felt and loudly broadcast. These dramatic individuals can be daunting at first, but colleagues have confessed that they find it easier to mediate with people in this quadrant than with those in the opposite (bottom left) corner, because "at least you know where you are."

The Dimensions

One important point needs to be emphasized: it was the experience of dancing, and thus opening ourselves to physical expression, that drew our attention to the nuances of emotion. Our rational, science-based culture tends to sideline both bodies and emotions. The risk here is that this approach diminishes our ability to analyze them with any subtlety. The grid is a way of enhancing that ability. So volume largely corresponds to the outward expression of emotion, and intensity equates to the strength of inner feelings. And yet, as with everything in the world of emotions, there is no precise line. An intense emotion may "leak out," so that, although the volume of speech remains low, other telltale signs are evident, such as a quivering voice or flushed face.

Conversely, people may express their feelings volubly, perhaps overwhelming the listener/ observer at first. After a time the listener/observer can recalibrate the volume scale (perhaps from loud to very loud!) as it becomes clear that there is still variation within the discourse. Volume does not refer only to sound. People may wriggle, their palms sweat or eyes dilate, or the atmosphere may just feel tense

Uses of the Grid

1. Developing Cultural Fluency

Even if there are universal emotions, the relationship between volume and intensity is almost certainly culturally mediated. We learn from earliest childhood when it is acceptable to display our feelings. Families, friendship groups, regions, and nations all have distinct norms. For example, while sitting in a park in Italy, I observed an encounter among three people on the street beside me. There was a lot of shouting and finger-jabbing as the noise of the conversation began to increase alarmingly. In my hometown of Glasgow, Scotland, this volume of emotion would be a fairly reliable predictor of violence, and I readied myself to witness a fight. And yet two minutes later, they embraced, said "Ciao," and walked off, apparently content. My cultural script gave me poor guidance as to the meaning of a particular emotional volume.

By using the grid regularly, I can plot the volume/intensity relationship of my encounters with others. This allows me to recalibrate my perception over time. If conversations regularly move within the top half of the volume range, I can adapt my expectations and responses, thus limiting the problem of experiencing the wrong emotion. Table 2 illustrates such a range.

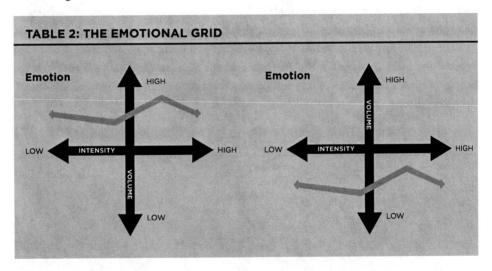

TABLE 2: THE EMOTIONAL GRID

Likewise, if I am operating in a culture where the volume of emotional expression is habitually low, I can use the grid to help me read emotion in a volume range that would normally go below my radar.

By consistently using the grid we can build our self-awareness. How do we respond to loud emotional displays? Is this culturally attuned (that is, conveying the meaning that we intend)? Equally, how do we respond in a low-volume culture? Does the mediation value of curiosity come across as intrusive and even insensitive? All of this will help mediators develop a keener sense of their impact on the conflict system they are entering.

PRACTICE TIPS

- In a new or unfamiliar setting, use the grid to plot the emotional range of the people you meet.
- Compare your own responses.
- If they are different, try adjusting your "volume" to mirror those around you.

In applying this scheme to international cultures, I am aware of the risk of confirming sweeping stereotypes. There is huge variation within any country or ethnic group. More locally, each family, workplace, and group of friends has its own setting, the unspoken norms of "how we do things round here." Mediators, like anthropologists, have to work as visitors to other people's worlds, and the grid may help us with this task of interpretation.

2. Plotting the Flow of Emotion over Time

I am grateful to my students at the University of Strathclyde for providing the next insight: the grid can also be used to plot the relationship between emotional intensity and volume over time. Someone may start a mediation session calmly but quickly raise the volume as he or she rehearses the sources of conflict. The other person reacts defensively to this rise in volume, which in turn increases the first person's emotional intensity. Then perhaps the volume gradually lowers while the intensity remains high, as the mediator helps to manage the process by providing procedural fairness.[45] Finally some sort of resolution is found, decreasing both poles.

TABLE 3: THE EMOTIONAL GRID

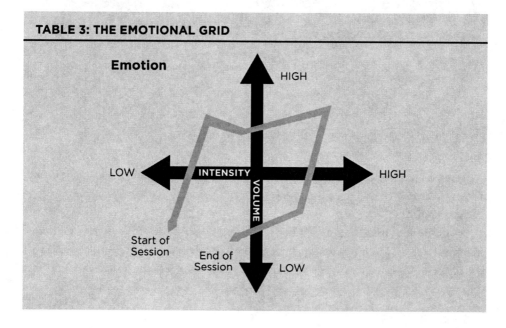

This is perhaps the classic hope of mediators, but the reality is surely more complex. My perception is of constant fluctuation throughout the sessions. For example, someone may arrive at mediation emotionally aroused and express it straightaway. That outburst leads to a slight reduction in volume and intensity, but the other party's resultant counteraccusation drives him or her upward again. This pattern can shift back and forth for a time, and the mediator's job becomes one of "holding:" creating an atmosphere safe enough for people to express their emotions without leaving the room. Techniques would include active listening, validating, affirming, appreciative inquiry, summarizing, calibrating between parties, checking out understandings, or simply sitting back and witnessing the interaction. Sometimes, as represented below, there is a key moment of emotional intensity, allowing for a form of catharsis before the volume reduces prior to resolution.

TABLE 4: THE EMOTIONAL GRID

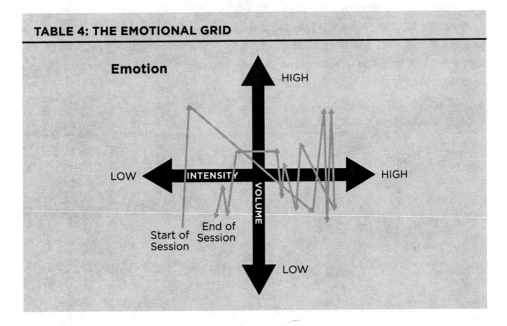

Becoming aware of our emotional change over time may help to counteract a tendency recently noted by Movius and Wilson to make errors in remembering past feelings and predicting future ones.[46] For example, we are demonstrably influenced by our current feelings when recalling a previous mood or predicting a future one.[47] The grid can provide evidence of our actual emotional condition.

PRACTICE TIPS

- Try plotting a client's emotional range throughout a mediation session.
- Note which mediation techniques or "moves" you used at particular moments.
- Use this to evaluate the effectiveness of different interventions.

3. Developing Mediator Practice

While experienced mediators probably get a feel for emotional volume and intensity, one perennial issue in the field is the difficulty in helping learners develop such capacities quickly. A recent article makes the case for daily skills practice.[48] Just as musicians practice their instruments *before* rehearsing with the band, so mediators can develop their skills as a regular discipline.

One use of the grid, then, is as an aid to self-reflection. By tracking our daily emotional volume and intensity, we develop a familiarity with our own triggers as well as with situations where volume is no guide to intensity. This would complement the practice of mindfulness, which Riskin argues will enhance a mediator's ability to address emotional concerns. He contends that "the ability to observe one's own thoughts, emotions and body sensations, without judgement, may help develop a sensitivity to these phenomena as they arise in others."[49]

Returning to my experience at Dancing at the Crossroads, if I examine it through the lens provided by the grid, I discover something of interest: my actions led to my emotions, reversing conventional wisdom. My emotional condition throughout the Bach piece would look something like this:

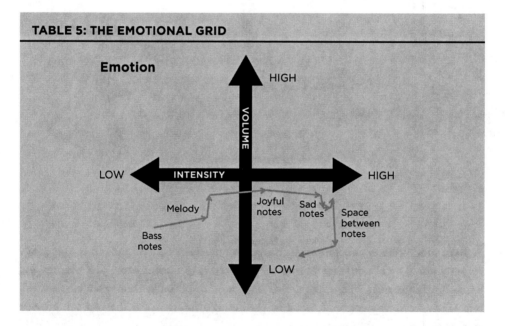

TABLE 5: THE EMOTIONAL GRID

The external face of emotion, volume, remains relatively low, though not invisible (because my body is manifesting the emotions that it is also creating). The internal dimension, however, rises quickly to a crescendo. Others may not see it, but the physical manifestation of emotion both expresses and fuels that state in a feedback loop: when you show your feelings, you feel them all the more. So, if in mediation an angry person jumps up and shouts, this enactment of emotion may well both express and fuel that person's anger. Conversely, showing patience and nondefensiveness can both express and fuel a cooperative problem-solving approach to disagreement.

This raises challenging questions for mediators. Can we, by embodying a particular emotion, help to bring it about for others?[50] Clients sometimes comment that mediators model calmness by their stance and tone of voice. Could we go further than current practice permits in harnessing the physical dimension of human interaction in the interests of peace? A mediator could enact the emotions he or she is witnessing, giving parties faster access to their own somatic markers; for example, by registering shock, surprise, dismay, or pleasure. This may challenge conventional notions of mediator neutrality, but if done transparently and respectfully, such a move could enhance self-regulation by offering people a glimpse of their own emotional states. By using the grid to record our own and the parties' emotional states, we may be able to plot causal links between such experiments and subsequent outcomes.

Finally, the grid can be used by groups of practitioners. Over time they can share the mappings of their own and others' emotional worlds with colleagues, alerting them to different perspectives and highlighting misinterpretations. This could be a rich tool for learning, helping mediators critically assess their interpretation of the emotional realm and their own responses to conflict.

PRACTICE TIPS

- Plot your own emotional volume and intensity during a mediation session.
- As above, note which techniques or "moves" you used and when.
- Develop your emotional fluency by tracing the link between what you feel and what you do—in other words, between emotion, perception, and action.

---

4. Using the Grid with Others

The grid can also be viewed as a game or puzzle to be played with. Since Dancing at the Crossroads, I have used it with different groups, and each has suggested new ways of applying it. One suggestion was to simply offer it to people in conflict and invite them to track their own emotional intensity or volume. The resultant insights can help them understand the dynamics of intractable conflict, where people are often unaware of their own contribution to the situation and are therefore mystified by others' responses. Someone may spot times when his or her volume was high (and perhaps alarming) or where it was low but masked intense feelings. Here the grid can help develop parties' capacity for self-regulation, whether or not they resolve their particular dispute. As one negotiation pioneer puts it: "*Become aware of your emotions* and, in so doing, take control of them rather than let them take control of you."[51]

PRACTICE TIPS

- Give the grid to the parties.
- Ask them to plot their emotional state before and after a mediation session.
- Discuss any changes and what lessons they can learn from the changes.
- Ask how they managed to control (regulate) their emotions.

Limitations

The grid is an abstraction—an attempt to systematize something inherently dynamic. It has its limitations. If it enhances emotional literacy, that's well and good, but I am not proposing that mediators override their well-honed instincts about when to dwell on emotions and when not to. I commend a spirit of "kindly curiosity"[52] both in relation to others and in considering our own emotional world.

Perhaps the grid is most safely used on ourselves. It might be seen as impertinent or unethical to attempt to divine someone else's inner state from external evidence. Conversely, however, it could be argued that it is unethical not to try to understand those in conflict, who are often confounded by their own actions and reactions.

Conclusion

This chapter began with a physical experience (actions) leading to an emotional state (feelings). It then turned to the cerebral world of academic scholarship (thoughts) in an attempt to make sense of what had happened during a week of dance. Three significant strands emerge. One is the folly of attempting to draw a bright line between reason and emotion. Accurate judgment relies on both.

A second strand portrays emotion as a source of conflict. Conflict literature tends to concentrate on the negative side of emotion: anger, fear, hatred, contempt, guilt, shame, and frustration. Somewhat neglected are positive emotions in conflict. And more work needs to be done in understanding the way emotions help in the resolution of conflict.

This links to the third strand, self-regulation, which allows us to make choices about the cocktail of feelings, thoughts, and actions involved in conflict. While this notion has found broad acceptance, there is less consensus on how it is to be achieved, and a number of writers speculate about possible techniques. I propose a grid with four possible uses: supporting cultural fluency, tracing emotional change over time, helping with the formation and development of conflict intervenors, and working with clients.

To return to Dancing at the Crossroads, this chapter underlines the unpredictable nature of that experiment. To confess for a moment my own Enlightenment prejudices, when the idea of spending a week on conflict and dance was first suggested, I was a bit wary and had no inkling that my enduring recollection would be of emotion. Creativity, perhaps; as a former musician, I have long wished to integrate that part of my life with my work as a mediator.

Or possibly technique: there was a lot to learn from how dance can be bold, swift, and intoxicating. How many mediation sessions can boast those qualities? I also thought I might learn from my colleagues and was not disappointed. And yet the project's most significant discovery for me was something far closer to home and, perhaps as a result, so often taken for granted: emotions.

The grid emerged from an honest and vulnerable conversation in which a group of us acknowledged how tough it can be to become immersed in conflict. It has led me to reexamine the way I engage with the world of feelings. In encountering the work of Damasio and others, I have come to realize that much of my own practice could be characterized as an attempt to mediate from the neck up. Dancing at the Crossroads brought the rest of my body to the table. It yielded other insights too: how mediators might use their whole selves (body and all) in conflict resolution; how to escape the "still life" scenario (three chairs and a table) presented by most mediation rooms; how we might harness what movement does to our thoughts and feelings to unlock tightly knit conflict. But it is the (re)discovery of emotion that has been the most powerful experience, offering significant potential for enhancing conflict resolution.

So if this grid—tool/heuristic/game/doodle—is useful, that's good. If not, no matter, for this piece of work has made me reconsider the practice of peacemaking. The older our field becomes, the more we become conscious of variables. The idea of a one-size-fits-all model seems neither necessary nor desirable. The huge variety of humanity's emotional and cognitive responses combine with other factors such as culture, time frame, social norms, subject matter, and values to create an almost infinite range of settings for our work. Rather than relying on models, perhaps we need to approach our work as dancers might: engage in daily practice and discipline so that when we rehearse we can use our whole range without inhibition. Then when it is time to actually perform, we interact afresh with a new audience, tailoring our moves to the nuances and minute details of each human interaction. Thus we can expand the "choreography" of conflict resolution, implicating mind and body to attain greater presence, responsiveness, and flexibility. To jump art forms, we need to develop our palette, perhaps adding this grid to the vast range of ideas and techniques from the conflict-resolution canon, so that when it really matters, when the sheer weight of conflict threatens to overpower even the mediators, we do the right thing at the right moment.

Dancing through Conflict

Developing Intuition for Mediation

SIMON J. A. MASON, SUSAN ALLEN NAN, AND VIRGINIE VAN DE LOE

Introduction

The aim of this article is to improve mediation practice by exploring how mediators can develop intuition through expressive dance exercises. At its simplest, mediation can be defined as "assisted negotiations" and negotiations as "interdependent decision-making." As mediators support negotiators making joint decisions, they themselves also make decisions on how to structure the process, how to clarify the conflict issues, and how to deal with the relationship dynamics and emotional atmosphere. Intuition is one form of decision making, often used in highly complex and uncertain situations—such as the ones mediators typically are dealing with. We argue that mediators can improve their mediation practice by reflecting on and developing intuition. Professionally guided expressive dance exercises can heal mediators by releasing emotional blockages. Expressive dance exercises can also be used in mediation training to help mediators embody key aspects of mediation and develop awareness of the dynamics of nonverbal communication. The guiding question of this article is: How is intuition related to mediation, and how can dance help mediators develop intuition?

Intuition

What is intuition and how does it work? Gigerenzer defines intuition as "a judgment that appears quickly in consciousness, whose underlying reasons we are not fully aware of, and is strong enough to act upon."[1] Intuition is knowing without fully knowing where we got the knowledge from. The words "not fully" means we may have some rough idea of the source and logic of our intuitive knowledge, yet this will never be 100% verifiable, otherwise it is not intuition. Some of the different aspects of intuition are summarized below, moving from the simpler and more plausible uses and misuses of intuition, to the more complex use of intuition to make sense of emotions in human relationships.

Two ways of thinking: Kahneman[2] differentiates two types of thinking: the "system 1" way of thinking is fast, intuitive, metaphorical, impressionistic, emotional and unconscious, while the "system 2" way of thinking is slower, more logical, more conscious and more deliberate. System 1 is useful in many situations, e.g. in the face of danger when one has to react quickly, as it can pick up on subtle environmental cues. Yet system 1 thinking may lead to numerous biases. For example the "framing effect": how a problem is framed, influences our response, even if the facts are the same, i.e. more people accept surgery if they are told they have a 90% survival rate, than if they are told that they have a 10% mortality rate. Kahneman highlights how we tend to wrongly identify ourselves with our rational way of thinking, our "system 2" being, while we are often actually more shaped by our "system 1".

Rules of the thumb: How can we make sense of this "system 1" being, and how can we conceptualize how intuition works? According to Gigerenzer,[3] intuitions arise out of a combination of three factors, 1) a "rule of the thumb", a simple "if this, then that" type rule; 2) an environmental structure or situation a person reacts to, 3) evolved capacities of the brain to merge and select information. There is no good or bad intuition per se, it is more a question of appropriate fit to a given context, and more or less useful "rules of the thumb" to make sense of it. A "rule of the thumb" aims to hit at the most important information, and disregard the rest. For example, when guessing what a person likes when presented by diverse options, we may use the rule of the thumb: "if a person looks at one alternative, it is likely the one the person desires" (gaze heuristic). However, we do not know if this is the case, and some people may also use different "rules of the thumb" and come up with different answers. In highly complex situations, where there is insufficient information, focusing on one good reason and using a simple heuristic approach to make a judgment can sometimes lead to better judgments than the more logical, statistical approach. Gigerenzer also shows how people who are experienced in a field (e.g. medicine) have better intuitions than those who are not experienced. Intuition can be trained and improved.

Core concerns: In the context of human relations, the way we read and react to emotions —be these our own or the person we are interacting with—has an enormous impact on if we and the other person experience the relationship as beneficial or harmful. Fisher and Shapiro[4] argue that it is too slow and cumbersome to analyze and react to individual emotions, but that a simple framework can help us understand emotions and react more appropriately. The framework they suggest argues that most emotions that arise in the context of human relations are related to five core concerns: appreciation, affiliation, autonomy, role and status. To deal with emotions, they suggest using two "rules of the thumb": The first one is: "If you hurt the core concerns of the other person, or they hurt your core concerns, negative emotions will result." The second one is: "If you satisfy the core concerns of the other person, or they satisfy your core concerns, positive emotions will result." These "rules of the thumb" can help fine-tune our intuition when dealing with emotions in relationships.

Nonverbal communication: Many of the cues that we use to make sense of emotions in interpersonal relationships are related to nonverbal communication. Thus intuition has also been defined as "a nonlinear process of knowing perceived through physical awareness…".[5] Nonverbal communication can be broadly differentiated into kinesics (body motion including facial expression, eye movement, posture, gestures etc.), vocalics (how something is said, including the pitch, rhythm, vocalizations etc.), haptics (touch, kiss, hand-shake, punch etc.) and physical appearance (hair, dress, make-up etc.).[6] The relationship between verbal and nonverbal communication shapes how we intuitively make sense of it. If the nonverbal message complements or accentuates the verbal message, the receiver will have more trust in the message.[7] If the nonverbal message contradicts the verbal one, however, the receiver may be confused and disoriented. For example, a manager that proclaims the good news that the budget will not be decreased in the next years, but he is frowning while saying it, is sending mixed messages to his audience. The nonverbal message may indicate his own hidden concern about the sustainability of the budget, or may not be related to the budget discussion at all, but to some other personal issue he is concerned about.[8] Intuition that arises from a mismatch between verbal and nonverbal communication is not a proof of anything, but it can flag something that may be worth following up. Special care is needed in intercultural settings, where we are not familiar with the specific cultural style of nonverbal communication, and are more likely to misread nonverbal signals.[9]

Projections: The way we react to other people is not just shaped by how we "read" the other person through verbal and nonverbal communication, but also by the past. One way the past influences our intuitions is through the mechanism of projection, where an internal feeling or desire is located outside the person and projected onto another subject.[10] For example, when looking for a partner, psychoanalysis argues that we carry a template of the person we are looking for, and that falling in love is the process of projecting our wishful fantasy onto another person. "Whatever part, even bodily part, or characteristic excites our fetishistic obsession becomes the trigger of our automatic spray-gun, which then paints the other whichever way we want that person to look."[11] Extreme fascination and extreme hate towards another person can be explained by such projections, which may have more to do with our own past experiences, socialization and upbringing, than with the actual person who is loved or hated. Thus it can be very hard to have access to the other person as they really are. The intuition that such and such is a wonderful or diabolical person may be totally misplaced if it is fed by such projections. If our intuition is fed by projections, wishful thinking or fear rooted in our own experience, it is less likely to fit the reality of the person or environment we are responding to.[12]

Before moving to the use of intuition in mediation, some general points regarding intuition are summarized:

Limited accuracy, but useful to deal with uncertainty: Knowing that intuitions can be wrong is useful in order not to use them blindly. Nevertheless, intuitions can be useful to create a good working hypothesis, a calculated guess, and sufficient clarity upon which to base action. This is especially the case in situations of uncertainty, minimal information, limited time and high complexity.

Experience improves performance: People experienced in a specific field tend to have better intuitions related to their field of expertise than inexperienced people. Intuition can be seen as our brain making an unconscious synthesis of all we have learnt and experienced. Thus intuition can be trained and developed.

Relationships are shaped by core concerns, nonverbal communication and projections: Using intuition to make sense of emotions can benefit from "rules of the thumb" regarding core concerns (appreciation, affiliation, autonomy, role, status). Nonverbal communication is fundamental to this process. Knowing about the process of psychological projection can help us realize how our intuitions about other people may be shaped by our own past and upbringing, rather than necessarily by the other person as they really are.

In summary, intuition per se is not bad or good, right or wrong, it is more a question of when and how to use it in relation to a given context. Intuition and rational, cost-benefit analyses should not be pitted one against the other. In the words of Albert Einstein: "The intuitive mind is a sacred gift, while the rational mind is only its faithful servant... but our society honors the servant and has forgotten the gift."[13] Ideally a decision is made that is both supported by intuition and by rational, logical thinking.[14]

Intuition in Mediation

Mediation is no hard, mathematical science, and mediators rely on intuition for a variety of insights and decisions. There are mediation skills, techniques and conceptual models that can be learnt rationally and are useful to guide a mediator. Ultimately, however, the quality of the mediator does not depend on knowing these skills and concepts, but being able to decide on how and when to use them. As these decisions happen in the context of uncertainty and often under time pressure, intuition plays a key role. Intuition is needed to merge and synthesize multiple skills, theories and experiences, read and understand a complex situation, and then shape an adequate response. A technocratic approach to mediation that only applies skills and theories to a conflict in a standardized manner has severe limitations, because building processes, relationship and trust is ultimately case-specific, personal and calls for a tailor-made approach. Bowling and Hoffman[15] show how in the end the various skills and schools of mediation are not the crucial factors that make mediation effective or not. They argue that it is rather the presence of the mediator, understood as the combination of psychological, intellectual and spiritual qualities of a person, which determines outcome.

Mediators use intuition in designing the process, relating to the parties, and clarifying the issues. These three aspects are elaborated:

Process design is a highly complex, situational and evolving activity. Simple approaches that argue for "if this, then that" answers do not work, as they do not sufficiently take into account the interdependency of various process design dimensions.[16] Intuition needs to be combined with rational thinking to make sense of the complexity and keep the larger context and evolving dynamics in mind. Once underway, mediators use intuition especially for contingent mediation moves, i.e. interventions that mediators undertake depending on the way the mediation process unfolds,[17] as well as to adapt the process if it is not leading to the intended results.

When relating to the parties, the guiding idea of many mediation approaches is to understand the parties, not just rationally, but in the sense of "Aha, that is a plausible motive for what they are saying or doing". By the mediator understanding the parties and being partially able to "walk in their shoes" the mediator can create understanding between the parties that will contribute to finding a mutually acceptable resolution to the conflict. Rooney[18] argues to use intuition so that the mediator bases his or her decisions on "the parties' needs in the here and now of their experiences and awakenings rather than from a mediator's speculation prior to that awakening."[19] Intuition in mediation can therefore lead to more immediate and appropriate responses, which helps to foster relationships and trust.

In clarifying issues, mediators also need intuition, especially as the parties often start with issues that are not related to their core concerns and grievances. Easy issues may be brought up to test the other side and the solidity of the mediation process. In international peace processes, the way a conflict is framed internationally may be accepted by the parties, who show up at the mediation table to satisfy international pressure, rather than because they want to actually negotiate. In such cases the "real" issues may remain hidden for some time. For example, in the Burundi peace process between 1997 and 2000, both the international community and the conflict actors framed the conflict as an ethnic Hutu-Tutsi conflict. It did not take much intuition from the side of the mediators to realize there was more to it than that, e.g. strong regional cleavages amongst the communities that went well beyond the Hutu, Tutsi cleavage, and in some cases situations where the regional cleavages were more important than the ethnic ones. More intuition was needed to decide when and how to deal with these other underlying issues, rather than pushing for it before the parties were ready.[20]

In summary, mediation involves numerous decisions related to process, actors and issues, and these decisions are normally taken in the context of stress, high complexity, great uncertainty, and limited time. Rational approaches are good for learning some of the mediation basics, but when it comes to applying these in real-life situations, intuition is needed to synthesize past experiences and theories and shape case specific responses. For these reasons, intuition is a prime tool for the mediator. Intuition can be learnt in a variety of ways, experience probably being the best teacher. The following approach, expressive dance, is explored as a complementary approach, which fits into the growing field of arts-based conflict transformation approaches.[21]

Using Dancing to Develop Intuition

Expressive dance exercises can help mediators themselves, thereby empowering mediators and minimizing the danger of them projecting their inner messes onto the people they are working with in two ways: (1) by supporting healing processes in the mediator her- or himself, thereby empowering the mediator and minimizing the danger of projecting one's inner mess onto the people one is working with; (2) by embodying key ideas of mediation and becoming more familiar with one's own physical sensations and responses, thereby being able to better read and make sense of nonverbal communication. We illustrate these dimensions using the authors' experiences as participants at the 2010 "Dancing at the Crossroads" workshop in Saas-Fee with dancer and choreographer Margie Gillis[22], and conflict practitioner/ scholars Michelle LeBaron and Andrew Acland.[23] The aim of the workshop was to explore how dance and movement can be combined with dialogue for conflict transformation.

Healing through Dancing

Why is it important to heal mediators? Mediators are often faced with a range of unpleasant experiences: stress, being the target of aggression, or being shut out by the parties, to name a few examples. Mediators need to find ways to deal with stress and heal their inner wounds in ways that are tailor-made to their individual needs. There is not one perfect way. While dancing is surely not the only way, we argue it can be transformative for healing and inspiring practitioners who work in conflict settings. Healing is needed to clear the chaos in ourselves to be clearer for others.[24] If we neglect ourselves, the danger is that we project our inner turmoil onto the actors in a conflict, and try and mediate or heal them as a substitute for dealing with our own inner turmoil. This is why it is important to care for our own psychological health, or what C.G. Jung calls "the least amongst the lowly in ourselves,"[25] with patience, honesty and kindness.

The importance of healing peace practitioners, and how physical movement can lead to emotional release, was illustrated during the Saas-Fee workshop. One of the participants, working as a delegate of the International Committee of the Red Cross in the Balkans, had seen people spreading petrol to burn down the village they were visiting—probably as part of an ethnic cleansing campaign. He and his colleagues told them to stop, and they surprisingly did. Then later when back at home during a massage, the person massaging him asked him to think of a color. He saw the color red, and then the emotions flushed out in a tidal wave. When in the field of violence, we often have our barriers up, and then later feel the pain or anger when it is safe enough to do so. Making space for these suppressed emotions to be dealt with is foundational for healing practitioners.

One possible explanation for how dance can heal is given by Joan Chodorow:

> "An emotion, by definition, is at once somatic and psychic. The somatic aspect is made up of bodily innervations and expressive physical action. The psychic aspect is made up of images and ideas. In psychopathology, the two realms tend to split. By contrast, a naturally felt emotion involves a dialectical relationship—a union of body and psyche."[26]

This conceptualization of emotions clarifies that you can approach "healing" from two angles: working on the psychic/emotional level can lead to a physical reaction, such as crying at the thought of someone you love and have lost. Yet the other entry point is also valid: by moving and perceiving a physical pain in your body, often something that you have forgotten was even there, you can enter into contact with it, and emotions and psychic images can be triggered and released.

How did healing of peace practitioners happen through dance in the Saas-Fee workshop? Arts based approaches have a structure, for example a three step sequence of engaging (introduction, setting the guidelines, clarifying the facilitation), decentering (experiencing the arts in a way that shifts people from where they were before) and harvesting (reflecting, linking the experience back to daily life or professional fields).[27]

Engaging: The healing experiences of the Saas-Fee workshop happened in the middle of the week, after people had become used to expressive dance movements and become fully engaged, but before they were getting ready to go back to their daily life. In the dance session,

Margie explained what she meant by the "plumb line." In a moving object, or moving dance group touching each other, there is the point of gravity, and from this point of gravity to the earth is the plumb line. This was embodied by the workshop participants dancing in pairs, back to back. By leaning on the other, the individual points of gravity merge: when they move, their joint point of gravity moves. Without knowing why, this exercise slowly brought many of the participants to an emotional level. Perhaps the dual psychic-somatic nature of emotions is part of the answer. Margie talked about physical pain, points of tension or blockages, as "knots" in one's body, which may have been caused by a physical or psychological experience or shock. The body remembers, the "knot" stays even after it was caused, and we do not relate so well to ourselves, or to others; it is as though our energies are at least partially blocked.[28]

Decentering: Through dance, participants approached their emotions through the physical entry point that then triggered psychic images, releasing emotions. In this way the energy that was blocked by the "knot" is released, and the person can relate more freely and fluidly to themselves as well as to others. The irrationality of Margie's words helped to guide people in their movement and toward their unconsciousness:

> "Let it be there, let it change, listen and fulfill
> From your head to your body, listen to your body
> Don't stop the chatter of your head with force
> Distract it, slowly softening it, slowly bringing silence into it, slowly moving out of it
> Don't know, discover
> Feel a part and see where it wants to take you, let it be, let it change
> Walk from your hips, not from your head
> Effortless passion
> See and hear the knot, go to it gently, gently
> Feel the colors in your body, see where it wants to take you
> Effortless passion
> If you do not know where to go, rise and stay still, till your body tells you a thousand touches in a cold cool mountain breeze rushing over old words
> Small movements, small movements, cool water, cool water, shake it out…"

The participants first danced without music, listening to their inside, but then they danced with music, and it pushed them over the brink, beyond the rational, reasoning plane. Margie moved around, giving moments of healing to people, by being with them, feeling where they were, touching them, for example by placing her hand on someone's back, or telling them to move in a quieter or wilder way.

Harvesting: The actual experience of healing is hard to capture in words. Most workshop participants needed some time alone and silence after the experience, before then sharing what they had experienced:

Susan: "I felt a freedom of movement from fingertip to my little toe. All parts of the body connected as a whole. However, in between the shoulder blades there was a knot I had known from my earliest years of engaging with conflict. This place of tension was physically located close to my heart, and was capable of absorbing a lot, even as I remained otherwise relaxed even in the toughest conflict situations.

Dancing gently around that tension, I moved my torso around the edges of the knot. I breathed more deeply and let my vertebrae gently stretch. I toyed with the possibility that there might be some movement in between those two vertebrae, even after years of holding them tight as the solid spot in highly unpredictable conflict dynamics.

I asked my dancing partner to hold his hand on that spot, as I breathed into it. Margie offered a gesture of support and held her hand near. A pathway began to slowly open that had been previously closed. I could breathe more deeply, feel more deeply, and move with ease.

I felt an overwhelming sense of letting go of all that I had been holding from accumulated conflicts. This was replaced with a new strength and a greater sense of flexibility. The guardedness had relaxed. The injury that had tightened those muscles, ligaments, tendons, and restricted movement had shifted and I no longer needed to hold on so tightly.

Later that day, I played a song for Margie that expressed my experience of the morning. It puts Rumi's words to music:

'Awake, my dear, be kind to your sleeping heart,
Take it out, to the vast field of light,
And let it breathe.'"[29]

Virginie: "Working with our "pain du jour", my focus was on the pain/tightness in my shoulders and throat. When we had finished the exercise, which I hadn't managed to do fully by myself, Margie walked up to me and without words helped me to stay connected to the pain and guided it down until it reached my belly. In this short process there was shock, fear, anger, fury and a big release. I remember Margie saying after the knot shifted to my belly: "…and now it is your strength!" This revelation felt new to me but I was able to see how it was so true. First it was stuck there in my throat, and I used my throat to keep the pain there. Once it moved into my belly, I could feel its potential. While Margie worked with me these few seconds I remember how present she was. Her eye contact was deep, as though she was looking into my soul and knew what was needed. I could feel my resistance to letting go of something that had been there from early childhood. Her ability to "see me" and stay connected helped me to trust and move it.

Afterwards I felt emotional and wanted to be held. It was a huge release followed by a flood of tears.

Later, I realized the shifts and turning points that occurred in this experience. The movement revealed anger, the beauty of assertiveness, and the energy to act in the world. Movement catalyzes transformation when there is a safe container and skilled guidance. I believe that such work requires a very qualified, intuitive, and highly sensitive dance facilitator. We should not underestimate these qualities when we integrate dance into mediation healing or training sessions."

Dance heals because it re-creates a union of body and psyche. However, this type of healing through dance needs professional support, as dance movements can tap into unknown emotional depths extremely quickly. Professional support does not just mean the trainer has theoretical knowledge, but rather has had personal experience. Many pioneers in the field of dance therapy experienced the healing power of dance on themselves.[30] Without a professional supporter who they trust, people will hesitate to let go of their conscious barriers and truly engage in the experience.

Using Dance Elements in Mediation Training

Dance elements can also be used in mediation training to embody certain ideas of mediation, as well as develop awareness of nonverbal communication and thereby intuition. This complements mediation literature that focuses on the role of nonverbal communication within the mediation session.[31] The following exercises were used in the Saas-Fee workshop, and could also be used in mediation training courses. While they do not need a professional dance therapist to facilitate them, we suggest people experience the exercises themselves before trying them on others.

Universal and focused vision: The trainer asks people to move around the room, first using focused vision: "Target a spot somewhere in the room, focus on it and walk towards it. Once you have reached that spot, choose a new spot; focus on it and walk towards it". In this mode, people normally end up bumping into each other, as they are focused on their goal, rather than keeping the entire room in their vision. The second approach is to walk around the room with no focus: "Walk around the room with wide angle vision, no focus". Here things flow much better, even if people never reach a precise point in the room. The idea is to clarify and embody the different types of "vision" you need in mediation, and when they are most useful. In co-mediation, one mediator may use focused vision, while the other remains aware of the broader picture, ready to react if something unexpected arises.

Stone in water: In this exercise, two people pair up. One person is the stone, the other person is the water flowing around the stone. In relation to mediation, this can practice the idea of flowing flexibly around obstacles, rather than conflicting agendas leading solely to clashes. Another version of this exercise is to have one person initiate a movement, and the other react to it. Here the idea is to experience the balance between independence and relatedness, between initiative and receptivity. In discussion after the exercise, one can explore which of the two characteristics comes more naturally to oneself, and how they relate to one's mediation style (directive vs. facilitative).

Awkwardness in integrity: Awkwardness and stupidity gives space for creativity and imagination, something that is often lacking in the midst of conflict. In this exercise, two people walk across the room doing "stupid" movements. The idea is to create a safe space to test ones creativity, ones "awkwardness," but to do so within limits; if the mentor or participant feels it is going too far, they should stop the exercise. In mediation we need to be creative, but within limits; we need integrity, a co-mediator can often help us find the limits, such as while discussing the mediation plan in preparation for a meeting.

Spinning: Two people from opposite sides of the room walk or run to each other, and spin off each other before they collide. They can touch or not; that is up to them. The spin movement avoids the clash, the direct confrontation. They have to negotiate who is going to spin off in which direction; they have the time it takes to walk or run to each other to sort this out. The spin is less controllable than a planned avoidance, following rules or a pre-determined map, but much faster and more dynamic than such a regulated, rigid and brittle approach. The spin is more controllable than a full confrontation and rebound: the circular movement has a pattern to it, and once the spin is started, the energy runs its course. In mediation, the mediator can shape and form the process, even if she or he cannot fully control it. This is the reason why some mediators speak about mediation as the art of creating a positive "spin."[32] This is a simple exercise that emphasizes the need for mediators to create a positive dynamic, rather than over-controlling the process or assuming the role of an impotent bystander.

Embodying words: In this exercise, the trainer says a word, and the participants associate another word to it. In pairs they embody the two associated words in a movement. In the Saas-Fee course, Michelle spoke the word "flexibility" that was associated and embodied in the following manner:

> Simon: "What comes to our mind in association with "flexibility" is "elasticity" (Kai) and "bounce" (Simon). We dance this convergence first with an approach towards one another. I put all my weight on his back as he bends over, and he bounces me off. The first few times it does not work. I feel I have to bounce. Then Kai says: "Let go, I will bounce you, you do not need to do anything." So I wait and listen, and when the bounce comes, I take the energy up and let myself spring forth. We repeat this pattern a few times: I wait for the bounce and only amplify the energy once the initial impulse comes from Kai. Kai's movement was an embodied symbol for the impulses of life and health, which often come even in the depth of conflict. Our task is to listen, discern and amplify these impulses, rather than create them."

The practice of listening to our bodies' intuition in a protected environment of a mediation training can help us to become more comfortable with using intuition in real mediation settings. In listening through the whole body we can be attentive to what is surfacing from parties moment by moment.

Conclusions

Mediators make decisions all the time in the context of uncertainty and high complexity. To do this, they rely heavily on intuition. Intuition, especially related to how we deal with emotions, can be fostered through expressive dance exercises. This can happen through professionally supported self-healing in retreats for peace practitioners, as well as through dance exercises in mediation training courses.

Emotions have a psychic and somatic dimension. By moving, we tap into our emotions through the somatic entry point. Movements thus often lead to a deep emotional level more quickly than if we talk about emotions. Tapping into emotions through movement is one way of releasing tensions caught up in the body, which is then experienced as a moment of healing. The "knot" of tension is infused with movement and the emotional blockage is released. With a newly found greater range of physical and psychic motion, peace practitioners can be more aware of themselves and those they are working with.

In mediation training courses, expressive dance exercises can address several lacunae caused by the field's overreliance on words and rationality: it offers clues to "embody" key mediation ideas and develop the intuition to foster relationship and trust which are fundamental to building peace. Our bodies are with us in conflict, and in conflict resolution. Tensions are often first felt physically before we react mentally to them. By also training physical awareness in mediation training courses we can prepare mediators to listen to their own body, listen to the nonverbal cues from the parties in conflict, and thus better dance through conflict.

Acknowledgements: Thanks to all the participants and trainers of the Saas-Fee workshop, as well as to Adrian Muller, Chris and Margrit Mason for their helpful comments on a draft version of this text. The financial support of the Mediation Support Project at the Center for Security Studies ETH Zurich, and the Swiss Federal Department of Foreign Affairs is acknowledged.

An Embodied Pedagogy for Conflict Transformation

Stepping into New Practices

MARGIE GILLIS

How can we begin to learn new movement patterns? An intended outcome of the Dancing at the Crossroads project was to develop a responsive and relevant pedagogy for an embodied approach to conflict transformation. To date, there has been very little documentation on how movement vocabularies can interface with conflict-transformation interventions. I have addressed this knowledge gap by creating a repertoire of somatic approaches that can be applied in a myriad of conflict dynamics. In the process, I have created a comprehensive map that encourages us to think not only *about* the body, but *with* the body.

This chapter outlines a series of accessible approaches for those who intend to facilitate movement-based exercises for peace building and conflict transformation. When it comes to learning how to apply these frameworks, cultivating capacities for physical engagement is of greater importance than precision of form. These approaches depend on both verbal and visual instructional techniques and focus on how somatic thinking can begin to transcend the fragmentation of the mind-body split. The aesthetic frame of dance creates the possibility for increased receptivity as new solutions arise from mobility. It is optimal for participants to stay with the physical experience for as long as possible without jumping into dialogue. This embodied approach offers its own form of insight, and coming to conclusions prematurely could inhibit learning that arises directly from the physical engagement.

The body is a constant teacher and presence in our lives, as our neuromuscular system receives, stores, and processes information that comes to us moment by moment. Embodied conflict transformation asks us to mobilize our muscles to reorganize the neural pathways that influence habitual responses. In developing and refining movement-based capacities, we can begin to notice how our patterns of thinking are inextricably connected to our physicality. Underdeveloped body consciousness leads to underdeveloped conflict intelligence, and choreography is itself a form of cognition.

A basic understanding of sensorimotor systems is necessary for this applied theory and praxis. Investigating connections between neuromuscular responses and movement patterns will help illuminate how the physical is a constituent of the mental. Facilitators will benefit from further training in movement-based approaches that acknowledge the centrality of the neuromuscular skeletal system. Physical health and safety are the basis for this work and must be considered at all times. It is important to highlight this with participants at the outset, before engaging in a collaborative process that requires risk, trust, and transparency. If unsafe conditions arise in the process, it is vital to stop, change, or shift the exercise immediately. Asking participants to be vigilant in assuming responsibility for their own and others' physical safety is a priority. Additionally, to ensure cultural sensitivity, each framework requires attention to how, when, and where it is applied.

Two Important Aspects to Keep in Mind as a Facilitator

1. **Softening of the joints will result in more fluidity and safety.** The aim is to carry out each action with a sense of ease, with an image of sustainable health as the guide. It is remarkable what people can do, even with disability and pain, if they are encouraged to underachieve—to keep their joints soft and use small movements, especially when their bodies are still warming up.

2. **Generally the problem is the solution:** the possibility of the solution exists in the movement but needs to be explored and discovered. Immobility is a physical and mental state that can be shifted and transformed if there is focus and intention.

Basics Phase I: Deepening the Experience

The following exercises include experiential and reflective components. The questions may serve as an inner guide for participants or may act as a catalyst for collaborative dialogue at the culmination of a workshop. The content of the reflective pieces comes from participants who were present at the weeklong Dancing at the Crossroads training in Saas-Fee. The chronological progression of exercises as they are listed below is recommended. However, facilitators are encouraged to use discernment according to specific needs of the context in which they are working.

Invitation to the Dance

- To begin, it is optimal if participants position themselves in a circle or in a formation that faces the facilitator in full view. The invitation to the dance is initiated through welcoming participants, explaining how the wisdom of the body informs the experiential nature of this work, and clarifying key parameters that will promote safety and health for all. Allowing time for questions during this initial period may help ease uncertainties about participating in movement-based practices.

- After introductions and setting the framework and intention for a session, have participants stand and place their hands on their chests while inhaling with a deep breath. Allow the hands to separate and expand while breathing in, and then as the chest compresses with an exhalation, let the fingers fall back together. Repeat this three times.

- Place the hands on the lower abdomen. Breathe in and expand the abdomen and then breathe out. Repeat this three times while synchronizing the mind and body with these expansive movements. In this subtle interchange of breath and movement, become aware of yourself as a pole of light. Envision the light coming up from the abdomen, through the spine, and out through the top of your head. Similarly, envision the light coming down from the abdomen, out through the bottom of the feet, and deep into the earth. This imagery helps to facilitate an extension of vertical energy through the body.

- Next, place both hands on your hips and begin to do small knee bends (pliés in parallel position is the ballet term). Feet are parallel to each other, in alignment with the hips. Then lift one leg and notice the crease that develops at the hip. Do this several times with each leg to assure that you experience the independence of the pelvis from the leg. Experiment with knee bends and lifts to feel how the pelvis can remain stable while the leg moves entirely independently of the upper body.

- Play with the range of the joints by bending, creasing and lengthening. Create small circles first with the feet and then the legs. Notice the release and suppleness of the ankles, knees, and hip sockets. Soften the leg joints while shifting the weight and placement of the feet. Continue to notice the energy flowing down from the legs and out of the feet, and also up from the abdomen, through the spine, and out the crown of the head. Find places of ease in each area and retain a sense of curiosity throughout the exploration.

Facilitator's Note: Making reference to the intricacies of the neuromuscular system will help introduce the concept of somatic logic. Explaining the physical mechanics of how electricity runs through the body as both contraction and release will also help illuminate how muscles respond to stimuli. In these explorations, it is vital that all participants recognize their own limits and work within them. The underlying foundation of the process is to ensure health and to highlight the miracle of who we are in motion. It is optimal if facilitators note that each person has different parameters for what constitutes this baseline of health. This inquiry could be retained throughout the sessions with the simple question: Is this healthy? If it is not healthy, modify and begin again.

Body Inventory

- Find your own space in the room that does not interfere with anyone else's space.
- Initiate a somatic inventory of your body by focusing on the patterns of your breath as you inhale and exhale. Relax into the rhythm of your breathing by releasing your muscles. Loosen your jaw and drop your arms to the sides of your body. Pay attention to the timing of your breathing and the subtle changes that occur in your body as you inhale and exhale.
- With each inhale and exhale, observe and sense how your bodily sensations shift and change in response to your breathing patterns. Focus your mind and body on the nature of the shifts. What rises? What falls? What can you let go of? What remains blocked? Include another dimension to this sensory exploration by adding movement. Follow the breath as it expands and contracts your lungs, and as you move through the space at various tempos. Keep your eyes open and be aware of others who are also moving around you.

- Begin to create an improvised conversation between your gestures and your breath. How do your gestures respond to your breath and vice versa? As you relax into this improvisation, add variations such as shifting your weight from side to side, creating more momentum with your arms, etc.

- Find points of tension in your body as you investigate the range of motion and elasticity of various joints and muscles. Concentrate this focus on the space inside your toes, feet, and ankles. Then add layers of movement into your knees, hips, shoulders, spine, elbows, wrists, and fingers. Maintain the integrity of your movement while observing the fluctuating sensations that follow your lines of attention.

- Explore the range of possible movement patterns as you generate momentum from different sources in the body. What happens when you lead with the pelvis? What direction are you pulled if you lead first with your shoulders or head? What parts of the body are lagging behind if you lead from certain areas? When does your movement find greater ease? Is your movement overcompensating for any weaknesses?

Facilitator's Note: This activity is useful in calming or centering the energy of a group as well as creating awareness of one's emotional state through subtle physical cues. It may be used to begin or end a workshop or as a way to offer a gentle closure after a particularly intense activity. Encourage participants to welcome shifting states. This can be articulated through the simple lines "Let it be there, let it change." Scanning the body will help support a participant's observer consciousness. If someone is injured or has severe scar tissue, it is also important that the person does not remain fixated on that area. Remind participants to intentionally scan those injured areas so that they can begin to move through them.

Reflections

All of the systems in the body are constantly working toward health and homeostasis. Our neuromuscular system receives, stores, and renews all of the information that we process. In shifting the locus of attention to very specific points in the body, it is possible to monitor how physical cues are pointing toward wellness. Focus follows from not only what the eyes are seeing but also what the body is sensing. This proprioceptive awareness will assist in rerouting neuromuscular patterns that no longer serve a greater sense of well-being and health. As we become more perceptive in these somatic realms, we will be more able to identify origins of entrenched habitual rhthyms. Our movement patterns are essentially thought patterns in motion.

Lines of Energy

- Work in partners. Partner A stands with one arm fully extended in front of the body and imagines that lines of energy are coming up from the lower abdomen and into the fingers. Partner A should hold the image of air filling up each finger as if it were a balloon. Partner B stands next to Partner A and presses Partner A's arm down. Both observe the levels of energy and resistance in this moment.

- Partner A now brings their energy up from the abdomen, out through the arm, and sends the energy to the other side of the room. While Partner A is in this state, partner B again presses down on Partner A's arm. Both observe how the levels of energy and resistance change throughout the process.
- Partners switch roles.
- Add another dimension and begin to move as if colors of paint were swirling around the pelvis area and flowing out through the legs, arms, and head. Move across the floor and between others as the images of colors flow out of these different body parts. Envision this energy coming out like water through a hose. Notice where the hose is being pinched or blocked and where the flow of energy is stopping and starting.
- After a few minutes, reverse the flow of energy and have the source come from the external environment, but envision it coming from a long distance away. Have the energy flow into the body through the extremities and back into the lower abdomen. This surge of energy can vary in color, texture, density, etc.

Questions
- How did the change in focus and intent influence the strength of your arm?
- What surprised you about this shift in focus while working in partners as you moved about the room?
- What does this exercise teach you about focus and the mind-body connection? In what conflict scenarios could such insights be applied?

Reflections
A person is generally stronger when the momentum of energy is flowing out of the arm. Impasse in conflict often arises from energy being swamped or people becoming too fixated on specific points within the problem. Although intense focus can be generative, it can also create limitations. To expand lines of focus, it helps to imagine problems on a larger grid of perception. As perspective broadens, the problem becomes smaller and smaller and is not at the center of the universe. This intentional act of "de-swamping" has a physical response in the body. We often naturally focus on breathing in, but we can forget to exhale with the same level of energy and intention.

Meditative Moving
- Begin moving slowly in the room and notice the sensations on your skin as you move through the space. Note how your body instinctively shifts and responds as you move alongside other bodies.
- Be aware of how your somatic responses correspond to the subtle shifts in your body. Notice how your body shifts in relation to your changing tempo. You can start to form an inquiry by asking: What changes when I focus my attention to certain parts of my body (for example, feet, knees, hips, shoulders, etc.)? Pay attention to the timing of your breathing as it relates to the textures of your movement.

- Slowly improvise with new movement patterning and be attentive to how the joints are moving. What new surfaces can you discover in the room from a place of curiosity? Make contact with the floor through body parts other than your feet. How can your arms, shoulders, back, and legs make contact with the floor in new ways? Be curious and make contact with the walls, chairs, and windows as if it were the first time you had ever seen them. Feel the change of temperature. What new sensations can be discovered? Pay attention to your proximity to others. Do you default to being close or far from the group? Are you commonly in the center or on the periphery? Cultivate curiosity for your own movement patterns and observe how your natural tendencies become part of your commonsense movement vocabulary.
- Discover where the places of greatest ease are in your body. With movement as the guide, begin to transition into these places. How does your body respond?

Reflections

Moving with somatic sensitivity ultimately creates a greater capacity to experience how we naturally place ourselves in relation to others. In the midst of chaos, bringing the focus back to subtle movements can have a calming effect and can open up the possibilities for new choices. Our relationships to space, tempo, and time are frequently disoriented in the confines of conflict. The momentum that builds in conflict is often rooted in our physicality. Our concepts of time, space, and energy all influence how we are able to coexist with one another.

Stone in My Water/Everywhere You Aren't

- In partners, move to fill the empty spaces (*negative space* is the term in sculpture) that are around and between both of you. Each person is in constant motion and maintains a relationship with his or her partner by dancing into a place or space where the partner's body is not present. This part of the exercise takes up the entire room.
- Partners come closer together to explore the empty space around each other. This exploration involves stretching through space and pivoting between and around each other's arms, shoulders, legs, behind the back, above the head, etc. The aim is to create fluid movement patterns in the ever-changing empty spaces.
- As comfort levels continue to increase, move closer to each other until there is an arm's length in between, and closer still (without touching) if appropriate safety has been established. Discover new variations in the movement patterns as you are in closer proximity. Play also with doing this at a distance with partners on opposite sides of the room.
- Move with your partner in variations of tempo and energy. The visual image of water moving around a rock can spark the momentum for this patterning. Each person imagines being fluid water around the partner's mobile stone. Be attentive to habitual responses. Do you usually move toward or away from the other? Is your default to initiate or to respond to the movement? Are you more comfortable with exploring the space in front, beside, or behind the other person?

- After ten minutes of exploring the potential of negative space, join another set of partners to continue this exploration in a group of four. In the larger constellation, all group members have the responsibility to look for the negative space between each person.
- After five minutes of exploring movement patterns in the larger group context, participants "find their conclusion" one by one when they feel their own dance has come to a natural end. They settle into a place of stillness until all group members have found a point of rest.
- Allow ten minutes for debriefing in these groups of four. Consider the challenges and discoveries that emerged in the smaller and larger groups.

Questions
- Do you habitually move toward or away from empty spaces?
- Is your default to initiate new patterns or to respond to what is given?
- What challenges did you experience with additional group members? What variances emerged as you moved with different partners?

Variation: One person can begin as a stone by creating a still shape, while another person creates and sculpts a range of shapes in the empty space around that person's stillness. Participants join in, one by one, adding new movement possibilities around the "stone." This can be performed with as few as three people and/or in very close quarters with an emphasis on micromovements filling smaller spaces. This variation would benefit from slowing down the movement to cultivate attention to these subtler possibilities. If the patterns become too chaotic, ask dancers to step back from the stone one at a time.

Facilitator's Note: This can be done with varying paces or proximities between participants, depending on levels of comfort, safety, and/or physical awareness. Encourage participants to move at a slow, easy, fluid pace to begin. Remind them to use their sides and backs, keeping a sense of connection to the empty spaces while in full rotation (often very difficult to do at first since people do not wish to "turn their backs" on conflict). If you see someone moving backward repeatedly to make space for a partner's movements, invite the person to move into the empty space first. Encourage partners to sense the seam between stone and water with the whole body.

Reflections
This dance can facilitate mindful perspective taking in situations of conflict. Obstacles that may be perceived to be intractable could actually be catalysts for another kind of response. In honing in on these sensibilities, it becomes possible to maneuver *around* and *between* points of conflict. Welcoming the unfamiliar is essential for understanding the potential that exists within negative space. Instead of focusing on the problem of opposing elements, a more-generative response can arise from moving *around* the given problem. When there is danger in the room, people can become destructive and self-destructive. This exercise is designed to investigate how polarities can be named and shifted.

Pain/Joy du Jour

- In partners, one person identifies a place of pain or tension in his or her body. This may be a long-term pain, but it is better if it is a place of pain that is present in that moment.
- The other person identifies a "joy" spot in his or her body—a site that feels most open, healthy, and happy.
- Moving from these respective places, have the "point of joy" engage in dialogue with the "point of pain." Have each person observe and listen to what is emerging from the fluid exchange between the two points. Partners do not have to be in close proximity to each other but should remain in constant communication. To ensure a level of continuous connection, they can imagine an energetic elastic band between these two points. Attention moves from the area of pain or joy to the lively space in between.
- "Shake it out," meaning to shake the body to refresh the nervous system and reset the ability to focus, and then switch roles.

Facilitator's Note: You may want to draw attention to how the points were signaled—for example, with a full hand, with a fist, or with a finger. This gives further clues as to the shape or quality of the joy or pain and invites another level of curiosity and nuanced understanding of the respective qualities of each. If you have an uneven number of participants, position two participants who are moving joy with one who is moving pain.

Questions
- How did the contrasting qualities of joy and pain serve each other?
- How did the experience of your own point of pain or joy shift during the exchange with your partner?
- What new discoveries emerged from the sensory information given in between the two points?

Reflections
This responsive exercise allows for engaged action and observation. In working with the tension of opposites, generosity can be infused into places of scarcity and health into areas of sickness. Rather than become overidentified with pain or joy and further entrench injury, an evolving responsiveness enables that injury to be transformed even as it is communicated. Health is the natural default of the body. An effective way to understand this abundance is to draw energy from the physical vocabularies in the body that are always evolving. Our will toward health finds its form through the body.

Being Centered in Motion

- Move your body however you wish while traveling across the room, keeping the mind focused on being centered.
- Experiment with where your "center" is in the body—sending it up, down, and from the pelvis. Notice how the energy is moving "up and down" through the spine and into various body parts as you shift your weight and focus of intent.

- Continue to create movement sequences that integrate repetitive patterns. Explore the potential of these discoveries first on your own, then in partners, and finally in the larger group.

Questions
- How does the center of gravity shift in relation to the pace of movement?
- How does repetition and familiarity influence your center of gravity?
- Was it easy or difficult to reorganize your center of gravity?

Facilitator's Note: There will be many variations as participants interpret this exercise. Ensure that each person retains a sense of the central line that runs from head to floor, whatever the motion. Explore what being centered in motion might be from a physical sense and how "centering" in different parts of the body is more or less effective. Note that the center of the dance emanates from the hips. Lower chakra, stomach, bundy (yoga), pelvic floor, tan dien: different cultures articulate this source in various ways but all point toward the hip area as the locus where movement begins.

Reflections
The force of gravity governs our movements, and yet often we are unaware of how this core plumb line grounds us. It is easy to become imbalanced by the pull of strong emotions and intentions of others while losing our own sense of gravity and center. This exercise draws attention to how the body offers a place of return where we can regain our core strength. In the midst of conflict it is particularly important to be alert to this infinite resource. Otherwise we can easily lose our bearings amid contradictory messages that can move us off center.

Not To, But Through
- Individually or as a group, identify a point in the room where you want to go. This can be symbolic of an individual or a collective goal in the context of conflict. It may be named or not. Once you choose this point, consider how your approach would alter if you were to go *through* this point instead of directly *to* it. Begin to move with this image in mind.
- When you reach the identified point in the room, go through it and continue until you cross to the other side of the room. Turn around and pass through it again as you return to the initial starting place.
- Imagine alternative ways of going around, backward, forward, and sideways around the point.
- Add another level of exploration and imagine an idea in the room. Circle around this idea in a group. Each person moves through and around this idea in various levels and tempos—forward, backward, and sideways.

Variation: As you move in or across the room, imagine energy pouring out of your hands, feet, and head. Once you are comfortable with embodying this idea, extend this perception of energy out to the walls and floor. Dialogue afterward about the different sensations that arise from the two dances.

Questions

- Does the notion of working *through* something instead of *to* change the intention? What qualities of perception are added?
- How can alternative ways of perceiving space expose new systems of meaning?
- Why could it be valuable to push the boundaries of our perceptions of space in situations of conflict?

Reflections

This movement approach supports the idea that dispositions may be more flexible than we think. Positions are not permanently rigid but are dynamic states that accommodate evolving fluctuations. This exercise can be used for representatives within a conflict and can reflect the task of trying to find alternative solutions amid plurality, ambiguity, and multiple vantage points. Sometimes it is necessary to enter into an unorganized space to be able to reorganize in a more cohesive manner. We can't know unless we are willing to face the unknown. Knowledge comes through discovery, and we can depersonalize by going into abstraction and away from the "point" or the "problem" to find solutions.

Elbows to Knees—Four Corners

- Notice your elbows and knees and create lines of focus between these four points. Imagine that the points are connected with a line through the inside of the body and/ or on the outside of the body.
- Begin to move these four points around in space like geometry. You are scanning and keeping track of four abstract points as they are moving at the same time while continuously altering the distance between these points.
- After a few minutes, start shifting the quality between the spaces. Envision the space as being dense, thin, etc. Observe how the movement corresponds to the changes in quality.

Variation: You could name four different ideas that you are grappling with, relegate each idea to a corner, and observe how mobility and fluidity can be achieved between each idea. What thoughts arise as these points are brought into different relations with one another?

Questions

- What was elicited as you worked with four points of focus? How many points did you keep in focus, and how did that vary as you moved?
- Did you focus more on the four points or on the spaces between them?
- What competencies could this exercise help develop for conflict interventions?

Reflections

This exercise builds on the notion of working with several points or ideas that are related to one another. In focusing on both the points and the space between the points, elements of embodied knowledge become revealed through action. Being conscious of how we move in relationship to key points and ideas helps reorganize our sense of spatiality, focus, and movement patterns. When we are accustomed to moving in certain ways throughout our lives, it becomes more difficult to see how kinesthetic cues can serve as prime indicators in relationships. The body is capable of opening, shaping, and concealing possibilities for relational shifts. Our capacity for embodied thinking is a foundational element in both micro- and macro-negotiations.

Moving Amongst

- Begin by simply walking at a normal pace in the room. Create your own pathways between others while being intentional about moving into empty spaces that are emerging. Keep your eyes open as you navigate to find openings and start to become aware of your movement patterns in space.
- Move clockwise, counterclockwise, backward, forward, horizontally, etc. Be attentive to how the movement patterns of others influence your own. Observe the subtle energy (body heat or coolness) of others as you pass them.
- Notice the relationship between intention, energy, and the tempo of your own rhythm as it relates to the collective momentum in the room. Everyone is responsible for movement without a designated leader.

Facilitator's Note: The movement should be easy and slow. Be aware of the needs of the group, as there will be different comfort zones experienced within different group dynamics. Succinct directions will be essential if aggressors are moving in the same space as those who are being targeted. For instance, you may want to say, "Hold concentration in the center of your body." This heightened level of focus can channel energy into new directions. Clear frameworks will help give a sense of safety to those who are feeling vulnerable, uncomfortable, or unsafe.

Questions

- How did you respond as the qualities of movement shifted in the room? Did you conform to the momentum of the group or retain your own center?
- Was it difficult to maintain your own tempo as your energy intersected with others? What are your default responses when others speed up? Do you slow down or follow the overriding momentum of the group?
- Where did you situate yourself in relation to the group? Do you have a tendency to move to the periphery or to claim space in the center of the room?

Reflections

This exercise powerfully demonstrates what can be revealed through simple movement patterns that often go unnoticed. Subtleties in pedestrian movements offer insights into "given" ways of relating to one another and can expose why we experience resonance or dissonance in relationships. This exercise acts as a mobile meditation: feeling, sensing, and moving in a reverential texture. Working with these subtle dynamics is also useful when there is an escalation of energy in the room. Simply slowing down movement can bring a group back to a calmer state.

Moving Amongst with Vision

- This version of Moving Amongst integrates diverse points of focus into movement patterning. The first task is to walk with a *universal* vision, taking in all that the eye is capable of through a wide-angle perspective. To do this, spread your arms and stretch your hands out to the sides—to the point where it is still possible to see your index fingers through the peripheral vision of both eyes. Allow your gaze to stretch between those two points.
- Begin to move through the space with this expanded universal focus. Notice how this expanded lens changes the quality, pace, or patterns of your walking.
- The next task is to walk with a pointed vision that focuses on the smallest details possible. To do this, choose one focal point in the room.
- Begin to move the body toward this focal point and observe the quality of movement.
- The last task is to walk with a vision of *economy* that is between universal vision and the pointed vision of focus. To do this, move around the room, deliberately alternating between necessity and universal focus.
- Spend five minutes in dialogue discussing the distinctions in movement patterns.

Questions

- What is your default mode of vision? Universal? Necessity? Economy?
- When does your focus shift from universal to economy, from necessity to universal? What catalyzes these shifts for you?
- What are the strengths and weaknesses of these different lenses? When would each be beneficial in conflict dynamics?

Reflections

Our gaze often leads us to move in certain directions. What we choose to see directly influences the nature of our interactions. The quality of our seeing becomes our visual ledger for reading one another and the world around us. Each context calls for diverse lenses. Focusing on points of contention may appear to be confrontational in certain contexts and appropriately to the point in others. In some scenarios, a wider vision of what is possible from a more-universal perspective may be necessary to shift narrower visions. If we choose to see through our kinetic body, we will have a greater capacity to understand dispositions that exist outside usual frames of reference. Harnessing a greater repertoire of responses will be possible if our attentiveness comes from a range of possible viewpoints.

Basics Phase II: Deepening the Experience

Front Body/Back Body/Side Body

- Begin to dance as if you are in front, behind, and within yourself. Continually shift your levels of consciousness between these perspectives as you move. Notice how your movement changes as you "place" yourself in your own dance from different angles.
- Find a partner and choose either front, back, or side body perspectives without telling your partner which one you have chosen. Observe the quality of the encounters. Continue to change the perspectives through which receptivity takes place.

Questions

- Where is your somatic consciousness centered in your body?
- What new insights did you gain as your focus shifted between front, back, and side?
- In what situations might it be useful to assume multiple positions of mind-body consciousness?
- Is it difficult to be in and/or outside your body? How can you shift this?

Reflections

We may experience a perpetual sense of fragmentation if we find that we are one step ahead, constantly beside, or lagging behind ourselves. A common expression that arises from anxiety or tension is "I was beside myself." Until people consciously explore how they situate themselves in relation to the awareness of their physicality, they may not realize how they default to a particular perception of themselves. We can experience the interdependence between intention, action, and proprioception if we are exercising our capacity for somatic navigation. With this awareness it will be more possible to understand the source of our impulses. The sensory information available through proprioceptive lenses can be a key informant for determining generative responses.

Balance, Off Balance in Fall and Recovery

- Begin shifting your weight side to side between your feet and notice specific places of comfort and discomfort in relation to your center of gravity. Find a posture that requires balance and stay with this posture for a couple of seconds. Look for the exact moment when you are off balance and keep returning to this point.
- Slowly begin to shift the weight of your posture until you find your own limits and parameters. Then return to center.
- Find additional points of balance, off balance, and recovery as you explore spaces above, below, beside, around, and behind you.
- Try standing on one foot first, then the other foot.

- Sit on the floor and play with varying levels of balance (such as relaxing and contracting your stomach muscles). Allow the body to roll when it needs to.
- Experiment with different ways of traveling across the room as you move between points of balance, off balance, and recovery. Focus on the relationship that your body has with each point.

Balance, Off Balance in Partners

- Stand face-to-face with a partner. Partner A begins to explore the points between balance and off balance, and Partner B assists Partner A in the subtle recovery in moments when they begin to lose their center of gravity. Both partners focus on the nonverbal communication that takes place with each movement.
- Partner A continues to explore various points of off balance and adds variation in tempo, levels, etc. The partners begin to travel across the room with each other.
- After five minutes, partners change roles. Partner B now explores the points between balance and off balance as Partner A assists with the subtle places of recovery.

Sensing Balance

- Stand back-to-back with a partner. Align your feet so they are shoulder-width apart. Find a natural point of stability and balance there.
- You and your partner begin to lean slightly back to feel the weight of your backs against each other. Begin to shift the weight of your feet while allowing the contact to let you to sense where the other person is leaning. Retain contact with your partner at all times. Find the points where you can shift your weight together and points where you can rest up against each other in between. Listen to the information that is coming directly from this contact.
- Continue to coordinate shifting of weight with each other as you begin to move through the space with your partner (still retaining the back-to-back posture). Neither partner is leading the movement. The movement comes from listening kinesthetically to the momentum of starting and stopping. Give your partner more and more of your weight as you continue investigating the shifts. Sensing how much weight each of you can carry and how to shift easily to the floor is a way to cultivate mutual responsibility with and for each other. Learning how to shift your hands and feet to reclaim your weight or to give in to gravity may also be necessary. Play with the ease, mobility, and places of support.
- If you lose contact with your partner, smoothly return to the original position of standing back-to-back and begin again. Remember to focus on softening the joints whenever possible.
- Once you are familiar with listening in this way, begin to share the weight of your body by slowly leaning against your partner. Bend your knees and have one partner lean back while the other partner bears the weight by leaning forward a little. Return to a standing position after and reverse roles. Try to end in a sitting position at least once as you both

find greater points of support with each other. Always work within your physical health boundaries. For instance, if you cannot go to a seated position, work within a smaller range. A little movement that is carried out with full intention can create a big change in perspective.

- After you have found a point of weight sharing that you are both comfortable with, slowly reduce the amount of weight you are sharing and return to a standing position. Allow yourself to be rooted again in your own weight.

Questions

- How is it possible to rely on kinesthetic sensibilities in the middle of upheaval or chaos?
- What are some of the challenges or joys you faced in sharing weight with another person without making eye contact?
- At what point in the process did you begin to relax and feel more comfortable with your partner?

Reflections

The notion of balance, fall, and recovery is vital for conflict transformation. The mind is not a static entity, so creating parameters for responsive action is foundational for knowing how to support one another through formidable challenges. It is difficult to transform a situation when paralyzed by fear of the unknown, but nuanced cues in the body help to reorganize patterns that may be fueling an impeded relationship. In shifting in and out of balance and imbalance in a contained environment, fall and recovery will be more attainable in real conflict dynamics.

Third Person

- Dancers find partners. Identify the empty space between you as the "third person," which you both observe as the combined synergy of your unique relationship. As you move together, observe how the third perspective informs the evolving movement patterns. Include as many levels and tempos as possible as you both listen to the third for guidance on movement.
- Switch partners several times and observe how this relationship with the third continues to change the quality of the movement. Notice what messages are being delivered.
- The dance can evolve into groups (for example, a "fourth person" for three people dancing together, a "fifth" person for four people, etc.).

Facilitator's Note: Dancers should switch partners often and easily to promote a variety of experiences. Continue to support the idea that the third person is not each partner individually but the combination of energy between two people. Encourage curiosity, mobility, and safety. Draw attention to the importance of retaining an observer's consciousness while in motion.

Safety parameters are as follows:

- Be ready at any time to recover your own weight or "fall easily."
- Each partner is responsible for listening and for his or her own actions.
- Strive for fluidity and try to move from a supple musculature. Your ability to "hear" and "respond" will be restricted if you are tense.
- Do not limit the other person's movement. Partners must always have a way out. This could be modeled by holding another person's wrists lightly with open fingers so the person can move away easily. The opposite of this can be modeled by tightening the fingers until movement is restricted.
- There must be permission to stop at any time if one partner feels overpowered in any way, with an understanding that it can be possible to restart at any time. High levels of sensitivity and supple strength are required from both partners.

Questions
- What qualities were you able to sense from the third person?
- How did the third person enhance your own understanding of your partner?
- How did your experience shift with multiple partners and with different partners?
- How did the third person influence your awareness of your own physicality in relation to spatial dynamics?

Reflections
Investigating the energy that arises between two people brings a new perspective to the forefront. Rather than focusing solely on what the other person is doing, the focal point becomes what is emerging in between. This third space promotes curiosity as the emergent dance reveals relational challenges in an alternative form. The gift of this dance is its ability to reinforce the idea that new information can arrive from the energy between people and that issues we face can be looked at collectively—side by side—rather than directing the problem at the other. Impasse often occurs because a certain position is in some way beneficial and is giving a person something. The focus on a dance adds a lens of objectivity around relationships, shared problems, and experiences. This in-between space offers a convergent point and facilitates pathways of safe risk taking that can extend beyond a formulaic approach.

Dancing "No" and "And"
- Begin to develop a movement sequence with the image of "no" in the body. Explore "no" through horizontal, vertical, lateral, and twisting movement patterns. Discover physical phrases in the body that correlate with verbal phrases such as "Dance what you don't want." "This is my stance and I'm not going anywhere."
- Spend a couple of minutes discovering this movement in your body, and move with all of the embodied material that comes from "no." Allow yourself to be surprised through the body's capacity to find "no."

- Focus without judgment on what arises from the movement. Stay with the experience of "no" as it shifts and transforms over time in various positions and stances.
- Once "no" is explored from various angles, find another movement that encompasses "no" and "and." Continue this exploration until you begin to find where the "and" lives in the body.
- Alternate between the "no" and "and" states.

Variation: Participants are invited to dance two conflicting sides of a controversial topic. For instance, one partner could dance a pro-life position while the other partner dances a pro-choice position. Partners first dance these opposing words, and after a few minutes they are invited to insert an "and" or "if" into the dance and to observe the changes in the dance. This exercise draws attention to the broader context surrounding the narrow focus in many situations of conflict and the complexity of issues that is often neglected through that focus. You may want to use other directives, such as "maybe," or "possible."

Facilitator's Note: Once dancers are comfortable with each state, alternate directions between "no" and "and." Move between people while drawing out either the "no" or the "and" if dancers are too deeply entrenched in one word or the other or if they switch too quickly out of one of these states. This can be communicated through a whisper, a tap on the shoulder, or eye contact. Ask participants to be aware of how qualities of the "and" physically shift to the "no" and vice versa.

Questions

- Did you find yourself staying in one state for a prolonged period or were you continually shifting your stance?
- How did your experience of "and" influence your experience of "no"?
- How would you describe the transition between words? What did the place of transition reveal?

Reflections

This exercise helps move the focus away from the rigid position of "no" into a place of curiosity and discovery. Allowing "and" to enter into one's own perspective or the broader context can leverage deeply lodged positions in new ways. Introducing new rhythms makes it possible to shift from one state to the next. Moving from certainty into an open-ended state of possibility can be challenging for those who are threatened by the unknown. Phrases such as "I can't do that" or "I will never go there" become sources of security. A textured dance can facilitate new levels of insight on the tensions within and between the individual and social body. We do not have to give up our position of "no" but can instead open up space and possibility around and within the transitions and textures.

Stability/Mobility

Part One

- Move in response to a word cue. Begin with the word *position*. Say the word in your own language to the group. Each person replies in any language desired. Repeat the word under your breath or in your mind as you begin to move. Allow your movement to respond to the word. Concentrate on the qualities and the rhythm of the word rather than what you assume you know about the word.
- After a few minutes, repeat the activity in response to the word *shape*.
- After a few minutes, repeat the activity in response to the word *pathway*.
- Try dancing to other words, such as *form, inertia*, etc. Keep the impressions shifting and active.
- Debrief as a group about how these words or states are different and how they are the same.

Part Two

- Individually, begin to explore various tempos, textures, and levels that span the full range of movement in your body. Start this exploration with stillness and gradually create momentum through different parts of the body. While spontaneously starting and stopping, be attentive to your own points of stability and mobility as you shift focus, timing, and energy level. Notice how stability can hold a dynamic sense of fluidity and vice versa.
- Choose a partner and begin to experiment with dimensions of stability and mobility. Find mobile postures for each word chosen and begin to create a movement pattern as you shift in between words and each other. As you become more familiar with your partner's limits, design repeatable movement phrases that are based on images of these words.
- Introduce a new set of partners to this movement patterning to create a group of four. Continue in the exploration with four people.
- Add another set of partners to your group and notice how the words take on new meaning with more negotiation required.
- Debrief as a group about the insights gained throughout each phase of the exercise.

Questions

- How does stability complement mobility and vice versa?
- How did the earlier exploration of *shape, position*, and *pathway* inform your movement?
- What did you discover as you shifted levels of focus with your partner? How did this change when more dancers joined in the shared movement patterning?

Facilitator's Note: Here two words are used and can be exchanged for other opposing words (*stability, instability, blockage, pathway*, etc.), or a third word can be added. Participants dance the qualities of each word and then compare experiences. Words that have been contentious for the group and words that have helped facilitate understanding can also be introduced in this process.

Reflections

A shift from the language of *position* to *shape* and *pathway* can reveal sources of stability that are more able to support exploration. *Stability* is a very different experience than *stop*. Shifting from inertia to generative places of mobility is challenging in conflict, and initial movement is often felt to be destabilizing. Conflict escalation is often linked to levels of instability. Embodied responses can serve as a guide for reorganizing patterns of thinking and relating, making it possible to reframe our experiences and attend to habitual responses in new ways. Both stability and mobility demand heightened levels of readiness, concentration, and focus. This exercise lets the meanings rise authentically from the movement itself.

Basics Phase III: An Inventory of Possibilities

Bowing

- Form two lines and face one another from opposite sides of the room. One side will be designated the bowers, the other the receivers. The lines do not need to be equal in number.
- Notice those who are positioned across from you. Begin to walk toward one another and to the opposite side of the room. Walk through the heels of your feet. Allow the energy for the movement to come from the top of your head and down through the legs. The body becomes centered through the pelvis. Placing a hand on your stomach can serve as a physical reminder of where the source of your movement comes from.
- Focus the intention of your movement on what you are leaving behind and what you are moving toward.
- When you pass one another near the center of the room, only one side acknowledges the other with a bow. The other side just receives the bow. The proximity, timing, entry, and exit of the bow are all negotiated nonverbally. After the exchange is finished, continue walking until you reach the other side of the room.
- Switch roles and repeat the exercise.
- Dialogue collectively for about ten minutes, in small groups or with partners, about the mutual experiences of approach, bow, and exit.

Facilitator's Note: Offer enough guidance to provide a framework while still allowing for spacious discovery. There are many variables to consider when approaching the entry and exit of the bow. You may want to have participants focus on the energy they are leaving behind them, or walking into, while keeping the line from head to floor centered. Participants may feel too close for comfort when they encounter the other or perceive the room as too small for such an intimate exchange, etc. The point is to negotiate the bow with awareness and intuition. Receivers should be a smaller number so that the emphasis is on the gift bestowed.

Questions

- What are some cues to observe in the subtleties of physical negotiation?
- How can embodied rituals contribute to the restoration of relationships?
- What happens to the quality of interactions when gestures become the focal point rather than words?

Variation: You may want to repeat the exercise, leaving the guidance open as to who will bow and who will receive.

Reflections

This ritual exchange can support contexts where reconciliation or a deliberate recognition of an apology is needed. Nonverbal negotiation is an invaluable skill set when encountering the other in conflict, and a ritualized gesture can overcome barriers that may hinder a sense of exchange and mutuality. Our ability to navigate through the various facets of conflict is often obscured by the way we think. Tensions that are diffuse and unnamed can find a new form of inquiry and analysis through gestures. Moments of reciprocity and recognition arise as the body seeks to find its own relational logic.

Lines and Circles

- The group is divided in half. One half walks individually in lines throughout the room, with the other half observing. Movers: You may switch the direction of your lines whenever you wish, as long as linear trajectories are generated. This may include forward and backward lines, zigzags, square corners, and sharp angles. You are encouraged to feel free to pause and start again when you have an intention to move.
- Movers: After five minutes, you may move in circles as well as lines, alternating between circles and lines however you want. Tempo may also alternate between fast and slow for both lines and circles. Observe your responses as circles intersect with lines and as you come into relationship with others in the space.
- Movers: After five minutes, you will now use only circles but can switch to any direction, size, or tempo you want.
- After five minutes, the facilitator can choose people to replace certain movers, invite more movers to join the group, have fewer movers, or have the entire group replaced by those observing. Continue this exploration for another five to fifteen minutes.
- Create a dialogue with the whole group and begin to share what emerged as the varying movement patterns intersected with one another. Those who observed may want to comment on the story lines that seemed to develop from intersecting patterns.

Facilitator's Note: The number of people moving on the floor should depend on how volatile the group is. The more volatile, the fewer on the floor; the more connected or peaceful a group, the more people on the floor. It is usually best to begin with three to six movers. You may also want to call out specific instructions for movement rather than have movers decide.

Movement generally will accelerate as the exercise progresses, though it is recommended that you encourage a neutral walking pace for awareness. As participants become more accustomed to the exercise, they can determine the timing of movement as safety, respect, and physical agility inform the process. Reminding participants to continually focus on health will serve the process well.

Questions

- Did you notice any recurring patterns in your movement in the group?
- How did the choice of stopping and changing direction influence your perceptions of others?
- Did moving in lines or circles feel more natural to you? How might this speak to your approach toward conflict or chaos?

Reflections

This is a more-formal and advanced version of Moving Amongst, where participants move with more fluidity around the room. In contrast to Moving Amongst, this exercise requires more spatial dexterity. Safety and trust can be attained through stopping, pausing, and shifting movement patterns to minimize danger around potential collisions. The task to move in straight lines creates opportunities to focus on the relationship between intention, action, and consequence. The tensions of this exercise are both symbolic and literal as conflicting purposes intersect when circular shapes encounter linear patterns.

Revolving Doors

- Partners approach each other from opposite ends of the room. Just before coming into physical contact, spin clockwise or counterclockwise away from the point of intersection, using the momentum of the approach, without touching the other person. This encounter may vary in tempo and range, depending on the comfort level you have with your partner.
- For five minutes, explore this notion of revolving from various distances and directions. Be aware of your partner's timing and comfort level with the spin as it relates to your own.
- Keep your focus on the hips as the center of the spin rather than the chest or head.

Questions

- How did your encounters shift as you approached each other from greater distances? When did you experience more anticipation or trepidation?
- At what proximity did you begin to spin off each other? How did the change of tempo in the approach affect your intent?
- How did shifting the center of the spin to the hips change your balance or encounter?

Facilitator's Note: Determine the pace of this exercise in light of the group dynamics. Most people tend to spin from the solar plexus. Chest and head tend to be rooted in a place of desire and can lead to confrontation and imbalance. Moving from the hips keeps the body centered while spinning, making for an easier and smoother transition. Explore new ways of spinning through the back of the hips for greater agility and range of motion, with a focus farther from the solar plexus.

Reflections

Somatic habits are encoded within our bodies in a complex manner and are often taken for granted until we are able to observe our patterns. Learning how to be fluid and responsive within the realms of the unexpected increases the potential for creative problem solving. Movement instigates mobility and fluidity, even within perceived limitations, and expands our range of possible choices. Repositioning ourselves changes our locus of attention and can lead to an enhanced awareness of how perspectives are always contingent upon our chosen dispositions.

Space Holds/Conflict Points

- Work with a partner and face each other directly. Choose an abstract point of "conflict" or immobility between both of you. This point of tension could exist between the solar plexus, hips, chest, arms, etc. If there is a different point identified by each person, find the space between the two points. The point identified becomes a "conflict point" around which everything else will move.
- Shift your weight toward, around, and away from that perceived point of conflict.
- Begin to shift and pivot around this point of conflict in various ways, with altering levels and tempos, while still having the perception of the point intact. Look for ways to change, rotate, smooth, texture, and interact with that point by moving until solutions begin to reveal themselves.
- As you move together, you both breathe into the immobility point and observe how movement patterns respond to your collective focus.

Variation: The point can also be imagined in the space between two different points of conflict, around which both partners move and shift; it can also be chosen based on areas of the body that participants find most conflict oriented, or places of weakness and strength.

Questions

- How can pivoting around points of conflict increase connectivity between people?
- How do deep social fissures and entrenched positions begin to transform from our embodied standpoints?
- Why is transparency important for negotiating through conflict? What are the potential risks?

Reflections

Leveraging mobility to overcome immovable points is a challenging task. How does one redirect, change, or dissipate the force of conflict dynamics? By abstracting conflict into a point outside of oneself, the nature of the dynamics can be observed with greater objectivity. When people engage in conflict in this more-objectified way, patterns can be reorganized in response to new information that is given in the moment. The solutions may arise in the choices that are instinctively guided by the movement. Impulses for empathy begin at the level of our corporeal sensibilities.

Primordial Ooze

- Either with or without music, begin to move very slowly and incrementally, letting exaggerated gestures emerge. Allow this movement to be exploratory in nature, moving in and out of areas that are slightly uncomfortable. When you think that you've found the slowest movement possible, try to find an even slower one. Keep the movement continuous as you thoroughly explore what can be discovered from incremental transitions.
- Find a way to integrate the words *maybe, possible,* or *almost* into the movement patterning. Start with small movements and gradually expand them. Be patient and stay in this lagging tempo for as long as possible without halting the movement or committing to a definite place of arrival. Concentrate on moving into spaces that are unfamiliar.
- As soon as you sense you are about to fulfill a movement phrase in one direction, shift again into another direction. Observe the signals of both ease and discomfort in the body that emerge from adapting to the physical transitions.
- Initiate small improvisations with other dancers with slow movement patterns—in duets, trios, and groups. Observe the opportunities that arise as the groups become larger.

Questions

- How did variations in the tempo affect the intention of your movement phrase?
- How do the qualities of gestures change with slow movement?
- In what conflict scenarios could it be vital to slow down physical responses?
- How can allowing a time of not knowing help new sensibilities emerge?

Facilitator's Note: This dance focuses on moving and releasing into areas of the body that feel awkward, different, strange, uncomfortable, or unfamiliar. The idea is to focus on what is possible and emerging; to sense and stay with a "primordial becoming"; to not jump forward to conclusions but instead find ease in what is sensed as new. The dancer is invited to move only in healthy ways that feel slightly unfamiliar. "You know what you know, what don't you know" is the phrase that can be repeated here. "Slow and slower until you are barely moving" can also be articulated until participants are moving at a glacial speed.

Reflections

Valuable communication cues will be missed if our relationships are guided only by reactive energy. Slowing the pace down to facilitate greater clarity is vital when conflict becomes escalated. Through the physical vocabulary of movement, it is possible to begin exploring incremental shifts from a sensorimotor understanding. The quality of a shift that is vital for sustainable transformation cannot simply be theorized from a detached mindset but must be experienced with the whole body.

Touch

- Partners begin at one end of the room. Partner A lightly touches an area of Partner B's body to communicate the direction and quality of movement intended for Partner B.
- Partner B responds to the perceived intention of Partner A's gesture by moving with the quality and in the direction it implies. Partner A continues to direct the movement of Partner B in this nonverbal dialogue across the floor to the other side of the room.
- When partners have traveled across the floor together and have reached the wall, they switch roles so that Partner B leads Partner A across the room through touch. Each partner becomes aware of how his or her intention relates to that which is embodied by the other.
- After both partners have had a chance to lead, they dialogue with each other for ten minutes and consider how the quality of the movement responds to the touch.

Questions

- If the touch was strong and directive, what was the response? If the touch was gentle, what was the response?
- How clear was the connection between intention and response?
- Did you feel "heard" by your partner? Was the intention clear in your partner's touch?

Facilitator's Note: The appropriateness of the touch will depend on the cultural context and/ or gender dynamics. The facilitator is responsible for providing verbal guidance on the extent of the touch and may wish to guide participants on touching more or less. Encourage touch through the fingers, palms of the hands, wrists, backs of hands, feet, or hips. These can be varied in accordance to the level of physical dexterity and comfort with touch. The Intended Touch exercise below may be more appropriate for those whose experience or culture makes the nature of this contact inappropriate.

Intended Touch

- Partners decide who will be the first (Partner A) to initiate the intended touch. Partner A then gestures an intention to Partner B. This gesture, which does not actually touch the body, becomes the impetus for an embodied response from Partner B. Partner A continues to direct intended gestures toward Partner B, who responds. Both travel across the room in this pattern of offer and response.
- Roles are then reversed.
- Participants debrief with each other on their experience.

Variation: Double-Intended Touch or Double Touch. Partners simultaneously intend and respond to each other's intentions. This variation is generated without physical contact (double intended) or with contact (double touch). One person can intend softness to another person's intensity, a faster pace to languorous movement, a grounded intention to a light-headed response, etc. Given the complexity of this variation, it should be preceded by one of the simpler versions to allow participants to become familiar with responding to their partner's directions. You may also want to begin this variation at a slower pace.

Be sure to debrief regarding how this added complexity affects the capacity to listen and respond and how this relates to situations of conflict where we are almost always performing these simultaneous roles.

Questions

- What effect did your partner's intention have on your body?
- How did your experience of intended touch differ from the exercise where touch was permitted?
- Were there moments when you were given either too much information or not enough?

Reflections

We are exchanging physical signals both consciously and subconsciously. When intention is harnessed through gesture, our actions respond accordingly. Communication cues often begin with nonverbal impulses. Movement articulates the plurality and complexity of our intentions as knowledge is drawn from all of the senses. To discern through cultural nuances, it is important to sense what is hidden behind language. Gesture amplifies our thoughts as we affirm, accompany, or deny one another. Our neuromuscular responses can renew the power of subtleties in communication, revealing overt ideas and the subtexts that inform them.

Dictionary

- Begin with a meditation, lying on the floor to empty the body of thoughts. Then stand up and begin to move into directions and shapes called out by the facilitator.
- Envision these images as states of being and add varying qualities, rhythms, and tempos to these correlating movement patterns.
- Begin to improvise with words that arise from your own movement. Allow the mix of these words to become phrases in the body, and observe how the movement in the body changes accordingly.

Variations: You might want to offer words rather than have these emerge in response to the movement. This could include moving in a particular color, shape, direction, position, rhythm, etc. Questions to enhance the movement exploration may include "What movement does red, blue, orange, etc. evoke?" "What happens if you shift into another color?"

You also might have participants envision themselves moving through water and allowing the weight of the water to alter their stances, positions, and perspectives.

Another variation may include "dancing a sentence." Have people move to different words in a chosen sentence. Tell each person privately their word but do not tell them what the sentence is. Afterward, reveal the sentence and debrief on the nature of the shifting movement qualities, noting how this connects to or changes the meaning of the sentence.

Facilitator's Note: You will want to move through words quite quickly after the meditation (thirty seconds to one minute) to prevent becoming bogged down. It is easier to start with colors, then shift to movement-oriented words (*horizontal, shape, articulation*), and then add any words you find appropriate. You might begin by integrating words that the participants are using themselves and then add variations. Exploring different languages also provides a new sense for discovering qualities in words.

Reflections

There is a neuromuscular response to everything, and language predisposes us to certain perspectives. This is especially the case when using language around conflict, which can hold us to certain dispositions. Internally we hold a muscle memory for words that act like a stimulation. In moving through words, it becomes possible to observe our shifting neuromuscular responses to words. If we work with these responses with compassion, we can learn how to carefully infuse health into them. This can also allow people to explore the meanings and effects of words that are commonly used in certain conflict contexts or cultures. What are the liberating and restricting rhythms around certain words? What are the textures that give life to the words? This can help negotiators discern which words they might want to use. For instance, framing a whole negotiation in the quality of a deep blue may shift perceptions and expand what can be voiced. Adding other dimensions, like transparent or opaque, also could alter the quality of a dialogue as new textures or rhythms influence the cadence of expression.

Discovering Delicacy

- If you have access to music that has delicate qualities, play it in the background. This is optional, but it can help the body discover the qualities of delicacy with more ease.
- Begin to invent delicacy in the body. What are the rhythms, tempos, textures, and nuances of delicacy? If you don't know what it is, invent it. Move with your uncertainties first to make room for discovery.
- Focus on finding delicacy in the joints. Allow the discoveries of delicacy to be isolated in small body parts; then expand the discovery to include full body movement. Experiment with levels of momentum and add varying degrees of energy, weight, and focus to each movement.

Facilitator's Note: As participants are moving, invite them to say words that are associated with delicacy. Words may include *precious, vulnerable, fragile*, etc. If they are uncomfortable with this at the outset, you can prompt them with words of your own. Have them explore how these words move in their physicality. Once participants are comfortable with certain words, have them explore how the words become animated as they encounter others in the room. How does vulnerability meet vulnerability? What shifts in these encounters? We may culturally perceive delicacy as feminine. Encourage the discovery, expansion, and exploration of masculine delicacy as well.

Questions

- What challenges did you encounter when searching for delicacy in movement?
- In what contexts would you introduce qualities of delicacy? Why? What are the risks?
- How does changing the quality and dynamics of delicacy change the intent? How might delicacy be used to achieve shifts in conflict?

Reflections

Delicacy is a foreign concept for many people. This quality is often regarded as being unattainable, especially in the midst of conflict dynamics. If people are capable of inventing delicacy, then it is likely that they can invent anything. As we experiment with delicate qualities from different angles and perspectives of focus, we can investigate our natural tendencies and dispositions. Our somatic habits not only influence physical postures and positions but also reveal attitudes and perspectives that we hold on to. If we can become attuned to the more vulnerable aspects of ourselves, we can begin to access a greater range of human experience.

Dance What Is Hidden

- The only guidance for this movement is to dance what is hidden or not yet revealed. Depending on the level of safety and comfort in the group, this could be initiated by two or three participants dancing what is hidden while the others watch or by all participants dancing simultaneously.
- Allow several minutes for the dance to reveal what is hidden, and continually bring new dancers into the center if two or three are dancing in front of the others. This dance may embody something that is personal or collectively hidden within the group. The point is not to judge or make conclusions from the dance. Simply allow the dance to reveal textures of what hasn't yet surfaced and then provide a way to shift those aspects revealed.

Questions

- How does somatic reflection help reveal hidden nuances in relationships?
- Are there risks involved with identifying hidden dynamics?
- In what contexts could this approach be productive? When could it be detrimental?

Reflections

Conflict often escalates when agendas, sentiments, and emotions remain hidden for a prolonged period. Small issues can become complicated controversies over time when emotional investment builds and is not able to be expressed. However, words alone cannot always adequately articulate what remains under the surface. A multisensory approach is needed to address both the explicit and implicit, and movement has a way of filtering through preconceived ideas as attention is directed toward what is being revealed through the body. The immediacy of physical responses stimulates a greater accountability to the present moment, but care must be given to those who find it difficult to "stay in the body" because the threat or experience of violence may have reinforced the notion that the body is not a safe place to come home to.

Around the Table Dances

- Sit around a table to start. Begin with simple stretches overhead, shaking out the arms to stretch the lungs and chest, breathing deeply. Visualize this movement extending through the whole body, beginning with the feet.
- Move your legs under the table however you wish.
- Mirror the movement of your legs with your hands on top of the table.
- Move your hands along the table, alternating so that they move toward and away from each other, extend outward along the table, or come toward the chest. Observe the patterns of movement of the person across from you at the table.
- After moving separately, begin to move your hands in response to the person across from you. This may be a mirroring of the movements or a counterbalance; for example, you move outward as your partner moves inward.
- Play with rhythms as they emerge. See if any patterns surface.
- Begin to shift the whole body backward and forward toward the table or person opposite. Then shift side to side and rotate the upper body, alternating between these movements as you wish.
- Shake the body, breathe deeply, and return to dialogue.

Variations

- **Eyeball-in-head dances:** Leave your head in the same place but move your eyes; then do the opposite: let the eyes rest in one place while the head moves.
- **Model in motion:** Take something that was said at the table and model it in motion. Objects on the table may serve as props for the movement.
- **Leave the table and return:** Stand up and leave your seat, then take the same chair; or, upon suggestion, take a different chair when you return to the table. Alternate leaving the table and returning, using different chairs, until asked to return to your original chair.

Questions

- What is not being presented at the table? What needs to be at the table?
- What does it mean to say fluidity is at the table? What might fluidity look like?
- How can simple gestures extend your range of sensory vision?

Facilitator's Note: As the exercises start feeling right, they have come to their own conclusion. Move on, leaving the dancers with a positive body memory. Start where your room "is."

Observe the prevalent rhythms and then identify them, enhance them, and consciously shift them (encourage simplicity, economy, and efficiency until comfort and creation can be easily explored).

Reflections

Meetings around the negotiation table often emphasize a cognitive and analytical approach. However, impasse can result from the simple lack of movement. Tensions, desires, longings, and resistances are all rooted in our physicality. The bodily dimension of thought cannot be overlooked, because our perceptions are directly linked to our kinesthetic encounters with the world. Movement oxygenates the body and mind, and thinking becomes more animated and reflexive if there is space for flow. Our capacity for receptivity and overall health will increase if movement vocabularies can be included at the table.

Suspend the Criticism

- Stand in the room wherever you wish. Begin to move in ways that might feel awkward, silly, or odd. At all times, keep the movement healthy for the body.
- When you hear the voice of internal criticism, shift your focus from knowing what you're going to do to *discovering* what you're going to do. In this process, find new ways of transitioning from comfort to discomfort through different parts of your body as you cultivate curiosity through movement. Begin at one side of the room and experiment with these transitions repeatedly until you have traveled across the room.
- After five minutes of physically exploring these transitions, begin to embody larger ideas, concepts, and/or desires. For example:
  — Health: invent what health would feel like. What positions, stances, or postures would health take?
  — Delicacy: invent delicacy in your bones.

Variation: This can be integrated into other exercises that highlight the importance of a kinesthetic inquiry. If you see participants being self-conscious or critical of themselves or others, suspend criticism by emphasizing the need for everyone's participation in a collective sense of discovery. Alternatively, you may have participants move collectively as each person embodies his or her own self-criticism for a few moments before shifting. Keep this honest and full of play.

Facilitator's Note: In the beginning, be sure that all are moving simultaneously to minimize the feeling of being observed. Once comfort levels and safety have been developed, this exploration could be extended into partner work. Have participants repeat movements that may seem extraordinary to extend their range of what is conceivable. This could be carried out in larger groups as well, as participants discover one another through nonverbal communication.

Questions

- How can movement create opportunities for inventive problem solving?
- When could suspending the criticism, or moving through the criticism, be particularly useful in heated negotiations?
- How can novelty, creativity, and spontaneity assist with seeing past limitations in relationships?

Reflections

As identities become threatened in conflict dynamics, the tension between surrender and control becomes heightened. The expectation to know can be its own obstacle, and the desire to control can lead to greater fear and eventual impasse. Shifting the focus from position to possibility and from knowing to discovering has the potential to replace suspicion with curiosity. If we can train our bodies to assume positions of curiosity rather than closure, we will be more equipped to be able to discern reactive behaviors. A deep sense of play can facilitate an overall sense of health. Imagining shifts and transformation involves a commitment to mediate the present moment through the senses.

If I Don't Have It, I'll Create It

- Imagine something that you desire but don't currently have. Envision how you can begin to invent this in the body. How will it begin to take shape? If you could imagine it, what would it feel like? Keep the invention real—in other words, sensed rather than intellectually constructed. You do need to know how to get there. Allow space and permission to invent and manifest it, no matter how amorphous, abstract, or partial the terrain may seem.
- If you are working in a large group, allocate half of the group as observers and half as dancers. Dancers begin to shape what they envision as they ask themselves, "What is needed?" Examples could include peace, harmony, unity, an abundance of resources, reconciliation, etc. Dancers may surprise themselves with the invention of a new dance. Observers are to be both supportive and discerning as they "hold" the space for the person inventing.
- First, individually explore the physical dimensions of this desire for a couple of minutes. Then, once a new movement pattern has been invented, find a partner and create a duet that uses the new creations as a conversation between two dancers. Switch partners and experiment with various encounters in the room.
- Begin to form groups of three or four and observe how each creation intersects with the other. Develop this convergent movement patterning for five minutes.
- Dialogue in small groups afterward to discuss what you've observed.

Questions

- How can imagination through a somatic lens help generate new insights?
- How did the shape of your desire shift and change when you encountered others?
- What were you able to discover as your divergent desires intersected?

Variation: The whole group can collectively embody one desire. Each person's embodiment— through a myriad of gestures, levels, tempos, textures, and movement sequences— gives this one desire individual shapes and forms. To add the additional role of a witness, it may be useful to create an alternate sequence that has some participants moving while others attentively hold space for the others.

Reflections

Imagining an outcome can facilitate the necessary conditions to find what is needed to create the vision. Without the capacity to imagine first what can be possible, creating solutions will be difficult. This can be particularly useful for practitioners who feel overextended. Through embodying what is not present but desired, it can be possible to transition from a sense of lack to a sense of possibility and even abundance. Movement sequences can offer solutions that were not previously known or even conceived of. If people who are living the problems are simultaneously moving through them in an embodied sense, deeper seeds of truth will surface through the wisdom of somatic intelligence.

Smallest Dance Possible

- Choose one person to stand in a designated spot in the room, with the rest of the group observing.
- If you are the mover, imagine you are in a big field, stadium, etc., and do the absolute smallest dance that is possible to be seen from a great distance. You may want to choose one specific body part—a part not usually associated with performing in dance, such as an ear, a nose, an eyelid, a knee, a shoulder, or a specific finger—and do the smallest dance possible with this part.
- After some time, another person takes the mover's place and chooses a different body part to perform the smallest dance possible.
- Change roles until everyone has had a chance to dance with a different part of the body.
- Debrief with the group, either after each dance or after all have had a turn, about what you saw.

Variation: Start without a specific person chosen to dance. Call out different body parts. If someone feels there is a dance for it, the person may run up to the designated space and do it. If movements are too big, give the direction to go smaller (such as "as small as you can get away with, that others can read" or "think it, don't do it").

Questions

- How much were you able to observe in others' dances?
- Were you surprised by how much range or expression was possible in your own or another's choice of body part?
- Did you see or experience any stories arising from the small dances?

Reflections

It is astonishing what can be accomplished through the smallest movement patterns. A layered and complex narrative can be generated from the most compact experiences. The transmission of key worldviews is not solely derived from an intellectual stance but through subtle gestures. Even the slightest movements can increase or decrease levels of receptiveness in relationships. What slips through the cracks in communication can be recovered through somatic sensibilities.

Dance and Resilience: Select International Examples

*T*his section of the book moves from exploration of why dance matters and what it can teach to a series of chapters that document the extent to which dance works in specific contexts. Hard experience from two contrasting countries, Ireland and Cambodia, which suffered from some of the most intractable conflict of the last century, demonstrates the vitality and usefulness of dance.

Maureen Maloney, a former deputy attorney general of British Columbia and—in a previous incarnation—a champion Irish dancer, walks us through the origins of traditional Irish dance and its relationship to the armed conflicts that have been so potent in the formation of contemporary Irish identities. The Irish scholar-practitioner Geoffrey Corry complements Maureen's approach through a moving narrative of enmity and humanity arising from a particular trauma of Northern Ireland's bitter war, reflecting on the lessons for resilience and reconciliation.

The focus in the subsequent three chapters moves across the world to Cambodia and Liberia, lands devastated by conflict and displacement. The dance ethnologist Toni Shapiro-Phim documents the way that dance has been used in Cambodia and Liberia to preserve the aesthetic and spiritual histories and cultures that the long years of internal conflict and refugee camps came near to destroying. John Burt, the founding chair of Cambodia Living Arts and producer of the Khmer rock opera Where Elephants Weep, writes with Andrew Dilts, a legal scholar, about how dance and other artistic traditions can be woven into the fabric of a nation being restored, through both the rebuilding of personal relationships and the transforming of cultural identity.

Carrie Herbert, a Welsh psychotherapist and director of arts therapy services for the Ragamuffin Project, also bases her chapter on her experience in Cambodia, but her focus is on the therapeutic role that arts such as dance can offer to the survivors of conflict. In celebrating this role for the expressive arts, however, she also emphasizes the need to create safe conditions and practices for using such powerful tools with those who are most vulnerable.

11

Ireland

Finding Meaning: Dancing Out of Conflict
MAUREEN MALONEY

> *"O body swayed to music, O brightening glance,*
> *How can we know the dancer from the dance?"*
> *Among School Children*, Yeats[1]

Introduction

What is the relationship between dance and conflict? Although I was a competitive Irish step dancer as a youth and have been a student and practitioner of conflict resolution as an adult, this question occurred to me only recently, when I was invited to participate in a project exploring the role of dance in conflict resolution. Working on this project introduced me to the limited body of academic literature on the subject, which caused me to search for answers in my own background and culture. As a woman of Irish descent, dance was a major preoccupation and an important part of my identity while growing up.

In the process, I have discovered that I am not alone in seeking an understanding of dance in personal as well as academic realms. As Wulff has noted, dance, like all bodily activities, contains knowledge in the practice of it. This is why virtually all dance, music, and sport scholars at some point take part in the activity they study, although they do not always make an explicit methodological point about it.[2]

In my case, the activity preceded the study,[3] but the ways that activity has informed my thinking are no less significant. My history and experience with Irish dance profoundly affects the way I perceive and interpret it. In this respect, I identify strongly with Bourdieu's observation, quoted in Wulff, that the practice of dancing reveals dispositions, or perceptions and actions that are being inscribed in a dancer's body. Such dispositions consequently have an impact on the dancing, the social life of dancers, and the dancers' movement patterns *outside* dancing.[4] Wulff tested this theory by asking Irish choreographers how Irish people move. Some responded that there were significant differences between the movement patterns of people in the north and people in the south. According to these choreographers, people in the north tend to move in a more-restricted way than those in the south, and "Catholics tend to move more softly than Protestants."[5]

These insights prompted me to explore further my own experiences and what they disclose about the relationship between dance and conflict. That exploration has drawn my attention to three methods through which conflict stories have been, and continue to be, communicated and perpetuated through Irish dance. One such method is by dance itself being an expression of Irish cultural identity and resistance to colonial influence. A second method is by imprinting upon dance conflict stories that utilize the power of dance to reinforce national pride, foster anticolonial sentiment, create shared memories, and perhaps reclaim Ireland's conflictual past as a way of mediating the pain and loss of those conflicts. More recently, dance theater, the third method, is providing a safe and comedic venue allowing Irish people on both sides of the religious divide, Protestant and Catholic, to meet and mediate their current and troubled past in a shared manner.

In what follows, I will illustrate the first two of these methods with reference to two forms of Irish dance in which I have engaged, the first as a child and the second as a child and an adult. For the third method, I will draw upon a contemporary example—one that, while outside my personal experience, shows how modern Irish dance theater continues to be a vehicle for communicating conflict stories and creating a place and space to mediate the loss and pain associated with those conflicts. Given that my analysis draws heavily upon my personal experiences and perceptions, I will begin by briefly describing my background and positioning myself.

Positioning Myself

I am one of the diaspora of Irish around the world. I spent most of my childhood in England in Irish neighborhoods, spending holidays on a farm in rural Ireland in the southwestern corner of County Clare, where my parents were born and spent their childhoods. Encouraged by my mother and father, I was an Irish step dancer as a child and a young woman, winning cups and medals in competitions all over England. I won my first medal dancing on the back of a truck at a country fair in the little town of Cross, County Clare. I cannot remember how old I was, but there is a photograph of a young girl dancing a reel on a truck, back straight as a ramrod, both feet seemingly hanging in the air. Her face is earnest and determined.

I gave up competitive dancing around age sixteen, but at my father's insistence I continued to show-dance at various Irish houses or at halls featuring Irish dancing, especially on St. Patrick's Day.

I have as an adult made yearly visits to Ireland to see my parents and siblings, who live in County Clare. During such visits, I have participated in ceili and set dancing, a much more-relaxed and communal form of dancing that takes place with ceili bands in public houses and dance halls. My favorite set dance is the Siege of Ennis, which I have danced countless times over the years with my father, who has very light feet of his own. Now in my fifties, having been a legal academic for decades and involved in peace building, I have recently returned to one of my first loves in an effort to understand how dancing has been used in Ireland to physically embody and communicate conflict narratives. I have shared this brief personal history because it both informs my understanding of Irish dance and influences my motivation for exploring it further.

Dance as the Embodiment of Irish Identity and Conflict Stories

Modern Irish dance began to be used in the late nineteenth century as a means of promoting Irish identity and nationhood and as a form of resistance against English colonization. In 1893, the Gaelic League was established with the express intention of conserving Irish culture, which is very distinct from English culture. While the League's main ambition was to preserve the Irish language, it recognized the essential role of dance in Irish culture and identity, and it sought to promote and regulate dance to be assured of its "Irishness."[6]

As part of its desire to see Irish dances flourish throughout the country, the Gaelic League sent out dancing masters, who were usually accompanied by Irish musicians. They would stay in a place for a few weeks and teach dances to the local people, incorporating variations as appropriate for different counties.[7] Dance was selected because it was "a malleable, inherently portable art form that could easily transfer from one place to another."[8] It was also "universal in every cabin" of the poor people of Ireland.[9] The League organized *feisanna* (festivals) to encourage competition and shared dancing experiences among different counties. In 1929, the League set up *An Coimisiún le Rinci Gaelacha*, the Irish Dancing Commission, which to this day regulates dancing styles and examines teachers and adjudicators for competitions.[10]

As these activities make clear, dancing has long been regarded a central feature of Irish culture and identity. Thus nationalists have looked to dance as a bulwark against colonial culture and as an important step in nation building. I will illustrate this by discussing two different types of dance that were spread throughout Ireland by the dancing masters: step dancing and ceili dancing.

Irish Step Dancing

Irish step dancing is the style of dance most recognized and associated with Ireland, particularly following the astounding global success of *Riverdance*. Traditionally, it is danced solo as a performance or in competition. It is a stylized form of dance in which dancers maintain a stiff back, with arms carefully controlled, while the upper body, including the head, is kept straight and immobile. The emphasis is on the feet, which perform very fast and intricate steps. Step dances are divided into two forms: soft shoe (reels and slip jigs) and hard shoe (hornpipe and double jig).

The historical origin and significance of the immobile upper body are unknown. Yet the stories told concerning its genesis reveal the importance of dance as resistance and identity. The most common tale (and the one I grew up with) is attributed to times when Irish dancing in houses was not allowed as a matter of English colonial policy, and subsequently as a matter of Catholic religious practice. According to this story, when people danced in their homes, the upper body remained immobile to prevent the prying eyes of English landowners, and later, Catholic priests, from seeing that dancing was taking place when they passed by. Wulff references another tale (which I had not heard) concerning the origins of this practice:

> Once upon a time, the Irish used to dance with their hands in the air and the smiles on their faces. But the English kidnapped some dancers and took them to dance for the Queen. In protest they danced with deadpan faces and their hands at their sides.[11]

These two stories explicitly portray step dancing as a form of resistance to oppressors and the dance itself as an act of liberty and defiance. It is a portrayal that gave romanticized meaning to how step dancing was viewed within the Irish community of my youth, and I have no doubt that was what motivated me to embrace this form of dance as a child. To be a step dancer made me much more than a performer or a competitor; it made me a participant in an act of community solidarity and national pride. At a deeper level, it engaged me in and made me an instrument for the preservation of shared memory of historical conflict and resistance. At the time I lived in England, the Irish were not always welcomed there, particularly when the struggle for a united Ireland once again turned violent in Northern Ireland and bombs were also detonated in England. To engage in specifically Irish activities could be construed as identifying with Irish nationalism.

Step dancing in performance and competition is still very popular in Ireland and among the Irish diaspora around the world. In addition to its entertainment value, such dancing serves to perpetuate Irish identity and to play out conflict rituals and remembrance for the benefit of both dancers and observers.

But it is not only step dancing that has played a role in promoting Irish solidarity and resistance; there are also social or community dances that frequently take place in dance halls, public houses, and on festive occasions such as weddings, anniversaries, and birthdays. These ceili dances "were adapted as ideal for large social occasions, because they involved large numbers and traversed the whole floor (unlike traditional [step dancing] which valued the ability to 'dance on a sixpence' in tightly restricted domestic space)."[12] I will now consider how these dances have also been used to record historical events (even those that did not actually happen), to perpetuate shared memories, and to relive and reaffirm conflict stories throughout the generations. I will do this with reference to a specific ceili dance, probably the most popular in County Clare: the Siege of Ennis.

The Siege That Never Was

Ceili dances are group dances, unlike step dances, which are usually danced solo in competitions or shows. Step dancing is complicated and not easily danced by all. Ceili dances are much simpler and more communal. They are danced primarily for social enjoyment by communities at festive events. These dances were also designated by the Gaelic League to be taught (where necessary) by the wandering Irish dance masters and to be danced instead of the quadrilles and set dances popular at the beginning of the nineteenth century. The League specifically delineated which dances were ceili dances and therefore deemed to be real Irish dance; set dances were not, as they were drawn from outside influences.[13] The term *set dance*—Irish steps combined with French movements—literally means "a set of quadrilles."

Quadrilles were originally brought to the large Protestant houses by the English military. They were adapted in the eighteenth century by dancing masters, who choreographed them to Irish music. (The dancing masters apparently used ceili dancing to occupy the less talented masses while they introduced step dancing to their most promising students.)[14]

The Siege of Ennis is a familiar ceili dance in County Clare. Ennis, the capital of Clare, is a lovely medieval town with a strong political history. Dance and music are common in the public houses and county halls and homes, and none are more popular than the Siege of Ennis.

Imagine a cold and dreary winter night in Moyasta, West Clare, where the pub nearest to my parents' farm is located. We have been told that local musicians will be playing tonight, so, facing strong Atlantic winds and pouring rain, we make our way to Taylor's. Despite the weather, there will be a good crowd and good *craic* (a good time). (These were regular events at least one night a week, usually Saturday or Sunday, up until a few years ago. The pub would invariably be packed with local people gathering to review the happenings of the week, to share the latest gossip, and to exchange tales of happiness and sorrow.) The music starts, and we hear the tune associated with the Siege of Ennis.

People of all ages (eight-year-olds to octogenarians) grab a partner and move onto the floor to do this fast but relatively simple dance. Everyone knows how to do it, so people of varying abilities, of all ages, and in various degrees of sobriety, join in. It is great fun as we advance, retreat, and enter the arch. We move to different partners and thus dance with many. Throughout the dance, there is an enormous feeling of shared community, common culture, and physical and psychological solidarity. The music and the dance together transform the room into a place of shared joy, hope, and experience, affirming Martin Stokes's assertion that collective dances to music "evoke and organise collective memories and present experiences of place with an intensity, power and simplicity unmatched by any other social activity."[15]

Instructions for *Ionsaí na hInse*, Siege of Ennis[16]

This is an Irish jig for eight people. Line up with two couples facing two couples. The man should be on the left in each couple.

Bars	Figures
8	Advance and retreat twice, all four on each side taking hands.
8	Center people drop hands (but keep the partner's hand). Slip sides as couples, (left lead, right rear). Change back.
8	Everyone drops hands. The center four people dance a right-hand star followed by a left-hand star. (Put your right hand into the center, dance clockwise for 4 threes, then turn around, put your left hand in, and dance back). The end people do a cross-hand or around-the-waist swing for all eight bars.
8	Advance, retreat, advance, pass through. On the pass-through, the couples with their backs to the music raise their hands, making an arch. The other couples drop hands and pass right shoulders with the people opposite them. One person doesn't get to go under the arch.

Repeat, having advanced one set—when you get to the bottom, you get to sit out one.

How did this dance get its name? I had always assumed, without ever being told, that the name related to a historical siege of Ennis and that the dance is a bodily enactment of this local conflict history between the English and Irish in County Clare. And it seems I was not alone in this belief. The Internet attributes the name to a siege of Ennis that took place in the 1680s.[17] However, with further inquiry and research at the County Clare library and archives, I discovered that there never was a siege of Ennis! There were two sieges of Limerick (the largest town to the north of Ennis, the capital of the adjoining County Limerick). Interestingly, there is no dance titled the Siege of Limerick, although there is the popular Walls of Limerick, which presumably is a reenactment of the event. So what is the history behind these sieges, and why was the name appropriated for Ennis? The history is easy to describe, since it is well known to most, if not all, Irish Catholics as a defining time in the long and bitter conflict between Ireland and England, which continued in various forms through the centuries until the Northern Ireland Peace Accords of 1998.

In 1660, Charles II, a Catholic, ascended the throne of England. This caused hope and excitement for the Irish, who thought that a Catholic king might return the lands that had been taken from landowners by English Protestants on Cromwell's orders. However, Charles feared displeasing the English Protestants and did nothing. Hopes rose again in 1685, when James II succeeded Charles as king. James appointed Catholics to prominent positions in government—as judges, for example. However, the promise of land returns did not materialize, and relationships between Catholics and Protestants deteriorated further.

In England there was also unrest, brought to a boiling point by the birth of a son to James II. English Protestants, fearing a succession of Catholic kings, urged the Dutch Protestant William of Orange to become king of England. He took up the invitation and drove James out, moving on to Ireland. James went to France, where he raised a Jacobite army in hopes of defeating William in Ireland. Irish Catholics took the side of James II; Irish Protestants in Ulster sided with William of Orange. After the Irish Catholics suffered a major loss in the north of Ireland at the infamous Battle of the Boyne in 1690 (celebrated to this day by northern Irish Protestants), they retreated south, deciding to hold the line at the River Shannon in County Limerick. William's army laid siege to Limerick but failed to take the city. A subsequent siege a year later did succeed, and the war ended.

Whether one of these sieges is the origin of the Siege of Ennis is uncertain. A more-intriguing question is why the dance was named for a historical event that did not happen. It expressly enacts a siege with "advances" and "retreats." My hypothesis is that the name was specifically created to give County Clare's residents and their descendants a sense that they had fought in the Williamite wars in their own county. It may also signify a reclaiming and reshaping of the conflict as a battle bravely fought by Clare men, since there is no clear "winner" in the dance. However, while it is true that the Clare Dragoons fought bravely, albeit poorly, at the Battle of the Boyne, "it would appear that no substantial military action was fought in County Clare. . . . although the last desperate action of the war was fought on Thomond Bridge—the bridge that connected Co. Clare to the city of Limerick."[18]

There is also speculation that both the Walls of Limerick and the Siege of Ennis were created (or at least named) by Fionan MacColuim, an activist in the Gaelic League, in partnership with an old dancing master, Patrick Reidy.[19] Another version attributes the naming to Sheain O'Cuirrin, the secretary of the Gaelic League in Limerick in the early 1900s.[20] There are also questions about whether these two dances were old Irish dances that were popularized by the League or new dances created by the League—or by one of its dancing masters—with the express intention of building Irishness and solidarity. The League's aim was to create an Irish identity, and the main identity of Ireland at the time was one of oppression, conflict, and colonization, resulting in displacement, loss of identity, and pain, in which the Williamite wars played a central role. Ensuring that each county felt it was part of this shared heritage and shared conflict would be a powerful way of building collective identity. Dance could be employed as physical metaphor, creating shared history (even if mythical) and embodying the hurt and pain of past conflict, then passing that shared history down the generations over several centuries.

Dance is also a powerful and joyful way to mediate the pain and loss associated with centuries of conflict. As Wulff comments: "Community is sometimes used in Irish dance to heal the hurt of history."[21] While the origins of the Siege of Ennis remain shrouded in mystery, it is powerful to observe how creative history is imprinted on this ceili dance, just as creative dance was imprinted on history in step dancing, both with extraordinary effect.

Having used historical conflicts and historical dances for my first two illustrations, I will now turn to more-modern conflicts and dances to explore how new forms of dance are being used to transmit conflict narratives among Ireland's residents and diaspora. Modern dance theater is very much central to Irish cultural identity, and many performance pieces continue the long tradition of the retelling and remembrance of Ireland's conflict stories past and present. Narratives of emigrations, pain, and loss followed by a reconciliation and homecoming are woven into *Riverdance*; the powerful exposition of the heartbreaking potato famine of the 1840s (brought about by English colonization and laws) is told in *Ballads* and also *The Leaving*.[22] The rich history of telling conflict stories through, by, and with dance continues along the centuries to the current day. The illustration that I will use here is a short eight-minute contemporary physical movement/dance titled *Hanging in There*.

Hanging in There

Hanging in There[23] is a production of Legitimate Bodies Dance Company, operating out of County Offaly in southern Ireland. It is a short interpretive dance that depicts the negotiations over the Northern Ireland Peace Accords, signed on April 10, 1998, often referred to as the Good Friday Peace Agreement or the Belfast Agreement. The historic treaty marked the culmination of years of negotiation to end the Troubles, a period of intense violence and conflict in Northern Ireland and to a lesser, but still deadly, extent in England and southern Ireland. The conflict existed between the northern Irish Protestants (backed for the most part by the British army) who wanted to maintain the existing connection and citizenship with

England decisively gained at the Battle of the Boyne centuries before and the northern (and many southern) Irish Catholics who wanted the six counties making up Northern Ireland—a result of the 1921 Anglo-Irish Agreement between England and southern Ireland—to be reunited as one Ireland. Given the intensity and level of violence that had been going on for decades in Northern Ireland, and the bitterness and distrust on all sides, the peace negotiations were lengthy (at times tortuous) and took many unexpected turns that were both positive and negative. They were closely monitored by the Irish in the north and south.

As in many peace processes, terms of movement or immobility are related to these negotiations. It is frequently said that negotiators are "caught in conflict," "bound in disagreement," or "locked in dispute." They are said to be "in step," "out of step," "unable to move on," or "frozen in time." These phrases portray conflict as something that is identified as much by the character and limitations of movement as by the presence and nature of cognitive disagreement. Such was the case in the Irish peace talks, where there was "speculation about 'body language' and damage to 'the body politic.'" Negotiators chose to "hold hands across the sectarian divide" or to "withdraw the hand of friendship."[24]

Hanging in There interweaves language taken from the peace agreement with physical movement to depict the Northern Ireland peace process. Two politicians from opposite sides of the divide attempt to work together. Shouting out phrases from the agreement, such as "shared and peaceful future," "respecting each other's dignity," and "building solid structures," they are physically challenged to embody the words of the peace agreement in front of the glittering new Assembly building. The dance conveys political nervousness and duplicity, or inability to trust each other, in stark contrast with the optimistic words of the peace agreement. The bodily movements, jerky and difficult, stand in contradiction to the spoken words. The dancers attempt seemingly impossible balancing acts; for example, one dancer climbs up on the other, teetering precariously while, hilariously, guaranteeing the stability and soundness of the legislative structure. At another time, the politicians turn toward each other and then pointedly move away while talking of common causes and new beginnings.

Perceptively, the dance reviewer Jane Coyle notes that although the combination of spoken word and dance worked well together, "[d]ance came out on top, guiding the audience through the tangled process. Our dancers take one step forward, two steps back (or vice versa) before propping each other up in a series of complicated U-turns and back bends. They laugh, josh, frown and squabble, striding ahead purposefully before retreating in tiny, hesitant steps. They confront each other face to face, and then turn away, unable to make eye contact."[25]

This formidable short piece highlights the duplicity and machinations of the politicians in the peace process but also, according to Gareth Vile, "[h]ighlights the importance of definitions, co-operation and the gap between rhetoric and reality. . . . [A] witty political statement and a profound comment on language's ability to hide or reveal physical reality.[26] Nick Bryson, the choreographer and one of the dancers in Legitimate Bodies Dance Company, explains the origins of the dance: "It is inspired by the kind of political speech which is deliberately and constructively ambiguous, so that both sides of the community can go along with it. We turn that speech into a physical language that informs the dance. Thus there emerges a parallel between the language of the dancers and that of the peace-making politicians."[27] Overall, the piece literally reveals points of connection and disconnection for all who were involved in the talks and brings observers an embodied sense of that conflict and its messy movement toward resolution.

Hanging in There is a modern-day creation and representation of the power of dance or movement to embody and express deep-rooted conflict and the difficulties, intricacies, ambiguities, and duplicities of peace processes and the negotiators. With an emphasis on moving on, but haltingly, forward or sideways and sometimes backward, the dance embodies the contradictions and discomfort of the conflict in the observer. Moreover, to the Irish observer the dance embodies memories of a painful and troubling time, reliving the fears, doubts, and insecurities. It also mirrors the ambiguities and fears that the peace process will become frozen again and that there may not be movement to a shared future.

Importantly, the dance also creates (or re-creates) shared memories of this time for both Catholics and Protestants, allowing the two communities to have collective, not separate, memories. The dance theater provides a safe place and space to process these painful emotions and recollections. In a dark theater, an individual can explore the embodied emotions that the dance generates, but in the midst of and along with the community observers. At the same time, the pain and loss that arise from the reliving of these embodied memories is mediated by the wickedly funny movements of the politicians, allowing the observer to laugh through the pain and share communal joy at experiencing this witty art form. The observance of the dance creates unity and a shared sense of the conflict narrative for both Catholics and Protestants. Unlike my first two illustrations, this interpretive dance, although performed throughout Europe, may not last as a living embodiment of the potential resolution to centuries of violence and conflict. However, the episodic nature may be as important, if not more important, to the observers who will carry this new embodiment (and perhaps a shared embodiment) into different realms and practices as the peace process unfolds.

Dance in its many expressions has the potential to solidify as well as to dynamize conflict within and over generations. My first two illustrations, step dancing and ceili, emerged as fixed forms from a specific time and context and gave lasting shape to the time, place, and events. In my third illustration, dance theater, we see dance as a process, moving parties and observers through shifts and playful discoveries, and one of many stepping-stones for building peaceful coexistence.

Conclusion

There is an old saying that the Irish have a long memory, meaning that Irish people are very conscious of their history, particularly of colonization and the misery and conflict that was imposed on them and their ancestors for centuries. My thesis is that this memory has also been deliberately cultivated and embodied in the culture in various ways, one of the most important being dance. Dance is central in Irish culture and identity and, as such, an important means by which conflict narratives are embodied and passed from generation to generation. Dance has also been used to promote and embed collective shared memories of the same events. As Wulff notes: "Collective or social memory may be distributed unequally in the minds of the members of a group, but it can be united at rituals and performances. . . . Because of the multivocality, of the many possible interpretations of a dance performance, it provides a versatile forum for investigation of the past,"[28] which is capable of producing unity, identity, and purpose through experiencing shared memories of conflict stories through the power of dance.

Irish dance plays an equally powerful role in ensuring that conflict stories are lived and embodied events whether they are historical or current. However, a distinction must be made between dances that portray historical memories and those that express lived experiences and memories of conflict. "The nature of these types of memory is by necessity different, even though both may have passed through official academic and political reformulations. But lived history, in its individual forms, should be recognised as crucial parts to consider in any analysis of the past. . . . Such individual personal memories can shed new light on larger historical processes."[29]

For example, experiencing *Hanging In There* depicting the Northern Ireland peace process may evoke memories and embodied feelings not only of living through the Troubles but also of their connection to long historical conflicts and oppression between the English and Irish. The three illustrations in this chapter are part of an unbroken connection of dance conflict narratives through the centuries—from the Williamite wars in the 1690s embodied in the Siege of Ennis to the step dancing cultivated in the 1890s to keep alive Irish tradition and identity in the face of continuing colonization to the interpretive dance embodying the peace agreement ending the pain and misery of the more-recent Troubles. One dance may reinforce or reinterpret other events and certainly provides vital links in the continuity of the conflicts through the centuries.

Dance has expressly been used in Ireland to collect shared memories and share collective memories, to mediate the pain and loss associated with those memories, and to provide a space and place to reenact and share those memories across generations and centuries. People experience dance from different perspectives, particularly so as either observer or participant. Dance is personal and fills the entire body with meaning, although the dance itself may be set in a much broader social and political conflict. Dance has also been used to transform and create unity out of conflict stories—to reach across divides of pain and loss to embody the resistance and build a nation. And yes, dance is also fun. It is a great leveler and mediator of the painful memories of loss and conflict.

Ireland

Finding Meaning: Melting the Stone in Relational Disputes
GEOFFREY CORRY

> *"Too long a sacrifice*
> *Can make a stone of the heart.*
> *O when may it suffice?"*
> *Easter 1916*, William Butler Yeats

When the Irish poet and Nobelist W. B. Yeats penned the lines above, he was thinking of the sacrifice of the lives of the men who staged a rebellion at the Dublin GPO[1] in the Easter Rising of 1916 against the colonial power of Britain. The British saw the rebellion as a stab in the back at a time when their country was embroiled in the Somme trenches in France. Yeats felt within himself the pain and suffering and was troubled by the demand for blood sacrifice, whether for Irish national freedom or for Britain's war to end all wars. His cry of despair was about how many more lives would have to be sacrificed before someone shouted, "Enough is enough!"

In conflict-resolution theory, this moment is called the mutual hurting stalemate,[2] the point at which leaders lose faith in obtaining a military victory and begin to think seriously about initiating a peace process to bring the political violence to an end and begin negotiations. That is no easy task. It requires the protagonists to think the unthinkable: to make peace with their enemy[3] and to "re-imagine their relationships."[4] For Nelson Mandela and F. W. de Klerk, it took considerable courage and leadership to start a peace journey together in 1989–91. Mandela refused to allow the long African National Congress sacrifice to make a stone of his heart. De Klerk's strength was thinking strategically and searching for a way out of "a seemingly hopeless downward spiral of violence and repression."[5] For both men, the journey involved a huge shift in their mindsets, requiring each of them to dig deep into their own moral values and spiritual reserves.

A similar hurting stalemate happened in Northern Ireland in the mid-1980s when Sinn Fein and the British government realized they could not defeat each other militarily, and each side somehow had to find a political solution. In May 2011, the Northern Ireland peace process culminated in the visit of Queen Elizabeth II to the Republic of Ireland, an event unimaginable back in the 1980s. Yet it happened. People now look back on the Troubles and ask, "What was that about?" When you get to the milestones that are difficult to get to—and go beyond them— you often wonder, "Why did we not think of that before?"[6] Somehow, everyone has been able to move on and find themselves in a new political space and in a new relationship with each other.

So what is it that happens in protracted disputes and long-standing struggles that causes the stone, in effect, to melt; the parties to make the shift; and the people to summon up the heart to get emotional closure and move on from the past hurt? The 2010 Saas-Fee workshop threw new light on these questions by exploring how body movement and creative dance, without using words and often without music, can open up the flow of energy blocked inside. By switching off the head (cognitive processes), dance can work with the feelings around hurt and trauma to unblock them and offer the first stepping-stone on the journey of recovery.

When Hurt Hardens into Stone

When you look at a hard stone in your hand and feel its texture, it is easy to forget that it has a very long history. Way back in time, it came from a volcano of red-hot molten lava erupting out of the bowels of the earth and flowing down the side of a newly created mountain. As it began to cool and stopped moving, it solidified and transformed itself into permanent hard igneous rock. That may not be the end of the story. It may get transformed again in later generations into new marbled colors or folded into mountainous vistas arising from more hot moments under the earth's surface.

Similar to the volcano, our fight-or-flight responses to "hot" moments of conflict can result in the eruption of volatile emotions—anger, rage, aggression—that can do a lot of damage, creating victims and impacting bystanders. Conflict-resolution skills such as counting to ten, active listening, and assertiveness can help us in those hot moments to respond in a proactive problem-solving way rather than reacting to events with blame and counterattack, causing further escalation and emotional eruptions. But the aftershocks of these eruptions—stress, hurt, shame, fear, and even signs of post-traumatic stress disorder (PTSD) such as insomnia or lack of concentration—must also be addressed. If these aftershocks go unacknowledged or unprocessed, they can lead to a sense of helplessness and hopelessness; they can sit in silence in the emotional brain like a weighty stone under the surface. Parties are not always aware of how the aftershocks of the volcanic trigger event can affect their emotional brain—the body's trauma center—in so many ways, both physically and emotionally. Simply put, the body remembers. Recent advances in neuroscience teach us that working through trauma and processing the hurt in the aftermath of abuse or violence can play a huge part in the body recovering its full energy and strength. This is true whether you are a direct victim of the event, a witness to it as a second party, or the abuser or victimizer who has engaged in the harmful behavior.[7]

Interpersonal Hurt

When a frustrated manager says to Helen, a frontline worker who has made a mistake in the calculation of a financial transaction, "You're so stupid. You are really stupid!" it comes as a shock, especially when overheard by her female colleagues. It is like having the wind knocked out of her, leaving her breathless. The manager's verbal assault consists of only seven words said within a few seconds. The moment goes so fast that Helen says nothing at the time. She goes back to her desk not knowing what happened, let alone what to do. In the days and weeks that follow, she is not able to concentrate at work and finds she is not sleeping at night. She goes to her doctor, who gives her medication and a note allowing her to stay home from work. Four months later, the company's human resources manager calls in a mediator to see what can be done. The company supports Helen's return to work, but having been out on sick leave, she is unwilling to return without the matter being resolved. She is surprised that the event has affected her in such a deep way. Over the past few weeks, in talking with a counselor, she has slowly discovered how those seven words hurt her to the core and shook her self-esteem. Her body did not allow her to forget the incident. She needed time to process the hurt lodged inside the emotional brain and to understand the significance and meaning of the trigger event. Thus began her journey of recovery to take back control and regain her sense of dignity.

Helen's symptoms of headaches, sleeplessness, and difficulties in eating are those of simple PTSD. They are better described as a shock and a stress injury (PTSI)[8] that blocks the ability to live in the now than as a disorder. Of course, there may have been other things going on in Helen's life that turned this into an event that evoked fragility.

Intergroup Hurt

People living in divided societies like Northern Ireland who have experienced violent conflict for decades may not realize how they have been affected directly or vicariously. They hold the shame, injury, and trauma in themselves as well as unknowingly in the body politic. In the safer post-Troubles situation, with the help of community-based self-help groups, victims from across the religious/political divide are now able to talk about their experiences. From a transcript, we hear the voice of a former British Army soldier talking about his new awareness of the impact of the conflict on himself and his family:

> I suffer from PTSD and I had a crack up about five or six years ago. Up to that point I did social work. . . . and I talked to other people about trauma but I bottled mine up. I said I was in a car accident, I wanted to put it behind me. It was denial, denial, denial. I was seething with resentment . . . If the subject came up I never wanted to talk about it. But I kept getting flashbacks and had problems with booze. The doctor diagnosed me with combat stress, PTSD, 30 years later. The mental health side of it—it came out years later. The IRA and UVF people I meet—they are going through the same thing I went through, PTSD. It has the same effect on their families. I was pushing my wife away, biting the head off my son . . . That's the ripple effect of conflict.[9]

If the trauma is not addressed and transformed, it can get transferred within the body and passed on to the next generation "to produce a range of social and psychological pathologies, such as self-harm, suicide, anti-social behavior, anomie and inter-personal violence."[10]

One of the big lessons of the Troubles was how stones of hurt, resentment, and revenge held in the emotional brain and the body politic on each side created a climate of dehumanization[11] and became the basis for the struggle against injustice. Strong, authoritarian religious and political leaders emerged to protect communities from the perceived threat on the other side. Through invoking fear, they turned their opponents into the demonized other, an enemy to be overcome, thereby distancing them and turning them into a legitimate target.

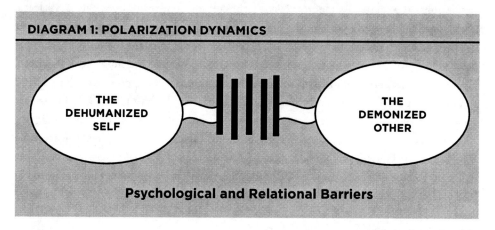

DIAGRAM 1: POLARIZATION DYNAMICS

THE
DEHUMANIZED
SELF

THE
DEMONIZED
OTHER

Psychological and Relational Barriers

An incisive reflection was made by the late Israeli psychoanalyst Rafael Moses: "Each group loses its own humanity in dehumanizing the other for otherwise it could not act so savagely toward other human beings."[12] From his own experience under the apartheid system, Mandela found that "oppression dehumanizes the oppressor as it hurts the oppressed."[13] Both sides experience dehumanization. One side reclaiming its loss of dignity and humanity frees the other to regain its self-respect. This is a relational process predicated on dialogue and interactive storytelling.

Judith Herman's groundbreaking book *Trauma and Recovery*, about working with survivors of post-traumatic stress disorder, suggests that shared stories can bring about healing. In retelling a story, not ruminating over it, the victim gains more control because the story is different each time it is told.[14] New bits about what happened are recovered from memory, or new nuances are understood. Through storytelling, each party gains the capacity to bring to the surface the hurt lodged in the emotional brain, leading to its eventual cognitive reframing. Along the way, the emotional and relational obstacles that need to be overcome are identified, such as disgust/revulsion, hatred, suspicion, and fear of the other. The diagram below depicts the three phases of the storytelling journey, extending Herman's work into not just emotional connection with others but face-to-face interactive dialogue with the other. Each side is supported to make the shift to take on the other's story and to see the other's part in the bigger picture or mosaic of what happened.

I have witnessed victims and ex-combatants on all sides of the Northern Ireland conflict take extraordinary journeys of survival in various storytelling and dialogue workshops at the Glencree Center for Reconciliation outside Dublin.[15] Many dehumanized individuals came to terms with what had happened and developed their inner strength to engage with those whom they once knew as the demonized other. It can often be a painful encounter with truth, but also a liberating experience, as the stone melts through the reckoning with each other.[16]

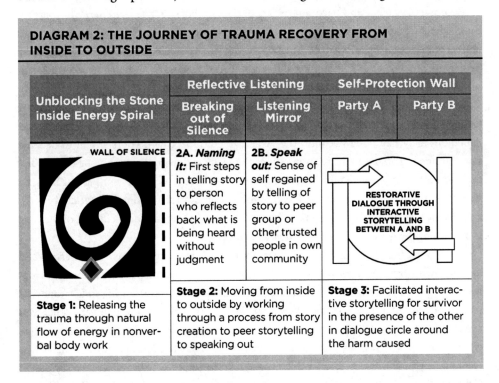

DIAGRAM 2: THE JOURNEY OF TRAUMA RECOVERY FROM INSIDE TO OUTSIDE

Unblocking the Stone inside Energy Spiral	Reflective Listening		Self-Protection Wall	
	Breaking out of Silence	Listening Mirror	Party A	Party B
WALL OF SILENCE	**2A. *Naming it:*** First steps in telling story to person who reflects back what is being heard without judgment	**2B. *Speak out:*** Sense of self regained by telling of story to peer group or other trusted people in own community	**RESTORATIVE DIALOGUE THROUGH INTERACTIVE STORYTELLING BETWEEN A AND B**	
Stage 1: Releasing the trauma through natural flow of energy in nonverbal body work	**Stage 2:** Moving from inside to outside by working through a process from story creation to peer storytelling to speaking out		**Stage 3:** Facilitated interactive storytelling for survivor in the presence of the other in dialogue circle around the harm caused	

Not everyone is able to start the journey or to complete each stage. The diagram suggests the journey is a sequential step-by-step process, but in reality it is rarely as smooth as that. There is bound to be regression backward to a previous stage or circular recycling of angst within a stage. No pressure should be placed on the sojourners; the next stage of the process is there only if they feel ready for it. For some, completing stage 1 is sufficient and in itself a major achievement to restore a sense of their own harmony. For others, deepening their self-understanding throughout stage 2 is enough to enable them to feel free of the trigger event's grip. But there are some who want answers to the difficult questions going around in their minds or to confront the abuser about the harm that was caused. They want the other to hear their truth face-to-face and to take responsibility for what happened.

Stage 1: Working with Silence inside the Dehumanized Self

In 1984, two days after her father, Sir Anthony Berry, was killed by a bomb planted by the IRA in the Brighton Grand Hotel, Jo Berry found herself in St. James Church off Piccadilly Square in London with a huge need to pray that she "would have the strength not to become bitter and angry and that out of the appalling tragedy, some peace would come." It was like her whole world had gone crazy, and she needed to be in a sacred, safe place. For four years she went back periodically to the church to play the grand piano for hours, just allowing what she felt inside to flow through the music: "The piano was a way of expressing all sorts of feelings." Learning to play that piano at school turned out to be her salvation.[17]

Carrying the silence and becoming aware of the numbness inside both play a big part for those who are grappling with what has happened to them. The silence comes from not being able to put the feelings into words. Most likely, the wound is just too painful and raw. These people are not able to talk about it and need the emotional wall of silence to protect themselves from re-experiencing the trauma or to avoid any new hurt.

Jo found music to be the best nonverbal medium, but healing can equally be achieved through dance, art therapy, or finding sacred space while walking in the woods or by the sea. An emotionally safe place becomes the vehicle to reconnect with yourself and to become mindful once again, moment to moment, of the feelings flowing through your body.[18] The body cannot be bypassed. Peter Levine calls this process embodiment "gaining, through the vehicle of awareness, the capacity to feel the ambient physical sensations of unfettered energy and aliveness as they pulse through our bodies."[19] Later, in stage 2, comes the act of "naming it" by finding the words to express what you are feeling.

In the postconflict situation of Northern Ireland, focus groups of victims/survivors and ex-combatants have given us an insight into the instinct of keeping the past secret for fear of becoming upset. A family member of a former British soldier revealed the awkwardness of protecting himself in ordinary casual conversations when meeting new people: "When you start a new job or something, people ask, so do you have any brothers or sisters? I never know what to say. Do you say, yes just 3 sisters, or do you say yes I did have a brother too but he was killed by an IRA bomb. It will start me again. Sometimes I'm brave enough to say that."[20] Others deliberately did not bring up the Troubles in conversation: "I would say I deliberately never talked about it; not consciously, but in my actions and deeds I avoided talking about it. . . . people in my local pub didn't know until Remembrance Sunday. I said about not forgetting the soldiers who were killed in Northern Ireland. They didn't know."[21]

Silence is part of the effort to normalize the situation. One women's group participant said, "I don't like to talk about it—it is the past. You have to get over it."[22] However, by actively avoiding talk and bottling things up, the silence maintains and strengthens confusion and fear. Is this fear of the other, fear of the truth, or fear of self? Silence also plays a crucial role in passing trauma and shock from one generation to the next.[23]

Repression of Feelings

When people over a period of time are bullied, abused, and dehumanized by the other, they may not be aware of the extent to which they become less than human and feel powerless to do anything about it. Consequently, people often have difficulty being in the present moment and find that prior events still control their behavior, making them prisoners of the past. What gets repressed then becomes, in Dan Bar-On's words, "undiscussable and indescribable."[24]

Repression buries hurtful and threatening events in the unconscious memory so people can avoid having to grapple with the terrible feelings arising from the trauma. The painful memories lie unprocessed in the unconscious. Freud taught us that the repressed material or unprocessed traumas threaten to erupt in bodily symptoms.[25] This happens in two ways: through individual illness, such as cancer or depression, or through projecting the unresolved psychic struggle onto others through racist, misogynistic, homophobic, or other types of hurtful behavior, with acute personal, social, and collective consequences. We need to constantly remind ourselves of the physical and emotional price that our bodies pay for continued conflict.[26]

According to Bar-On, the lesson is to not continue repressing and silencing past events. We have to work with the silenced facts that are inside.[27] Herman reminds us that traumatic memory is wordless and static.[28] It is preverbal and exists as feelings. So we must acknowledge that feelings are in fact emotional realities and find new ways to work with the undiscussable and the indescribable to dissolve the emotional wall of silence.

Shift to Body-Based Work

Taking into account the new understandings from neuroscience, the psychiatrist David Servan-Schreiber believes that we must move beyond a reliance on the cognitive psychoanalysis—talk therapies—developed by Freud as well as move away from the overuse of medication, such as the antidepressants favored by Western medicine.[29] He wants us to give much greater consideration to a holistic approach—body therapies—based on Eastern medicine, which emphasizes the harmony of body, mind, spirit, and emotion when all come together to support healing and trauma recovery. He helps us understand the different roles played by the higher cognitive brain of the neocortex, which is the center of language and thought, and the lower emotional brain of the limbic system, which governs psychological well-being and most of the body's physiology. We now know that the emotional brain—the older, animal part of the brain located at the top of the spinal cord—holds repressed trauma.

This older brain is responsible for the instinctive fight-or-flight reaction when the brain perceives danger or threat; the cognitive brain remains "off-line." Servan-Schreiber believes we have to find ways "to 'reprogramme' the emotional brain so that it adapts to the present instead of continuing to react to past experiences."[30] He is convinced we need "to use methods that act via the *body* and directly influence the emotional brain rather than use approaches that depend entirely on language and reason, to which the emotional brain is not receptive."[31] Because the emotional brain contains natural mechanisms for self-healing—effectively its own instinct to heal—we need to elicit these innate abilities through balance and well-being to support self-healing in the body. Servan-Schreiber wants to divert from cognitive talk and instead use natural treatments such as nutrition, acupuncture, regular exercise, and emotional communication.

One group that respects the inherent instinct or wisdom of the body to return to balance and wholeness is Capacitar, a popular education approach to heal trauma and empower wellness. Patricia Cane, Capacitar's founder, has devised simple circle dance and body movement activities that combine personal healing and peace building as two sides of the same coin rather than using an individual therapeutic method. Capacitar places in people's hands simple body-based skills they can use to release stress, manage emotions, and live with balance amid conflict situations. Regular use of tai chi, acupressure, and breath work helps to alleviate traumatic stress symptoms. Cane believes that "healing occurs through the release of undischarged energy as well as through a strengthening of the natural flow of energy. . . . When energy is flowing freely and without obstruction through the channels and energy centers of the body, the person experiences good health, emotional balance, mental clarity, and overall wellbeing." Wellness is seen as a process. It is a developing awareness that there is no end point but that health and happiness are possible in each moment, here and now.[32]

Implications for Mediators

Through dance and neuromuscular movement, victims of conflict and workplace bullying can be supported to explore in nonverbal ways the pain and hurt locked inside the emotional brain. By releasing feelings and going with the natural flow to see where it might lead them, people prepare the body for the next step of putting into words what they are feeling. It would be productive for mediators in a basic training course to have an evening session to explore emotion through dance and movement, with or without the support of music.

Stage 2: Finding Voice and Humanizing the Self

For Jo Berry, after several years of holding and working with the pain of losing her father, she began to realize that she could transform her pain by using it in a positive way to build peace. Having lost her father through violence, she would not wish it on anyone else. She started a journey to understand why people resort to violence and traveled to Ireland to meet people caught up in the political struggle, mainly on the Republican side. Much later, she expressed this wish: "If only we could listen to people before they use violence."[33]

Weingarten strongly asserts, "The antidote to silence is the creation of story."[34] She believes the past must be worked through before new energy can be released and the self can be humanized: "People who fail adequately to mourn their losses and to work through the pain of their suffering are more likely to repeat their past." Bar-On used his storytelling work with children of Nazi leaders in Germany's Third Reich to explore the difficult first step in the process of searching for and finding the words by which feelings become facts.[35] Telling your story initially helps to form the feelings into thoughts. As you tell your story a second and third time, you can gradually recall the sequence of events. With the emergence of the bigger picture comes the ability to process the traumatic event in terms of new meaning. Finally you begin to come to terms with what happened in the past.[36] There may well be a gender issue here since women often have more emotional fluency than men when it comes to self-disclosure and expressing feelings.

Restorative justice facilitators have developed three very simple but profound questions to support the dehumanized person in this naming process:

1. What happened?
2. What were you feeling at the time?
3. Looking back at it with the distance of time, how do you see it now?

People need the time to describe and process what has happened to them. This involves going through the detailed facts of the incidents(s) and recovering from memory those things regarding past trauma that have remained unprocessed and repressed. It is equally important for them to discharge the emotions of fear, shock, and horror that accompanied the experience. When every detail has been worked through, probably a couple of times, listeners can help people make sense of what they have been through in terms of loss, helplessness, anger, and humiliation. As with Jo Berry, the person may want to discover why the other did a certain act and to understand the human meaning embedded in the conflict. It is important to remember that a person may be under social pressures from a work group to not tell the story or from a hostile society to maintain social silence.

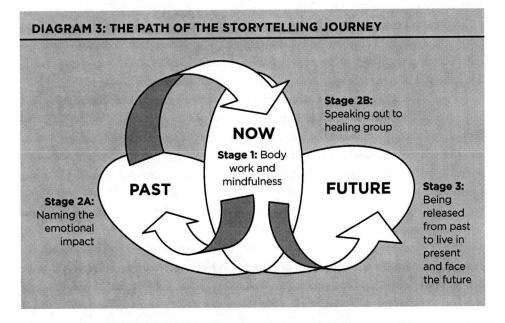

DIAGRAM 3: THE PATH OF THE STORYTELLING JOURNEY

NOW

Stage 1: Body work and mindfulness

PAST

FUTURE

Stage 2B: Speaking out to healing group

Stage 2A: Naming the emotional impact

Stage 3: Being released from past to live in present and face the future

Storytelling brings disputants into the now and supports them to talk at their own pace about what they recall from their past memories. It is a highly subjective process of self-acknowledgment. It is through the actual telling of the story that the victim eventually gets to the meaning of it. The more a person tells the story to a supportive listener, the clearer the meaning becomes. Diagram 3 shows the path of the journey through three time zones while the body and the brain hold all three in tension with one another.[37] For the storyteller, there are choices to be made about what gets expressed:

- What do you choose to talk about in detail? . . . because it is important to you or emotionally difficult?
- What do you find the need to talk about at length? . . . because perhaps you have not yet figured it out and you need to go around it a few times?
- What bits do you choose to omit intentionally? . . . or unintentionally, thereby becoming the "untold story"? Is there another story within the story?
- Which piece do you decide to skip over? . . . because perhaps you have not yet found the words for it?

Story-Listening Mirror

The story listener is anyone who is entrusted to hold up the mirror and take on the discipline of being a reflective, empathic listener: to suspend judgment, support the emergence of the story from inside out, and not add anything to the story. The listener can be a friend, a fellow victim who acts in a peer role, or a trained counselor who may be more able to understand the layers of the repressed trauma.

The metaphor of a mirror highlights a number of aspects of the journey of recovery. First, the listener turns the emotional wall of silence in the victim's mind into a mirror so the dehumanized self can actually hear his or her own feelings and thoughts and be accepting of them. The listener is not a sponge who soaks up the feelings but reflects them back.

Second, facilitators create and maintain a safe emotional space for the sojourners so that they can find their voice and put into words what they have experienced. Behind the silenced facts, their suffering will need to be heard and acknowledged. Bar-On points out that "words are relatively poor transmitters of feelings."[38] Watching the visible nonverbal facts expressed in the body language becomes a skill: the tone of voice, facial expression, gestures, body postures, eye contact, social distance. By following bodily movements, facilitators get clues beyond the verbal. Because the stories are heard in relationship, tellers find themselves mirrored by the listeners, receiving validation and support.

Third, Weingarten draws attention to the skill of holding the hope for the sojourner, because hope makes life purposeful and meaningful. When a storyteller feels helpless, it is the listener's task to hold the hope until such time as the teller can hold it again. This is a "reasonable hope" that retains optimism while being careful not to set up unrealistic expectations or being unable to also recognize feelings of despair; this kind of hope discerns "what is within reach more than what may be desired but unattainable . . . Reasonable hope softens the polarity between hope and despair, hope and hopelessness."[39]

Fourth, for the story listener, there is the question of what might be missing in the story. Bar-On found the storyteller filtered out parts of the story. He distinguished between "directed filtering," such as when a grandparent refrains from describing what happened in the Holocaust, and "subconscious filtering," such as when the victim does not talk about it perhaps because the victim is not asked about it. Bar-On found there was a tension for the storyteller between two things: on the one hand, wanting to crystallize exactly what had happened yet wanting to hold on to the memory of it; on the other hand, the need to put the experience out of one's mind to be able to move on.

In these four tasks, the facilitator plays a bridging role between the two sundered brains. The agitated emotional brain is dominated by binaries—"us versus them" distinctions and black-and-white thinking—whereas the province of the cortex/cognitive brain is more about sorting out the shades of gray. By reflecting back the trauma story, the facilitator is therefore doing the work of the cognitive brain, externalizing the emotional content and enabling the three essential processing tasks:

- to put emotional experiences in a verbal and coherent narrative form
- to dampen inappropriate fear responses
- to connect current events with the sojourner's autobiography[40]

The Speak Out

"All the things that we do not dare or cannot talk about must not stay unsaid because they will destroy our soul." Groups of twenty to thirty victims of the Bosnian War (1992–96) have mobilized their own "people support" for telling their story in self-help psychosocial workshops held in a safe space in the mountains of northern Bosnia.[41] Similar to the Glencree workshops, they enable victims to break out of isolation behind the wall of silence to find a new sense of community with one another in the listening circle. Group members confirmed that the "whole pain does not come out at once." Melting and dissolving the hurt—not dissipating it—can be a slow process. It takes many years to become comfortable with the identity of being a survivor, talking about that experience to others.

There comes a point when survivors are ready and want to speak out to tell their story to others in front of a camera or to people in their own community (see stage 2B in diagram 2). Giving their testimony makes them stronger inside. The Bosnian group encouraged each survivor to return to his or her community and take on a leadership role. This supports what Herman found: "[T]he survivor has regained some capacity for appropriate trust . . . and is now ready to risk deepening her relationships"[42] with family, friends, and community.

Implications for Mediators

In conclusion, too much of the discussion in mediation has focused on what happens in the mediation room and not on all the preparatory work that needs to take place in enabling parties to come into that space. This is normally referred to as the premediation phase, or "getting parties to the table." First, the recent growth of conflict coaching[43] in workplace disputes has brought the spotlight back on how disputants gain a better understanding of their own trigger points and "hot buttons" before engaging in negotiation. They prepare for those difficult conversations by envisaging their own behavioral reactions and seeing how they can respond in a more positive way to tension-filled matters.

Second, the storytelling approach does not avoid the past by not talking about it. John Haynes was an early pioneer in family mediation in the 1980s and showed how to work face-to-face in the room jointly with disputants rather than going into a caucus. He also taught mediators not to go back into the past but to stay in the cognitive present[44] and ignore or interrupt the emotional past by asking a future-focused question to get the parties to think about their situation as opposed to how they felt about it. This works when you are at the problem-solving stage of the mediation process and up against time constraints. However, when dealing with hurt and fear, it is important to stay with the three restorative questions to help parties process what happened. It does, of course, involve more time, which becomes a cost factor.

Third, is "storytelling" the right way to describe this work? There is a danger that it becomes a jargon word used by practitioners. At times I have urged, "Tell me your story!" and gotten feedback as if to say, "My story is not some kind of fiction! It is a real-life experience that has to be acknowledged!"

Stage 3: [Re]humanizing with the Other

When Patrick Magee was released from prison under the terms of the Good Friday Agreement in 2000, Jo Berry was left with a dilemma. "You don't go to talk to the person who has killed your father! You don't sit and talk to him!" What would her extended family think? They might see it as betrayal and never speak to her again. She discussed the matter with people who had known her father, and gradually she realized that she had no choice. "If I do not do this then I feel I choose to stay a victim."[45] As she faced the thought of meeting Pat, feelings of elation came with the realization that there was a whole new journey starting. Here are her own reflections six years later:

> I wanted to meet Pat, to hear his story and see him as a real human being. At our first meeting I was terrified but as soon as we met we talked with an extraordinary intensity. I shared a lot about my father, while Pat told me some of his story. . . . It has been challenging and inspiring and I have learnt much about the roots of violence and how to communicate without blaming. Over the past six years of getting to know Pat, I feel I've been recovering some of the humanity I lost when that bomb went off. Perhaps more than anything I've realized that no matter which side of the conflict you're on, had we all lived each other's lives, we could all have done what the other did. I still have feelings that are painful. I still get angry but I have learnt that these feelings can be transformed into passion for change. My passion for change starts with me wanting to stop the cycle of violence and revenge in me and has grown into helping create a world in which violence is not seen as a viable way of resolving conflict. . . . For me, the question is about whether I can let go of my need to blame, and open my heart enough to hear Pat's story and understand his motivations. The truth is that, sometimes I can and sometimes I can't and this choice is always there.[46]

In 2009, on the twenty-fifth anniversary of the bombing, Pat and Jo sat together in the House of Commons in London at an unprecedented meeting to speak of their journey. Pat came under pressure to show his repentance and replied to the members of Parliament:

"I don't understand repentance. I think it has a religious meaning . . . but I can regret . . . I don't think even a room full of people can agree on a meaning of that word [repentance] . . . I have never asked for forgiveness. Why should I? Meeting Jo was never about forgiveness. It was always about trying to explain and trying to understand the hurt we have caused . . . I did what I did with full conscience. I did what I felt needed to be done. Why do I need to ask forgiveness for that? But I can feel regret."[47]

He explained that he had joined the IRA as a 21-year-old and insisted to the surprised gathering that he had been a pacifist. However, all options became closed, and that was why he turned to violence: "I wondered was I even up to the task. I did a lot of soul searching about that. I was not a violent person. I had to convince myself that I could kill . . . I'm sorry that I killed Jo's father . . . I wish there had been another way . . . If there were other options open, I would have jumped at them."

For Pat to engage with Jo in the first place and then to appear so publicly with her in Westminster took considerable courage, because he could be accused of betraying his former comrades in arms. He wanted to do it for himself; he felt obliged to speak about what he had done: "There's a political obligation . . . to try and undo harm."[48] The fact that Jo and Pat continue to meet and appear on public platforms can be very unnerving for other victims and ex-combatants. The two of them were ready to meet after having had many years on their own to think about it. However, for others it is a bridge too far and puts huge moral pressure on them. Of course, there are huge risks in engaging fully and investing time in the dialogue, because there are no guarantees that it will work. In her own journey, Brene Brown stumbled on her "excruciating vulnerability" when she invested in the relationship and found that the uncertain was made certain. For full interactive dialogue, somehow heart-to-heart moments must be present. In fact, she discovered that "whole heart" means "courage," derived from the French word *coeur*, meaning "heart."[49]

The Double Wall

Dan Bar-On created the concept of the double wall to explain the emotional and relational obstacles that have to be overcome to engage the other in any journey out of dehumanization.[50] The wall represents psychosocial impediments or barriers to discourse. He believes that each side constructs an emotional wall of self-protection for different reasons. The dehumanized person (Party A), who has already made the journey out of the zone of silence in stage 1, now faces the challenge to move beyond the zone of safety among friends. Having lost the sense of self in the trauma and regained it through the storytelling, Party A has slowly built the capacity to identify and work with the other.

The demonized other (Party B) senses the wall of the victim and builds one to be insulated from accepting responsibility for what has been done. The existence of the two walls sends both parties the message that certain subjects must not be discussed, because they are not yet ready to talk about them. The self-protection wall keeps them both at a distance. When one side is willing to open up a chink in the emotional wall or tries to open an emotional window in its wall on the relationship, there stands the wall of the other side.

Interactive Storytelling

So how do you get there? What are the steps for melting the stone and creating the humanizing moment? Coming from a southern Irish relational culture where the art of telling your story—called the *scéil* in the Irish language—is part of everyday life in the family, in the shop, at work, and in the pub, it just struck me as making eminent sense that people in conflict need to be able to tell their story about what happened. The story is a social construct of what was experienced, perceived, and felt. It probably is not the whole truth, but embedded in it are the grains of truth waiting to be elicited.

Known for their tradition of talking circles, Native Americans have a saying: "You talk and talk until the talk begins." Somewhere in this ancient wisdom is the notion of three layers of dialogue that start out as parallel talking and listening. As the talking stick goes around the circle and everyone has a turn to speak, a talking process builds. It is only when you get to the third layer—after the hot storming and venting of emotion—that the true engagement begins and the breakthrough in human vulnerability allows the real talk to happen and the heart to soften. This creates the platform in the fourth layer for humanization to emerge.

Diagram 4 attempts to visualize the face-to-face journey through the layers of the story and the interactive back-and-forth taking of turns. The facilitator/mediator holds the hope and balances the power.

Layer 1

At the outset of the facilitated dialogue, mediators hear the parties' first thoughts on what is important for them or what is on the surface, often described as the presenting issues. A lot of story is packed into those first few minutes. It can come fast and furious as parties want to get things off their chest. The story might be positional, containing demands and exaggerated facts. If it is a "saturated story" of blame, accusations, and projections against the other as named by narrative mediation,[51] then facilitators need to be ready to hold the dripping sponge and let the water pour out at the same time they have a go at dissolving the toxicity. They also work with the story to discern what needs are being met through it being presented in such a saturated form. It could be a rehearsed and polished story where feelings, issues, and assumptions are compacted together in sequence. On the other hand, the story may be very authentic and spoken from the heart, with a lot of thought and reflection. Or it might just be very polite, and the party is holding back on saying it all straight-out.

Layer 2

Layer 1 usually gives way to layer 2 after perhaps two to three turns of a few minutes each. Here begins the most important phase of storytelling, where both parties are fully and accurately *heard, understood, acknowledged, and validated* to each one's satisfaction in the presence of the other. Throughout, the mediator is listening with the whole body, particularly with the eyes, following the body movements of the parties, because they give clues in advance of the verbal.

DIAGRAM 4: FOUR LAYERS OF MELTING THE STONE

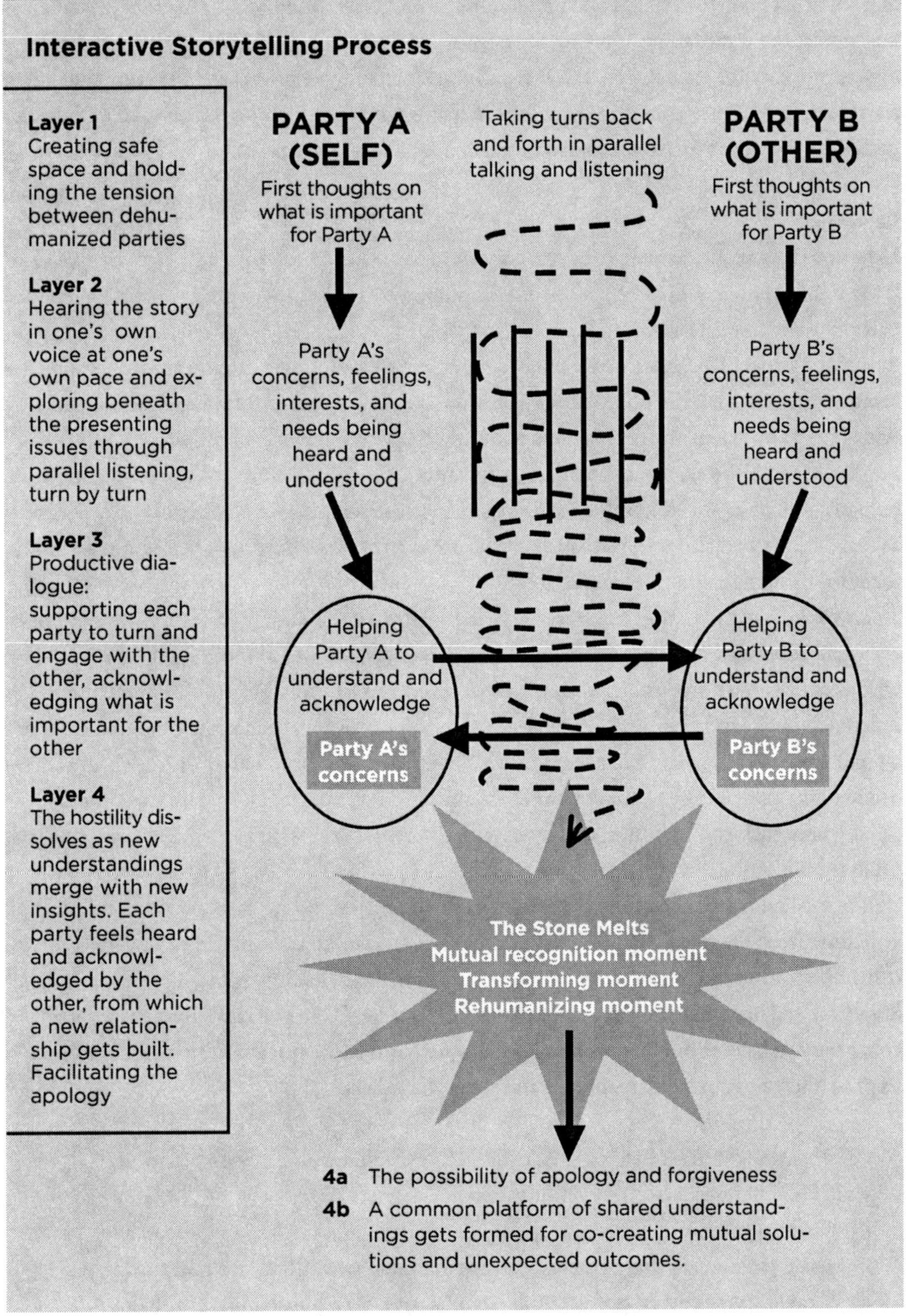

Interactive Storytelling Process

Layer 1
Creating safe space and holding the tension between dehumanized parties

Layer 2
Hearing the story in one's own voice at one's own pace and exploring beneath the presenting issues through parallel listening, turn by turn

Layer 3
Productive dialogue: supporting each party to turn and engage with the other, acknowledging what is important for the other

Layer 4
The hostility dissolves as new understandings merge with new insights. Each party feels heard and acknowledged by the other, from which a new relationship gets built. Facilitating the apology

PARTY A (SELF)
First thoughts on what is important for Party A

Taking turns back and forth in parallel talking and listening

PARTY B (OTHER)
First thoughts on what is important for Party B

Party A's concerns, feelings, interests, and needs being heard and understood

Party B's concerns, feelings, interests, and needs being heard and understood

Helping Party A to understand and acknowledge

Party A's concerns

Helping Party B to understand and acknowledge

Party B's concerns

The Stone Melts
Mutual recognition moment
Transforming moment
Rehumanizing moment

4a The possibility of apology and forgiveness

4b A common platform of shared understandings gets formed for co-creating mutual solutions and unexpected outcomes.

For Parties A and B, which comes first: to understand the other or to be understood? Because of the many barriers of suspicion and assumptions, it is much harder for Party A, for example, to reach out emotionally to understand Party B before Party A has been understood—and vice versa. The point at which one party is ready to give recognition to the other is when that party has been fully heard and understood, either by the mediator or the other. Mediators must resist the temptation of trying to get one party to understand the other's point of view too early in the storytelling process. Instead, parties need to be given the opportunity to get to the issues that are important to them and to name how they see them. It is often difficult for parties to put words on things and to be exact about what they mean.

Layer 3

How does a facilitator know when the parties are ready to move from layer 2 to layer 3? This is the point when the crossover takes place, and one party reaches out to the other; when one party is ready to make a shift in perspective by being able to take on or consider the perspective of the other. Mediators often see it coming when one party actually shifts in his or her seat and turns to hear the other, asks a question, or offers a concession. Weingarten identifies this as the point when one party is able to listen carefully to the other without defensiveness.[52] For Bush and Folger, "the hallmark of a recognition shift is *letting go*—however briefly or partially—of one's focus on self and becoming interested in the perspective of the other party as such, concerned about the situation of the other as a fellow human being, not as an instrument for fulfilling one's own needs."[53]

Layer 3 gives the parties the possibility to work with the difficult questions they want to ask each other that have been going around in their minds for some time. Will the person who asks the question be able to listen respectfully and to really hear the answer? This is the difference between layer 1, where the question is being used to get at the other and to score a point, and layer 3, where the pace is much slower, perhaps punctuated with silence, and the listener takes some time to think before attempting to respond. The parties have reached the point where each can be honest and open with the other. Fear is dissolving and respect for the other is building.

The facilitator will need to support each party in understanding what the other is saying by switching from parallel listening (party to mediator) to interactive listening (party to party). It may help to use language with physical cues, such as: "Paul, I would like you to turn to Susan and tell her what you have just told me." Or maybe: "Can you show Susan the particular concerns you have about this proposal?" Here are some more questions that are useful at this stage to elicit and consolidate understanding of the other:

- What do you think Paul does not yet fully understand about your situation?
- Which bit does Susan not yet fully appreciate?
- What do you now understand about the incident that you did not appreciate before?
- Susan, is there anything you want to ask Paul that you still have a question about?
- What is it that you do not yet understand about what Susan said/did?

There is a powerful sequential link between three elements arising out of these interactions: new information can lead to new understandings by one party about the other, which in turn can lead to new shared insights. When this process also becomes circular, one building on the other within a positive integrating spiral of self-understanding and mutual respect, these elements provide the key to unlocking the door in the wall on each side.[54] New information contributes to getting behind hidden intentions, expectations, and assumptions. New understandings arise when the story of the other reveals the context and thinking of that party's situation and helps to reframe both perspectives. From the dialogue, new insights give new and deeper meaning, opening the door to a humanizing and breakthrough experience.

Layer 4

Insights have been called "aha" moments or eureka moments—when the light bulb switches on for people. Melchin and Picard believe that "insights, once achieved, reshape the way we experience the sensory data the next time around."[55] It is a profoundly experiential moment that changes feelings and thought. *Affective insights* change feelings about the other when parties hear what matters to them in ways they were unable to before. *Cognitive insights* are moments of discovery and clarity following periods of confusion, allowing a party to accept the necessity for change.

Adam Curle, a Quaker mediator, told me back in 1981 that "reconciliation involves the building of a new relationship of understanding through an act of love, compassion, or restitution."[56] Since then, my understanding of the rehumanization process has deepened in three ways: first, it must be worked out relationally through each party opening up to the other and accepting the other within them; second, it arises from new understandings generated by interaction between the parties; and third, it involves something freely given by the other, such as a reassurance, an apology, or something tangible.

The moment of rehumanization is made possible through a complex and often lengthy process, yet it appears as a sort of magic. It enables the melting of the stone, which in turn allows people to reach out to one another. The stone may not melt all in one go but might instead dissolve over a period of time.

The Journey Never Ends

In conclusion, the metaphor of the stone has helped us understand that the hurt and trauma caused by dehumanization in intergroup conflict and workplace relational disputes cannot be resolved without hearing and acknowledging the inside pain and suffering. The storytelling process, working its way through three stages, allows the warm, supportive water to build up around the solitary stone to eventually melt the frozen position. It works in a different way from interest-based resolution by putting in place a listening process drawing on affective and cognitive empathy by the facilitator as story listener. When the dehumanized person feels sufficiently safe to come into the room with the other and then feels heard, acknowledged, and understood, it enables a shift to take place inside the person's perspective. The pain dissolves within and frees that individual to let go of the burdens of the past and live in the present. Each party frees the other. Then they are both able to use their energy to reshape their chosen future.

Once started, the journey never really ends because the journey itself opens up new destinations. However, the new journey is qualitatively different. People are personally and collectively changed by the storytelling process; they rediscover themselves, reimagine themselves, and redefine their place in society. And in the process, the humanizing dialogue interrupts the trauma from being passed on to the next generation.

Cambodia and Liberia

Finding New Futures: Dancing Home

TONI SHAPIRO-PHIM

> *"I always long to go back to Liberia where I can dance with the women,*
> *because that's where the actual work takes place."*
> Leymah Gbowee, during her acceptance speech for the Adela Dwyer-St. Thomas of
> Villanova Peace Award, Villanova University, Pennsylvania, September 15, 2011.
> The following month Ms. Gbowee was honored with the Nobel Peace Prize.

> *"You don't know what it's like not to be able to go home—to have to live on **their** land . . . The*
> *international agencies give us food, but we have two stomachs: they only feed our lower one.*
> *The other nourishes the soul, connecting us with our home. We feed that one with dance."*
> Meas Van Roeun, director of the fine arts service of Site 2 (Cambodian)
> displaced persons camp in Thailand, 1989.

Geographical displacement ruptures connections on numerous levels; community, family, nation, livelihood, a shared past, hopes for the future, and a whole way of life may all be in tatters. Migration during war adds violence and chaos to the mix, compounding loss with danger. In this chapter, I relate stories of how dance among Cambodians and Liberians in refugee camps was vital in people's search for a way to make a return home possible, both symbolically and practically. Dance functioned, in these cases, to re-create fundamental connections; it helped foster alternatives to the horror, trauma, and hopelessness experienced by victims of political scheming and military aggression. Dance was powerful enough to create an environment in which hope for positive change could be born and sustained.

Aesthetic, Political, Social, and Spiritual Resonance of Dance

In 2010, an envoy, reportedly from the office of Bun Rany Hun Sen, president of the Cambodian Red Cross and wife of Cambodia's prime minister, contacted the renowned Thai dancer and choreographer Pichet Klunchun about a possible collaboration between the two countries' dancers as a way of easing tensions around competing claims to an ancient temple that straddles their respective borders. "Artists can talk to one another," explains Pichet. "The Thai and Cambodian prime ministers don't get along. But through the dance we can get along."[1]

In 2008, the eleventh-century Temple of Preah Vihear had been inscribed on UNESCO's World Heritage List. UNESCO describes the temple as "unique" and "an outstanding masterpiece of Khmer [Cambodian] architecture, in terms of plan, decoration and relationship to the spectacular landscape environment."[2] Dedicated to the Hindu deity Shiva, the temple was built as part of the Khmer Empire, which covered much of what is now the countries of Cambodia and Thailand, and even parts of Vietnam and Laos. The empire lasted from about the ninth to the fourteenth century. Thailand and Cambodia long disputed ownership of the temple on their mutual mountainous border, and in 1962 the International Court of Justice had awarded Preah Vihear to Cambodia. But when Cambodia applied for recognition of the temple as a World Heritage Site in the early twenty-first century, the embers of disagreement reignited. Since then, Thai and Cambodian soldiers and civilians have died in sporadic fighting.

Unfortunately, the suggested dance collaboration never took place. Hostilities have since erupted anew, with each side claiming the other has instigated the fighting; each country's nationalist politics help keep possession of the sacred site a prominent emotional issue. Citizens of Thailand and Cambodia want their flag flying above land surrounding the temple that they claim is rightfully theirs.[3] Bun Rany Hun Sen's initiative for an artistic exchange or collaboration arose from a belief that dance matters: its spiritual, aesthetic, somatic, and political potency is believed by Khmer people to make a difference for individuals, communities, and even nations. In this chapter, I explore dance as a means through which to approach a study of peace-seeking processes as played out among and by those who value its strength and meaning. I will examine work that prioritizes dance in the midst of destruction and detail experiences of its transformative capacity.

Movement is both a repository and a form of cultural knowledge that encompasses histories and belief systems. The polyvalent meaning making in and through dance occurs kinesthetically, intellectually, visually, emotionally, and (for some) spiritually within temporal, spatial, and societal/cultural contexts. The potency of dance has also been clear to colonizers and other oppressors, some of whom have historically worked toward its destruction as a tool to further their goals. For example, in the nineteenth century the Canadian and U.S. federal governments felt so threatened by indigenous dance practices that they banned them across North America. As the dance scholar Jacqueline Shea Murphy writes:

> Dance practices and gatherings threatened assimilation policies based on classroom education and literacy, as they affirmed the importance of history told not in writing or even in words, but rather bodily. Praying through bodily movement and ritual practice rather than through sitting, reading, and believing threatened colonizers' notions of how spirituality is manifested . . . In short, the federal governments of North America sensed and feared the importance of Indian dance as a social, political, and ideological agent, and the threats it posed.[4]

In some cases, people in positions of political authority have stipulated how, where, and when to dance, in an attempt to co-opt the power and meaning-making impact of such activity. Following the orders of President Mobutu Sese Seko (1965–1997), people in Zaire (now the Democratic Republic of the Congo) were forced on a daily basis to participate in public dance events honoring the president, his family and ancestral home, or particular political initiatives. Dance, which has far-reaching social, cultural, and spiritual force for many ethnic groups in Zaire, became a tool of nationalist ideology and, in some instances, humiliation. People who didn't participate, or didn't participate enthusiastically enough, were punished severely. Further, according to historian Joan Huckstep: "As one informant stated, 'It was really like being raped. I wept when I saw my father being forced to dance on the podium . . . .' His outrage went beyond observing his father forcibly dancing, embodying an ideology and political praxis with which he fundamentally and morally disagreed. In [their local] tradition, given his social status, his father would not have danced publicly for others; others would have danced for his father."[5]

Memory embodied in performance contributes to the sharing of local knowledge across generations because of the enduring nature of the kinesthetic intelligence embodied in movement. Ness points out that "[t]he dancer's body's tissues are structures that mold and are molded by thinking in action. The performative monuments into which traditions of dancing render their dancers' bodies . . . are forms that bring symbols to life."[6] For this very reason, manipulating or forbidding certain types of or contexts for dance, then, as Mobutu did in Zaire and as governments did in Canada and the United States, inverts the social order and deprives people of stories and rites through which they find and make meaning, thereby reinforcing their subjugation. The implications of dance's proscription are epic, as are the implications of its practice and performance. Dance's power to foster a sense of historical or cultural continuity, to anchor individual and group identity, and to transcend the mundane positions it to be a force for peacemaking.

Dance also maintains the potential to cultivate vibrant change—along with continuity. For example, a "reformulation" of the traditional dance-drama form *kooththu* took place in eastern Sri Lanka following the 2002 cease-fire. Associated with Tamil-speaking communities, *kooththu* "is performed as an all-night event [with] . . . . sections of Hindu epics . . . sung and danced . . . to large village audiences."[7] Civil war had made it impossible to stage these dance dramas for two decades. The cease-fire allowed space for reconnection with aspects of traditional knowledge through performance and for engagement with issues whose direct acknowledgment might be dangerous. Elders taught dances and stories while communities rewrote some episodes from the *Ramayana* and *Mahabharata* epics[8] to reflect contemporary reality, including social fissures and caste conflict. This occurred in a region that "has suffered violence and disappearances and, since 2004, . . . [has] been the site of a violent split in the Liberation Tigers of Tamil Eelam."[9] These danced stories highlighted resistance to power imbalances and discrimination, obliquely offering suggestions for the transformation of conflicts, including those related to gender and caste. Ultimately, "reformulation was not a movement from one fixed tradition to the creation of another: it refreshed a tradition and exemplified a shift from the closed and repressed places of war to a form of cultural practice that was active, dynamic and open to ongoing change."[10] Because of the depth and breadth of dance's communicative potential and the value accorded *koohthu* in this community, such a reformulation was efficacious. The roles for dance in potentially enabling change are intimately related to a given cultural context.

Dance and the "Enabling" of Change

In his 2006 article on the notions and practices of change and conflict, Christopher Mitchell outlines the complex intersections among the development, perpetuation, and escalation of conflict; the attenuation or resolution of conflict; and structural and environmental change. Calling change agents "enablers of resolutionary change" as opposed to "drivers" of transformation, he suggests that "members of parties in conflict have to be placed in a position where they can contemplate alternatives" and construct "road maps" of realistic paths pointing to resolution.[11]

In the stories presented below, Liberian and Cambodian dancers were addressing attitudinal adjustment and, in the Liberian example, the actual laying down of arms during lengthy, bloody battles. While constrained within the larger complex web of a specific protracted conflict, the individuals and troupes I discuss were inspired and determined to make a difference—to foster change—through what they knew to have resonance in their cultural, historical, political, and aesthetic contexts. The stories highlight nuances and implications of dance's pivotal role *on the ground* in these particular contexts.

Liberia: Dance and Guns

Liberia suffered two rounds of civil war in the late twentieth and early twenty-first centuries. A 1980 military coup headed by Samuel Doe was followed by increasing domestic turmoil, culminating in a brutal war from 1989 to 1997.[12] Armed rebel factions tore the country apart again between 1998 and 2003, when the Comprehensive Peace Accord was finally signed in Accra, Ghana. "Along with its neighbor Sierra Leone," writes anthropologist Mary Moran, "Liberia in the 1990s gave the world ghastly images of child soldiers, 'warlord' politics fueled by 'blood diamonds,' and utter, region wide devastation."[13]

The dancers and musicians of Liberia's National Cultural Troupe had lived, worked, and danced as one, even though they were from a number of ethnic groups, until the day in 1990 when the war reached Kendeja (a kind of artists' village in which members of the troupe resided). Fatu Gayflor, a principal singer and dancer with the company, said in a published interview that "[o]ne striking feature at Kendeja were the various examples of indigenous architecture. Traditional houses were built [there], including homes in the Vai, Kpelle, Bassa, and Mandingo [ethnic] building styles, all of which are different. Many were built with the same materials, including thatch roofs, but with vastly different designs."[14] The repertoire drew from all corners of the country as well, including a diversity of languages, movement styles, stories and instrumentation.[15]

The inclusiveness represented by the professional performing community was called upon at the end of the war when—with 200,000 dead, half a million internally displaced, and perhaps more than 300,000 Liberians in nearby countries as refugees[16]—the National Commission on Disarmament, Demobilization, Reintegration and Resettlement (NCDDRR) sought to take guns away from more than 50,000 combatants, some of whom were as young as nine.[17] Tokay Tomah, domestically and internationally recognized as one of Liberia's finest singers and dancers, had studied and performed at Kendeja. She participated in numerous disarmament ceremonies, performing songs and dances for the youths who were being asked to hand over their guns. Some of the boys and young men said they would do this only if they could place their weapons directly in her hands, so strong was the authority of her presence and her art.[18] (The launch of the NCDDRR program took place in the town of Buutuo, which was not only where the civil war had begun in 1989 but also Tomah's hometown. She performed as part of the program's inauguration.)[19]

Inside refugee camps, Zaye Tete, another well-known Liberian singer, dancer, and member of the National Cultural Troupe, had been performing during the war as a way of asking displaced Liberians to put down their anger and resentment. She recalls that she also tried to get people to "pick up their spirits and come together as one. Some people were literally going out of their minds because of the losses they suffered. This was leading to even more violence. I wanted all Liberians, no matter whose relatives were fighting whom, to focus on the possibility of peace."[20]

Zaye was born into a Dan (also known as Gio) family in northeastern Liberia. The Dan have been noted by the art historian and dance scholar Robert Farris Thompson to be highly attuned to an "awareness of bodily motion," with one Dan village situated on Liberia's border with the Ivory Coast especially "famed for its critical code." If performers didn't meet the expected caliber, they could be told to stop and then sent to be reprimanded by elders.[21] Zaye first learned dances and songs from her father, a coffee and cocoa farmer who was also the leader of the local dance troupe. She joined with him in ceremonial performances honoring a child's birth or a dignitary's visit, or on feast days following a death.

Zaye became a professional dancer at Kendeja, as well as a national recording star, singing both traditional and original songs. She used the power of her name and the impact of her art to attract crowds in each refugee camp she visited, performing songs and dances of her Dan heritage or those of the Vai or Kpelle or other peoples. Refugees came from all ethnic groups. When they saw her perform, "[a] lot of them cried," she says. "Our forefathers sang some of those songs, and did those dances. I re-worked them for contemporary times, and wrote new songs about peace."[22] Those in the audience wept, according to Zaye, thinking of what they had left behind at home; they also wept at the elusiveness of peace.

Zaye herself was a refugee who, having run away from Kendeja in 1990, made her way on foot and then by canoe to the Ivory Coast. Her husband, Gbahtuo Comgbaye, established himself as a teacher in a camp school and, with his meager salary, bought a drum. That was the beginning of Zaye's cultural troupe, formed in the Gbinta camp in 1993. She started out by recruiting some children resident in the camp and teaching them traditional dances and songs. They performed to the accompaniment of that one drum and a *sasa*, a traditional beaded gourd instrument that

Zaye made herself. During their initial performances in traditional contexts of funerals and other rites, as well as staged shows, they wore only whatever they had brought with them to the camp; sometimes they fashioned large empty rice sacks into costumes.

The renowned choreographer, dancer, and anthropologist Pearl Primus, who served as director of Liberia's national dance company in 1959 and 1960, writes of African dance in general that it "turns the body to liquid steel. It makes it vibrate like a guitar. The body can fly without wings. It can sing without voice." She also notes that people who watch a performance may be "snatched, plucked up by an invisible force and hurled into the ring of the dance, their own heartbeat matching the crescendo of pulsing sound, their bodies becoming one with the sweating dancers."[23] In the refugee camps, audience members might have experienced a kinesthetic convergence with the polyvalent messages of the rhythms, movements, and lyrics. Through participation in these performances of ethnic and national identity in the camps, observers and dancers alike had the potential to reframe their relationship to their present and their future. In a recognizable and valued expressive medium, Zaye was modeling respect for traditional culture as well as openness to new ways of imagining and enacting social and political relationships.

Zaye took advantage of a short cease-fire in 1994 to slip back across the border to Liberia to perform. She selected seven children and three drummers from her troupe to accompany her. The audience that day consisted of civilians and numerous soldiers, some with guns slung over their shoulders. She began with songs recognizable to the crowd. Then she sang newer ones—her own compositions about the importance of putting down weapons. As she sang, she also danced. The children with her formed the dance chorus, holding their torsos forward and their hips back, moving their legs and arms in synchronized choreography, reinforcing the rhythm with each placement of a foot flat against the earth. In Zaye's words:

> I remember it so clearly. After we finished, a soldier thanked us for the program by taking the microphone and saying publicly, 'She's telling us we should put down our arms. Yes, we should listen to her. But it isn't easy. If they attack us, we have to defend ourselves. But we pray it won't come to that.'[24]

Zaye and others were putting into play what perhaps is akin to Ilana Shapiro's reference in describing theories of change as requiring "a cohesive internal logic."[25] In these examples, cohesive internal logic took form in dance and music performances reflected upon by the artists themselves as influential in forging trust in a future of peaceful coexistence between the warring factions. Zaye and her associates could invoke this logic because of the kinesthetic/aesthetic and symbolic import of the melodies, rhythms, movements, and lyrics they were sharing.

They performed the traditional *Zamalay*, one of a variety of moonlight dances, done in the evening hours during the dry season after the harvest. The lyrics, sung in Zaye's native Dan tongue, refer to a greedy boy who, unbeknownst to his parents, is in the habit of going around to beg for food after eating a meal at his own house. The song presents the perspective of his younger sister, who spots him on his escapades and informs the parents, asking them to take responsibility and teach him right from wrong. "I chose that song and dance," recalls Zaye, "because they would remind them about the times before the war," when, as a peaceful village or community, they could celebrate or simply enjoy the light of the full moon. "Oh, yes, we know this song,"[26] the soldiers at that military post, most of whom were Dan themselves, said during the show as they moved their shoulders and hips to the beat. She also selected *Zamalay* because it highlights the responsibility (of members of a family, a community, a nation) for making constructive change. *Zamalay* brought the audience back into a traditional mode of storytelling that set social imperfections against "implied criteria for perfect living".[27] The newer peace songs also posited a contrast, this time between the surrounding reality and a life without the maiming caused by land mines, the ripping of youngsters from their childhoods, and constant fear and distrust.

Zaye told me that she and her husband and everyone else she knew in the camps wanted to go home. For that to be possible, they needed "the soldiers to put down their arms and the leaders of all warring sides to agree to some kind of peace plan."[28] Zaye, however, wasn't seeking a nostalgic or romanticized return to prewar existence, though she missed terribly what she had left behind. Through teaching and performing, she was hoping to encourage a shift in attitude *and practice*. She was anticipating the development of a new educational system in Liberia, one that would foster critical thinking skills and the responsibility and accountability of leadership.

"Lack of education on the part of the leaders and everyone else is part of how we got into that mess," she explained. "When we were in refugee camps we started to see the importance of education. So many women hadn't been given the chance to study. So many of the soldiers were so young, they didn't know what they were doing, and they didn't know how to question what was in front of them. They were easily brainwashed by grown-ups who took them from their villages and gave them guns."[29]

While living in refugee camps, Zaye and others became more attuned to systemic inequities and the need fo broader knowledge and new skills to forge a better Liberia. They took their dances and songs "on the road," engaging fellow refugees and combatants alike in shared moments of opening up to aspects of tradition that might underpin the future advancement of their homeland.[30]

After Zaye performed for the soldiers just across the border inside Liberia, she and her troupe of artists headed back into exile. The war continued for many years. After spending a decade in various camps, Zaye, Gbahtuo, and their children eventually immigrated to the United States before peace accords were signed.

Cambodia: Dance and Flags

Just as some Liberian refugees did, displaced Cambodians engaged with dance in the midst of profound loss and ongoing uncertainty. The what-if of peace and coexistence *at home* became an aspect of the practice of dance and music in Cambodian war zone camps. Instead of a concentrated effort to encourage the laying down of arms, the emphasis of artists in the stories that follow was on a shift in the attitude and loyalty of a war-weary populace. The arts were focused on invoking divine guidance and support through danced prayers for a home to which they could return with dignity, security, and hope intact.

Late-twentieth-century Cambodia had been the setting for civil and international war, revolution, and genocide. Civil strife erupted in what was then the Kingdom of Cambodia in the late 1960s. A 1970 coup d'état, undertaken with the support of the United States, sent the royalty into exile and established the Khmer Republic. Meanwhile, the antigovernment communist insurgency grew at the same time that the Vietnam War, in which the United States was engaged, spilled over into Cambodian territory. The United States ultimately "dropped over half a million tons of bombs on Cambodia, more in six months of 1973 than had been dropped on Japan in World War Two."[31] In April 1975, the communist Khmer Rouge declared victory in the civil war, ushering in an era of unprecedented horror. During the Democratic Kampuchea years (1975 to early 1979), with the Khmer Rouge in charge, between one-fourth and one-third of the country's entire population perished from forced hard labor, malnutrition, starvation, disease, and torture and execution. The Khmer Rouge were ultimately ousted by the Vietnamese army, also communist, attacking from the east. Numerous Khmer Rouge deserters joined forces with the Vietnamese to install yet another new government in Cambodia, the People's Republic of Kampuchea (PRK), in January 1979. While in power for the next ten years, the PRK fought armies loyal to each of the former regimes: the royalists, the republicans, and the Khmer Rouge. Each faction had at least one encampment on Cambodia's western border with Thailand, from where they launched attacks.

Until the 1970 coup d'état, Cambodian classical dance had grown, with royal support, as a symbol of the nation and its identity. Mention of dance, long connected with monarchs and spirituality, can be traced back to sixth- or seventh-century stone inscriptions at temples, listing names of dancers associated with those houses of worship. Cambodian royalty eventually moved dance behind the palace walls, keeping the spiritual potency for itself. After the coup, the country's professional dancers, no longer "royal," were now called "classical." Though performers practiced the traditional repertoire of mytho-historical tales; stories of magic, love, and revenge; and short discrete pieces without story lines, the lyrics and thus the meanings of some of the dances changed. They couldn't sing about "princes and princesses" anymore; the lyrics had to refer to "boys and girls" instead. Just as they had done throughout the twentieth century, however, the dancers continued to travel overseas as representatives of the nation-state of Cambodia.

Everything changed once the Khmer Rouge came to power in 1975. Small-town and city dwellers were sent on forced marches to the countryside, where collectives of agricultural workers were to make up the core of the new, supposedly class- and corruption-free Cambodia. Dance as Cambodians had known it was forbidden. The connections it fostered to heritage, community, and spiritual elements were a threat to a regime that demanded obedience to one authority and punished displays of love and loyalty focused elsewhere. Only new formulaic dances that praised the Khmer Rouge revolution and its new society and declared war on the former rulers were performed. Fists thrust before them, marching in linear formations to songs of blood and revenge, revolutionary dancers embodied the brute nature of the regime as a whole. Many dancers who had trained at the palace or university hid their identities for fear that their connection to previous regimes would mark them for death.[32]

When the PRK took over in 1979, pushing the Khmer Rouge to the west, government officials immediately put some of their meager resources into re-creating Cambodia's artistic heritage. Representatives scoured the provinces, looking for surviving dancers, musicians, actors, and poets. They estimated that in less than four years, 80 to 90 percent of Cambodia's professional artists had died.[33] Although survivors were encouraged to recall, perform, and teach as much as they could from the old repertoire, new dances were added to the classical idiom. Some of these had a political bent—for example, praising the friendship of the communist countries of Cambodia, Laos, and Vietnam.[34]

Throughout the 1980s, civil war raged inside Cambodia and along the border with Thailand. Hundreds of thousands fled the fighting and poverty to camps on that volatile border. These camps for displaced persons—both those affiliated with the royalists and those loyal to the Khmer Republic—had dance companies. In each place, thousands of residents would come out in the sweltering tropical heat to watch their fellow refugees perform the old dances. Sometimes artillery shells would fall in the middle of a performance. Seeking safety in trenches or just running in panic, the crowd would scatter. When the shelling ceased, an audience would form again, and the show would go on.[35] (While initially the Khmer Rouge refugee camps had no troupes, they eventually created folk dance ensembles in the late 1980s that also performed one or two short classical pieces.)

Dance was a way for Cambodians cut off from their homeland and in harm's way to create momentary order and beauty. Those performing and observing were able to counter loss by regaining meaningful links to community, history, and home through story, movement, and music. Site 2, the largest of the Cambodian camps inside Thailand has been described as follows:

> [T]wo hundred thousand people without the right to earn money. It's thousands of rice farmers without land to farm, without even a natural water source. It's flat land with very few trees . . . It's huge red water trucks barreling down the central road, orange dust flying. It's United Nations and CARE and Red Cross four-wheel drives filing past the checkpoints at 5:00. It's Americans named Andy wearing cowboy boots and G.I. Joe radios strapped to their green webbed belts. . . . Site 2 is a city of one-legged husbands and fathers. It is the painfully real remainder [and reality] of war.[36]

And yet some people danced, and many came to see them. Dance in Site 2 was practiced amid a baneful power structure that left the displaced dependent on foreign aid and vulnerable to unfathomable domestic, community, and military violence. In this way, it was a force for resistance to the surrounding circumstances, an assertion of people's will to control some aspects of their lived story.

In 1989, when the Vietnamese army withdrew from Cambodia, forces loyal to the Khmer Republic (run by the Khmer People's National Liberation Front, or KPNLF), with whom Site 2 was affiliated, made a push into Cambodia from the border, capturing some villages. As a way of marking their territorial gains, they sent for a dance troupe from the Site 2 camp. With the exception of the Khmer Rouge years, leaders of Cambodia had for centuries enlisted classical dancers as emblems of the kingdom's or the state's prowess. Planting the dancers in this newly liberated region in 1989—in addition to planting their flag—was the forces' way of claiming legitimacy to rule that slice of the country. Indeed, in one of the dances performed for area villagers, performers used fans with the image of the KPNLF flag, which differed slightly from the flag of the central Cambodian government.[37]

The KPNLF military and political leadership may have been connecting themselves to people through dance to "prove" a right to govern Cambodia as they asked the local populace to turn their backs on other warring factions and honor their recent tenuous victory in an ongoing battle for control. But the dancers spoke to me of what they felt was their mission: to beseech the spirits for peace in the region through performance of sacred dance so that they could return to their homeland and be welcomed with open arms by their compatriots. Moeun Srey Peau, a teenager at the time, said she felt excited and nervous to have the honor and responsibility to "dance well enough so that enemies would become, instead, loving family, and Cambodia could be my home again."[38] For the artists, dance, accompanied by sacred melodies, had the power to encourage such an outcome.

When Khmer classical dancers enter and exit a performance space, they often trace a figure-eight-like pattern as their feet guide them almost soundlessly across the stage or ground. The pattern's curves—said by artists to represent the S shape of the naga, the sacred serpent who inhabits the land and waters of Cambodia—are echoed in the dancers' arched backs and flexed toes and fingers. Nagas are thought to connect humans with the heavens, and carvings of them at ancient temples lead visitors from mundane to sacred territory. Dancers embodying the naga also communicate with the heavens on people's behalf, making requests for blessings and well-being.

The ethnologist Ang Choulean has written about the profound connections between territory, history, and the sacred for rural Khmer communities. Each village has a sacred identity, defined by its spirit.[39] If an individual or a family moves to a new home, a ceremony is performed to ask permission from the resident spirit or spirits to live on that land. The Site 2 dancers were doing just that through their performance in the zone that had been captured by the KPNLF troops.

Conclusion

Whether under the initiative of the powers that be or an independent artist, dance became, in these examples, part of the choreography of negotiation and peace seeking, serving as a kind of alternative or parallel platform for reconciliation. Dance was already suited for such a role, in part because of its own intrinsic and necessary negotiation. "[Dance's] required attention to shifts in weight, rhythm, relation to other bodies, and available space, and to the shifting circumstances experienced, theorized, and recorded in embodied form," as noted by Jaqueline Shea Murphy,[40] was particularly relevant to the Liberian and Cambodian people who witnessed and participated in these traditional cultural expressions. Performers reimagined dances that informed, reflected, and constructed multiple and fluid identities within new, dangerous contexts to help bring about a transformation. They did this through engaging a local population traumatized by war, on one hand by inspiring the handing over of guns and on the other by the beseeching of spirits and the "planting" of dancers.

The potency and potential of dance are broad reaching; they touch multiple contexts (geopolitical, economic, social, spiritual, and many others). They begin to offer the glue and social cohesion so needed as antidotes to deep ruptures caused by years of armed violence, lack of access to land and productive livelihoods, malnourishment, harassment and abuse, and systemic disenfranchisement. In the Liberian example described above, Zaye Tete and Tokay Tomah embodied a reconciled nation. Each, transcending her own ethnic background, mastered movements, melodies, and languages of Liberians from different ethnicities and regions. When people in the audiences turned over their weapons, or even momentarily considered ways to rethink their circumstances, they partook of the potency of dance and music to enable movement toward transformation of entrenched violence and displacement. These moments were turning points toward restoring hope and social cohesion, although people had to wait for structural/institutional and leadership changes to begin rebuilding their lives without the reality and/or threat of war.

For the displaced Cambodians, classical dance, with its connection to spirituality and imaginings of the nation, created an emergent space for trust and positive expectations. However, only after a United Nations–brokered peace accord was signed, and logistics were put in place for the repatriation of hundreds of thousands of refugees, could permanent movement home take place. The KPNLF dancers' work in a long-contested area was a statement about the possibility of peace, beauty, and order (and return), even as it was an outgrowth of being manipulated as part of the KPNLF war machine. The dances were important catalysts in the ultimate de-escalation of violence. The work of conflict transformation and peace building is ongoing, with legal, artistic, and other undertakings aimed at fostering accountability and peaceful, respectful coexistence.[41]

Just as the Preah Vihear Temple on the Thai/Cambodian border features carvings of nagas that mark the transition from the everyday to the divine, dance can be seen as something that bridges worlds and states of being. Perhaps in proposing dance as a way to diffuse political and military tension at that border, Bun Rany Hun Sen was hoping to tap its potency as a cohering and transcendent force. The displaced artists did the same when they went into western Cambodia from the Site 2 camp, seeking not only to lay claim to the site but also to embody the naga, beseeching the heavens for peace.[42]

Cambodia

Children of Bassac—A Case Study of a Dance and Music Association in the Tonle Bassac Community

JOHN BURT WITH ANDREW DILTS

"Dancing has to come from the inside out. If a student understands this from their experience of learning to dance and play music, then they have a chance to become a heart-felt citizen."
Ieng Sithul, master of the Tonle Bassac Dance and Music Association

This chapter details the rebirth of the traditional dance and music forms in Cambodia—and the country's coincident return to health and vitality—after the Khmer Rouge genocide. A case study of the cultural revival of the nongovernmental organization (NGO) Cambodian Living Arts, and one of its leading dance associations in a Phnom Penh slum, reveals that dance is not only a marker of social resilience and a tool of postconflict cultural reconstruction but also a carrier of hope.

Cultural Peace Building: Arn Chorn-Pond and the Cambodian Living Arts

In 1984, 18-year-old Cambodian American refugee Arn Chorn-Pond delivered an impassioned keynote address to nearly 20,000 people at the Cathedral for St. John the Divine in New York City, a gathering convened by Amnesty International. A former child soldier, Chorn-Pond was the first such individual to speak out publicly about the atrocities of the Khmer Rouge and the ensuing genocide in Cambodia in the late 1970s and 1980s. He initiated the human rights campaign Children of War, bringing to the United States young war survivors from around the world so they could tell their stories to other young people.

Since then, Chorn-Pond and the organizations he has worked with have been models and catalysts for reconciliation and cultural peace building. Defined by Boutros Boutros-Ghali, the former secretary general of the UN, as "action to identify and support structures which will tend to strengthen and solidify peace in order to avoid a relapse into conflict,"[1] peace building has taken many forms around the world. Explored here, the dance-focused and other cultural methods employed by Chorn-Pond in Cambodia serve as excellent examples of postconflict strategies for contemporary conflict resolution: fostering peace and conflict awareness, education, and training; supporting cultural exchanges and initiatives; solving problems as a means to an improved future; and using dance as a means of reconciliation.[2]

As a social worker in Lowell, Massachusetts, in the years following his Amnesty International advocacy, Chorn-Pond worked with violent street gangs formed by the children of the second-largest Cambodian refugee community in the United States. He helped establish a sound studio—partially with donated equipment—to channel these youths' energy into artistic endeavors; they recorded their own music while being introduced to songs and music of their Cambodian cultural heritage. Within months, the gang members were composing their own hip-hop and pop songs and also playing ancient Cambodian instruments. Consistent with an established body of research on the arts and conflict resolution,[3] Chorn-Pond's experiment began to show how a greater involvement in their artistic and cultural heritage might divert the otherwise violent behaviors of these youths. Such programs have been repeatedly recognized as helping participants to recognize risk factors in their lives, learn problem-solving and conflict-resolution processes, and survive in a chaotic world.[4] In Lowell, participants in these artistic endeavors were able to rebuild relationships and work toward overcoming the differences that had once polarized them.

Involving traditional Cambodian arts for reconciliation and peace building has been a key theme of Chorn-Pond's work. He would soon take one approach, similar to that used in Lowell, home to Cambodia. In that country, his family had owned, operated, and performed in a traveling opera company for at least four generations before the Khmer Rouge targeted Cambodian artists as being subversive and having ties to the West. Nearly 90 percent of Cambodia's artists and intellectuals were targeted and killed by the Khmer Rouge or fled the country.[5] Chorn-Pond recalls meeting elder artists—people who had known his parents' traveling opera company—who were selling cigarettes and beer on the streets in the postconflict period after the Khmer Rouge regime fell. He was determined get these unemployed, homeless artists off the streets, supporting them while they taught the younger generation of Cambodians their core cultural traditions.

A living-room gathering in New York featuring Chorn-Pond, and hosted by one of the authors of this chapter, raised $50,000 toward this goal, and a small delegation of committed human rights workers made the journey to Cambodia to meet the elder master artists and try to find ways for them to teach and perform again. The goal was to establish a national school "without walls" that would teach music, dance, theater, and puppetry to the surviving younger generations in every province around the country. The news program *60 Minutes* aired a segment on the initiative, which provided invaluable coverage for the project, its team, and its mission.

That initial trip established the humble roots of an organization that started by supporting a few elder artists and has since grown to become one of the largest arts NGOs in Cambodia.[6] Cambodian Living Arts (CLA) now has an annual budget of nearly $500,000 and employs thirty-five master artists and instructors, who teach traditional Khmer (Cambodian) performing arts to more than five hundred students in seven provinces and in all major Cambodian cities.[7] CLA now commissions and produces contemporary music, dance, and theater works, including a fusion hip-hop band formed by the refugee youth from Lowell, Massachusetts; shadow-puppet plays that tour the rural Cambodian countryside with an AIDS prevention message; and the Cambodian Youth Arts Festival, produced with the cooperation of more than twenty allied arts organizations.[8] These efforts are aided by CLA's sound and video production studio, which also archives ancient art forms and records new works.

Recently, CLA commissioned and produced a large-scale rock opera by a Cambodian composer, which told the love story of a Cambodian refugee returning to his postgenocide homeland. Premiering in Phnom Penh, the opera played to sold-out houses, becoming one of the largest Cambodian cultural events of the last forty years.[9]

CLA's goals are ambitious, but its accomplishments have been as well. Cultural dance and music are believed to carry the link to the religious underpinnings of Cambodia, to the memory of the past, to the aesthetic beauty of the present, and to the world of hope for the future. The interactivity and problem-solving opportunities offered by dance and music education are essentially the same as those recognized as playing a key role in overcoming entrenched historical enmity between opposing groups[10] and fostering a healthy national culture.[11] Giving participants the chance to engage in such creative processes as music and dance—art forms that require a discipline of study and an adherence to form but also allow for experimentation and novelty—helps promote fundamental behaviors and thought processes that are essential to social development.

CLA's efforts harmonize well with a model of sustainable peace building put forward by Reychler. This model has five essential components: an effective system of communication; peace-enhancing political and economic structures and institutions; an integrative political-psychological climate; a critical mass of peace-building leadership; and a supportive regional and international environment.[12] While CLA may not do explicitly political work per Reychler's model, many of its activities help knit together the cultural and communal underpinnings that promote sustainable peace building. CLA's dance and cultural programs improve the level of communication between participants and between others in the community; they enhance economic aspects of Cambodian dance and related Cambodian industry; they develop leadership (within the dance community); and they increase international attention to Cambodian culture.

Each dance and musical form fostered by CLA carries with it a morality tale. Some of these stories are admittedly outdated, but they expose to contemporary society a past that many of the younger generation would otherwise have no link to, having lost so many of the people who would have passed on these stories and traditions. In Chorn-Pond's words, "we will reach out and support one master artist and one student at a time until my country's culture is knitted back together."[13]

Tonle Bassac: After Conflict, the New Epicenter of a Blossoming Cambodian Dance Community

When the violent Khmer Rouge took political power in 1975, they forcefully evacuated the population of Phnom Penh into the countryside, leaving buildings and communities abandoned.[14]

When the Vietnamese overthrew the Khmer Rouge in early 1979, many survivors returned to cities where many of the buildings had been looted and were in ruins.

One of the communities in Phnom Penh, called Tonle Bassac, was home to many artists, who had lived and worked in this area since the 1960s, when the internationally renowned Cambodian architect Van Molyvann's residential White Building was built for civil servants, many of them also artists.[15] The National Theater was built in this famous "post-French" region of the city.

During Cambodia's period of upheaval, the people from this community—and from Phnom Penh in general—posed a threat to Khmer Rouge ideologues who were attempting to force the nation back to its agrarian roots. The urban artists had been active in the brief cultural renaissance in the 1950s and 1960s after Cambodia's independence from France, when the Cambodian royal government encouraged cultural exchanges with the West. These artists began to emulate Western music, dance, and in particular, rock and roll.[16]

After the horror of the Khmer Rouge regime, there remained—perhaps surprisingly—evidence of this brief cultural renaissance, even twenty years later. Many of the families of these master artists settled back in and around the National Theater, where most of them had once been employed. They lived in squatter shelters made of blue plastic or in the abandoned White Building. The masters and teachers began instructing and performing in the lobby of the burned-out National Theater as well as in their makeshift apartments and huts. Some of them also began teaching again at the government-run Royal University of Fine Arts, which had reopened immediately after the Khmer Rouge fell. CLA began sponsoring many of the elder master artists and teachers living in the Tonle Bassac community who were too old or ill to teach. The association also was supporting master artists in the rural countryside, where nearly 90 percent of the population worked in agricultural fields,[17] to reach young people who would never have access to the university system for education or arts training.

The story of the post Khmer Rouge era Tonle Bassac is one of a transformative peace-building movement within the Cambodian community. In peace-building theory, such a movement finds its foundation in terminating something undesired and then building something desired, through the transformation of relationships and construction of the conditions for peace.[18] In this case, the undesired states are those that flowed from the destructive legacy of the Khmer Rouge regime. The desired states, and the methods though which they have been introduced, greatly focus around the constructive relationships and ameliorative approaches of the dance and cultural initiatives discussed here.

Master Sithul and the Tonle Bassac Dance and Music Association

Master Ieng Sithul (b. 1957) is the youngest of the masters in the Cambodian Living Arts. He is one of the most celebrated experts in ancient Khmer cultural dance and music and has officiated many national religious ceremonies. Master Sithul lived in Tonle Bassac, with his wife, Pich Kuntheary, in the early 1980s. They became very concerned about the youths in and around the community. Children from very poor families were on the streets begging, prostituting themselves, selling drugs, and sniffing glue. From the couple's experience teaching dance and music to children in the impoverished countryside after the Khmer Rouge regime, they believed that a vigorous, demanding arts training program would give urban youths a place to learn the values of rigorous hard work. Master Sithul and Pich Kuntheary aspired to elevate them to a higher national cause: "Our aim is that we want these young people to succeed us and safeguard our cultural heritage. They need to know about their country's greatness, not only their immediate loss of family and nation."[19] The impacts of this knowledge and cultural heritage would be considerable in postconflict Cambodia. According to Master Sithul, "[W]hat makes survival worth it, we had to ask ourselves. It's not just food and water."[20]

With such goals in mind, Master Sithul started the Tonle Bassac Dance and Music Association in the late 1990s, along with Bassac teachers Thida and Vuthy—two other instructors of dance and music living in the White Building. The association teaches children in the community traditional dances dating back to the ninth century (the Angkor Empire), together with more-modern Cambodian folk dances made popular in the 1950s and 1960s. In the dance classes, the generations are completely interconnected. Younger teenage dancers teach the children. Older students, most of whom are members of the dance troupe Children of Bassac, run drills and routines with the teenagers. Many of the Tonle Bassac students have essentially grown up in the dance studio, rehearsing and dancing together for nearly a decade. Such close-knit participation in artistic programs is well recognized as supporting and enhancing community engagement, not just among members of the artistic group but among those members and others in the greater community as well.[21]

The association's facilities are humble, and the attendees come from challenging backgrounds. Housing and income are key hurdles for these students, most of whose parents are single wage earners in a country where the median annual income is $650.[22] Some of the students are living on their own, a few of them on the floor of Master Sithul's classroom. Many of their families have been evicted from the squatter community, which was demolished in 2009. Most still live in a building that is slated for demolition as soon as titles can be bought (or bribed). Master Sithul notes that "the students have so many financial problems. They do not have the strength and resilience for international travel and performance. They are generally malnourished and therefore have related health issues and lack fully functioning brain capacity."[23] He further notes that "every month, I have to find one or two bags of rice for those staying at our place, the dance classroom that used to be our living room. Some of my students don't have anything to eat, and I give them my own money to buy food . . . without all we do, they will fall apart. Without me helping them, everything will be finished."[24] The students themselves also worry about what will happen once they finish their educations and are obliged to start supporting their families, a primary challenge and concern in a still-recovering nation.

Despite the problems, Master Sithul and the Dance and Music Association recognize and foster potential in the young people. The resilience of the teachers and the capacity of the students appear to override the despair and overcome many obstacles. This ability to overcome obstacles is in accordance with a wide body of academic literature on the arts, conflict resolution, and resilience. Whether dealing with inner-city youths,[25] challenged immigrant populations,[26] rural communities,[27] or groups overcoming major national trauma,[28] participation in the arts has repeatedly been shown to be a successful means of resolving issues and fostering social participation among those who face challenges in doing so.

The teachers anticipate that 70 percent of the students could become professional dancers or musicians, further passing on the cultural and individual lessons learned, if there were enough work in the city to support them. Master Sithul states passionately and often that dance and music are not just about learning technique; they are a way into the heart and soul of a being. The teachers go out of their way to instill strong values and civil practices in their students. In the face of Cambodia's high levels of corruption, in a country where the black market is simply a way of doing business, the discipline and structure of the dance classes demand courtesy and respect for others. The motivation these students have for building a stronger culture elevates their immediate needs in daily life to a larger commitment to the whole of society. Students note that they could be forced into corruption to support their families, but as one said so eloquently, "Master Sithul and the teachers teach us to have respect for our culture. We believe we can be great again."[29]

Students who have had more than a decade of dance classes also enjoy secondary benefits of enormous exposure to other areas of study, including learning English and acquiring computer skills; they also can take part in international travel and receive introductions to international visitors attending their classes. Many of the foreign visitors to the dance classes over the years have contributed to the CLA scholarship fund that enables gifted students to further their studies in a variety of fields, including dance, media, and the arts. But perhaps most significantly, these students are maturing with confidence and an ability to express themselves.

Outcomes and Impact of Dance in Cambodia

Peace building and postconflict social change are essentially social and associative processes that rebuild fractured relationships.[30] Just as other civil society groups may be explicitly aimed at healing some particular part of a community following a major conflict or trauma, so too are dance- and culture-rebuilding initiatives such as those discussed here. Further, such initiatives help embed cultural rebuilding at the level of the local community.

In a country that lost a sixth of its population[31] and had very little economy to rebuild, the idea that Cambodia's arts and culture have become central to its new core capacity and strength is very exciting. Tourism and international trade have contributed significantly to this optimism, however fragile it may be. The teachers and students in the Cambodian dance community can earn wages in their particular art form to contribute to their families and their economy. They have become passionate, electrifying performers on national and international stages. Many of the students have established savings accounts for their education. Some have been able to buy motorbikes to commute to school; others have received scholarships to study at various institutions both in Cambodia and abroad. To support the students, CLA has begun a competitive scholarship program for university and advanced arts training. Teacher Vuthy explains the benefits of his students earning income as dancers: "Before studying dance with me, those students beg their parents for money every day. But when they take our classes and have learned the necessary skills, they can earn money to support themselves and their parents. This is what I have observed on how studying arts has helped young people. The art gives my students hope."[32]

The true value of this growing artistic community, however, runs much deeper. The students of dance programs mature while developing enormous artistic competencies. The students have secured a place of respect in their society. They are wage earners. They have dignity within their family systems. They are regarded as living protectors of the nation's resolute pride in its religion and culture, often considered as one in the same.[33] Consistent with previous research on the role that the arts can play in fostering a resilient postconflict culture,[34] both the students' and the teachers' participation in the various Cambodian cultural programs allows them to prepare to be, and to become, active leaders and healthy participants in their own lives.

Not all of the students remain in the dance programs, but all still carry a deep appreciation for the arts. Some have moved on to other artistic disciplines, such as media studies or documentary filmmaking. Regardless of their chosen fields, the students express a strong sense of family and national pride. Master Sithul declares, "[T]he students who now perform each week in front of their national museum are considered as important as the national treasures inside."[35]

The Tonle Bassac Dance and Music Association, along with other CLA arts classes, has provided a sustained environment for young people to build consistent relationships with mentors, most of whom are old enough to be their grandparents. The programs have connected youths to their cultural history and practices, which had been badly interrupted by war and genocide. For a nation whose cultural traditions are still passed on orally, these mentor-student relationships have been key to reconstituting civil society. Arts and culture were transmitted quickly by the few remaining elders after the Khmer Rouge regime. Dance and the other living arts connected the public to positive memories and history that potentially counterbalance the traumatic past. Focusing on individual and national capacities elevates the possibilities for hope, for healing of hurts caused by past conflict, and for resilience.[36]

In 2003, UNESCO recognized traditional Khmer royal dance as a "masterpiece of oral intangible heritage of humanity."[37] It is difficult to begin measuring the significance of this honor bestowed upon a nation that nearly lost its religion and primary cultural forms during the Khmer Rouge regime. The Cambodian government now recognizes "the importance of art and culture as a force for reconciliation and social bonding and as a source of national pride which transcends political divisions, giving the Cambodian nation its unique character and identity." Since the signing of the Paris Peace Accord in 1991 and the reorganization of government in 1997, the Ministry of Culture and Fine Arts has been charged with overall responsibility for the development of culture and fine arts in Cambodia, for nurturing creativity and innovation and for promoting the diverse Cambodian cultural heritage.

Cambodian Living Arts serves as one of the leaders in the public dialogue about what role the arts have in the economic and social development of a postconflict nation. At the same time, Ministry of Culture officials have recently been involved in international discussions of arts policy and the role of government. At present, there is very little financial support from the government for arts and cultural education. Some assistance comes from outside the country; there are currently forty-five independent arts NGOs in Cambodia receiving foreign aid. Public-private partnerships could help build the infrastructure needed to bring Khmer arts and cultural training to all the schools and universities in Cambodia.

Still, there are signs of hope. Organizing around the arts and culture has so far been a winning formula for institutional funders and individuals alike. CLA declared a bold vision thirteen years ago that by 2020, Cambodia's national and international signature will be its art and culture. Now, a little more than halfway to that deadline, the possibility of this goal being realized is apparent. Nearly 20,000 Cambodian youths are engaged in visual and performing arts training or employment through forty-five arts organizations.

The successes of the Cambodian dance community have also begun to have an impact around the world. In 2009, the renowned musician Peter Gabriel sponsored the Children of Bassac dance troupe to perform at a major cultural and music festival in Bath, England. That same summer, the troupe won the Best Pick Audience Award at Scotland's Edinburgh Fringe Festival, following a five-week performance there.

CLA initiated and produced "Season of Cambodia," the first international festival of Cambodian performance and art, in New York during the spring of 2013. Thirty-three of New York's major cultural and educational institutions partnered with CLA to present contemporary and traditional dance, music, and art in a celebration of the cultural tension between preservation and innovation through the curatorial theme "Living Arts Festival." One hundred twenty five Cambodian artists participated in this prestigious event, advancing their nation's agenda of preservation, while celebrating twenty years of groundwork that methodically transmitted the skills of an ancient culture into contemporary society.

Cambodia's dancers are building a new legacy. They have embraced, learned, and performed the nation's traditions related to its key historical moments: the golden Angkorian era, in which the traditional Khmer royal dance flourished; the cultural renaissance of the postindependence period, when many folk dances depicting rural Cambodian life were commissioned by the royal government; the tragic times under the Khmer Rouge regime; and the current postconflict period of reconstruction. Out of the slums of Tonle Bassac and the rural temples in the poor countryside, a remarkable momentum has been achieved in the postwar mission to revive and preserve Cambodia's greatest legacy to the world: its living arts and culture. There is no question that those arts will endure as long as—or longer than—the inanimate stones of Angkor Wat.

Cambodia

"Dancing in the Eye of a Storm"—Principles of Practice When Working With the Arts Therapeutically with Traumatised Communities
CARRIE HERBERT

> *"You can dance in the eye of a storm*
> *All around voices and memories rage*
> *There's a still quiet calm*
> *Peace lives there, peace in your pain."*[1]
> *Eye of a Storm*, Carrie Herbert

The eye of a storm holds the paradox of both stillness and intense turmoil. It is perhaps the same in any conflict where extreme and chaotic psychological states also hold the potential for transformation, change, growth, and, ultimately, peace. Dance, and the therapeutic use of the arts, can provide opportunities to transform potentially destructive energies resulting from internal and external conflict into acts of creation. Drawing from my practice in arts psychotherapy, training and clinical supervision in postconflict, mental health, and trauma recovery, this chapter explores the principles of practice that need to be in place to safely and effectively navigate conflict through the arts. The chapter will offer case studies that show how the arts have been integrated into displaced communities that have experienced conflict in the Middle East and Cambodia. Accounts from therapeutic literature, in conjunction with the application of arts-based therapeutic approaches, demonstrate the imperative need to cultivate a sense of safety and security. I will highlight key strategies to achieve these foundational elements in contexts where trauma prevails.

"Braving the Storms": What Is Needed for Effective Therapy with War Refugees?

For asylum seekers who have endured conflict, torture, or violence, experiences of perpetual hostility significantly undermine their capacity to cultivate a sense of safety and trust. They may perceive internal and external security as foreign and unattainable. In the midst of perpetual upheaval, people are often alienated from their own culture and belief systems. Working with those who have endured a series of losses has made it clear that conflict and traumatic experiences are multilayered and interwoven with beliefs, values, and embodied experiences. This complex weave can, over a period of time, make it challenging to navigate through inner and outer conflicts. Individuals separated from their family, community, or culture often become isolated and attempt to negotiate such losses on their own. Some authors suggest that trauma is psychocultural and recovering from trauma largely depends on how the injury is interpreted through a cultural lens. For example, if the terror or loss is interpreted as heroically meaningful in certain contexts, the effects of trauma will be minimized,[2] whereas if it is reinforced by superstition and fear, the effects are potentially exacerbated.[3] Such insights from conflict and trauma theory provide important frameworks for understanding the complexities surrounding trauma. Therapeutic approaches can effectively address the challenges that accompany such complexities.

The starting point for a therapeutic approach begins with a willingness of both the therapist and client to engage with the inner and outer conflicts that mutually inform one another. Winnicott states, "If only we can wait, the client arrives at understanding creatively with immense joy. I now enjoy this joy more than I used to enjoy the sense of having been clever."[4] A sense of humility is foundational for letting go of preconceived agendas and expectations and requires deliberate acts of waiting. When we find a still point in ourselves, we can gradually begin to hold a place of peace for others.

> *At the still point of the turning world. Neither flesh nor fleshless;*
> *Neither from nor towards; at the still point, there the dance is,*
> *But neither arrest nor movement. And do not call it fixity,*
> *Where past and future are gathered.*
> *Neither movement from nor towards,*
> *Neither ascent nor decline. Except for the point, the still point,*
> *There would be no dance, and there is only the dance.*
> *I can only say, there we have been: but I cannot say where.*
> *And I cannot say, how long, for that is to place it in time.*[5]

The innate desire for safety and trust is central to human nature, and the longing to be healed and to heal is at the core of human dynamics. In every culture these instincts have given rise to a repertoire of traditional healing practices dating back thousands of years. The therapeutic relationship involves creating the right conditions for healing to take place. The critical question that remains is: What determines whether a relationship is therapeutic, and how can it transform inner and outer conflict? One answer lies with existential and person-centered therapeutic approaches, which focus on the "therapist's 'being' qualities rather than 'doing' skills."[6] Carl Rogers, one of the founders of psychotherapy research, stated that unconditional positive regard, empathic understanding, and congruence are essential qualities in the therapeutic relationship.[7] In psychotherapeutic literature, congruence is understood as a way of being genuine, transparent, and true to one's emotions, beliefs, and values.

Congruence is particularly pertinent in conflict-ridden environments where chaos and confusion are the norm. It challenges therapists to be genuine, honest, and aware of how their own internal conflicts, beliefs, and values unfold and shift as they navigate through external conflicts. Congruence is central to therapists' depth of therapeutic presence and influences their ability to facilitate and catalyze change. It is a delicate balancing act of recognizing internal responses in relation to the external environment. This degree of awareness fosters congruency and *presence*. Along with Rogers, the noted psychotherapists and educators Bugental and Yalom emphasize a psychotherapeutic method that cultivates presence and its role in effecting intra- and interpersonal change.[8] To cultivate a therapeutic presence, the therapist is open to being with others at the deepest level of their experience. Such witnessing involves a balance of listening, reflection, and articulation. It could be said that congruence is the living practice of this wisdom; the dance of balancing inner and outer awareness. It is humbling to recognize the heightened levels of self-awareness and attunement that are required to build and sustain trust amid self-disclosure and vulnerability.

If "the relationship is the therapy," then this elucidates what such relationships require. In short, the therapist cultivates what the philosopher Martin Buber calls I-Thou rather than I-It relationships, where clients are engaged in "dialogical encounter . . . and through which they encounter inter-relational meaning where untold possibilities unfold themselves to both of us."[9] As a person's essential identity can be threatened and confined in conflict, it is necessary to create spacious frameworks that accommodate increased capacities for choice when anxieties are heightened. This deep-rooted work beckons toward a relationship that relies on a mutual vulnerability.

The arts have a primary role to play in the center of relational uncertainties. With the capacity to hold what is both dynamic and vulnerable, the arts convey the breadth and depth of what remains unspoken in our lives. By evoking the senses, the arts can begin to humanize encounters across borders and complex identities while holding multiple contradictions within a framework. The following sections will explore the various dimensions of artistic practices that lend themselves to cultivating the therapeutic relationship.

The Ability of the Arts to Hold Paradox and Internal Conflict

In situations of internal and external conflict, we are pulled between perceived polarities of good or bad, past or future, affirmation or negation, empowerment or disempowerment, control or surrender. The tension between polarities can offer a generative source of creative momentum and is the very substance of life. The multivalent nature of art images or metaphors can hold the extremes of human experience, making it possible to work between polarities. Just as an image can convey opposing symbols and conflicting emotional states, the body can similarly generate enormous insights through the simple use of gestures and postures. Through creative interventions that support embodied awareness, rigid polarities can shift and be understood from multiple vantage points.

The Centrality of the Body in Storing Memory, Identity, Emotion

Anna Halprin, the dance and expressive arts therapy pioneer, aptly claims that the imprints of life are housed within the body.[10] Since the 1950s, experts in medicine and neuroscience have similarly pointed toward the mind-body connection and the complex interrelationships of the neurons of the brain with the cells of the whole body.[11] In situations of conflict or trauma, especially early traumatic experiences, thought-emotion pathways are laid down in the physiological system. When these experiences are suppressed, communication patterns become altered over time. Through images and metaphors, a therapist can help create an awareness of the blocks in the person's physical body. Such approaches create a vital distancing from the original traumatic event, and the complexity of a person's story can be encapsulated in a single image or gesture. In contrast to conventional modes of dialogue, the arts offer frameworks that illuminate nonverbal modes of expression. Through the reflexive process of dialoguing with art forms, a new-found sense of safety can be cultivated that is set apart from the trauma narrative.

Therapists can heighten their capacity for presence by drawing from the wisdom of their own embodied experiences. Embodied awareness not only assists clients in discovering and negotiating their own experiences but also contributes to the capacity of therapists to provide adequate support. Kleinman[12] describes the three specific skills drawn from concepts underlying dance/movement therapy that allow therapists to understand on a kinesthetic level what their clients are experiencing:

- **Rhythmic Synchrony:** the ability of therapists to be in tune with, and to cultivate relationship and connection with, their clients. For example, a therapist might move or breathe in the same rhythm as a client.
- **Kinesthetic Awareness:** the ability of therapists to sense themselves physically on both an internal and an external level. For example, a therapist might ask a client a question and simultaneously focus on his or her own embodied states and somatic sensations.
- **Kinesthetic Empathy:** the ability of therapists to foster shared expression. For example, the ability of the therapist to identify with the embodied experiences and sensations of the client whilst maintaining the capacity to differentiate their own experiences, reactions and responses from that of their clients.

Therapists' use of these skills can enable them to become highly sensitive to the internal and external states of conflict. In refining these skills, therapists will be better equipped to listen to the stories that live in somatic memories. Then they can help clients create new pathways of thinking while rehearsing alternative physiological patterns, making it possible to reshape old identifications with past traumas.

Utilizing the "Imaginal Realm" in Postconflict Settings

The arts can help individuals and communities draw from their own resources of resilience as they recover from conflict. Cultural knowledge and correlating practices can be restored through symbols as individuals struggle to communicate events that may be traumatic or difficult to articulate. In a synthesis of the literature of peace building and the strategic use of the arts, Shank and Schirch[13] explain how the arts are uniquely suited for nonverbal expression and thus powerful assets in peace-building work. Though the exact percentage of nonverbal expression in communication is widely debated by experts, there is relative consensus that its role is substantial. Wood cites that between 65 to 93 percent of all communicated meaning is nonverbal.[14]

This evidence challenges all those working in the field of peace building to reconsider how they respond to nonverbal behavior and communication, to what extent they rely on a verbal approach, and how they might expand their repertoire of skills with an embodied approach. Many art forms communicate through metaphor, the human body, the senses, and the experience and expression of emotion. Art can also make it possible to reclaim the body in the imaginal realm when the body has been the deliberate target of acts of oppression, abuse, or violence. Through imaginative modalities, the arts can reveal what has yet to be named or defined. Once given shape, these hidden or even unconscious aspects of identity, emotion, and experience can be witnessed and understood through the artistic approach of the "traumatic imagination."[15] Trusting this gentle, creative guide is like focusing on a distant light. Artistic renderings of what is otherwise ineffable emerge like a talisman, holding the essence of the experience while creating sufficient distance and safety.

Arts-Based Therapy in Practice: Case Studies from the Field

1. Refuge from the Storm: Arts Therapy with Asylum Seekers from the Middle East

Saiya (a pseudonym) left her home in the Middle East for political reasons. Living on the border of Iraq as an Iranian was no longer safe: her husband was being tortured in prison, she had been attacked, and her life was threatened. Saiya fled the country with her three children, enduring a long and dangerous journey. She eventually found sanctuary in South Wales, although she did not know how long, or even if, she would be allowed to stay. Saiya did not have a way of contacting her husband and was not certain if he was still alive.

When I first met Saiya, her shrouded head hung low, and she was always staring at the floor. She would nervously turn her keys round and round in her hands as she described her bleak reality: "Nowhere is safe anymore, nothing is certain, all hope has fled from me and my family." She spoke of her despair, desperation, and hopelessness. Her symptoms of distress were a concern for local health providers, who became alarmed by her increasing tendency toward isolation. The therapy and community arts team visited Saiya at home to explore whether she might want to join Incredible Journey's arts psychotherapy and community arts program for asylum seekers, run by the Ragamuffin Project (Creative Arts Therapy) and Arts for Us (community arts team, City and Council of Swansea).

Visiting asylum seekers in their homes created an opportunity to build bridges. Establishing foundations of trust and safety at the outset became essential as we navigated personal and political terrain. The complexity of working through translators also impacted communication and relationship formation. Setting specific times to debrief became paramount as we acknowledged the role that translation played in both verbal and nonverbal communication. The translators were not claiming to be neutral in their professional role, and it became important to recognize when they might be putting their own interpretation on what a client is trying to express.

Tapping into core values and belief systems through arts-based interventions began to anchor tumultuous experiences. In joining the arts psychotherapy group, Saiya found a new community of fellow asylum seekers where there was mutual understanding. Her recognition that many in the group had similar stories to tell created a sense of collective support, and her confidence slowly returned when she immersed herself in the visual arts and dance processes. Rather than framing dialogue around the pervading trauma and conflict, the arts mediated the traumatic memories of Saiya and the others. Clay sculptures made from household objects created a connection to their lives before the conflict. Just as a kiln transformed the clay, the arts created an alchemical process that slowly refined/transformed the group members. Working diligently with textiles offered a tangible platform for creative decision making. Metalworking was also significant; small silver pendants became symbolic talismans of hope against the skin.

The celebration of cultural dances with music and food also strengthened the relational threads between participants whose countries were at war with each other. Collaborative choreography slowly shifted strained relationships in nonthreatening ways. We composed a song together, and the original words became a symbolic anthem in the group:

> *Because we're all just the same underneath*
> *'cause we're all just the same under skin*
> *A river of hands now*
> *No more at war.*

The ritual of community singing offered a collective experience that could be shared and celebrated. We lit a candle to symbolize this mutuality and explored the significance of the fire from diverse cultural perspectives. The intersection of stories and rituals from the Middle East and Wales emerged, and it became apparent that fire was a powerful symbol of transformation, cleansing, and renewal. Poetry surfaced from this interaction: "Each time we light the candle it's like the light in the dark leading me home"; "The fire has made us closer." The ritual gathering helped the group create a place of mutual belonging as untold histories surfaced. Saiya began to be less withdrawn after her stories were witnessed in community and this collaborative exchange provided a new consensual frame for encountering one another. Active listening was a vital component of this witnessing. The potential for transferential processes also became a critical point of discernment. If I had tried to make things easier by finding instant solutions, this would have interfered with Saiya's learning and undermined her potential. She was heard, seen, and valued without a rational explanation for what had taken place. Simply surrendering to this stark reality created a lull in the storm. This artistic process surpassed conventional limits of representation and created a space in which she could be received.

Saiya recognized that although her situation remained unchanged, she was no longer solely a victim of her experience. She began to reclaim her body with a sensory language, and from this place she could translate unspeakable losses without a reliance on words. Her symptoms of trauma decreased; she began to sleep and eat well, her anxiety lessened dramatically, and her panic attacks stopped. Saiya had found a safe community and culture of care in which to begin her recovery.

2. Storms within Storms: Post-conflict Arts Therapy with Cambodians Evicted from Their Land

In Cambodia, land wars are unfortunately becoming another destructive experience layered upon historical traumas that are all too familiar to Cambodian people. Families and communities are being forced from their homes and land as a result of regional development. A refugee recalls one such event:

> In the early morning hours of Saturday January 24, 2009 approximately 500 demolition workers escorted by 300 mixed police in full riot gear surrounded the community of Dey Krahorm. Their mission, to forcibly evict the approximately 400 families that were living on the disputed land in the heart of Phnom Penh . . . families had erected barricades and stood defiantly in front of their houses. The police were able to break through the villagers' lines and disburse them with the use of tear gas, water cannons and rubber projectiles. In a matter of hours the demolition workers completely destroyed houses and market stalls. . . . At least 18 people were injured includ[ing] 5 seriously during the forced eviction.[16]

The community became refugees in their own country, and there has not been any legal or political action to date that compensates for these losses.

The Ragamuffin Project was asked to work alongside an international human rights organization with this community. The task was to explore the impact of the conflict from individual and communal perspectives. Initial assessments of the community showed symptoms of trauma that included nightmares, panic attacks, illness, unemployment, hopelessness, depression, and despair. This process took two months and involved creating conditions that could facilitate meetings with the community leaders.

This section draws from the experiences of three members of the community who joined an arts therapy group. Chea (a pseudonym) wanted to show the group when she felt the most disempowered and "frozen," as she called it. Creating a static image with people's bodies, Chea physically sculpted the moment when the bulldozer hit her home and knocked her mother to the ground. She stood in a posture of shock and described her life as being frozen since then.

In converging movement, breath, and sound, she began to find her voice and was able to express her deeper emotions about her experiences. She was angry, enraged, grief stricken, and felt utterly hopeless and powerless to respond. This visible embodiment made it possible for her to be witnessed, heard, and supported by the group. Repeating the movement with sound brought her into deeper and deeper contact with her own voice and power. Chea was expressing both the eviction and her life during the Pol Pot regime, where she had witnessed the brutal killing of her husband. With her body as the compass, she was able to draw closer to her experiences and could begin to safely grieve her deepest losses. The wisdom in her body knew how to navigate through the significant moments of inexpressible pain and sorrow. Though Chea was illiterate, words flowed from her poetically as we worked together with the movement. The end of the poem she created reflects the slow thawing of her frozen body:

> *Finding my voice unfreezing my body*
> *I can now reach down*
> *Pick up my heart and*
> *Hold it in my arms*
> *Until it heals again*
> *Until it heals again*
> *(Chea's poem)*

To accompany her poem, we created a simple dance from her gestures, each movement reflecting different facets of longing. Raising her fists in short, sharp movements, she punched at the air, turned and twisted around in a fury, and then dropped to the floor in a collapse. The movement patterning enabled her to shape new perspectives around her suffering. The energy shifted visibly in her body from contorted postures of despair to open postures of hope. We explored how the dance between the two could help her manage her everyday challenges. I witnessed Chea becoming the creator of her healing as her dance and words revived her.

Fifty-year-old Vann (a pseudonym), a member of the same group, sat in the only clothes he had saved from the eviction. His shirt, now too big from weight loss, hung off his gaunt body. As each member of the group was invited to check in, Vann cried as he spoke:

> I am holding a huge mountain, it's too heavy; I feel disabled because I have no job, no home, no land. My wife is nearly blind, they used tear gas, my blood pressure is high, and I have lost half my body weight. I have a five-month-old baby and two children, five and nine years; I am so very sad—my heart is dead. They killed my heart.

Vann was a key community leader who fought to save his village from the eviction but couldn't; subsequently he felt he had failed everyone, including himself. His symptoms of post-traumatic stress were acute, and he was often found wandering in the streets, with his baby left unattended. His distress had reached a peak point of crisis. I suggested to Vann that he create a movement to depict a visual image of the huge mountain. He readily did so by embodying the enormous pressure of the mountain in his hands until he could barely stand up. I asked him what he needed. "I need help, it's too heavy, I need other people!" he exclaimed. I asked the group to respond through their own self-selected movements, and people created movements that supported either Vann or the imaginary mountain he was holding. They all became connected through this embodied exchange, which gave them the capacity to identify with the weight of his suffering. We deepened his experience with words of support: "You are not alone, let us help you, let's share the load." Many more words of support and encouragement were added spontaneously as others became part of his solution. Vann looked down and saw a green crayon at his feet. He picked it up and said, "In my black, dead heart, I see a small green tree growing. I thought my heart was dead, they took and destroyed everything, but maybe they cannot destroy my heart."

Staying within the imaginal realm, Vann was able to engage in another life force. The metaphor of the mountain enabled him to reconnect to his body through an alternative mode of understanding. There were very few words spoken, no analysis or explanations, and no case history. Instead, the imagination reminded him that he was still alive and could be witnessed by others. Vann experienced such a release when he discovered that his heart was not dead and there was green life growing. It was as if he could finally "breathe like a released prisoner."[17]

"I can't talk about it." Satha, 67 years old, was present in the same group but could not speak about what had happened. In one session the group presented a still body-sculpture depicting the conflict of the eviction. The roles they represented included the community, the company forcing people off the land, and the officials instructing them what to do. The image was initially motionless. We then "pressed play," and the frozen image came to life. An intractable conflict played out between the two sides. Satha became increasingly agitated, and I invited her to join the drama and take whatever role she wanted. She stood on the side of the community. Seeing this, I gave her permission to communicate anything that she wanted to say. This invitation instantly shifted her whole stance, and her fragile frame transformed into a warrior's, full of power and strength. I then invited her to find her voice in the momentum of this new movement. She made her way toward the people who were forcing her to be evicted, and a torrent of words flew out of her. The person playing the role of the official was shocked. We explored this further through a movement-based dialogue and then swapped roles between the antagonists and the defenders of the land. This embodied relationship created a deeper understanding of the socioeconomic and political context of the situation. Investigating the antagonist's story from multiple perspectives created mobility in previously static relationships. This process enabled Satha to make connections to her own untold story:

> My heart is black, full of the black Khmer Rouge soldiers who took my husband away and killed him. I became a widow for thirty years living alone, and then I found I could buy a small piece of land with my grandchildren, I was so happy, it was like life had come back again. When they bulldozed my house, they threw a gas barrel at my chest; it was the same level of physical pain as when they took my husband away all those years ago and killed him. They beat me up and hit me. I was there and I was in the past at the same time. My heart filled up with all the blackness again.

Satha began to express the detail and depth of her experiences as she connected the past with the present in creative ways. In doing so, she recognized the sources of impasse that fueled her internal conflicts. We continued to deliberately explore points of resilience through movement, and she spoke with strong emotion: "When I showed the official how I really felt, it unlocked the fighter in me. I could understand him all locked up inside."

A New Weather System: Creating Conditions for Safe Therapeutic Practice in Navigating Conflicts

In each of the case studies above, there are specific conditions being fostered that are foundational for safe and effective therapeutic practice: the creation and building of trust, a place of psychological safety, confidentiality, absence of judgment, and a process where a client's creativity and inner world are central. Specific techniques will assist in achieving certain dimensions of therapeutic practice. However, the qualities of the therapist's "being" will influence whether a relationship is safe, beneficial, and ultimately transformative. I was deeply moved by my encounters with Saiya, Chea, Vann, and Satha. Meeting people who had lost everything challenged my own consumerism and attachment to possessions. Additionally, my experiences of home and belonging surfaced, and this awareness provoked my outrage toward the socioeconomic injustices. The ability to navigate these complexities without getting lost in the process is our collective challenge as therapists.

The therapeutic use of the arts can bring the most vulnerable and fragile states of being to the surface. Therefore, it becomes essential to cultivate a safe framework that can hold a range of emotions and varying states of being. To draw out intense and volatile memories and vulnerabilities and then leave them unacknowledged can cause the recurrence of traumatic experiences. Trust can easily be shattered if retraumatization results from an intervention. There is an ethical obligation in this work to acknowledge the power of the arts and the corresponding responsibility that lies at the heart of such initiatives.

Navigating Storms: The Importance of Professional Supervision and Self-Care in Therapeutic Practice

How can we be in the eye of the storm and at the same time tolerate the emotional and psychic disturbance that is being experienced? How can we integrate ourselves without unconsciously becoming entangled in another's conflicts? As an arts therapist, I draw on my own imagination and creativity to reveal the unconscious dialogue both with others and within myself. Satir uses the metaphor of an instrument to describe the artistry and fine-tuning involved: "How it is made, how it is cared for, its fine-tuning, and the ability, experience, sensitivity and creativity of the player will determine how the music will sound."[18]

Just as artistic modalities mediate, clarify, and create new systems of meaning, they also provide such strategies for the therapist's awareness and fine-tuning. My own creativity is a constant source of wisdom when working therapeutically. Supervision is also essential in the creative therapist's work and is an ethical requirement for practice. In essence, supervision is a relationship, where the supervisor acts as a third person and offers a different perspective outside of the client-therapist relationship.

My clinical supervisor and I considered many issues during client work. Some of the recurring themes included the impact of belief systems and cultural norms on recovery from trauma; the multiplicity of traumatic experiences and varying levels of impact on resilience and coping; psychiatric referrals; management of acute symptoms of distress, including dissociation, self-harm and suicidal ideation; influences from the political environment; Western and Eastern approaches to mental health; personal and professional support; and working with crisis and impasse. It is vital to step back and consider the underlying dynamics that may be influencing the processes. For example, while working with the evicted community, I began to feel a heavy weight, like a depression. In exploring this with my supervisor, I became connected to the impotence of the men in the group, who were essentially voiceless. In the protest it was the women who stood on the front line. The men were not allowed, because it was feared that their confrontation would become too violent; they were disempowered to protect their land, their homes, and their families. The cultural belief was that the men needed to be able to appease and free the spirits that were still locked in the stolen land. They had experienced a severing of both their masculinity and their connection to the spirit world, and their rage at this injustice masked their deepest pain. I wrote a song to reflect back to them how I had received this aspect of their story. Sharing the song served as a catalyst to unlock their own songs, and over time the men slowly began to find their voice in the community again.

Concluding Remarks

Carl Jung presented the following challenge as the world emerged from World War II, and it is perhaps as relevant today as it was then, challenging our duties as therapists, mediators, and advocates in a world in conflict:

> We are living in times of great disruption: political passions are aflame, internal upheavals have brought nations to the brink of chaos. . . . This critical state of things has such a tremendous influence on the psychic life of the individual that the analyst . . . feels the violence of its impact even in the quiet of his consulting room . . . The psychologist cannot avoid coming to grips with contemporary history, even if his very soul shrinks from the political uproar, the lying propaganda, and the jarring speeches of the demagogues. We need not mention his duties as a citizen, which confront him with a similar task.[19]

There are many across the world committed to engaging in this similar task, yet the need is not diminishing. This duty goes hand in hand with the challenge presented in this chapter: to fully engage the imagination in the complexities of conflict. Carrying this work out in a safe and ethical manner is one of our primary responsibilities. The arts offer rich resources that enable individuals and communities to meet challenges and facilitate the relationship of therapy that catalyzes both healing and transformation. The arts can offer a new language for indescribable events when words cannot convey the severity of traumas.

In the "imaginal realm," new alternatives can be conceived beyond the constrictive narratives that are often associated with trauma and conflict. The arts naturally serve us in reconnecting with our inner resources, resilience, and ability to build relationships with others. However, the practice of healing begins within our own roles as professionals. The artistry of walking with others through the storms requires our own humanity, vulnerability, and preparedness to step into the unknown. Self-care, support strategies, and professional supervision are imperative if we are going to bear witness to the fullness of life's experiences. The question remains not how we can replace one approach with another, but how we will work to bring a new level of consciousness to our practices as peace builders, conflict mediators, and therapists.

Organizations: Finding Coherence

*T*his final section looks at the relevance of dance to organizations. The first chapter is by Mark McCrea, an American workplace mediator and trainer, and focuses on the importance of mindfulness. He examines how physical movement, when paired with more conventional approaches to managing conflict, can bring new perspectives to conflict rooted in differing worldviews. Mark looks in particular at bullying and discrimination in the workplace and how movement can help victims find reserves of mental resilience, along with how movement can help mediators cultivate the calm and detachment needed to operate in sometimes trying circumstances. He also explores the value of kinetic facilitation in helping groups develop trust and increase mutual support when tackling complex issues.

In the second chapter, Clemens Lang, a Swiss-German physicist and an organizational consultant with a particular interest in corporate social responsibility, also sees the body as a potential bridge to better understanding different worldviews. He reflects on the formality and efficiency of Swiss business culture and how this can also lead to a reluctance to express emotions and, consequently, difficulty in unlocking conflict that is rooted in emotional differences. Clemens describes how he has used movement to bypass this problem and discusses the challenge to use it in ways that are not so culturally uncomfortable that they create new barriers to progress and that also reveal to those involved aspects of their problems that may previously have gone unrecognized.

Finding Coherence I

Observations on Movement and Worldview Conflict in the Workplace
MARK MCCREA

> *"We stand in parallel position, our arms by our sides, head aligned, back and chest lifted. We take a deep breath, lifting our arms up to the sides of our torso as we inhale. Journeying to Mother Earth, we release through the back, bend our knees and roll to the floor. We touch the earth, paying homage to Mother. We stretch our arms, fingers and palms, caressing earth. We begin a tracing with our fingers from earth upward through our body until we reach the sky, paying homage to the ancestors. We arch, releasing both our torso and pelvis to the back, stretching our torso, arms in parallel position above the head, hands flexed, fingers pointing toward the back. We release our torso to the earth, keeping our torso flat and parallel to earth Mother. Torso and legs at right angles. We stretch. With a release of breath we continue rolling to the floor, rebounding in a roll back up to our original position. We take a deep breath and contemplate our completeness and connectedness to Mother Earth and Father Sky."[1]*
> *African Dance: Divine Motion*, Ferne Caulker

Dancing at the Crossroads

The words cited above describe the movements of a salutation (Finding the Ashé in You) used at the beginning of African dance classes taught by Ferne Yangyeitie Caulker, founder and artistic/executive director of Ko-Thi Dance Company in Milwaukee, Wisconsin. Ko-Thi is an international African dance and music ensemble. According to Caulker, the Yoruba people of Nigeria believe that ashé represents a divine gift that is expressed in each person through movement. Caulker says that the salutation provides an opportunity for students to commit their awareness and their bodies to seeing and experiencing the world in a new way. It is an invitation to let go of safe and familiar notions, perceptions, and preferences and allow a flow into new shapes, rhythms, and levels of understanding.[2]

The participants in the Dancing at the Crossroads workshop in Saas-Fee, Switzerland, were essentially invited to find their ashé. The event was a unique opportunity to spend several days intensely interacting with conflict intervenors, academics, and performing artists from around the globe, exploring the utilization of movement and dance as conflict management modalities. We were encouraged to let go of our dependence on lectures, PowerPoint presentations, and safely choreographed discussions and, instead, experience a new aesthetic that merged body, mind, and spirit through the use of dance, creative movement, music, and critical reflection. Under the masterful guidance of our facilitators, our bodies were unleashed to sense, feel, and be creative. We were encouraged to feel our breath; to allow our brains and other organs to rest inside our skeletons; to feel the relationship between body parts and then to move with focus and awareness of that relationship; to locate our movement prohibitions; to move with sound; and to trust the wisdom of our bodies to know more than our conscious understanding about what is safe and what is threatening.

It has been suggested that movement and breath signify life.[3] Havelock Ellis has written: "If we are indifferent to the art of dancing, we have failed to understand, not merely the supreme manifestation of physical life, but also the supreme symbol of spiritual life."[4] In some societies, dance is as essential as eating and sleeping, and it provides a means to commune with nature or to perform extraordinary feats of endurance and strength.[5] Dance may involve rituals, stories, myths, and symbols that preserve and transmit cultural values essential to the fabric of community life.

The dance and dialogue sessions in Saas-Fee created a context in which a group of strangers and sojourners celebrated the divine, without judgment or censoring. The creative, spontaneous, and improvised movement workshops in conjunction with periods of critical reflection formed pathways that facilitated awareness of our own deeply ingrained thought patterns, biases, and feelings. These movement activities literally pushed to the surface some of the flawed assumptions underlying my own habitual thought patterns. The resulting dissonance and openings enabled me to take in an exciting embodied perspective that has profoundly influenced how I perceive and understand my personal and professional context.

Creative Movement and Dance

Creative movement and dance are linked to a mind-body-spirit frame that honors personal discovery and transformation over risk assessment, tactical maneuvering, and problem solving. This frame seems to be based on the widely accepted notion that our minds and bodies influence each other in ways that can promote healing and resilience. In Saas-Fee, our minds and bodies were connected in astonishingly powerful ways through the use of creative and improvised movement. This leads me to the following observations:

- Without being aware of it, individuals often communicate with their bodies.
- Listening to the body is another way to access inner experience.
- The body expresses inner experience much more adequately than verbal communication.
- Significant change in movement affects total functioning and behavior.

In essence, the dance and movement frameworks in Saas-Fee established a foundation for the participants to become consciously aware of habitual thought patterns and emotions and understand how these factors impact appraisals of and responses to conflict.

This chapter explores the notion that mindfulness, cultivated by an intervention approach that uses creative physical movement in conjunction with conflict management and critical reflection, might be useful in addressing workplace conflict linked to worldviews. Worldview conflict in the workplace can be characterized by physical and emotional trauma linked to tyranny and aggression. This encompasses bullying, harassment, and discrimination involving groups or individuals targeted on the basis of sex, age, religion, ethnicity, race, occupation, body shape, and many other factors. These conflicts often involve deeply ingrained conflict-supporting beliefs that combine with powerful emotions to distort and rigidify communications. This makes it almost impossible for parties and dispute resolvers to take in information that could clarify issues, enhance participation, and possibly improve organizational outcomes. The chapter is essentially framed around two questions:

- Why is creative physical movement an important factor in the design of interventions intended to manage workplace conflict attributable to worldviews?
- What are the specific components of an effective workplace conflict intervention that would use such techniques to address conflict regarding worldviews?

Worldviews and Workplace Conflict

The U.S. workplace is increasingly becoming a site for intense political activity, where workers challenge and reinforce structures of power reflected in the society at large. As more people from diverse cultures acquire jobs formerly held almost exclusively by members of dominant groups, workers in those groups have expressed fears regarding perceived violations of their rights or privileges. These dynamics often contribute to creating work environments that are permeated by threats, intimidation, ridicule, insults, physical assaults, and other offensive conduct.[6]

According to the U.S. Equal Employment Opportunity Commission (EEOC), total charges regarding discrimination in the United States increased from 93,277 in 2009 to 99,992 in 2010. As shown in the chart below, most protected group categories under the EEOC's jurisdiction experienced an increase.

	2009	2010
Total Charges*	93,277	99,992
Race	33,579	35,890
Retaliation	33,579	36,258
Sex/Gender	28,028	29,029
Age	22,778	23,264
Disability	21,451	25,165
National Origin	11,134	11,304
Religion	3,386	3,790

*Note: An individual may face charges of more than one type of discrimination.

Also, the key findings of an August 2010 study regarding bullying in U.S. workplaces, conducted by the Workplace Bullying Institute, indicated that

- 35 percent of all workers have experienced bullying firsthand;
- 62 percent of bullies are men, and 58 percent of targets are women;
- in 80 percent of cases, women bullies target other women;
- bullying is four times more prevalent than illegal harassment; and
- the majority (68 percent) of bullying is same-gender harassment.[7]

Conflict associated with workplace bullying and harassment may be either predatory or dispute related.[8] Predatory bullying and harassment involve situations in which victims have done nothing provocative that may reasonably justify the conduct of bullies. In such cases, the victim may be a member of a certain out-group or simply an easy target for a predator's need to demonstrate power. Predatory bullying has been linked to organizational cultures in which harassment, aggressiveness, and hostility are institutionalized as part of leadership and management practices.[9] Organizational tolerance of bullying and harassment is communicated by the lack of sanctions for individuals engaging in this type of behavior.

Dispute-related bullying and harassment are typically based on specific workplace interactions in which a party's identity or self-image is at stake. The alleged transgression is perceived as deeply offensive by the recipient. Dispute-related bullying involves extreme distrust, fear, suspicion, contempt, and anger.

Predatory and dispute-related bullying involve patterns of multiple negative acts, such as isolation, humiliation, and intimidation, occurring over extended periods of time. These acts prevent targets from satisfactorily performing their job duties and seriously jeopardize their personal health and well-being.[10]

Victims subjected to predatory and dispute-related bullying are more likely to adopt avoidance or resignation coping styles than problem-solving styles, which can increase their likelihood of suffering long-term negative effects or leaving the organization.[11] Both types of bullying may also involve elements more typically associated with unlawful discrimination and harassment, which have been linked to anxiety, depression, and obsessive-compulsive disorder;[12] decreased motivation to achieve goals; increased emotional discomfort, anger, and emotional problems;[13] and chronic health conditions, such as high blood pressure, heart disease, cancer, and diabetes.[14]

The dynamics of bullying, harassment, and discrimination and their effects in the workplace may reflect conflict involving deep differences in values or worldviews. Worldviews have been defined as sets of assumptions about physical and social reality—what is considered "true or false," "good or bad," "desirable or undesirable"—that may powerfully affect cognition and behavior.[15] LeBaron has indicated that "worldviews are deeply rooted in the human psyche, encompassing multiple dimensions of culture; they primarily exist at an unconscious level where our identities are created; and they implicate spiritual, imaginative, emotional, and somatic channels in our meaning-making processes."[16]

As such, worldviews influence our perceptions, judgments, and overt behaviors, particularly spontaneous behaviors such as nonverbal reactions, which frequently occur in conflict interactions. They can also activate stereotypical or prejudiced mental associations that are firmly entrenched in thought patterns that are ultimately automatic.[17] These automatic thought patterns support conflict when they are characterized by

- linear thinking—attempting to predict the future on the basis of a particular factor, attitude, or behavior in the past;
- hierarchical thinking—placing others or self in an inferior or a superior position; or
- dichotomous thinking—an either/or mindset (I am either good or bad, right or wrong).[18]

Conflict-supporting beliefs linked to worldviews are central, rigid, held with great confidence; they tend to produce certainty in decision-making situations. According to Bar-Tal and Halperin,[19] these beliefs are a major barrier to the management and resolution of conflict because they "freeze" individuals to their prior knowledge.[20] Freezing motivates individuals to view prior knowledge as being truthful and valid because it fulfills various needs for them. Several cognitive strategies—only attending to, interpreting, actively seeking, and less critically examining information consistent with supporting beliefs—are common in efforts to shore up prior knowledge.[21]

When the terrain is deepened by worldview differences, conflict easily becomes intractable. Although conflicts have objectively identifiable issues and circumstances, their perceived intractability is sustained by subjective meaning making and emotions, which may determine conflict behavior more than objective knowledge or the issues that began the conflicts in the first place.[22] These cycles of conflict may also involve actions that are not based on any discernible concrete goals and are sometimes completely dissociated from any prospect of success.[23]

Gaining conscious awareness of deeply ingrained automatic thought patterns is a critical first step in effectively addressing conflict involving worldviews. However, since these patterns are difficult to control and can efficiently operate without conscious awareness, access to them may be somewhat difficult. This difficulty is further compounded where cultural conditioning values direct forms of expression, rational analysis, and logical problem solving. The following sections explore facets of movement, dance, and mindfulness and identify how these alternative strategies might—and in some cases, already do—contribute to mediating "frozen" workplace conflicts based on worldviews.

Benefits of Dance and Creative Movement

Dance and creative movement could be used to enhance parties' capacities to more effectively manage the dispute-related stress and thought patterns that frequently block the emergence of more-mindful perspectives of conflict situations. Kabat-Zinn has defined mindfulness as "the awareness that arises through intentionally attending to one's moment-to-moment experience in a nonjudgmental and accepting way."[24] Mindfulness also means being aware of bodily sensations, thoughts, emotions, and consciousness.[25] According to

Langer, mindfulness prevents us from being trapped by categories, automatic behavior, and single perspectives.[26] Riskin has suggested that mindfulness helps negotiators and mediators in calming the mind, concentrating, experiencing compassion and empathy, and achieving awareness of—and distance from—thoughts, emotions, and habitual impulses that can interfere with making good judgments, building rapport, and motivating others.[27] Mindful interactions in the workplace may encourage candid, open, and honest conversations; reduce mistrust; promote dignity and respect; and possibly reduce conflict-related costs.

Certainly dance has been shown to yield positive mental and physical effects that contribute to such mindfulness. Believed to exist in all human societies, dance has been defined as "human behavior composed of (from the dancer's perspective, which is usually shared by other members of the dancer's culture) purposeful, intentionally rhythmical, and culturally patterned sequences of nonverbal body movements other than ordinary motor activities."[28] Cultural dance, associated with religious and social celebrations of cultures and ethnic groups, integrates the physiological, psychological, and sociological aspects of one's lived experiences and worldviews into highly personal movement.[29]

The incorporation of visual, tactile, and auditory stimulation in dance enables emotional release and creative expression of feelings and moods and has been linked to mental and physical health benefits. Dance has been shown to be quite effective in reducing back pain, cardiovascular risk factors, stress, physical tension, and problematic weight gain, as well as resolving symptoms of anxiety and depression.[30] In many African, Native American, and Middle Eastern cultures, dance ritual is rooted in traditional healing and is used to provide participants with spiritual and emotional well-being, consciousness-raising or mood-altering experiences, and self-healing powers over various evil and psychological forces.[31] Dance may also cause emotional changes and altered states of consciousness, inducing "the feeling of a qualitative shift in thinking, disturbance in sense of time, loss of control, change in body image, perceptual distortion, change in meaning, sense of the ineffable, feelings of rejuvenation, and hyper suggestibility."[32]

Additionally, Vetter et al. have described creative movement or dance improvisation as "a process of uncovering and describing one's lived experience through motion" intended to produce a cathartic moment, defined as release in tension and anxiety, by bringing repressed feelings or fears to the surface.[33] Creative movement and dance improvisation have been successfully used in reducing stress linked to the physical, emotional, and financial responsibilities associated with disability- or illness-related caregiving.[34]

Through dance, humans have the capacity to gain access to feelings that cannot be verbalized.[35] Essentially, it is a means of communication that serves to make the extraordinary and inexplicable in life understandable, manageable, and less threatening.[36] In this way, dance has the potential to transform the observer as well as the dancer.[37]

Moreover, the symbolic qualities of dance can capture the imagination in ways other forms of physical activity cannot, crossing language barriers to expand participants' knowledge of cultures outside their own.[38] It is clear that dance might yet be a powerful tool in creating a safe context for "unfreezing" and negotiating conflict-supporting beliefs and strong emotions.

Conflict intervention tools based on dance or creative movement principles could be effectively implemented by use of kinetic facilitation and mindful exercise techniques, which enable parties and intervenors to engage in a dialogue of movement, emphasizing verbal and nonverbal channels of expression to create trust, awareness, and understanding.

Kinetic Facilitation

Kinesics is increasingly being used as a facilitation tool in team building and strategic planning. According to Raymond Birdwhistell, kinesics refers to the study of all bodily motions that are communicative.[39] He suggests that movement exercises can potentially promote rapport and trust among group members.[40] Kawakami has indicated that movement exercises can create inclusivity while respecting diverse viewpoints by involving all members of a group in the same activity at the same time without requiring special skills; establishing common grounds of experience through engaging members in an exercise and eliciting feedback about it; and enabling facilitators to conduct group relationship formation activities in a shorter period of time than when not using movement.[41] Kawakami asserts: "Kinetic exercises fill the relationship gap in a group's formation by intentionally focusing on the building of mindful relationships among group members, which is especially necessary for individuals with a high context orientation."[42]

Mindful Exercise

Mindful exercise, described by La Forge as "physical exercise executed with a profound inwardly directed contemplative focus," is also being increasingly used to cultivate self-nurturance, stress minimization, and healing.[43] It consists of cognitively-based low-exertion activities that combine meditative mindfulness with slower movement or static exercise to induce affective changes.[44] Mindful exercise generally requires individuals to focus on the action they are doing, to feel their movements, and to develop a sense of their body and motion.[45] It relies on self-monitoring of perceived effort, breathing, the conscious relaxation of muscles, and internal awareness rather than cues from an exercise leader or peers, as in conventional group exercise classes.[46]

Mindful exercise may be more powerful in immediate mood enhancement than high-intensity rhythmical movements that are not cognitively focused.[47] It promotes cardiorespiratory benefits (decreased resting systolic blood pressure, increased pulmonary function, improved respiratory function), musculoskeletal benefits (increased muscular strength and flexibility, improved posture, increased neuromuscular balance), and psychophysiological benefits (increased cognitive performance, improved relaxation, decreased anxiety and expression).[48] Modalities include some forms of yoga, Qigong, tai chi, Pilates, neuromuscular integrative action, the Alexander technique, and the Feldenkrais Method.

Mindful Conflict Engagement

The gathering at Saas-Fee and research since that time have produced new insights about possible uses of dance and creative movement to address conflict related to worldviews. The remainder of this chapter describes an experimental workplace intervention that uses creative movement in conjunction with conflict management training and critical reflection to bring to the surface and shift deeply rooted value systems, allowing the emergence of more-viable approaches to toxic and hostile work environments. Creatively using movement to access the body's inner experience may facilitate critical thinking, encourage full participation, promote mutual understanding, foster inclusive solutions, and cultivate shared responsibility. Conflict management training and critical reflection could complement this by providing concrete skills that enable targets and perpetrators to address their differences in less hostile and more-productive ways.

The experimental integration of creative movement, critical reflection, and conflict management training will be referred to as MCE (mindful conflict engagement). This section explains the major components of MCE and provides a description of the process, which may be used at all levels of an organization. MCE is intended to address bullying, harassment, discrimination, and other severe workplace conflicts by changing the nature of daily interactions and conversations among workers. It is based on three key assumptions underlying shifts in thought and behavior:

- what individuals think and know affects how they act
- knowledge is necessary (but not sufficient) for prompting behavioral change
- individual perceptions, skills, and social context influence behavior[49]

MCE may

- create conditions for de-escalating tensions between individuals or work units,
- promote critical reflection and self-disclosure among individuals,
- help individuals identify moral and ethical blind spots,
- reduce mistrust between individuals or work units,
- allow conciliatory gestures, and
- lead to imagining new creative possibilities.

MCE is intended to prepare workers to better manage their own conflicts, without needing continued oversight and intervention from external experts. It is not a quick fix for recurring conflict issues but an attempt to manage conflict in real time by increasing the competencies of individuals who are closest to the day-to-day manifestations of particular conflicts. MCE activities can be included as part of team building, strategic planning, assessment, or problem-solving interventions. MCE could also be included in work-site health and wellness initiatives, leadership development programs, and diversity training.

MCE Process Design Considerations

The components of MCE are meant to increase participants' understanding of characteristics and behaviors associated with bullying, harassment, and discrimination; the effects of bullying and harassment on individuals' job performance and physical and psychological health; power dynamics between victims and perpetrators; and the links between bullying, harassment, discrimination, and organizational culture. The components are designed to be delivered in three segments: one full day followed by two half days. Facilitators should have substantial experience and training in dance/movement and workplace conflict management.

1. Enrollment Preparation

Each segment opens with movement activities involving cultural dance, creative improvisation, or mindful exercise. All activities are designed to cultivate participants' mindfulness. Enrollment materials for the program should include a screening questionnaire that helps participants determine whether they should confer with a physician prior to engaging in the movement components. The document should be similar to the following, based on the Physical Activity Readiness Questionnaire (PAR-Q) developed by Public Health Agency of Canada:

- Has your doctor ever said that you have a heart condition and should only do physical activity recommended by a doctor?
- Do you feel pain in your chest when you do physical activity?
- In the past month, have you had chest pain when you were not doing physical activity?
- Do you lose your balance because of dizziness, or do you ever lose consciousness?
- Do you have a bone or joint problem (e.g., back, knee, or hip) that could be made worse by a change in physical activity?
- Is your doctor currently prescribing drugs (e.g., water pills) for high blood pressure or heart disease?
- Do you know of any reason why you should not engage in physical activity?[50]

Due to emotional trauma associated with their workplace experiences, some MCE participants may have a high level of anxiety sensitivity to relatively benign bodily sensations during vigorous movement, such as faster heartbeat, rapid breathing, and sweating.[51] Such individuals may experience panic symptoms and fear, characterized by dizziness, numbness, tingling, breathlessness, heart palpitations, and chest pain, which may hamper their participation in creative movement activities.[52] Prior to movement activity during each segment, to avoid surprises or other unexpected developments, participants should be advised that some of them may experience uncomfortable sensations. Those who become uncomfortable should be encouraged to try to relax with the sensation or to withdraw from the activity if they believe they may be at risk for adverse consequences.

2. Facilitator Qualifications/Responsibilities

Ideally, MCE should be co-facilitated by persons with substantial experience conducting workplace conflict intervention training and professional movement training. Workplace conflict intervention trainers should have hands-on experience negotiating or mediating issues involving bullying, harassment, and discrimination. Movement training experts should have direct experience conducting dance or mindful exercise training that is safe, executed at low to moderate intensities, and is adaptable to groups with a wide range of functional capacities. The primary tasks of facilitators are to manage the delivery of all MCE learning content, encourage open discussions and full participation, and cultivate an atmosphere for safe and respectful communication of diverse points of view.

The legal protections and liabilities discussion should be facilitated by a lawyer with experience mediating or litigating workplace bullying, harassment, and discrimination disputes. Also, the cultural dance movement exercises should be facilitated by persons with experience performing or teaching particular cultural dance activities.

3. Physical Setting

The physical setting for MCE should be large enough to allow participants to safely engage in a reasonable amount of free-flowing movement. Physical settings away from the workplace are preferable in some instances to foster more active and autonomous engagement by all participants. The space used for movement activities should be accessible for persons needing physical accommodations and should be free of extraneous noise, strong smells, and other distractions.

4. Warm-Up/Cool-Down

Facilitators should lead the group in a warm-up immediately before movement activities to prepare participants' bodies and minds for more-vigorous physical exertion. Warm-ups should consist of light physical elements that essentially prepare muscles for stretching. Facilitators should demonstrate proper stretching techniques to increase participants' comfort, ability to move freely, and energy level; improve posture and relaxation; and lessen susceptibility to muscle and tendon injuries.[53] Stretching should also be conducted during cool-down periods to alleviate potential soreness and to return bodies to normal activity levels. Warm-ups and cool-downs may include shaking of body parts, foot exercises, spinal twists, moving with breath, tension and release, and arm swings.

5. Movement Activity

Each segment includes movement activity with requisite warm-up, stretching, and cool-down periods. Activities will consist of creative improvisational movement, mindful exercise, and cultural dance. Creative improvisational movement will be used in the first segment primarily to relieve any tension and anxiety participants may feel and to acquaint them with the idea that bodily movements may be used as a medium to connect with major life issues in a personally meaningful manner. This type of movement should include a number of fun and stimulating activities, such as those noted by Vetter et al., which include using soothing background music and facilitator voice inflections; having participants move only one body part with their eyes closed, then gradually adding more body parts until they are moving the entire body; asking participants to walk up to someone in the class at random and introduce themselves (repeating this several times); asking participants in pairs or small groups to have a "movement conversation," in which one person moves and another responds with similar or contrasting movements; and asking participants to create a story with movement, showing a beginning, a middle, and an ending with specific types of motion, such as walking, running, hopping, jumping, skipping, sliding, and so forth.[54]

6. Mindful Exercise Activity

Mindful exercise introduces participants to the notion of using physical activity executed with a "profound inwardly directed contemplated focus."[55] Mindful exercise is implemented in the second segment and is focused on meditation or contemplation, proprioceptive awareness, breath centering, anatomic alignment, and energetic awareness. These factors are the essential components of mindful exercise identified by LaForge.[56] Modalities that participants may engage in include, but are not limited to

- styles of yoga that are appropriate for participants who are nonambulatory, relatively weak, or fatigued;
- Qigong—movements executed in standing, sitting, and supine positions at very low levels, focused on balance, breathing, and good posture;
- tai chi—flowing, graceful martial-arts-type movements that emphasize breathing, power, or relaxation;
- Pilates—extremely orderly system of slow, controlled, and distinct movements that demand cognitive focus; and
- neuromuscular integrative action (NIA)—blended movements and concepts from diverse sources, including tai chi, yoga, martial arts, modern dance, and ethnic dance, that foster creativity, self-expression, and spontaneity.

7. Cultural Dance Activity

Cultural dance is defined as "dance particular to a cultural or ethnic group that stems from the purpose of celebration, whether it be religious, temporal or social."[57] It is included in the third segment because of its capacity to expand participants' knowledge of dance outside their own cultures. These activities should encourage enjoyment and social interaction; require no special equipment or clothing; and be noncompetitive, compatible with the music and dance tastes of the group, and designed to meet the needs of groups that may not respond well to traditional physical activity. Cultural dance activities may include folk dances, line dances, belly dances, step dances, break dances, praise dances, square dances, and other relevant genres, such as jazz, ballroom, and hip-hop.

    These activities are expressly intended to expand participants' cross-cultural knowledge of dance, promote the appreciation of cultural differences, and strengthen participants' ties with one another. Facilitators should endeavor to educate participants about the origins and meanings of the particular dance movements.

8. Case Study/Role Play

Facilitators present a case study based on a particular workplace conflict. The conflict should have key elements of bullying, harassment, and discrimination. The case study describes the main features of the work environment, the dynamics of pertinent interactions, the evolution of events precipitating the conflict, and effective conflict management approaches. Ideally, important aspects of the case study are phased in during each segment of the MCE process. Discussion should occur based on substantive content presented and discussed in each segment.

Facilitators should role-play critical parts of the case study to expand and deepen participants' understanding. Role plays should enable participants to more fully comprehend the situational and contextual dynamics of bullying, harassment, and discrimination and how to possibly navigate these challenging encounters. Role-play exercises will prompt dialogue and reflection regarding the issues, encourage participants to express whatever feeling they have about the enactment, and guide participants to speak their own truth. Each role play will be followed by a debrief to enable participants to note what captured their attention and what they learned.

The elements described above should be implemented during the three segments. Each segment has sections pertaining to the movement and content activities reflecting the core focus of the MCE process.

Segment 1

1. Introduction

Segment 1 introduces the MCE approach in addressing bullying, harassment, and discrimination in the workplace. The segment provides an orientation to the nature and effects of conflict associated with bullying, harassment, and discrimination; essential elements of the concept of mindfulness; and the application of movement to enhance participants' capacities to address these issues.

Segment 1 includes customary introductions and a review of ground rules. Suggested ground rules include confidentiality regarding personal information discussed in the segments, respect for everyone's movement efforts and class participation, freedom to not share an insight, permission to leave a session at any time, and other factors expressly solicited from participants.

2. Overview

This section provides an overview of the nature and prevalence of bullying, harassment, and discrimination; the effects of bullying and harassment on victims, witnesses, and family members; characteristics of victims and perpetrators; the impact of bullying, harassment, and discrimination on organizations; and legal protections and liabilities.

3. Warm-Up

Warming up with movement is a way to "bring everyone into the room," emphasizing commonality and mutual respect. It also adds an air of vitality to the process and helps people relax and engage.

4. Creative Improvisational Movement Activity and Cool-Down

This section fosters the realization that bullying and similar forms of behavior hurt the body as well as the mind because hurts are stored in the tissues, leading to physical as well as mental and emotional pain. As participants are encouraged to improve movement, they identify choice points in their day-to-day actions and find ways to stretch beyond habitual patterns of thought and behavior. Some of the Saas-Fee exercises are helpful here because they map conflict dynamics onto physical movement, teaching participants about how conflict can be held in the body. Cooling down prepares everyone for the next section.

5. Automatic Thinking Patterns and Conflict Styles

Section 5 primarily involves an overview of automatic thinking patterns and their relationship to conflict dynamics. The section will cover the formation and nature of automatic thought patterns; how they can lead to innumerable categorizations on the basis of criteria such as sex, race, age, occupation, body shape, and so on; how the presence of culturally devalued groups can trigger the activation of stereotypical thoughts and negative evaluations; and how conflict styles (such as avoiding, accommodating, competing, compromising, and collaborating) linked to automatic thinking patterns impact the dynamics of bullying, harassment, and discrimination. Participants will be given the opportunity to assess their own conflict style by completing a brief conflict style inventory.

6. Mindfulness—Self-Awareness (Assumptions, Values, Beliefs)

This module provides an overview and discussion of how participants see the world via their own assumptions, values, and beliefs. Participants will engage in a small-group exercise in which they will be asked to choose from a range of responses to indicate where they exist on values continua for concepts such as the following:

- fate/destiny (life is what happens to me) ↔ individual control (life is what I make it)
- indirect communication (maintaining harmony is critical) ↔ direct communication (telling it like it is, even if it hurts)
- stability, tradition, and continuity (accepting things as they are) ↔ change is natural and positive (challenging the status quo)[58]

Discussion will focus on how perceptions and definitions of abuse are largely socially constructed and reflect culturally defined norms and values regarding acceptable and unacceptable behavior.[59]

The section will also address basic elements of mindfulness and their application to workplace bullying, harassment, and discrimination, including concepts such as

- non-striving—not forcing things,
- nonjudging—observing the present without evaluation,
- acceptance—a clearer understanding of the present so one can more effectively respond (does not mean passivity or resignation),

- patience—allowing things to unfold in their time,
- trust—life is unfolding as it is supposed to,
- openness—creating possibility by paying attention to all feedback in the present moment, and
- letting go—not holding on to thoughts, feelings, or experiences (which does not mean suppressing those thoughts, feelings, or experiences).[60]

In addition, this section will also increase participants' understanding of the levels of mindfulness articulated by Epstein: denial and externalization (mindlessness); imitation (behavioral modeling); curiosity (cognitive understanding and emotions and attitudes); insight; and generalization, incorporation, and presence.[61]

7. Case Study/Role Play Regarding Conflict Styles

This section includes an overview and discussion of part 1 of the case study illustrating the dynamics of bullying and harassment in a workplace context. Facilitators will role-play selected aspects of the case study to show how early stages of unaddressed bullying and harassment impact thinking patterns and conflict styles. They will also demonstrate mindless versus mindful ways to address specific situations depicted during the role play and elicit suggested approaches from participants. All suggestions will be recorded on flip charts.

Segment 2

1. Warm-Up and Mindful Exercise Activity

2. Communication Styles

Facilitators provide an overview and discussion of communication styles and their effect on conflict dynamics, including assertive, aggressive, and submissive communication; verbal abuse; and hate speech. This section also covers various approaches to self-disclosure, setting boundaries, and identifying and responding to boundary violations.

3. Communicating Stories of Bullying and Harassment

This section discusses approaches for effective and safe engagement of personal stories regarding bullying and harassment. Suggested approaches include the following:

- expressing emotions appropriately
- providing consistent details
- inviting relevant observations
- emphasizing competence
- showing consideration for others' perspectives
- using language that is clear and easily understood[62]

4. Case Study/Role Play Regarding Communication Issues

This section continues the case study introduced in segment 1. During part two, participants are provided additional information regarding communication dynamics as patterns of bullying, harassment, and discrimination escalate. Facilitators will role-play selected aspects of the case to demonstrate effective approaches to escalation through setting boundaries and then identifying and appropriately responding to boundary violations. Suggested approaches to boundary issues will be elicited from participants and recorded on flip charts.

5. Debrief of Role Play

Segment 3

1. Warm-Up, Cultural Dance Activity, Cool-Down

2. Overview and Discussion

This section focuses on specific types of workplace conduct, such as silent treatment, social exclusion, verbal abuse, demeaning treatment, excessively harsh criticisms of performance, confidentiality violations, withholding work assignments, stealing or intentionally sabotaging or destroying work materials, and derogatory comments regarding racial or ethnic group status.

3. Discussion

Facilitators subsequently discuss characteristics of the revenge process noted by Jones, including triggering events, revenge motives (procedural, distributive, interpersonal, or informational injustice; mistreatment and disrespect), breaking points (identity threat, damage to core psychological needs, violation of moral code), and attributions (negative overly personalized thinking).[63] Specific categories of revenge behavior are also discussed, including actions intended to harm a perpetrator's career or reputation, actions that financially benefit an avenger, and actions that deliberately reduce the effectiveness of the work performed by the avenger.

4. Preventing Perceived Mistreatment

This section features a presentation and discussion of effective ways to prevent and manage perceived mistreatment, including notions of forgiveness, apologies, and resolution. Facilitators will offer definitions of forgiveness and ideas about the relationships between apology and forgiveness. They will also provide information about negotiating and how apology and forgiveness may be part of negotiation processes.

5. Case Study/Role Play Regarding Negotiations

This section continues the case study from segments 1 and 2. During part 3, participants will be provided case information with more details regarding specific types of mistreatment,

mistreatment-related revenge, and approaches to forgiveness, apology and resolution. Facilitators will role-play selected aspects of the case to demonstrate effective approaches to forgiveness, apology, and resolution. Suggestions elicited from participants regarding these issues will be recorded on flip charts, and an overall synthesis will be presented.

Conclusion

Implementing workplace interventions to address conflict regarding worldview issues is difficult and emotionally draining for intervenors and disputants. Increasingly, such conflict is characterized by costly, health-endangering bullying, harassment and discrimination, particularly for historically marginalized groups. A number of studies have noted the impact of these behaviors on physical and mental health. MCE is proposed as a movement-oriented approach that could possibly assist individuals and organizations in managing this type of conflict.

MCE is an experimental technique based on insights derived from the Dancing at the Crossroads sessions in Saas-Fee. The core features of MCE are body movements intended to cultivate mindfulness. Mindfulness skills enable individuals to translate feeling, sensation, and awareness into concrete action. Mindfulness decreases the power of fixed, narrow thinking patterns that are significant barriers to the management and resolution of workplace conflict involving bullying, harassment, and discrimination.

Creative movement and dance components of MCE are intended to build individuals' capacities to manage the extraordinary and inexplicable horrors of workplace bullying, harassment, and discrimination. These movement and dance activities awaken and invigorate sensing, feeling, and other inner experiences that enhance the effectiveness of the conceptual elements of the MCE process. The creative movement and dance activities also allow participants to escape the more-of-the-same patterns that reduce the viability of some workshop training experiences. In essence, MCE reflects an approach to learning that is multilayered, multidimensional, and values flexibility, patience, and sensitivity.

There is a compelling need for an evidence-based set of key theoretical principles to establish a foundation for movement-oriented interventions involving workplace issues. These principles should drive the development of effective techniques and approaches that reflect a wide range of cultures, ethnicities, racial backgrounds, and worldviews. This chapter has described an experimental training application that could be used to assess the benefits of incorporating movement to enhance the effectiveness of training intended to build individuals' capacities to address severe workplace conflict linked to bullying, harassment, and discrimination.

Finding Coherence II

Catalyzing Embodied Change Processes in Conflict

CLEMENS LANG

Cultural nuances are distinctive, yet they are often overshadowed by larger agendas that dominate conflict interventions. Conflict practitioners and intercultural theorists recognize this dilemma and have developed specific classifications to categorize cultural differences. These models may provide an appropriately structured framework for some contexts, but the risk of falling into stereotypes or generalizations has inherent limitations. As a Swiss coach and consultant, in the context of intercultural work I face the challenge of devising interventions that consider different systems of rationality. To understand the symbolic dimension of conflict dynamics, I propose that embodied approaches address diverse value systems and worldviews stretching beyond predictable frameworks. Culturally fluent strategies drawing from kinesthetic intelligence can foster a more in-depth understanding of the interplay between sensory experience, cultural identities, and conflict dynamics. Implicit cultural norms influence conflict dynamics, and effective interventions need to explore the roots of conflict behavior through an integration of the senses.

With reference to cultural frameworks, the Swiss are considered to have a cognitive-data and word-oriented culture.[1] Formalized documentation, efficient procedures and outputs, and highly structured meetings characterize our work environments. We are classified as linear-actives who plan, schedule, pursue action chains, and do one thing at a time.[2] Our dominant forms of individual and collective expression correlate with these cultural frames of reference. Swiss people often tend to express themselves with reserved and polite mannerisms, giving priority to logical and rational communication strategies.[3] With minimal allowance for physical expression or emotional behavior, the retention of emotional expression is a common result. There can even be an overt dismissal of emotional involvement in certain scenarios. While navigating through conflictive behavior, we tend to believe that rational arguments are a sufficient form of persuasion. As a result, we neglect our emotions and become limited in our capacity to express the tensions or contradictions that we are sensing.

Emotional responses can be unpredictable and difficult to regulate; inviting the expression of emotions into linear negotiation processes could be perceived as threatening or simply inappropriate. If emotions are integrated with greater awareness, they can add valuable insights in conflict interventions. Leading conflict theories indicate that emotions, when properly harnessed, can offer a way through turmoil toward a positive change process.[4] However, the ability to decode emotional responses is highly influenced by our capacity to relate to one another through an embodied lens. Many of us can account for the positive shift in our overall sense of inner health and well-being after physical exertion. Accumulated and potentially destructive forms of blocked mental and physical energy can become exposed and released through movement. If latent or unseen aspects of conflict have a chance to surface, areas of interpersonal dissonance may change. Engaging in movement patterning is a way to communicate more holistically and helps us discern how to access and shift emotions. When we are hindered by aggression or fear, certain muscle contractions can actually block energy, constrict breathing, and limit our capacity to think clearly. Such responses can be detrimental, holding larger implications if they become habitual over time. We can lose our ability to find our own ground when anticipatory reactions take precedence over what is being revealed in the moment.

With a lens of culture at the forefront of embodiment, it is important to acknowledge that just as cultures have varied communication styles, they also have diverse expressions of emotion.[5] Out of this diversity comes the need for emotional intelligence, which in simple terms is "how well we are able to recognize and manage our own feelings and read and deal effectively with other people's feelings."[6] Emotional intelligence cultivates the necessary relational threads needed to make collaborative decisions. Effectively regulating the power of emotions is pivotal for managing responses in volatile situations. Susan Podziba elaborates on the depth of these capacities and recognizes that "embedded within the chaos that fosters conflict is the powerful energy of passion, that, if properly harnessed, can lead to progress through actionable agreement."[7]

Harnessing this passion in a constructive, coherent, and culturally fluent manner remains a consistent challenge as belief systems transcend into embodied realizations. Although it may seem self-evident that physical engagement helps process or resolve emotions, *how* to locate and embrace cultural knowledge in the body is not always obvious amid the disorientation of conflict. When we become more attuned to the physicality of our responses, we can sense the rising or falling of our body temperature, the quality of our breath, and the tone of our voice. Our vocal range often fluctuates directly in correlation with tension felt in the body. However, despite the vast scope of insight that emotions carry, discourse around embodied expression continues to be discouraged within a structured work environment.

Although the physicality of negotiation may be more difficult to manage than verbalization, it is important to acknowledge how kinesthetic cues provide insights into cultural meaning systems. Para-verbal or nonverbal cues, said to make up about 80 percent of our communication,[8] can convey important relational information.[9] Differences in expressing nonverbal cues can create confusion and frustration in intercultural negotiations. Misunderstandings pervade when gestures are interpreted as having common meanings across cultural boundaries. Because such expressions are highly interpretive, understanding this aspect of communication can contribute greatly to promoting conflict resolution between parties.[10]

Multiple adjustments are necessary on every level as the language of embodiment becomes integrated into the framework of conflict interventions. Developing a culture of mutuality and trust is vital to restructure social and emotional patterning. This is especially critical in situations fraught with competitive dynamics; the temptation to revert to patterns of alienation can hinder one's ability to seek out new positions. In linear-active cultures,[11] it can be challenging to draw upon expressive elements or methods to work through change processes. However, dismissing body language is not a sustainable solution, because the body is always actively engaged in any conflict scenario. Shared principles, social networks, and power hierarchies are all contingent on physical positioning. In the midst of conflict, the renegotiation of cultural geographies can be an act of translation between these shifting elements.

Expressive methodologies could also be particularly effective and complementary in cultures where there is resistance around conventional interventions. In such contexts, the aesthetics that are woven into the fabric of a culture can provide invaluable cues about its internal logic. History lives in the body; therefore, archives of embodied memory cannot be dismissed in conflict analysis. When the body senses a level of crisis, body memories tend to resurface. Developing creative capacities that can work with the scope of emotional competencies will enhance the depth of conflict interventions.

Change processes in organizational contexts may particularly benefit from the added dimension of creative problem solving. Experience-based pedagogy serves as a powerful stimulus for transformation. Multimodal art forms that include dance, movement, visual art, theater, poetry, and music can offer a full palette of possibilities for determining the resources and limitations in a specific context. The arts can often offer mutual points of exchange, making it possible to renegotiate meaning systems when we reach the limits of our own narratives. Such forms of embodied knowledge can be a powerful form of individual and collective agency that supports identities and social relations to find threads of meaning. LeBaron asserts that the use of "kinesthetic metaphors," or the physical expression of metaphors, can be very effective in harnessing emotions and ideas to effect change.[12] The recognition of arts-based interventions in change processes is continuing to expand; nonverbal interventions add a layer of accessibility across linguistic and cultural divides. For example, the United Nations' Culture of Peace program acknowledges this potential and supports numerous arts-based change processes now occurring across the world.[13] The border-spanning Art Miles Mural Project offers collaborative murals from diverse societies as a way to "develop and advocate art rather than violence, [and] cooperation instead of war."[14] This type of arts-based change perspective offers embodied practices as ways to support noticeable shifts in communities.

Scholars such as Hall have emphasized the value of symbolic communication systems.[15] When considering the potential scope of creative interventions, it is vital to focus on ways in which to leverage symbolic systems of communication and power. The capacity to access symbolic realms will be contingent on a variety of factors. In highly expressive cultural contexts, creative forms of engagement may be able to generate and support larger-scale change processes. However, visible change can happen in subtle and incremental ways even in contexts that place less emphasis on outward expression. Simple metaphors or images might invigorate static processes and expose unrealized dimensions of conflict. Structural violence is often so intrinsic into societal patterns that it becomes invisible until another image interrupts the conceptual framework of "the way things are." Similarly, animating subtle gestures and shifting physical postures can create new openings for reflection and recognition. Embodied interventions can often override limitations created by monolithic thinking. I am frequently confronted with how to activate this level of cultural fluency in my work. Reflexivity and imagination are often needed to overcome prejudices and patterns of insularity. With these considerations, I offer the following paradigms for embodied transformative change processes.

1. All involved individuals should be able to express their experiences and participate in the transformation of a distressing situation.

Some individuals involved in a conflict may not have the opportunity to express their experience or be able to articulate their perceptions with clarity. Their limited vantage points may also make it difficult for them to understand how they are situated in relation to others in the conflict. (As mentioned earlier, the misinterpretation of perceptions can often be at the root of such conflicts.) Over the years, specific frameworks have been devised to address the tensions of multiple vantage points.

For example, the Johari Window is a self-awareness tool that has conveyed the importance of perception in facilitating change since its inception in the 1950s. Luft and Ingham coined the term to convey the way in which self-awareness and perception can be understood within quadrant "windowpanes." This model demonstrates the impact of both self-perception and group perception as people disclose information about themselves. It has been commonly found that people want to reveal only one aspect of the self in any given response. However, when they are more open with one another, especially in regard to their perceptions, a more-accurate depiction emerges, and confusion and conflict become less likely.[16]

I experienced this tangible shifting of perceptions through a multifaceted intervention in a kindergarten school. There was extensive conflict around relocating the school, which would lead to fewer children attending and thus to loss of revenue. The spiraling consequences manifested as structural leadership changes, resulting in the shifting distribution of tasks and responsibilities. In private interviews during and after the event, staff people and community members communicated how difficult and isolating this experience had been and how little support they had felt throughout the process.

In a community inquiry, those most affected were asked questions—primarily related to their emotional responses—pertaining to how they felt about their particular roles. They were challenged to consider their feelings before, during, and after the change and were asked to what extent they felt supported by others. They also had space to comment about the impact their shifting leadership responsibilities had on their feeling of security. This comprehensive inquiry included a nonverbal portion that was designed as an embodied grid. Every person had to find a position on the floor relative to a scale that went from zero to ten. Participants were encouraged to articulate how it felt to be situated on their chosen point in relation to others; they were also given the opportunity to explain why they had chosen their particular positions. From these physicalized standpoints, perceptions of scarcity became visible as unfulfilled expectations were voiced. However, participants gained a sense of strength from feeling connected with others on the floor, and they felt physically supported by those who shared similar perceptions and sentiments. People who found themselves in close proximity to others on the scale could literally see that they were not the only ones in a certain "position." Generative dialogue emerged as participants focused on how momentum could continue to grow from the expressed concerns, interests, and goals.

For groups with a capacity to easily embrace physical expression, sculpture work based on the approach of Virginia Satir[17] or the related organizational constellation approaches[18] based on concepts of Bert Hellinger can be useful.[19] Neither method organizes on a numerical scale as above. Instead, the intention of both is to systemically explore people's relationships to other people, objects, themes, institutions, or projects. Participants take positions within the space according to how they perceive themselves in relationship to one another or to a chosen subject. As participants pivot their bodies, moving toward or away from one another or the subject, a collective knowledge base begins to form through their varying degrees of proximity. This nonverbal dialogue creates a depiction of where people literally position themselves, and it becomes clear whether they are in the center or on the periphery of relationships.

2. All individuals should have the opportunity to express existing emotions.

Nonverbal modalities are particularly useful for directly expressing emotions that cannot be solely articulated in words. Certain body postures found in pantomime, a movement sequence, or a dance can reflect an extensive range of emotions. The body's responses can find points of specificity and shape subjective experiences beyond generalized claims. This has the potential to move individuals away from habits of judgment into ones of curiosity. The extent of creative engagement depends on a number of "trust factors," including safe affiliations, the awareness of underlying prejudices, overt or subtle hierarchies, and fluctuating power dynamics.

Practicing emotional expression in secure environments can begin to establish the necessary groundwork for building safety. The initial phase of exploring a range of emotions can be very insightful for those who are not accustomed to overtly expressing their emotions. A willingness to delve into unknown terrain tends to increase if this exploration is framed as a game. Through elements of play, which can be less threatening than verbal interrogations, the body can express new commitments, shifting identities, evolving roles, and aspirations. In the initial phase, it is important for individuals to first become aware of how their physical sensations and correlating reactions are linked to their various emotions. Those who are not accustomed to investigating the source of their emotions may have a tendency to suppress them. If emotional channels become blocked for a lengthy period of time, depression or prolonged anger may prevail and contribute even further to an impasse.

The following exercise has proved helpful for individuals who struggle to express a range of emotions. This approach is based on a workshop that I facilitated in Switzerland with a group of ten men ranging from age forty to sixty-five. The participants came from a variety of employment backgrounds, and the topic of the workshop was on discussing and experimenting with the current role of males in society. The goal of the seminar was to learn more about gendered behaviors, perceptions, and contradictions. We focused on the conditioning of male roles and on the societal expectations that lead to certain choices and actions. The group investigated various gender-based biases and collectively examined how such perspectives hindered different aspects of their relationships. Developing personal practices of awareness in physical, cognitive, and emotional realms became the foundation for exploring this work in depth.

In establishing the framework for the exercise, the space is divided into four areas. Each area is assigned a particular sensation (dry, wet, cold, hot). The participants are then invited to move through the space until they find a quadrant with which they resonate. Next, the four sectors are divided into emotions, such as joy, fear/insecurity, sadness, and anger/rage. As participants again find their "home space," they are encouraged focus inwardly and not concern themselves with where others are positioned. They then listen to the facilitator describe a specific situation. During this process, they are to be attentive to any emotions that arise in them. In the first role play that follows, volunteers act out "normal" behavior for the situation described. The second role play depicts a behavior that is typically considered inappropriate for that situation. The aim of the exercise is to help people learn how to express a range of emotions as contexts shift and change. During the allocated time for dialogue that accompanies these mini interventions, the facilitator can ask how the emotions that were acted out might be applied in the example situation.

When the space is divided, it is important to designate a neutral area where participants can go if they need a break. The facilitator marks the different areas with pictures or symbols and demonstrates how to move through the spaces while expressing a range of emotions that are emerging. Participants then explore their responses to the respective quadrants in their own time. Throughout this exploration, they remain focused solely on their own sensations and responses in each area. The facilitator should allow ample time for dialogue afterward so participants can reveal how easy and appropriate the expression of emotions was for them.

3. **Emotional expression is important because it not only helps parties hear or see the perspective of another person but also enables them to concretely experience it.**

The aim is to understand emotions not merely on an intellectual level but to know them experientially through the body. LeBaron calls this aim "body wisdom," stating that "[e]motional experience is body-centered, not intellectual . . . emotions, as we have seen, fire the nervous system, which triggers the release of the hormones that affect and produce emotions. . . . Given these physiological reactions, the possibility of being able to shift our feelings through physical channels opens up to us."[20] Body wisdom can be facilitated through organizational/

situational constellation exercises or through movement-based sculpture exercises that use shifting postures and positions to embody varying emotional states. This approach is to be initiated without prejudging or interpreting the meaning of the movement patterns. Remaining open-minded as insights surface through the body is the first priority. If the group seems interested, a mediator might further investigate a certain position or posture through an interactive role play. The potential for understanding empathy through this exercise might be enhanced by extending the play a little further, exchanging the tasks and responsibilities of certain roles for a limited time.

For instance, in larger companies with several departments, an employee may have the opportunity to work in a completely different area for a while. This exchange can facilitate an enriched learning about the other in a framework that is conducive to improvisation and learning. In Switzerland, we have a project called *Seitenwechsel* ("change of perspective"): managers from vastly different sectors in businesses and administration insert themselves into a social institution for one week. This exposure is a new learning curve for most, expanding their repertoire of management approaches. The change also heightens perceptions and has the potential to remove prejudices by introducing people to alternate work realities that demand different skills and leadership capacities. To uphold a sense of mutual respect, integrity, and transparency, the process requires significant explanation and debriefing. It might be suitable as a preliminary training phase to expand possibilities for creative thinking or as an initial intervention in a personal development seminar.

Past participants in this exchange stated that they learned to approach those from diverse backgrounds with more compassion and consciousness. They felt that they were able to have greater levels of empathy for the magnitude of challenges that others faced. Once they returned to their original jobs, they also had a greater clarity on the perspectives and situations of their own employees and collaborators. Such initiatives can enhance human resourcefulness and create ripe conditions for leadership development.

Within the context of a leadership program, dance could be another variation that could integrate the exchange of perspectives. For example, two people might participate in role training and focus on topics such as professional or gender-based roles. Since roles are normally prescribed or fixed, role reversals could facilitate lively dialogue on contrasting perspectives. Therefore, experiencing the situation of a dance could lead to a dynamic inquiry on leadership themes. Questions arising from the dance may be varied: Who is leading whom? Who is often the one being led? How do you feel when you take over the role of the leader? What is the impact of a reversal of the traditional roles of women and men? How can this be experienced and not simply theorized beyond the parameters of dance?

As a visible modality, dance can highlight one's self-assurances or insecurities through conscious exploration. I experienced the potential of dance when attending several classes that encompassed couples-based and individual dancing. Both forms involved heightened levels of communication between partners. What was pertinent in these contexts is that the dancers did not have the time to deliberate on what to do. Presence and concentration were needed in the moment, and each step depended on immediacy of focus. I had to cultivate a level of openness toward others and read the signals that they were giving. I could then decide whether to adopt these signals, react to them, or disregard them. If I doubted the steps or overanalyzed what I expected from a partner, the dance began to degenerate and the relationship to the other began to feel uncomfortable. I also noticed when my partner was feeling a level of discomfort. When I could cultivate the sense that the dance was important and what I was doing was good, a sense of fluidity emerged. This developed independently of whether the steps were in accordance to a particular sequence or whether I was upholding a certain standard in my dance.

4. **Entrenched situations often lack vitality where energy is blocked, retained, and not in flow. Embodied approaches can begin to break open the narrowness and the hurt/fear focus and activate a new sense of momentum.**

LeBaron states that "internal physical tension is a cue that something is stuck or blocked . . . [and often such emotions] will manifest in [the] body as a sense of being covered up, silenced, or held back from the center of things. If I can recognize the body sensation associated with feeling covered up, I can then make different choices about how to respond." Further elaboration refers to the potential of activating energies: "The dance can be interrupted if we realize it is unfolding and make a choice to step out of habit and into awareness. We can use our bodies to enact change or experiment with what change might feel like."[21] Playing dynamic or nurturing music, showing the "awakening experience" (see below) from a film clip or giving a short demonstration can activate blocked energy and leverage blocked motivation in new directions. I discovered this by playing a piece of choral music from a film while initiating an internal change process in a child-care organization. In the core scene of this film—this is what I would like to call "awakening experience," a previously withdrawn boy was able, with much patience and support, to express his vocal abilities in a beautiful solo.[22] The essence of this piece connected with the goals and visions of the organization and resonated with the participants on a nonverbal emotional level. A greater sense of openness and motivation spiraled out from this shared moment.

It is also worthwhile to consider how archetypal or mythological change processes may be expressed today. The phoenix rising from the ashes, the hero's journey of Jason or Hercules, the revival of a sleeping princess, or the resurrection of Lazarus could be interesting subjects to contemplate. When a fitting image for a desired change process is found, group members may become more emotionally responsive with one another. Collective competencies arise as they develop shared symbolic systems of meaning together. Louise Diamond illustrates just how impactful the expression of archetypes can be on facilitating change processes, especially those dealing with conflict. Her concept of the heroic journey is an "archetypal story of transformation found in cultures around the world—in myths, fairy tales, ancient stories, legends, books and movies"[23] and gives five archetype references as a guide for moving through conflict toward transformation.

The specific dance methodology of the 5Rhythms,[24] developed by Gabrielle Roth, seems noteworthy in regard to the individual activation of energies. It is rooted in the idea of a natural developmental and wave-patterned movement of life processes. The dancer moves through a map of five rhythms—flowing, staccato, chaos, lyrical, and stillness—tracking perceptions and memories, seeking out gestures and shapes, and tuning in to instincts and intuitions. The intention of these rhythms is to expand both physical and emotional expression and awareness. The unrestricted letting go, intentional action, chaotic overturning, lyrical celebration, and quiet resonance all serve to expand and release what is already present. A dancer experiences the energy and pulse that accompany each rhythm, supported by correlating music.

Simply changing the context or going for a walk can shift the energy of tension and literally allow for more breathing room. Problems are often solved when the focus is diverted elsewhere. Food can act as an important buffer when conflict escalates. Eating a meal together often provides a welcome point of shared connectivity and can serve as a common bridge across linguistic and cultural divides. Other roles are often temporarily suspended during a meal, and conversations can become animated in new ways. Having a social dance after intense meetings can have a similar effect, creating a context that supports release and rejuvenation through dynamic modes of communication and exchange.

5. Creative embodied modes of expression can assist in imagining possible outcomes from change processes.

This could also be referenced as vision work, and such visions may be relegated to the emotional realm. One question to spark the exploration might be: How would I like to feel after the change process? Alternatively, the question may be aimed at more-concrete results: What do I want the desired impact to look like? The methods mentioned in this chapter can be used to move through these inquiries. Taking on a body posture, performing a pantomime, or engaging in an organizational constellation may each lay the foundation for imagining a collective future. The goal is to reduce concerns about how the change process will happen and focus on what is unfolding in the present moment. With the wisdom of the body at the forefront, it becomes possible to physically disentangle the self from old patterns. This alone can be a catalyst for profound change processes.

6. After a transformational process, the last application of embodied approaches may lead to the affirmation and manifestation of the new situation in the form of a crystallizing ritual.

This ritual could be a conscious performing of agreed-upon processes. It may include an act that symbolizes closure through the integration of previous themes, such as figuratively laying down, storing away, or burning the old ways of doing things and celebrating the new agreements. Such rituals have taken on many forms in cultures across the globe. Particularly interesting is one reported from the Luba people of the Congo: rinsing the mouth and spitting to indicate a cleansing from previous insults and hostility.[25] Affirmation in a more-conventional context could be acknowledged with a ceremonial handshake, mutual bowing, or a big feast for all involved.

As embodied modes of expression are becoming increasingly recognized as legitimate in change processes, the ideas described here represent a brainstorming rather than an exhaustive account. More applications of this work in fields of coaching, leadership development, conflict transformation, and mediation will help create a concrete body of knowledge for this burgeoning area. Nevertheless, I hope these accounts will reveal the untapped modes of intelligence that can inform these respective fields in generative ways, and I anticipate more experimentation between the analytic and intuitive.

I am grateful for the opportunity to have participated in the Dancing at the Crossroads seminar in Saas-Fee, Switzerland, which moved me to write this chapter. The insights gained from the sessions involving dance and dialogue were both inspiring and challenging. Even though the participants were open-minded and keen to experiment with unconventional approaches, it became evident that some barriers still existed. For many participants, there was a natural tendency to revert back to dialogue approaches when uncertainties arose. Understanding how dialogue could complement embodiment and vice versa became a point of discovery and a high learning curve for many. In working through these issues, it was important to acknowledge the limitations of embodied practices also. If a group of people are interested in cultivating this level of self-awareness, they will come to understand that the body does not lie, and this realization may be disarming. Although the relationship between emotions and embodiment may seem obvious, the willingness to explore this terrain should not be taken for granted. Contracts within the group that will ensure safety are necessary, and ongoing process checks need to be established with care between participants and the facilitator. Retaining transparency throughout the process is beneficial for all, and it is especially vital in the midst of conflict, where suspicion and fear infiltrate.

Many considerations influence the effectiveness of change processes. Dance supports renewal, spontaneity, and innovation, and all of these elements are vital for working in organizational complexities. Mental and physical inertia may be the largest stumbling blocks to generative transformation, and a few steps toward dance may create the alchemy that is necessary for positive change.

The author would like to express his deep gratitude to thank Sabine Silberberg for translation and especially Carrie MacLeod, Kim Haiste, and Emily Beausoleil for editorial assistance.

Conclusion

New Choreographies of Conflict
CARRIE MACLEOD

This book explores the body as the prime place of return amid the shifting ground and up-heaval of conflict. It takes us across diverse conflict landscapes, digging below the imprints of violence to see how physical experiences can contribute to positive shifts, and describes how movement can effectively reframe and mobilize progress in the midst of numbing silences and stalemates in conflict. From their various contexts and disciplines, the authors have un-derlined the utility of an embodied vocabulary and related somatic strategies for handling conflict.

What follows when conflict practitioners understand the body as a primary site of social change? In a wide range of settings, from organizations to postconflict zones, physical engage-ment offers possibilities for realignment with the other. As bodies are literally disentangled from the narratives in which they have been confined, fragmented histories can be reassem-bled and reimagined, one gesture at a time. As autobiographies are enacted, grief, loss, and recovery find new channels of physical expression.

The practical movement exercises offered in this book constitute a new sensory compass for conflict practitioners. When awareness becomes stimulated from the inside out, habitual thought patterns can become visible through physical expression. Each author—from per-sonal experience—affirms the necessity of collaboratively cultivating physical reflexivity and flexibility in the face of defensiveness and resistance. Third parties who bring a spirit of curios-ity, a willingness to risk, and generosity to difficult conflicts can inspire these qualities in ways that elicit suppleness from all involved.

The book also introduces mediation and negotiation *as* dance, a metaphor that highlights how parties shape the choreography of conflict "ensembles." Conflict intervenors who see their work as a dance are attuned to the aesthetic domain and are more likely to be alive to the beauty emerging from the ashes.

Ethics of Somatic Interventions
Because dance and movement connect space, identities, and narratives in ways that may help mend torn relational fabrics, they function as conduits for recognition, reciprocity, and renewal. Given the potency of somatic interventions, it is vital to consider when and how they may contribute to "melting the stone" and when they entail risks. There are many un-known factors that influence conflict dynamics, and associated physical responses can be

unpredictable, powerful, and intense. Poorly designed interventions may heighten tensions or even contribute to conflict escalation. It is therefore essential that practices be sensitive to local input and external validation while upholding a high standard of integrity and ethics. Attentiveness to the safety and well-being of all involved must be central in this work.

A number of questions exist in relation to ethics and professionalism in somatic interventions, including the following:

- What are the ethical and aesthetic responsibilities in somatic interventions?
- How can miscommunication or offense be prevented or minimized?
- How can physical modalities be used in settings where physical contact is unusual or even proscribed? Should they be used in those settings?
- Which ways of describing this work are most accessible, given that communication always involves nonverbal elements that may alienate some listeners?
- What aesthetic responsibility, if any, should be among the goals of those who design and apply these approaches?

Paolo Knill, the originator of expressive arts therapy, suggests that "aesthetic responsibility"[1] should be a component of ethical practice. Stephen K. Levine elaborates on this and stresses the importance of being able to "use our own imagination in helping others to transcend their limitations and become aware of the unexplored possibilities that are available to them."[2] He suggests a transparent process of inquiry to create mutuality and shared accountability in process design. Further research on developing ethics of practice for embodied interventions is vital, as well as examining where, when, and for whom interventions may be most useful.

Where To from Here? Moving Forward in Healthy Ways

As we work with embodied theoretical maps that inform the choreography of conflict, we ask which central ideas will serve and guide us. It is important to consider a number of practical questions, including the following:

- How can we account for the subjectivity of physical experience in designing empirical research?
- How can we meld different ways of knowing and diverse lexicons in this evolving interdisciplinary field?
- What are the best ways to develop concrete strategies based on body-mind relations when our knowledge is abstract, partial, and contingent?
- How can we minimize the vulnerabilities involved in working physically with people in conflict?
- How can verbal problem solving and body-based work be brought into dialogue?
- How can kinesthetic interventions be developed, deepened, and taught, retaining the integrity of the exercises' origins, while also adapting them across cultures?

Combining traditional and somatic strategies may be difficult for many practitioners. It will be critical to not oversimplify somatic schemata or consider them to be less rigorous than traditional interventions. It will also be important to monitor, evaluate, and document how these emergent approaches translate into tangible practices across cultural boundaries. Rich, descriptive accounts will be useful in determining how such conflict interventions can be applied at complex intersections. Conflict analysis, too, will be deepened through the application of sensory-based methods to existing frameworks. We predict that embodied insights will serve as increasingly valued complements to traditional approaches to intervention.

As physical intelligence is welcomed into all aspects of mediation and dialogic practice, including assessment, intervention, and evaluation, new and original ways to teach it will emerge. Research and practice summarized in this book invite practitioners and scholars to examine their own—and their fields'—root assumptions and perceptual habits as these inform trainings and interventions. Effective pedagogy and curriculum will not proceed prescriptively but will arise from exploring and understanding the physical dimensions of conflict as it relates to emotion, thought, intuition, and imagination across cultures. Effectively integrating physical approaches in learning and teaching will texture conflict pedagogies in revealing and productive ways.

With the body at the center of both individual and collective health, one broader question remains: How can sustained states of health be maintained in adversarial and conflict-ridden environments? This book has suggested how our bodies can help us discern and design healthy strategies for conflict engagement. The authors have challenged us to create a living legacy in our work as conflict intervenors, generating vitality and responsiveness to the very real physical dimensions of conflict. By integrating the approaches from this book, we have the collective opportunity to truly and productively embrace differences, vulnerabilities, and—most important—our full humanity.

Notes

Acknowledgments

1. MOSAIC, a newcomer-serving agency in Burnaby, British Columbia, Canada, http://www.mosaicbc.com/.

Introduction: Let's Dance—Michelle LeBaron and Carrie MacLeod

1. Bernard Mayer, *Beyond Neutrality: Confronting the Crisis in Conflict Resolution* (San Francisco, CA: Jossey Bass, 2004).

2. John Paul Lederach, *The Moral Imagination: The Art and Soul of Building Peace* (Oxford, UK: Oxford University Press, 2010).

3. Cynthia Cohen, Roberto G. Varea, and Polly O. Walker, *Acting Together: Performance and the Creative Transformation of Conflict*, vol. 1, *Resistance and Reconciliation in Regions of Violence* (Oakland, CA: New Village Press, 2011). Cynthia Cohen, Roberto G. Varea, and Polly O. Walker, *Acting Together: Performance and the Creative Transformation of Conflict*, vol. 2, *Building Just and Inclusive Communities* (Oakland, CA: New Village Press, 2011).

4. See also CRANE (Conflict Resolution, Arts and iNtercultural Experience) Project Report and related publications, http://www.law.ubc.ca/pdr/crane/index.html; Michelle LeBaron and Christopher Honeyman, "Using the Creative Arts," in *The Negotiator's Fieldbook: The Desk Reference for the Experienced Negotiator*, ed. Andrea Kupfer Schneider and Christopher Honeyman (Chicago, IL: American Bar Association, 2006), 415–24.

5. Mark Patrick Hederman, *The Haunted Inkwell: Art and Our Future* (Dublin, Ireland: Columba Press, 2001).

6. Roger Fisher, William Ury, and Bruce Patton, *Getting to Yes: Negotiating Agreement without Giving In* (New York, NY: Penguin, 1983).

1 / Dance and Neuroscience *by* Emily Beausoleil

1. Candace Pert, *Molecules of Emotion* (New York, NY: Simon & Schuster, 1997), 188-89.

2. Robert A. Baruch Bush and Joseph P. Folger, *The Promise of Mediation: Responding to Conflict Through Empowerment and Recognition* (San Francisco, CA: Jossey-Bass, 1994), 2.

3. Candace Pert, *Molecules of Emotion*, 188-89.

4. Alvaro Pascual-Leone *et al*, "Modulation of Muscle Responses Evoked by Transcranial Magnetic Stimulation During the Acquisition of New Fine Motor Skills." *Journal of Neurophysiology* 74 (1995): 1037-1045.

5. Alan C. Tidwell, "Not Effective Communication but Effective Persuasion." *Mediation Quarterly* 12.1. (Fall 1994): 3-14, 4.

6. Kalila B. Homann, "Embodied Concepts of Neurobiology in Dance/Movement Therapy Practice," *American Journal of Dance Therapy* 32 (2010): 80–99, 87

7. Michelle LeBaron and Venashri Pillay, eds, *Conflict Across Cultures: A Unique Experience of Bridging Differences* (Boston, MA: Intercultural Press, 2006), 150, 131.

8. Lynn Koshland, J. Wilson and B. Wittaker, "PEACE Through Dance/Movement: Evaluating a Violence Prevention Program," *American Journal of Dance Therapy* 26.2 (2005): 69-90.

9. Chris D. Frith and Uta Frith, "Social Cognition in Humans," *Current Biology* 17 (2007): R724–R732.

10. Frank Bernieri, J. Steven Reznick and Robert Rosenthal, "Synchrony, Pseudo-Synchrony, and Dissynchrony: Measuring the Entrainment Process in Mother-Infant Interactions," *Journal of Nonverbal Behavior* 12 (1988): 243-53; Frank Bernieri and Robert Rosenthal, "Interpersonal Coordination: Behavioral Matching and Interactional Synchrony," in *Foundations of Nonverbal Behavior*, ed. R.S. Feldman and B. Rime (New York, NY: Cambridge University Press, 1991); Tanya I. Chartrand and John A. Bargh, "The Chameleon Effect: The Perception-Behavior Link and Social Interaction," *Personality and Social Psychology* 76 (1999): 893-910; Janet Beavin Bavelas, Alex Black, C.R. Lemery, and Jennifer Mullett, " 'I *Show* You How I Feel': Motor Mimicry as a Communicative Act," *Journal of Personality and Social Psychology* 50 (1986): 322-29; Robert R. Provine, "Yawning as a Stereotypical Action Pattern and Releasing Stimulus," *Ethology* 71 (1986): 109-22; Joseph N. Cappella and Sally Planalp, "Talk and Silence Sequences in Informal Conversations: Interspeaker Influences," *Human Communication Research* 7 (1981): 117-32; Roland Neumann and Fritz Strack, " 'Mood Contagion': The Automatic Transfer of Mood Between Persons," *Journal of Personality and Social Psychology* 79 (2000): 211-23.

11. Morten Christiansen, Giacomo Rizzolatti and Michael Arbib, *Language Within Our Grasp* (Oxford, UK: Oxford University Press, 2001)

12. Marco Iacoboni, *Mirroring People* (New York, NY: Farrar, Straus and Giroux, 2009)

13. Vittorio Gallese, "The Roots of Empathy: The Shared Manyfold Hypothesis and the Neural Basis of Intersubjectivity," *Psychopathology* 36 (2003): 171–80

14. Emily S. Cross, Antonia F. Hamilton, and Scott T. Grafton, "Building a Motor Simulation de Novo: Observation of Dance by Dancers," *NeuroImage*, 31(3): 1257-1267.

15. Steven Brown and Lawrence M. Parsons, "The Neuroscience of Dance," *Scientific American* 299, (2008): 78.

16. Bush and Folger, *The Promise of Mediation*, 2

17. Kenneth Cloke, *Mediating Dangerously: The Frontiers of Conflict Resolution* (San Francisco, CA: Jossey-Bass, 2001).

18. Lee Ross, "Reactive Devaluation and Negotiation in Conflict Resolution," in *Barriers to Conflict Resolution*, edited by Kenneth Arrow et al. (New York, NY: W. W. Norton, 1995), 26-42.

19. Jill Bolte Taylor, *My Stroke of Insight: A Brain Scientist's Personal Journey* (New York, NY and Toronto, Canada: Plume, 2009).

20. Charles J. Limb and Allen R. Braun, "Neural Substrates of Spontaneous Musical Performance: An fMRI Study of Jazz Improvisation," *PLoS ONE* 3.2 (2008): e1679.

21. Johan Galtung, "Peace, Music and the Arts: In Search of Interconnections," in *Music and Conflict Transformation: Harmonies and Dissonances in Geopolitics,* (London, UK and New York, NY: I.B Tauris in association with The Toda Institute for Global Peace and Policy Research 2007), http://www2.hawaii.edu/~kent /Unpeaceful Music.pdf accessed 20 August 2013

22. Ivar Hagendoorn, "The Dancing Brain." *Cerebrum: The Dana Forum on Brain Science* Vol. 5.2 (Spring 2003): 5

23. Dennis J. D. Sandole, *Capturing the Complexity of Conflict: Dealing with Violent Ethnic Conflicts in the Post-Cold War Era* (London, UK: Pinter, 1999)

24. Jane C. Desmond, "Introduction: Making the Invisible Visible: Staging Sexualities through Dance," in *Dancing Desires: Choreographing Sexualities on and Off the Stage,* ed. Jane C. Desmond (Wisconsin, WI: University of Wisconsin Press, 2001).

25. *Rize,* DVD, directed by David LaChapelle (Santa Monica, CA; Lions Gate Entertainment, 2005); Craig Zelizer, "The Role of Artistic Processes in Peacebuilding in Bosnia-Herzegovina," *Peace and Conflict Studies* 10.2 (2003): 62-75; John Paul Lederach, *The Moral Imagination: The Art and Soul of Building Peace* (Oxford, UK: Oxford University Press, 2004); Michael Shank and Lisa Schirch, "Strategic Arts-Based Peacebuilding," *Peace and Change* 33.2 (2005): 217-33; David Román, *Acts of Intervention: Performance, Gay Culture, and AIDS* (Bloomington, IN: Indiana University Press, 1998); Naomi Jackson and Toni Shapiro-Phim, eds, *Dance, Human Rights and Social Justice* (Plymouth, MA: The Scarecrow Press, 2008).

2 / Dance as Metaphor *by* Tara Ney and Emmy Humber

1. Daniel Rigney, *The Metaphorical Society: An Invitation to Social Theory* (Oxford, UK: Rowman & Littlefield Publishers, 2001).

2. Dennis J. D. Sandole, *Handbook of Conflict Analysis and Resolution* (New York, NY: Routledge, 2009).

3. Roger Fisher and William Ury, *Getting to Yes: Negotiating Agreement without Giving In* (Boston, MA: Houghton Mifflin, 1981).

4. Phyllis E. Bernard, "Rethinking Negotiation Teaching: Finding Common Ground in the Soil of Culture," *Hamline Journal of Public Law and Policy* 31, no. 2 (2010).

5. David B. Lipsky and Ariel C. Avgar, "The Conflict over Conflict Management," *Dispute Resolution Journal* (May–October 2010), 11–43.

6. Lode Walgrave, *Restorative Justice and the Law* (Portland, OR: Willan Publishing, 2002).

7. Judith L. Innes and David Booher, *Planning with Complexity: An Introduction to Collaborative Rationality for Public Policy* (New York, NY: Routledge, 2010).

8. John Forester, Dealing with Differences: Dramas of Mediating Public Disputes (New York, NY: Oxford University Press, 2009).

9. Vamik Volkan, *Bloodlines: From Ethnic Pride to Ethnic Terrorism* (Boulder, CO: Westview, 1999).

10. Nadja Alexander and Michelle LeBaron, "Rethinking Negotiation Teaching Project: Death of the Role-Play," *Hamline Journal of Public Law and Policy* 31, no. 2 (2010).

11. Christopher Honeyman, James Coben, and Guiseppe DePalo, *Rethinking Negotiation Teaching Innovations for Context and Culture* (St. Paul, MN: DRI Press, 2009); John Paul Lederach, *The Moral Imagination: The Art and Soul of Building Peace* (Oxford, UK: Oxford University Press, 2005); Jacqueline Nolan-Haley, "Mediation: The New Arbitration," *Harvard Negotiation Law Review* 17 (2012), 61.

12. Joseph P. Folger and Robert A. Bush, "Ideology, Orientations to Conflict, and Mediation Discourse," in *New Directions in Mediations: Communication Research and Perspectives*, eds. J. Folger and P. Jones (San Francisco, CA: Sage Publications, 1994), 3–25; John Braithwaite, *Crime, Shame, and Reintegration* (Cambridge, UK: Cambridge University Press, 1998); Honeyman, Coben, and DePalo, *Rethinking Negotiation Teaching Innovations for Context and Culture*; Michelle LeBaron, *Bridging Cultural Conflicts: A New Approach for a Changing World* (San Francisco, CA: Jossey-Bass, 2003); Rupert Ross, *Return to the Teachings: Exploring Aboriginal Justice* (Toronto, Canada: Penguin Books, 1989); Elizabeth Elliot, *Security, with Care: Restorative Justice and Healthy Societies* (Toronto, Canada: Fernwood, 2010).

13. Albie M. Davis, *Liquid Leadership: The Wisdom of Mary Parker Follett*, accessed January 30, 2012, http://sunsite.utk.edu/FINS/Mary_Parker_Follett/Fins-MPF-03.txt.

14. Honeyman, Coben, and DePalo, *Rethinking Negotiation Teaching Innovations for Context and Culture* (St. Paul, MN: DRI Press, 2009).

15. Michelle LeBaron and Mario Patera, "Reflective Practice in the New Millennium," *Rethinking Negotiation Teaching Innovations for Context and Culture*, eds. C. Honeyman, J. Coben, and G. DePalo (St. Paul, MN: DRI Press, 2009).

16. Roberto M. Chene, "Beyond Mediation—Reconciling an Intercultural World: A New Role for Conflict Resolution," in *Re-Centering Culture and Knowledge in Conflict Resolution Practice*, eds. M A. Trujillo, S. Y. Bowland, L. J. Myers, P. M. Richards, and B. Roy (Syracuse, NY: Syracuse University Press, 2008), XI.

17. Tara Ney, Jo-Ann Stoltz, and Maureen Maloney, "Voice, Power, and Discourse: Experiences of Family Group Conference Participants in the Context of Child Protection," *Journal of Social Work* 13, no. 2, (2013), 184–202; Andrew Woolford, *The Politics of Restorative Justice* (Winnipeg, Canada: Fernwood Publishing, 2009).

18. George Lakoff and Mark Johnson, *Metaphors We Live By* (Chicago, IL: University of Chicago Press, 1980).

19. Rigney, *The Metaphorical Society: An Invitation to Social Theory* (Oxford, UK: Rowman & Littlefield Publishers, 2001), 3.

20. Lakoff and Johnson, *Metaphors We Live By* (Chicago, IL: University of Chicago Press, 1980).

21. George Lakoff and Mark Johnson, *Philosophy in the Flesh: The Embodied Mind and Its Challenge to Western Thought* (New York, NY: Basic Books, 1999).

22. LeBaron, *Bridging Cultural Conflicts: A New Approach for a Changing World*; Lederach, *The Moral Imagination: The Art and Soul of Building Peace*; D. Druckman, "Intuition or Counterintuition? The Science behind the Art of Negotiation," *Negotiation Journal* 25, no. 4 (2009), 431–48.

23. Lederach, *The Moral Imagination: The Art and Soul of Building Peace*, 72.

24. Andrea K. Schneider and Christopher Honeyman, *The Negotiator's Fieldbook*, 1st ed. (Washington, DC: American Bar Association Section of Dispute Resolution, 2006), 20.

25. Niccolo Machiavelli, *The Prince*, trans. G. Bull (Oxford, UK: Penguin Books, 1981), 60.

26. Ibid., 56.

27. Ibid., 33.

28. "'Soul Force,' is the means of striving for truth and social justice through love, suffering, and conversion of the oppressor. Its tactic is active nonviolent resistance." John P. McKay, Bennett D. Hill, Buckler, John Buckler, Clare Haru Crowston, Merry Weisner-Hanks, *A History of Western Society, Volume C: From the Revolutionary Era to the Present* (Boston, MA: Bedford/St. Martin's, 2007), 859.

29. Mahatma Gandhi, *Hind Swaraj and Other Writings*, ed. Anthony J. Parel (Cambridge, UK: Cambridge University Press, 1997), 81.

30. Eknath Easwaran, *Gandhi, the Man: The Story of His Transformation* (Berkeley, CA: The Blue Mountain Center of Meditation, 1997), 43.

31. Rigney, *The Metaphorical Society: An Invitation to Social Theory*, 7.

32. Ibid.

33. Ibid., 205.

34. Agnes DeMille, *The Life and Work of Martha Graham* (New York, NY: Random House, 1991).

35. Bruce G. Douglass and Clark Moustakas, "Heuristic Inquiry: The Internal Search to Know," *Journal of Humanistic Psychology* 25 (Summer 1985), 40.

36. Rod Munday and Daniel Chandler, "Tacit Knowledge," in *A Dictionary of Media and Communication* (New York, NY: Oxford University Press).

37. John Paul Lederach , *The Moral Imagination: The Art and Soul of Building Peace* (Oxford, UK: Oxford University Press, 2005), 73.

38. Ibid.

39. Chris Gutherie, "I'm Curious: Can We Teach Curiosity?" in *Rethinking Negotiation Teaching Innovations for Context and Culture*, eds. C. Honeyman, J. Coben, and G. DePalo (St. Paul, MN: DRI Press, 2009).

40. Kenneth H. Fox , "Negotiation as a Post-Modern Process", *Rethinking Negotiation Teaching Innovations for Context and Culture* (St. Paul, MN: DRI Press, 2009).

41. Michelle LeBaron and Mario Patera, "Reflective Practice in the New Millennium," *Rethinking Negotiation Teaching Innovations for Context and Culture*, eds. C. Honeyman, J. Coben, and G. DePalo (St. Paul, MN: DRI Press, 2009).

42. Andrea K. Schneider and Christopher Honeyman, *The Negotiator's Fieldbook*, 1st ed. (Washington, DC: American Bar Association Section of Dispute Resolution, 2006).

43. Jennifer Brown, "Introduction: The Second Generation of Negotiation Teaching," in *Rethinking Negotiation Teaching Innovations for Context and Culture*, eds. C. Honeyman, J. Coben, and G. DePalo (St. Paul, MN: DRI Press, 2009).

44. Dan Shapiro, "Untapped Power: Emotions in Negotiation," in *Rethinking Negotiation Teaching Innovations for Context and Culture*, eds. C. Honeyman, J. Coben, and G. DePalo (St. Paul, MN: DRI Press, 2009).

45. Alexander and LeBaron, "Rethinking Negotiation Teaching Project: Death of the Role-Play" *Hamline Journal of Public Law and Policy* 31, no. 2 (2010).

46. Ted Shawn, "Dance Quotes," Dancer's Domain, accessed January 15, 2011, http://www.angelfire.com/oh2/chezsarah/bquotes.html.

47. Shanna LaFleur, "Dance Quotes," Dancer's Domain, accessed January 15, 2011, http://www.angelfire.com/oh2/chezsarah/bquotes.html.

48. John Paul Lederach, *The Moral Imagination: The Art and Soul of Building Peace* (Oxford, UK: Oxford University Press, 2005), 57.

49. Ibid., 69 (italics added).

50. Ibid., 67.

51. Ezra Pound, "A Few Don'ts by an Imagiste," *Poetry* 1, no. 6 (March 1913), 200.

52. John Paul Lederach , *The Moral Imagination: The Art and Soul of Building Peace* (Oxford, UK: Oxford University Press, 2005), 69.

53. Jimmy Carter, *Keeping the Faith: Memoirs of a President* (Fayetteville, Arkansas: University of Arkansas Press, 1995).

54. William B. Yeats, *Early Poems* (New York, NY: Dover Publications, 1993).

55. Charles W. Mills, *The Sociological Imagination* (New York, NY: Oxford University Press, 1959).

56. Ibid., 70.

57. Agnes DeMille, *The Life and Work of Martha Graham* (New York, NY: Random House, 1991).

58. Daniel Rigney, *The Metaphorical Society: An Invitation to Social Theory* (Oxford, UK: Rowman & Littlefield Publishers, 2001).

59. Doris Humphrey and Barbara Pollack, *The Art of Making Dances*, accessed August 21, 2013, http://www.dorishumphrey.org.

60. Agnes DeMille, *The Life and Work of Martha Graham*, accessed August 21, 2013, http://www.shahina.com/poetry/quotes.htm.

61. Michael S. Gazzaniga, *The Ethical Brain* (New York, NY: Dana Press, 2005).

62. Beatriz Calvo-Merino et al., "Seeing or Doing? Influence of Visual and Motor Familiarity in Action Observation," *Current Biology* 16, no. 19 (October 10, 2006), 1905–10.

63. Michelle LeBaron, *Bridging Cultural Conflicts: A New Approach for a Changing World* (San Francisco, CA: Jossey-Bass, 2003).

64. Martha Graham quoted in Kevin Nelson, *The Runner's Book of Daily Inspiration: A Year of Motivation, Revelation, and Instruction* (Chicago, IL: McGraw-Hill, 1999), 11.

65. John Braithwaite, *Crime, Shame, and Reintegration* (Cambridge, UK: Cambridge University Press, 1989).

66. Michelle LeBaron, *Bridging Cultural Conflicts: A New Approach for a Changing World* (San Francisco, CA: Jossey-Bass, 2003).

67. Michel Foucault and Colin Gordon, *Power/Knowledge: Selected Interviews and Other Writings, 1972-1977* (New York, NY: Pantheon Books, 1980).

68. James W. Walters, *Martin Buber and Feminist Ethics: The Priority of the Personal* (Syracuse, NY: Syracuse University Press, 2003), 16.

69. Michelle LeBaron and Mario Patera, "Reflective Practice in the New Millennium," *Rethinking Negotiation Teaching Innovations for Context and Culture*, eds. C. Honeyman, J. Coben, and G. DePalo (St. Paul, MN: DRI Press, 2009).

70. Amy Gutmann and Dennis Thompson, *Why Deliberative Democracy?* (Princeton, NJ: Princeton University Press, 2004).

71. Leah Wing, "Mediation and Inequality Reconsidered: Bringing the Discussion to the Table," *Conflict Resolution Quarterly* 26, no. 4 (2009), 383.

72. Lederach, *The Moral Imagination: The Art and Soul of Building Peace*, 14.

73. Daniel Rigney, *The Metaphorical Society: An Invitation to Social Theory* (Oxford, UK: Rowman & Littlefield Publishers, 2001), 4.

74. Leah Wing, "Mediation and Inequality Reconsidered: Bringing the Discussion to the Table," *Conflict Resolution Quarterly* 26, no. 4 (2009).

75. Roberto M. Chene, "Beyond Mediation—Reconciling an Intercultural World: A New Role for Conflict Resolution," *Re-centering Culture and Knowledge in Conflict Resolution Practice* (Syracuse, NY: Syracuse University Press, 2008), 39.

4 / Choreography of Conflict *by* Carrie MacLeod

1. Myriam Denov, *Child Soldiers: Sierra Leone's Revolutionary United Front* (Cambridge, UK: Cambridge University Press, 2010), 64.

2. "Sierra Leone: Reparations Program," Justice In Perspective, accessed January 5, 2012, http://www.justiceinperspective.org.za/africa/sierra-leone/80-country/mechanism/416.html#.

3. David Scheffer, *All The Missing Souls: A Personal History of the War Crimes Tribunals* (Princeton, NJ: Princeton University Press, 2012), 330.

4. Stephen K. Levine, *Trauma, Tragedy, Therapy: The Arts and Human Suffering* (London, UK: Jessica Kingsley Publishers, 2009), 32.

5. John Paul Lederach and Angela Jill Lederach, *When Blood and Bones Cry Out: Journeys through the Soundscape of Healing and Reconciliation* (Oxford, UK: Oxford University Press, 2010), 9.

6. Catherine Dauvergne, *Making People Illegal: What Globalization Means for Migration and Law* (Cambridge, UK: Cambridge University Press, 2008), 15.

7. Ibid., 17.

8. Myriam Denov, *Child Soldiers: Sierra Leone's Revolutionary United Front*, 15.

9. Conflict Resolution, Arts and iNtercultural Experience (CRANE). Michelle LeBaron, principal investigator; Carrie MacLeod, project coordinator. This project involved training and practice in diverse settings exploring the use of multiple arts-based strategies. Funded by the Social Sciences and Humanities Research Council of Canada, 2004–2008.

10. Dancing at the Crossroads. Michelle LeBaron, principal investigator; Carrie MacLeod, research director. This project explores how dance and movement, combined with narrative, can broaden peacemaking capacities in intercultural conflicts. Funded by the Social Sciences and Humanities Research Council of Canada, 2009–2013.

11. Robin Grove, Catherine Stevens, and Shirley McKechnie, *Thinking in Four Dimensions: Creativity and Cognition in Contemporary Dance* (Carleton, Victoria, Australia: Melbourne University Press, 2005), 90.

12. Vinashri Pillay, "Culture: Exploring the River," in *Bridging Conflicts across Cultural Divides*, eds. Michelle LeBaron and Vinashri Pillay (Boston, MA: Intercultural Press, 2006), 31.

13. Ibid., 32.

14. Homi Bhabha, *Location of Culture* (London, UK: Routledge, 1994), 53.

15. Paolo Knill, "Foundations for a Theory of Practice," in *Principles and Practice of Expressive Arts Therapy*, eds. Paolo J. Knill, Ellen G. Levine, and Stephen K. Levine (London, UK: Jessica Kingsley, 2005), 136.

16. John F. Dovidio, Samuel L. Gaertner, and Tamar Saguy, "Another View of 'We': Majority and Minority Group Perspectives on a Common Group Identity," *European Review of Social Psychology* 18 (2007), 301.

17. Gordon W. Allport, *The Nature of Prejudice* (Cambridge, MA: Perseus Books, 1954).

18. John Dixon, Kevin Durrheim, and Colin Tredoux, "Beyond the Optimal Contact Strategy: A Reality Check for the Contact Hypothesis," *American Psychologist* 60, no. 7 (2005), 697.

19. Larry E. Sullivan, "Contact Hypothesis," *The SAGE Glossary of the Social and Behavioral Sciences*, eds. Larry E. Sullivan, R. Burke Johnson, Cynthia Calkins Mercado, and Karen J. Terry (Thousand Oaks, CA: SAGE, 2009), 108.

20. Michelle LeBaron, *Bridging Cultural Conflicts* (San Francisco, CA: Jossey-Bass, 2003), 148.

21. Paolo J. Knill, "Foundations for a Theory of Practice," 123.

22. Ibid., 154.

23. Ibid., 158.

24. Tatsushi Arai, *Creativity and Conflict Resolution: Alternative Pathways to Peace* (New York, NY: Routledge, 2009), 5.

25. Ibid., 42.

26. Michelle LeBaron, *Bridging Cultural Conflicts* (San Francisco, CA: Jossey-Bass, 2003), 41.

27. Ian McClosky, "Human Proprioception," *Journal of Clinical Neuroscience* 1, no. 3 (July 1994), 173–77.

28. Imogen Walker, "Proprioception: Your Sixth Sense," *Dance Today* 53, no. 90 (March 2009), 54.

29. Katherine Linn Guerts, *Culture and the Senses: Embodiment, Identity and Well-being in an African Community* (Berkeley, CA: University of California Press, 2002), 73.

30. Corinne Jola, Angharad Davis, and Patrick Haggard, "Proprioceptive Integration and Body Representation: Insights into Dancers' Expertise," *Experimental Brain Research* 213 (September 2011), 258.

31. Ibid., 258.

32. Dean G. Pruitt, "Readiness Theory and the Northern Ireland Conflict," *American Behavioral Scientist* 50, no. 11 (July 2007), 1525.

33. Ibid.

34. Danielle Goldman, *I Want to Be Ready: Improvised Dance as a Practice of Freedom* (Ann Arbor, MI: University of Michigan Press, 2010), 22.

35. Ibid., 25.

5 / Choreography of Space *by* Andrew Floyer Acland

1. Betty Edwards, *Drawing on the Right Side of the Brain* (London, UK: Fontana, 1983).

2. Alan Fletcher, *The Art of Looking Sideways* (London, UK: Phaidon, 2001), 370.

3. Ibid.

4. Judith Hanna, *To Dance Is Human: A Theory of Nonverbal Communication* (Austin, TX and London, UK: University of Texas Press, 1979), 4, 5.

5. John Keats, letter to his brothers George and Thomas, 21 December 1817, Keats' Kingdom, accessed October 31, 2011, www.keatsian.co.uk/negative-capability.htm.

6. Gerard Manley Hopkins, *Poems and Prose*, ed. W. H. Gardner (London, UK: Penguin, 1953), xx.

7. Antonio Damasio, *Descartes' Error: Emotion, Reason, and the Human Brain* (London, UK: Penguin, 2005).

8. Michelle LeBaron, *Bridging Troubled Waters* (San Francisco, CA: Jossey-Bass, 2002), 126.

9. "What Is the Partnership Brokering Project?," The Partnership Brokering Project, accessed October 31, 2011, www.partnershipbrokers.org.

6 / Choreography of Negotiation *by* Christopher Honeyman and Rachel Parish

1. Christopher Honeyman et al., *Performance-Based Assessment: a Methodology for use in selecting, training and evaluating mediators* (Test Design Project, Washington, DC: National Institute for Dispute Resolution 1995). Available electronically at www.convenor.com/madison/method.pdf (accessed April 7, 2011).

2. See Howard Gardner, *Intelligence Reframed: Multiple Intelligences for the 21st Century.* (New York, NY: Basic Books, 1999) and "Using multiple intelligences to improve negotiation theory and practice," *Negotiation Journal* 16, no. 4 (2000), 321-324.

3. For a practical application of "interpersonal" intelligence, see Christopher Honeyman et al., *Performance-Based Assessment: a Methodology for use in selecting, training and evaluating mediators* 1995. For a practical application of logical-mathematical intelligence, see the note on the math problem included in a performance-based test of prospective labor mediators at p. 55.

4. Personal communication with Professor Rena Sharon, 2007–2012, regarding research on negotiation within string quartets.

5. Mark Twain, *The Innocents Abroad* (Oxford, UK: Oxford University Press, 1996).

6. Paul Ekman, *Emotions Revealed: Recognizing Faces and Feelings to Improve Communication and Emotional Life* (New York, NY: Holt 2007).

7. Rachel Parish, *StoryStation*, at http://storingstories.com. (London, UK: Firehouse Creative Productions (2007-10).

8. Christopher Honeyman, James Coben, and Andrew Wei-Min Lee, *Educating Negotiators for a Connected World*: Volume 4 in the *Rethinking Negotiation Teaching Series* (St. Paul, MN: DRI Press, 2012); Christopher Honeyman, James Coben, and Guiseppe De Palo, eds. *Rethinking Negotiation Teaching* (St. Paul, MN: DRI Press, 2009); Christopher Honeyman, James Coben, and Guiseppe De Palo, "Negotiation Teaching 2.0," *Negotiation Journal* (April 2009); Christopher Honeyman, James Coben, and Guiseppe De Palo, *Venturing Beyond the Classroom* (St. Paul, MN: DRI Press 2010); Christopher Honeyman and Andrea Schneider, eds, special issue of 25 articles, *Marquette Law Review*, 87/4 (2003); Christopher Honeyman, Robert Ackerman and Nancy Welsh, special issue of 17 articles, *Penn State Law Review*, 108/1 (2003); Christopher Honeyman, Scott Hughes, and Andrea Schneider, guest eds, special series of ten articles *Conflict Resolution Quarterly*, 20/4 (2003); Sandra Cheldelin, Melanie Greenberg, Christopher Honeyman and Maria Volpe, guest eds, *Negotiation Journal*, 18/4, 19/1 (2002/2003).

9. Christopher Honeyman, James Coben, and Guiseppe De Palo, *Venturing Beyond the Classroom* (St. Paul, MN: DRI Press, 2010) Christopher Honeyman, James Coben, and Andrew Wei-Min Lee, *Educating Negotiators for a Connected World*: Volume 4 in the *Rethinking Negotiation Teaching Series* (St. Paul, MN: DRI Press 2012).

10. Keith Johnstone, *Impro: Improvisation and the Theatre* (London, UK: Methuen 1979), 137.

11. Ibid., 110.

12. See http://www.tate.org.uk/servlet/ViewWork?cgroupid=999999961&workid=216 38&searchid=94 76 (accessed July 4, 2011) and http://www.moma.org/collection/browse_results.php?object_id=81795 (accessed July 4, 2011).

13. David Larson, "Adventure Learning: Not Everyone Gets to Play" in Christopher Honeyman, James Coben and Guiseppe De Palo, *Venturing Beyond the Classroom* (St. Paul, MN: DRI Press, 2010).

14. For why this is important, see Sandra Cheldelin, Melanie Greenberg, Christopher Honeyman and Maria Volpe, guest eds, *Negotiation Journal*, 18/4, 19/1 (2002/2003).

15. Jennifer Levitz "UPS Leaves 'Brown' for New Love" in *Wall Street Journal* September 13, 2010, available online at http://online.wsj.com/article/SB10001424052748704621204 575487840032479922.html (accessed 4/7/2011).

7 / Building Kinesthetic Intelligence *by* Nadja Alexander and Michelle LeBaron

1. Venturing Beyond the Classroom, *Rethinking Negotiation Teaching Series*, vol. 2, eds. Christopher J. Honeyman, James Coben, and Guiseppe De Palo (St. Paul, MN: DRI Press, 2010), 2.

2. Ibid.

3. Lenore Wadsworth Hervey, "Embodied Ethical Decision-Making" *American Journal of Dance Therapy* 29, no. 2 (2007), 91–99.

4. Dee Nolan, "Spain: A Food Lover's Pilgrimage," *Qantas: The Australian Way* (December 2010).

5. Sabine C. Koch, "Interdisciplinary Embodiment Approaches: Implications for Creative Arts Therapies," in *Advances in Dance/Movement Therapy: Theoretical Perspectives and Empirical Findings*, eds. Sabine C. Koch and Iris Brèauninger (Berlin, Germany: Logos Verlag, 2006), 17–28; Paula M. Niedenthal, Lawrence W. Barsalou, Piotr Winkielman, Silva Krauth-Gruber, and François Ric, "Embodiment in Attitudes, Social Perception, and Emotion," *Personality and Social Psychology Review* 9, no. 3 (2005), 184–211, 186; Lawrence W. Barsalou, Paula M. Niedenthal, Aron K. Barbey, and Jennifer A. Ruppert, "Social Embodiment," in *The Psychology of Learning and Motivation*, ed. B. Ross, vol. 43 (San Diego, CA: Academic Press, 2003), 43–92; Antonio Damasio, *Descartes' Error: Emotion, Reason, and the Human Brain* (New York, NY: Putnam, 1994); Antonio Damasio, *The Feeling of What Happens: Body and Emotion in the Making of Consciousness* (New York, NY: Harcourt Brace & Company, 1999).

6. See e.g., Niedenthal et al., "Embodiment in Attitudes, Social Perception, and Emotion"; Barsalou et al., "Social Embodiment," 186.

7. See e.g., Iris Marion Young, "Throwing Like a Girl: A Phenomenology of Feminine Body Comportment Motility and Spatiality," *Human Studies* 3 (1980), 137–56; Cressida J. Heyes, *Self-Transformations: Foucault, Ethics and Normalized Bodies* (Oxford, UK: Oxford University Press, 2007); Judith Butler, *Bodies That Matter: On the Discursive Limits of Sex* (London, UK: Routledge, 1993).

8. See e.g., Frank Coffield, David Moseley, Elaine Hall, and Kathryn Ecclestone, *Learning Styles and Pedagogy in Post-16 Learning: A Systematic and Critical Review* (London, UK: Learning and Skills Research Center, 2004); Gameet BenZion, "Prevailing the Dyslexia Barrier: The Role of Kinesthetic Stimuli in the Teaching of Spelling," in *Neurocognition of Dance*, eds. B. Blasing, M. Putke, and T. Schack (London, UK: Psychology Press, 2010).

9. See e.g., Hervey, "Embodied Ethical Decision-Making"; Cynthia F. Berroll, "Neuroscience Meets Dance/Movement Therapy: Mirror Neurons, the Therapeutic Process and Empathy," *The Arts in Psychotherapy* 33, no. 4 (2006), 302–15; Katya Bloom, *The Embodied Self: Movement and Psychoanalysis* (London, UK: Karnac, 2006).

10. See e.g., Robert C. Givler, *Ethics of Hercules: A Study of Man's Body as the Sole Determinant of Ethical Values* (New York, NY: Alfred A Knopf, 1924); Judith Butler, *Bodies That Matter*.

11. Martha Graham, http://www.quotationspage.com/quote/1579.html, accessed August 3, 2013.

12. Robert J. Lifton, *The Protean Self: Human Resilience in an Age of Fragmentation* (New York, NY: Basic Books, 1995).

13. John Wilson Foster, *Fictions of the Irish Literary Revival: A Changeling Art* (New York, NY: Syracuse University Press, 1993); See also Mary Clark, *In Search of Human Nature* (London, UK: Routledge, 2002).

14. Leonard Riskin, "Contemplative Lawyer: On the Potential Contributions of Mindfulness Meditation to Law Students, Lawyers, and Their Clients," *Harvard Negotiation Law Review* 7 (2009), 1–66.

15. Insa Sparrer and Samuel Onn, *Miracle, Solution and System: Solution-Focused Systemic Structural Constellations for Therapy and Organisational Change* (Cheltenham, UK: Solutionsbooks, 2007).

16. Augusto Boal, *Theatre of the Oppressed* (New York, NY: Theatre Communications Group, 1993; originally published as Teatro di Oprimido in Spanish, 1974); Paolo Freire, *Pedagogy of the Oppressed* (London, UK: Bloomsbury Academic, 2000; 30th Anniversary edition; originally published in Portuguese in 1968).

17. David Diamond, *Theatre for Living: The Art and Science of Community-Based Dialogue* (Bloomington, IN: Trafford Publishing, 2007); Augusto Boal, *Theatre of the Oppressed.*

18. Babette Rothschild, *The Body Remembers: The Psychophysiology of Trauma and Trauma Treatment* (New York, NY: Norton, 2000); Kalila B. Homann, "Embodied Concepts of Neurobiology in Dance/Movement Therapy Practice," *American Journal of Dance Therapy* 32, no. 2 (December 2010), 80–99; Allison F. Winters, "Emotion, Embodiment, and Mirror Neurons in Dance/Movement Therapy: A Connection Across Disciplines," *American Journal of Dance Therapy* 30, no. 2 (2008), 84–105.

19. Derrick P. Aldridge and James B. Stewart, "Introduction: Hip Hop in History: Past Present and Future," *The Journal of African American History* 90, no. 3 (2005), 190–95.

20. Jamie Cevallos, *Positional Hitting: The Modern Approach to Analyzing and Training Your Baseball Swing* (Minneapolis, MN: Mill City Press, 2010), 15.

21. Mark Young and Erik Schlie, "The Rhythm of the Deal: Negotiation as a Dance," *Negotiation Journal* 27, no. 2 (April 2011), 196–203.

22. Leonard Riskin, "Contemplative Lawyer" 2009; Clark Freshman, "Core Concerns, Internal Mindfulness and External Mindfulness for Emotional Balance, Lie Detection and Successful Negotiation," 10 Nev. L.J. 365 (2010).

23. John Grinder and Richard Bandler, *The Structure of Magic*, vol. 2 (Palo Alto, CA: Science and Behaviour Books, 1976), 4.

24. Judith Lynne Hanna, "Anthropological Perspectives for Dance/Movement Therapy," *American Journal of Dance Therapy* 12, no. 2 (Fall/Winter 1990), 117–120, here 118.

25. David L. Hall and Roger T. Ames, *Thinking from the Han* (New York, NY: State of New York University Press, 1998).

26. Andrew Wei-Min Lee, "Ancient Wisdom for the Modern Negotiator: What Chinese Characters Have to Offer Negotiation Pedagogy," in *Venturing Beyond the Classroom*, Rethinking Negotiation Teaching Series, vol. 2 (St. Paul, MN: DRI Press, 2010), 93–107.

27. Johan Galtung, interview, *One to One*, Al-Jazeera, March 27, 2010, http://english
    .aljazeera.net/programmes/oneonone/2010/03/201032311415403979.html.

28. Ni-Vanuatu refers to the indigenous population of the country Vanuatu.

29. Ellen G. and Stephen K. Levine, *Art in Action: Expressive Arts Therapy and Social Change*
    (London, UK: Jessica Kingsley Publishers, 2011).

30. See http://myartfullife.wordpress.com/category/dance/, accessed August 21, 2013.

31. Howard Gardner, *Frames of Mind: The Theory of Multiple Intelligences* (New York, NY:
    Basic Books, 1993).

32. Antonio Damasio, *The Feeling of What Happens: Body and Emotion in the Making of
    Consciousness* (Boston, MA: Mariner Books, a division of Houghton Mifflin Harcourt,
    2000).

33. Kalila B. Homann, "Embodied Concepts of Neurobiology in Dance/Movement Therapy
    Practice," *American Journal of Dance Therapy* 32, no. 2 (December 2010), 80–99.

34. Maurice Merleau-Ponty, *The Visible and the Invisible: Studies in Phenomenology and Exis-
    tental Philosophy* (Chicago, IL: Northwestern University Press, 1969); Rosalyn Diprose,
    Corporeal Generosity: On Giving With Nietzsche, Merleau-Ponty, and Levinas (Albany, NY:
    State University of New York Press, 2002), 174.

35. Carl W. Cotman and Christie Engesser-Cesar, "Exercise Enhances and Protects Brain
    Function," *Exercise and Sports Sciences Review*, 2002, Apr. 30 (2), 75–79

36. Allan N. Schore, *Affect Regulation and the Repair of the Self* (New York, NY: W. W. Norton,
    2003).

37. Robert C. Givler., *Ethics of Hercules* (New York, NY: Knopf, 1924).

38. Lenore W. Hervey, "Embodied Ethical Decision-Making," 99, 102–105.

39. Paul Ekman and Wallace V. Friesen, "A New Pan-Cultural Facial Expression of Emotion,"
    Motivation and Emotion 10, no. 2 (1986), 159–68.

40. Judith L. Hanna, "Anthropological Perspectives for Dance/Movement Therapy," *Ameri-
    can Journal of Dance Therapy*, 12, no. 2 (1990), 116–117.

41. Carrie Noland, *Agency and Embodiment: Performing Gestures/Producing Culture* (Cam-
    bridge, MA and London, UK: Harvard University Press, 2009), 13.

42. Marc Jeannerod, "The Representing Brain: Neural Correlates of Motor Intention and
    Imagery," *Behavioral and Brain Sciences* 17 (1994), 187–245; Marc Jeannerod, *The
    Cognitive Neuroscience of Action* (San Francisco, CA: Wiley-Blackwell, 1997).

43. Beatrice de Gelder, Josh Snyder, Doug Greve, George Gerard and Nouchine Hadjikhani,
    "Fear Fosters Flight: A Mechanism for Fear Contagion When Perceiving Emotion
    Expressed by a Whole Body," *Proceedings of the National Academy of Sciences* 101, no. 47
    (2004), 16701–706; Philip I. Jackson, Andrew N. Meltzoff and Jean Decety, "How Do
    We Perceive the Pain of Others? A Window Into the Neural Processes Involved in Empa-
    thy," *NeuroImage* 24 (2005), 771–9.

44. Erma Dosamantes-Alperson, "Experiential Movement Psychotherapy," in *Theoretical Approaches in Dance/Movement Therapy*, vol. 2, ed. P. L. Bernstein (Dubuque, IA: Kendall/Hunt, 1984), 257–91; Giovanni Berlucchi and Salvatore M. Aglioti, "The Body in the Brain Revisited," *Experimental Brain Research* 200 (2010), 25–35; I. Dosamantes-Beaudry, "Somatic Experience in Psychoanalysis," *Psychoanalytic Psychology* 14, no. 4 (1997), 517–30; Lenore W. Hervey, "Embodied Ethical Decision-Making," 98–99.

45. Carrie Noland, *Agency and Embodiment*; Homann, "Embodied Concepts of Neurobiology in Dance/Movement Therapy Practice," 3; Bloom (2006).

46. Kalila B. Homann, "Embodied Concepts of Neurobiology in Dance/Movement Therapy Practice," 3.

47. Malvern Lumsden, George Lakoff and Mark Johnson, *Philosophy in the Flesh: The Embodied Mind and Its Challenge to Western Thought* (New York, NY: Basic Books, 1999); Malvern Lumsden, "The Moving Self in Life, Art, and Community Mental Health: 12 Propositions," *Body, Movement and Dance in Psychotherapy* 5, no. 3 (October 13, 2010), 231–43, doi:10.1080/17432979.2010.518018.

48. Lenore W. Hervey, "Embodied Ethical Decision-Making," (2007), 102–104.

49. Janis P. Sarra, ed. *An Exploration of Fairness: Interdisciplinary Inquires in Law, Science and the Humanities.* (Toronto, Canada: Carswell, 2013). See also http://www.explore fairness.pwias.ubc.ca/

50. Malvern Lumsden, "The Moving Self in Life, Art, and Community Mental Health: 12 Propositions," 11.

51. Mark Young and Erik Schlie, "The Rhythm of the Deal: Negotiation as a Dance," *Negotiation Journal* 27, no. 2 (April 2011), 202.

52. *Ubuntu* is an African philosophical term that offers an explanation of the essence of what it means to be human and the individual's interconnectedness with others. According to *Ubuntu*, we affirm our humanity when we acknowledge that of others because our humanity is bound up in theirs. See Desmond Tutu, *No Future without Forgiveness* (Colorado Springs, CO: Image Books, 2000).

*8/*Building Emotional Intelligence—Charlie Irvine

1. Mary E. Clark, *In Search of Human Nature* (London, UK: Routledge, 2002), 155.

2. Giuseppe de Lampedusa, *The Leopard* (London, UK: Penguin Books, 1958), 50.

3. Well summarized in Tricia S. Jones, "Emotion in Mediation: Implications, Applications, Opportunities, and Challenges" in *The Blackwell Handbook of Mediation: Bridging Theory, Research, and Practice*, ed. Margaret S. Herrman (Oxford, UK: Blackwell Publishing, 2006).

4. Bernard Mayer, *The Dynamics of Conflict Resolution: A Practitioner's Guide* (San Francisco, CA: Jossey-Bass, 2000), 43.

5. Leonard Riskin, "Further Beyond Reason: Emotions, the Core Concerns and Mindfulness in Negotiation," *Nevada Law Journal* 10, no. 2 (Spring 2010), 290–337, 294.

6. Suzanne Retzinger and Thomas Scheff, "Emotion, Alienation, and Narratives: Resolving Intractable Conflict," *Mediation Quarterly* 18, no. 1 (Fall 2000), 71–85, 71.

7. Jones, "Emotion in Mediation," 278–79.

8. Kerry Patterson, Joseph Grenny, Ron McMillan, and Al Switzler, *Crucial Conversations: Tools for Talking When Stakes Are High* (New York, NY: McGraw-Hill, 2002), 99.

9. Jones, "Emotion in Mediation," 279.

10. Daniel Goleman, *Emotional Intelligence: Why It Can Matter More Than IQ* (London, UK: Bloomsbury, 1995), 78–95.

11. Antonio Damasio, *Descartes' Error*, rev. ed. (London, UK: Vintage Books, 1994), 139.

12. Ibid., p.xxiii; see also Clark, *In Search of Human Nature*: "Thinking is definitely powerful stuff, but it can go nowhere without guidance from the deep emotions built into us during our evolutionary past."

13. William Wordsworth, *Preface to Lyrical Ballads* (1800), paragraph 15, http://www.bartleby.com/39/36.html.

14. Damasio, *Descartes' Error*, 151.

15. Ibid., 160.

16. Ibid., 165–201.

17. Paul Ekman, "Basic Emotions," *Handbook of Cognition and Emotion*, eds. Tim Dalglish and Mick J. Power (Chichester, West Sussex, England: John Wiley and Sons, 1999).

18. Jones, "Emotion in Mediation," 279.

19. Bianca Beersma, Fieke Harinck, and Maria J. J. Gerts, "Bound in Honor: How Honor Values and Insults Affect the Experience and Management of Conflicts," *International Journal of Conflict Management* 14, no. 2 (2003), 75–94, 86.

20. David W. Augsburger, *Conflict Mediation Across Cultures: Pathways and Patterns* (Louisville, KY: Westminster/John Knox Press, 1992), 124.

21. Mayer, *The Dynamics of Conflict Resolution*, 10.

22. Aaron T. Beck, *Prisoners of Hate: The Cognitive Basis of Anger, Hostility, and Violence* (London, UK: Perennial, 1999).

23. Paul Ekman, *Emotions Revealed: Understanding Faces and Feelings* (London, UK: Phoenix, 2003), 40. Describes the "refractory state" that follows the triggering of an emotion, "during which time our thinking cannot incorporate information that does not fit, maintain, or justify the emotion we are feeling."

24. See Ohh Shoot, "Thinking There Was a Burglar, Man Shoots Girlfriend Who Had Gotten Out of Bed to Go to the Bathroom, *Ohh Shoot* (blog), November 22, 2010, http://ohhshoot.blogspot.com/2010/11/thinking-there-was-burglar-man-shoots.html.

25. Beck, *Prisoners of Hate*, 25.

26. Ekman, *Emotions Revealed*, 17.

27. Keith Allred, "Relationship Dynamics in Disputes: Replacing Contention with Cooperation," eds. Michael L. Moffitt and Robert C. Bordone, *The Handbook of Dispute Resolution* (San Francisco, CA: Jossey-Bass, 2005).

28. Jones, "Emotion in Mediation," 279.

29. Kenneth Cloke, "Bringing Oxytocin Into the Room," Mediate.com, January 2009, www.mediate.com/articles/cloke8.cfm. note 46, p.1

30. Daniel L. Shapiro, "Enemies, Allies, and Emotions: The Power of Positive Emotions in Negotiation," eds. Michael L. Moffitt and Robert C. Bordone, *The Handbook of Dispute Resolution* (San Francisco, CA: Jossey-Bass, 2005), 69.

31. Robert A. Baruch Bush and Joseph P. Folger, *The Promise of Mediation: The Transformative Approach to Conflict*, 2nd ed. (San Francisco, CA: Jossey-Bass, 2005).

32. Richard S. Lazarus, *Emotion and Adaptation* (Oxford, UK: Oxford University Press, 1991).

33. Uwe Herwig, Tina Kaffenberger, Lutz Jänckec, and Annette B. Brühl, "Self-Related Awareness and Emotion Regulation," *Neuroimage* 50 (2010), 734–41.

34. Damasio, *Descartes' Error*, 3–19.

35. Retzinger and Scheff, "Emotion, Alienation, and Narratives," 79.

36. Jessica Katz Jameson, Andrea M. Bodtker, and Tim Linker, "Facilitating Conflict Transformation: Mediator Strategies for Eliciting Emotional Communication in a Workplace Conflict," *Negotiation Journal* 26, no. 1 (January 2010), 25–48, 29.

37. Jones, "Emotion in Mediation," 293–96.

38. Jameson et al., "Facilitating Conflict Transformation," 34.

39. Herwig et al., "Self-Related Awareness and Emotion Regulation."

40. Jameson et al., "Facilitating Conflict Transformation," 45.

41. Riskin, "Further Beyond Reason,", citing Roger Fisher and Daniel Shapiro, *Beyond Reason: Using Emotions as You Negotiate* (New York, NY: Viking Press, 2006).

42. Ekman, "Basic Emotions." For an excellent summary of the relevance of individual emotions to mediation see *Mediation Ethics: Cases and Commentaries*, ed. Ellen Waldman (San Francisco, CA: Jossey-Bass, 2011), 56–63.

43. Harold Schlosberg, "The Description of Facial Expressions in Terms of Two Dimensions," *Journal of Experimental Psychology* 4, no. 4 (October 1952), 229–37.

44. Leonard Riskin, "Understanding Mediators' Orientations, Strategies, and Techniques: A Grid for the Perplexed," *Harvard Negotiation Law Review* 1 (1996), 7–52.

45. Charlie Irvine, Bryan Clark, and Rachel Robertson, *Alternative Mechanisms for Resolving Disputes: A Literature Review* (London, UK: Health Professions Council, 2011), 14–15. Available from http://www.hpc-uk.org/publications/index.asp?id=462.

46. Hallam Movius and Timothy D. Wilson, "How We Feel About the Deal," *Negotiation Journal* (April 2011), 241–50.

47. Ibid., 247–48.

48. Fiona McAuslan, "Performance-Based Conflict Resolution Training for Children," *ACResolution* (Summer/Fall 2010), 21–22.

49. Riskin "Further Beyond Reason," 322–23.

50. Ekman, "Emotions Revealed," 36, 37.

51. William Ury, *The Power of a Positive No: How to Say No and Still Get to Yes* (London, UK: Hodder & Stoughton, 2007), 33.

52. Riskin 2010, citing Zindel V. Segal, J. Mark G. Williams, and John D. Teasdale, *Mindfulness-Based Cognitive Therapy for Depression: A New Approach to Preventing Relapse* (New York, NY: Guilford Press, 2002), 322–23.

9/ Dancing through Conflict *by* Simon J. A. Mason, Susan Allen Nan, and Virginie van de Loe

1. Gerd Gigerenzer, *Gut Feelings, the Intelligence of the Unconscious* (New York, NY: Viking Penguin, 2007), 16.

2. Daniel Kahneman, *Thinking, Fast and Slow* (New York, NY: Macmillan Publishers; Farrar, Straus and Giroux Paperbacks, 2011).

3. Gerd Gigerenzer, *Gut Feelings, the Intelligence of the Unconscious* (New York, NY: Viking Penguin, 2007).

4. Roger Fisher and Daniel Shapiro, *Beyond Reason – Using Emotions as You Negotiate* (New York, NY: Penguin Books, 2005).

5. Anita J. Smith, Mary Ann Thurkettle and Felicitas A. dela Cruz, "Use of Intuition by Nursing Students: Instrument Development and Testing," *Journal of Advanced Nursing* 47, no. 6 (2004), 614–622, here 614.

6. Judee K. Burgoon, David B. Buller and W. Gill Woodall, *Nonverbal Communication: the Unspoken Dialog* (New York, NY: Harper & Row, 1989), 35; Mark L. Knapp, *Essentials of Nonverbal Communication* (New York, NY: Holt, Rinehart and Winston, 1980).

7. Mark L. Knapp, *Essentials of Nonverbal Communication* (New York, NY: Holt, Rinehart and Winston, 1980).

8. August Napier and Carl Whitaker, *The Family Crucible, the Intense Experience of Family Therapy* (New York, NY: Harper Collins, 1988).

9. David Matsumoto, "Culture and Nonverbal Behavior." In: Valerie Manusov and Miles Patterson (eds.), *Handbook of Nonverbal Communication* (Thousand Oaks, CA: Sage, 2006), 219–235.

10. Carl G. Jung, "Aion: Phenomenology of the Self." In: Joseph Campbell (ed.), *The Portable Jung* (New York, NY: Penguin Books, 1976), 139–162, here 146.

11. Mark Patrick Hederman, *Love impatient, Love unkind – Eros Human and Devine* (New York, NY: Crossroad Publishing Company, 2004), 35.

12. Francis Vaughan, *Awakening Intuition* (Doubleday, New York, NY: Anchor Books, 1979).

13. Quoted in Leonard J. Waks (2007). "Intuition in Education: Teaching and Learning without Thinking," in *Philosophy of Education*, ed. Daniel Vokey (Urbana, IL: Philosophy of Education Society 2006), 379–388, here 379.

14. Roger Fisher and Daniel Shapiro, *Beyond Reason – Using Emotions as You Negotiate* (New York, NY: Penguin Books, 2005).

15. Daniel Bowling and David Hoffman, "Bringing Peace into the Room: The Personal Qualities of the Mediator and Their Impact on the Mediation," *Negotiation Journal* 16, no. 1 (2007), 5–28.

16. Christopher W. Moore, *The Mediation Process, Practical Strategies for Resolving Conflict* (San Francisco, CA: Jossey-Bass, 2003).

17. Christopher W. Moore, *The Mediation Process, Practical Strategies for Resolving Conflict* (San Francisco, CA: Jossey-Bass, 2003).

18. Greg Rooney, "The Use of Intuition in Mediation," *Conflict Resolution Quarterly* 25, no. 2 (2007).

19. Greg Rooney, "The Use of Intuition in Mediation," *Conflict Resolution Quarterly* 25, no. 2 (2007), 248.

20. Julian T. Hottinger interviewed by Simon Mason and Damiano Sguaitamatti, Renens, Switzerland 2009.

21. Michelle LeBaron, "Creating Shifts: Using Arts in Conflicts with Religious Dimensions." In: Simon Mason and Damiano Sguaitamatti (eds.), *Religion in Conflict Transformation – Politorbis* no. 52 (2/2011), 53–58; John-Paul Lederach, *The Moral Imagination, the Art and Soul of Building Peace* (Oxford, UK: Oxford University Press, 2005); Ellen G. Levine and Stephen K. Levine, *Art in Action – Expressive Arts Therapy and Social Change* (London, UK: Jessica Kingsley Publishers, 2011).

22. See www.margiegillis.org

23. See http://www.law.ubc.ca/faculty/Lebaron/

24. Thich Nhat Hanh, *Peace is Every Step: The Path of Mindfulness in Everyday Life* (New York, NY: Bantam Books, 1992).

25. Carl G. Jung, "Psychotherapists or the Clergy." In: Carl G. Jung, *Jung: Modern Man in Search of a Soul* (Milton Park, UK: Routledge Classics 2001), 241.

26. Joan Chodorow, *Dance Therapy and Depth Psychology: The Moving Imagination* (London, UK: Routledge, 2005), 3.

27. Michelle LeBaron, "Creating Shifts: Using Arts in Conflicts with Religious Dimensions." In: Simon Mason and Damiano Sguaitamatti (eds.), *Religion in Conflict Transformation – Politorbis* no. 52 (2/2011), 53–58.

28. This blockage and the subsequent negative impacts may play out even long after it was caused. This is well researched in extreme cases of being wounded, often called a "trauma." The body memory of a psychological wound may also be a reality in less severe cases. See for example, Kim Etherington (ed.), *Trauma, the Body and Transformation: A Narrative Inquiry* (London, UK: Jessica Kingsley Publishers, 2003).

29. David Wilcox and Nance Pettit, "Awake My Dear." In: *Out Beyond Ideas*, Songs for Peace Project, Audio CD (University of Maryland, MD: What Are Records, 2005).

30. Examples of pioneers in this field in the West include: Mary Wigman, Rosalie Cladeck, Isadora Duncan, Rudolf von Laban, Martha Graham, Liljan Espenak, Trudi Schoop and Guy Ramet; see: Fe Reichelt, *Ausdruckstanz und Tanztherapie* (Frankfurt, Germany/M: Verlag Brandes & Apsel, 1987).

31. Ana Schofield, "Body Language in Mediation – Including Recuperation Patterns During Work Cycles for Mediators", *Mediate.com*, March 2004; Amy Starr and Norman Page, "Dealing With Nonverbal Cues: A Key To Mediator Effectiveness," *Mediate.com*, March 2005; Tricia S. Jones and Andrea Bodtker, "Mediating with Heart in Mind: Addressing Emotion in Mediation Practice." *Negotiation Journal* 17, no. 3 (July 2001), 217–244.

32. The "spin" idea in mediation was mentioned by Julian T. Hottinger in interviews with Simon Mason and Damiano Sguaitamatti, Renens, Switzerland, 2009.

11 / Ireland *by* **Maureen Maloney**

1. William Butler Yeats, "Among School Children," in *Collected Poems* (London, UK: Picador, 1990). Interestingly, dance used in Yeats's plays has been interpreted as a vehicle to bolster Irish nationalism and to depict both personal and national conflict. See e.g., Deng-Hui Lee, "The Evolution of Yeat's [sic] Dance Imagery: The Body, Gender and Nationalism" (PhD diss., University of North Texas, 2003), http://digital.library.unt .edu/ark:/67531/metadc4312/m1/1/high_res_d/dissertation.pdf.

2. Helena Wulff, *Dancing at the Crossroads: Memory and Mobility in Ireland*, vol. 1, *Dance and Performance Studies* (Oxford, UK: Berghahn, 2007), 18.

3. Although dance has played, and continues to play, a major role in Irish culture, there is a dearth of scholarly literature on its role in conflict narratives. Consulted works include J. G. O'Keefe and Art O'Brien, *A Handbook of Irish Dances* (Dublin, Ireland: McGill and Sons, 1902); Violet Alford, *Dances of France*, vol. 3, *The Pyrenees* (London, UK: Max Parrish and Co., 1951); Breandán Breathnach, *Dancing in Ireland County Clare* (Miltown Malbay, Ireland: Dal gCais Publications, 1983); Pat Murphy, *Toss the Feathers: Irish Set Dancing* (Dublin, Ireland: Mercier Press, 1996); Helen Brennan, *The Story of Irish Dance* (County Kerry, Ireland: Mount Eagle Publications, 1999); Finton Vallely, *The Companion to Irish Traditional Music* (Cork, Ireland: Cork University Press, 1999).

4. Helena Wulff, *Dancing at the Crossroads: Memory and Mobility in Ireland* (Oxford, UK: Berghahn Books, 2007), 46.

5. Ibid., 47.

6. Murphy, *Toss the Feathers*, 25. See also Diarmuid O'Giollain, *Locating Irish Folklore: Tradition, Modernity, Identity* (Cork, Ireland: Cork University Press, 2000), 120; Joe Cleary and Claire Connolly, *The Cambridge Companion to Modern Irish Culture* (Cambridge, UK: University Press, 2005), 144; Brennan, *The Story of Irish Dance*, 30–31; Vallely, *The Companion to Irish Traditional Music*, 346; Wulff, *Dancing at the Crossroads*, 80–82. Indeed, the debate continues to this day: see Victoria White, "Will the Real Irish Dancing Please Stand Up," *The Irish Times*, December 18, 1996, accessed January 17, 2011, http://www.standingstones.com/ceili.html.

7. Cleary and Connolly, *The Cambridge Companion to Modern Irish Culture*, 143; Brennan, *The Story of Irish Dance*, 30–31, Breathnach, *Dancing in Ireland*, 24; Vallely, *The Companion to Irish Traditional Music*, 346.

8. Cleary and Connolly, *The Cambridge Companion to Modern Irish Culture*, 143.

9. Arthur Young, a noted English agriculturalist and traveler, quoted in Breathnach, *Dancing in Ireland*, 23.

10. Irish Dancing Commission (formally known by the Gaelic name *An Coimisium Le Rinci Gaelacha*), accessed July 1, 2013, http://www.clrg.ie/.

11. Anecdotal conversation about a story told to the anthropologist Thomas Taaffe by his mother, quoted in Wulff, *Dancing at the Crossroads*, 98.

12. Cleary and Connolly, *The Cambridge Companion to Modern Irish Culture*, 144.

13. Ibid.

14. Murphy, *Toss the Feathers*, 29.

15. Martin Stokes, "Introduction: Ethnicity, Identity and Music," in *Ethnicity, Identity and Music*, ed. Martin Stokes (Oxford, UK: Berg, 1994), 3. Quoted in Wulff, *Dancing at the Crossroads*, 10.

16. "Irish and Scottish Dance Descriptions," Scott MacHaffie, last modified November 5, 1999, http://www.nonvi.com/sm/dance_list.html. To see the dance performed, http://www.youtube.com/watch?v=GBnda_SH-zU.

17. "When Was the Siege of Ennis?," Yahoo Answers, accessed December 10, 2010, http://answers.yahoo.com/question/index?qid=20070806085513AA57n9k.

18. Ibid., 2.

19. Cleary and Connolly, *The Cambridge Companion to Modern Irish Culture*, 144.

20. This story is attributed to Francis Roche, *Irish Dances, Marches and Airs* (1957) in White, "Will the Real Irish Dancing Please Stand Up?"

21. Wulff, *Dancing at the Crossroads*, 10.

22. Ibid., 24, 98.

23. Available at http://www.youtube.com/watch?v=zamzdlYARrs. On YouTube there are two performances: *Hanging in There* part 1 and *Hanging in There* part 2. This piece and associated reviews refer to part 1, although part 2 is equally interesting.

24. Jane Coyle, "Dance Review: *Hanging in There/Touching Distance*," CultureNorthern-Ireland, November 5, 2009, accessed December 17, 2010, http://www.culturenorthern ireland.org/article/2893/dance-review-hanging-in-there-touching-distance.

25. Ibid.

26. Gareth Vile, "Catapult Dance, Fearghus O'Conchuir, Legitimate Bodies Dance Company," *Ballet Magazine*, September 2008, accessed December 17, 2010, http://www. ballet.co.uk/magazines/yr_08/sep08/gv_rev_catapult_conchuir_legitimate_bodies _0808.htm.

27. "Dance Has Politics Down to Fine Art," *Belfast Telegraph*, October 28, 2009, accessed December 17, 2010, http://www.belfasttelegraph.co.uk/entertainment/belfast-festival /previews/dance-has-politics-down-to-fine-art-14544131.html.

28. Wulff, *Dancing at the Crossroads*, 34.

29 Ibid., 48.

*12/*Ireland *by* Geoffrey Corry

1. GPO is the general post office in O'Connell Street in Dublin.

2. William Zartman, "Ripeness: The Hurting Stalemate and Beyond," in *International Conflict Resolution after the Cold War*, eds. Paul C. Stern and Daniel Druckman (Washington, DC: National Research Council: National Academy Press, 2000).

3. The concept of making peace with your enemy is attributed to Nelson Mandela: "If you want to make peace with your enemy, you have to work with your enemy. Then he becomes your partner." It is often quoted by the former president Bill Clinton.

4. President Barack Obama used this language in Dublin on May 23, 2011, when he pointed to what had been achieved in Northern Ireland compared with the quagmire of the Israeli-Palestinian problem.

5. F. W. De Klerk, "Moving Beyond Victimhood" (speech, Summer School of the Glencree Centre for Reconciliation, Ireland, August 16, 2002). De Klerk is the former president of South Africa.

6. Thoughts of David Reddaway, British ambassador to Ireland from 2006 to 2009, on his departure from Ireland. See also Geoffrey Corry, "Peacemaking Lessons of the Northern Ireland Peace Process 1985–2007" (paper, annual conference of Association of Conflict Resolution, San Diego, 2011).

7. B. Rothschild, *The Body Remembers: The Psychophysiology of Trauma and Trauma Treatment* (New York, NY: W. W. Norton, 2000).

8. Peter Levine supports the redesignation of trauma as an injury (PTSI) and an emotional wound, which can be healed, and not a medical disorder like diabetes, which is managed. Peter A. Levine, *In an Unspoken Voice: How the Body Releases Trauma and Restores Goodness* (Berkeley, CA: North Atlantic Books, 2010), 34.

9. Irish Peace Centres, "Intergenerational Aspects of the Conflict in Northern Ireland," Experiential Learning Paper No. 2 (Irish Peace Centres: 2010), 52.

10. Ibid., page 78.

11. Rafael Moses, "On Dehumanizing the Enemy," in *The Psychodynamics of International Relationships*, vol.1, eds. Vamik Volkan, Demetrius Julius, and Joseph Montville (Lanham, MD: Lexington Books, 1990), 111–18.

12. Ibid.

13. Nelson Mandela (address to Dail Eireann [Irish Parliament], July 2, 1990).

14. Judith Herman, *Trauma and Recovery: The Aftermath of Violence—From Domestic Abuse to Political Terror* (New York, NY: Basic Books, 1992), 95.

15. I acknowledge the work of my colleagues at Glencree: Ian White, Jacinta de Paor, and Wilhelm Verwoerd.

16. Something similar is happening in the psychosocial workshops in Bosnia. See Ed Vulliamy, *The War Is Dead, Long Live the War* (London, UK: Bodley Head, 2012).

17. Interviews with Jo Berry (Tuffnell) on the BBC television documentary "Facing the Enemy" (2002) included the dialogue between Jo and Patrick Magee and the reflections of both of them.

18. Mark Williams and Danny Penman, *Mindfulness: Finding Peace in a Frantic World* (London, UK: Piatkus, 2011).

19. Peter A. Levine, *In an Unspoken Voice: How the Body Releases Trauma and Restores Goodness*, 279

20. Irish Peace Centres, "Intergenerational Aspects of the Conflict in Northern Ireland," Experential Learning Paper No. 2 (Irish Peace Centres: 2010), 48.

21. Ibid., 48.

22. Ibid., 49.

23. Kaethe Weingarten, *Common Shock: Witnessing Violence Every Day; How We Are Harmed, How We Can Heal* (New York, NY: Dutton, 2003).

24. Dan Bar-On, *The Indescribable and the Undiscussable: Reconstructing Human Discourse after Trauma* (Budapest, Hungary: Central European University Press, 1999).

25. Anthony Storr, *Freud: A Very Short Introduction* (Oxford, UK: Oxford University Press, 1989), 21.

26. Kenneth Cloke, *The Crossroads of Conflict* (London, UK: Janus Publications, 2006), 218.

27. Dan Bar-On, *The Indescribable and the Undiscussable: Reconstructing Human Discourse after Trauma* (Budapest, Hungary: Central European University Press, 1999), op. cit., 127, 146. By silencing the facts of past events, people may "unintentionally and unwittingly transmit the repressed violence" to the next generations through normalized discourse. Bar-On believes that this is what happened in Bosnia. On the collapse of Tito's communist regime, the old unresolved conflicts and memories of previous atrocities "resurfaced into a terrible and meaningless bloodshed."

28. Judith Herman, *Trauma and Recovery: The Aftermath of Violence—From Domestic Abuse to Political Terror* (New York, NY: Basic Books, 1992), 175.

29. David Servan-Schreiber, *Healing without Freud or Prozac: Natural Approaches to Curing Stress, Anxiety and Depression* (London, UK: Rodale International, 2005). See Chapter 1.

30. Ibid., 21.

31. Ibid., 21.

32. Patricia Cane, *Trauma, Healing and Transformation* (Santa Cruz, CA: Capacitar, 2000).

33. My personal conversations with Jo Berry at the Glencree Centre for Reconciliation.

34. Kaethe Weingarten, *Common Shock: Witnessing Violence Every Day: How We Are Harmed, How We Can Heal* (New York, NY: Dutton, 2003), op. cit., 235.

35. Dan Bar-On, *The Indescribable and the Undiscussable: Reconstructing Human Discourse after Trauma* (Budapest, Hungary: Central European University Press, 1999), op. cit., 4.

36. Herman, op. cit., 2.

37. Adapted from a nested egg concept devised by Máire Dugan, "A Nested Theory of Conflict," *A Leadership Journal: Women in Leadership* 1, no. 1 (1996), 9–20.

38. Dan Bar-On, *The Indescribable and the Undiscussable: Reconstructing Human Discourse after Trauma*, op. cit.

39. Kaethe Weingarten, "Compassionate Witnessing: Creating Moments of Healing for Ourselves and Others" (unpublished paper, presented at Belfast Conference on Trauma and Spirituality, March 2011).

40. Kaethe Weingarten, *Common Shock: Witnessing Violence Every Day: How We Are Harmed, How We Can Heal* (New York, NY: Dutton 2003).

41. Arnautovic Azra and Elmir Ibralic, *Socio-Therapeutic Work with Male Group in Konjevic Ploje 2008–2009* (Tuzla, Bosnia: UG Vive Zene, 2009), 7.

42. Judith Herman, *Trauma and Recovery: The Aftermath of Violence—From Domestic Abuse to Political Terror* (New York, NY: Basic Books, 1992), op. cit., 205.

43. Cinny Noble, *Conflict Coaching: The CINERGY Model, Cinergy Coaching* (Toronto: Canada: 2012).

44. John M. Haynes, Gretchen L. Haynes, and Larry Fong, *Mediation: Positive Conflict Management* (New York, NY: SUNY Press, 2004).

45. Twenty years after the Brighton bomb, Simon Fanshawe of the *Guardian* newspaper chaired a public meeting between Jo Berry and Patrick Magee and wrote about the story they told (October 13, 2004).

46. Jo Berry has set up a joint project with Pat Magee: www.buildingbridgesforpeace.org.

47. From a report of the meeting. "Brighton Bomber: I Don't Want Forgiveness but I Feel Regret," *Belfast Telegraph*, October 14, 2009. The meeting was organized by the Forgiveness Project, a British charity dedicated to conflict resolution. (For more information, visit www.theforgivenessproject.com.) Magee and Berry appeared under the auspices of the House of Commons all-party parliamentary group on conflict issues.

48. Quotations of Patrick Magee are from the report of Richard Allen Greene, "Bomber Who Tried to Kill Thatcher: 'Regret,' but not 'Sorry,'" CNN, last modified October 13, 2009, http://www.cnn.com/2009/WORLD/europe/10/13/britain.brighton.bomb.statement/.

49. Brené Brown, "The Power of Vulnerability," TED video, 2010, http://www.ted.com/talks/lang/eng/brene_brown_on_vulnerability.html.

50. Dan Bar-On, *Tell Your Life Story: Creating Dialogue Among Jews and Germans, Israelis and Palestinians* (Budapest, Hungary: Central European Press, 2006), 2.

51. John Winslade and Gerald Monk, *Narrative Mediation: A New Approach to Conflict Resolution* (San Francisco, CA: Jossey-Bass, 2000), chapter 3.

52. Kaethe Weingarten, *Common Shock: Witnessing Violence Every Day: How We Are Harmed, How We Can Heal* (New York, NY: Dutton, 2003), op. cit., 133.

53. Robert A. Baruch Bush and Joseph P. Folger, *The Promise of Mediation: The Transformative Approach to Conflict* (San Francisco, CA: Jossey-Bass, 2005), 77.

54. Kenneth R. Melchin and Cheryl Picard, *Transforming Conflict through Insight* (Toronto, Canada: University of Toronto Press, 2009), 67. Insight theory is based on ideas of the Canadian philosopher Bernard Lonergan.

55. Ibid., 58.

56. Adam Curle, "Reconciliation," (unplublished paper, presented to Glencree Centre for Reconciliation, 1981).

13 / Cambodia and Liberia *by* Toni Shapiro-Phim

1. Author interview with Pichet Klunchun, Phnom Penh, Cambodia, December 2010.

2. The term "Khmer" officially refers to the majority ethnic group of Cambodia. In common usage, "Khmer" is interchangeable with "Cambodian," accessed February 8, 2011, http://whc.unesco.org/en/list/1224/.

3. Seth Mydans, "Pause in Fighting between Thailand and Cambodia," *The New York Times*, accessed February 8, 2011, http://www.nytimes.com/2011/02/09/world/asia/09iht-cambo09.html.

4. Jaqueline Shea Murphy, *The People Have Never Stopped Dancing* (Minneapolis, MN: University of Minnesota Press, 2007), 29.

5. Joan Huckstep, "*Animation Politique*: The Embodiment of Nationalism in Zaire," in *Dance, Human Rights, and Social Justice: Dignity in Motion*, eds. Naomi Jackson and Toni Shapiro-Phim (Lanham, MD: Scarecrow Press, 2008), 62.

6. Sally Ann Ness, "The Inscription of Gesture," in *Migrations of Gesture*, eds. Carrie Noland and Sally Ann Ness (Minneapolis, MN: University of Minnesota Press, 2008), 24.

7. James Thompson, Jenny Hughes, and Michael Balfour, *Performance in Place of War* (London, UK: Seagull Books, 2009), 147.

8. The *Ramayana* and *Mahabharata* are both lengthy, complex epics of Indian origin, with numerous versions found in countries in South and Southeast Asia.

9. Thompson, Hughes, and Balfour, *Performance in Place of War*, 149.

10. Ibid., 152.

11. Christopher R. Mitchell, "Conflict, Social Change, and Conflict Resolution: An Enquiry," in *Social Change and Conflict Transformation*, Berghof Handbook Dialogue Series, no. 5, eds. David Bloomfield, Martina Fischer, and Beatrix Schmelzle (Berlin, Germany: Berghof Research Center for Constructive Conflict Management, 2006), 19, accessed February 8, 2011, http://www.berghof-handbook.net/documents/publications/dialogue5_mitchell _lead-1.pdf.

12. In the 1820s, the American Colonization Society purchased land on the west coast of Africa as a colony for returning freed slaves. Liberia, whose name means "free land," became an independent country in 1847.

13. Mary H. Moran, *Liberia: The Violence of Democracy* (Philadelphia, PA: University of Pennsylvania Press, 2008), 5. Leymah Gbowee recalls that it was during Doe's presidency that ethnicity began to be a major dividing force in Liberia. After he took office, "tribal identity began to matter. Before Doe, the split was between the elite and the indigenous. All of us had our tribal identities: our dances and traditions, our native languages. But we were equal to each other, and tribal intermarriages took place all the time. Doe changed that . . ." awarding coveted jobs to people of his own Krahn ethnicity, while completely excluding certain other groups. "Bitterness, then opposition, grew." Leymah Gbowee, *Mighty Be Our Powers* (New York, NY: Beast Books, 2011), 17.

14. Timothy Nevins, "An Interview with Fatu Gayflor," *Works in Progress*, The Philadelphia Folklore Project (2008), 7.

15. For a study of the history and politics of the formation of various national folk dance or cultural troupes around the world, see Anthony Shay, *Choreographic Politics: State Folk Dance Companies, Representation and Power* (Middletown, CT: Wesleyan University Press, 2002).

16. United Nations High Commissioner for Refugees, 2003 UNHCR Statistical Yearbook, data sheet for Liberia, accessed February 8, 2011, http://www.unhcr.org/41d2c182c.html.

17. Samwar S. Fallah, "Youth Unemployment Spells Trouble in Liberia," *Development and Cooperation International* 51 (July/August 2010), 294.

18. Author interview with Tokay Tomah, Philadelphia, Pennsylvania, July 2009.

19. United Nations Development Program, *Focus on Arms for Development* 3, no. 4 (March 2007), accessed February 8, 2011, http://www.lr.undp.org/Focus%20on%20AfD%20 -%20Vol%203%20NO.4.pdf.

20. Author interviews with Zaye Tete, Philadelphia, Pennsylvania, March 2007 and February 2011.

21. Robert Farris Thompson, "African Art in Motion," in *Art from Africa: Long Steps Never Broke a Back*, Pamela McClusky and Robert Farris Thompson (Princeton, NJ: Princeton University Press/Seattle Art Museum, 2002), 21–22.

22. Author interviews with Zaye Tete, Philadelphia, Pennsylvania, March 2007 and February 2011.

23. Pearl Primus, "African Dance," in *African Dance: An Artistic, Historical and Philosophical Inquiry*, ed. Kariamu Welsh Asante (Trenton, NJ: Africa World Press, 1996), 5, 3.

24. Author interviews with Zaye Tete, Philadelphia, Pennsylvania, March 2007 and February 2011.

25. Ilana Shapiro, "Extending the Framework for Inquiry: Theories of Change," in *Social Change and Conflict Transformation*, Berghof Handbook Dialogue Series, no. 5, eds. David Bloomfield, Martina Fischer, and Beatrix Schmelzle (Berlin, Germany: Berghof Research Center for Constructive Conflict Management, 2006), 3, accessed February 8, 2011, http://www.berghof-handbook.net/documents/publications/dialogue5_shapiro _comm.pdf.

26. Author interviews with Zaye Tete, Philadelphia, Pennsylvania, March 2007 and February 2011.

27. Pamela McCluskey and Robert Faris Thompson, *Art from Africa: Long Steps Never Broke a Back* (Princeton, NJ: Princeton Unversity Press/Seattle Art Museum, 2002), 33.

28. Author interviews with Zaye Tete, Philadelphia, Pennsylvania, March 2007 and February 2011.

29. Author interviews with Zaye Tete, Philadelphia, Pennsylvania, March 2007 and February 2011.

30. Leymah Gbowee, *Mighty Be Our Powers* (New York, NY: Beast Books, 2011), 127. Liberian peace and human rights activist Leymah Gbowee writes in her memoir about having "no idea where we were going next in our alliance, our quest" as she set out with a group of Liberian women, initially inside the country, envisioning a cessation of the civil war and full participation of women in Liberia's development. Clarity and articulation of demands came with time.

31. Ben Kiernan, *Genocide and Democracy in Cambodia*, Yale University Southeast Asia Studies Monograph Series, no. 41 (New Haven, CT: Yale University, 1993), 9.

32. For information about dance during the Khmer Rouge years, see Toni Shapiro-Phim, "Dance, Music and the Nature of Terror in Democratic Kampuchea," in *Annihilating Difference: The Anthropology of Genocide*, ed. Alexander Hinton (Berkeley, CA: University of California Press, 2002), 179–93.

33. Cambodian government officials estimated that the loss of life among artists was this high after putting out a call for surviving dancers, musicians, actors, playwrights, painters, and other artists to gather in the capital city shortly after the ouster of the Khmer Rouge. They wanted to see who had perished and what those who remained could do to re-create the country's artistic heritage. See interviews in Toni Shapiro, "Dance and the Spirit of Cambodia" (PhD diss., Cornell University, 1994).

34. See Shapiro, "Dance and the Spirit of Cambodia" (PhD diss., Cornell University, 1994) for material related to the re-creation of dance, music and theatrical repertoire following the genocide in Cambodia.

35. For more details about dance inside Site 2, see Toni Shapiro-Phim, "Mediating Cambodian History, the Sacred, and the Earth," in *Dance, Human Rights, and Social Justice: Dignity in Motion*, eds. Naomi Jackson and Toni Shapiro-Phim (Lanham, MD: Scarecrow Press, 2008), 304–22.

36. Ashley Thompson, "Oh Cambodia! Poems from the Border," *New Literary History: A Journal of Theory and Interpretation* 24, no. 3 (Summer 1993), 533.

37. There is evidence of a long history of dancers performing with fans decorated with the image of the national flag. See Shapiro-Phim, "Mediating Cambodian History" (Lanham, MD: Scarecrow Press, 2008), for more about the push by the KPNLF to retake some areas of western Cambodia.

38. Author interview with Moeun Srey Peau, Site 2 camp, Thailand, 1989.

39. Ang Choulean, "La communauté rurale khmère du point du vue du sacré," *Journal Asiatique* 278, nos. 1–2 (1990), 135–154.

40. Jaqueline Shea Murphy, *The People Have Never Stopped Dancing* (Minneapolis, MN: University of Minnesota Press, 2007), 29.

41. The Khmer Rouge Tribunal is now trying former Khmer Rouge leaders. See also Toni Shapiro-Phim, "Silences and the Staging of History" (unpublished paper presented at Cambodia, from Then to Now: Memory and Plural Identities in the Aftermath of Genocide Conference, Montreal, May 2011), on theatrical and danced representations of the Khmer Rouge era and its legacy; and Laura McGrew, "Reconciliation in Cambodia: Victims and Perpetrators Living Together, Apart" (PhD diss., Coventry University Center for the Study of Peace and Reconciliation, Coventry University, 2011), on the complexities of reconciliation in Cambodia in general.

42. Two decades earlier, in 1988, when Cambodia was embroiled in civil war and negotiations among the adversaries were underway, officials at the table referenced dance as a vehicle through which to help bring about, sanction, and/or mark the transformation of the conflict. Dr. Sina Than, an observer at one of the discussions in Jakarta, Indonesia, reported the following to me in a personal interview conducted that same year: Seeing a possible path to agreement, representatives from the four political and military factions with territory and power at stake stated that as a way to make effective an eventual peace treaty they would each bring a dance troupe to perform.

14/Cambodia *by* John Burt with Andrew Dilts

1. Boutros Boutros-Ghali, *An Agenda for Peace*, 2nd ed. (New York, NY: United Nations, 1995).

2. See generally Oliver Ramsbotham, Tom Woodhouse, and Hugh Miall, *Contemporary Conflict Resolution*, 3rd ed. (Cambridge, UK: Polity Press, 2011).

3. See e.g., Donna Crawford, *Conflict Resolution Education: Community & Juvenile Justice Settings* (Washington, DC: Diane Publishing, 1996), 63;

4. Ibid.

5. See e.g., Sam-Ang Sam, "Khmer Traditional Music Today" in *Cambodia Culture Since 1975: Homeland and Exile* eds. May M. Ebihara, Carol A. Mortland, and Judy Ledgerwood (Ithaca, NY: Cornell University Press, 1994).

6. It would be a worthwhile area of study to investigate factors that help arts-based conflict resolution and social change organizations thrive and those that hinder their success. That approach is beyond the scope of this current work.

7. See "Cambodian Living Arts," Marion Institute, http://www.marioninstitute.org/cambodian-living-arts.

8. See Cambodian Youth Arts Festival, http://cambodianartsfestival.org.

9. See Catherine Foster, "'Where Elephants Weep': A Cambodian Opera for Modern Times," *The New York Times*, April 26, 2007.

10. See e.g., Herbert C. Kelman, "Transforming the Relationship between Former Enemies: A Social-Psychological Analysis" in *After the Peace: Resistance and Reconciliation*, ed. R. L. Rothstein (Boulder, CO: Lynne Reinner, 1999).

11. See Ramsbotham, Woodhouse, Miall, *Contemporary Conflict Resolution*, chapter 16.

12. Luc Reychler, "Challenges of Peace Research" *International Journal of Peace Studies* 11, no. 1 (2006).

13. Interview of Arn Chorn-Pond by John Burt, Phnom Penh, 2011.

14. David Chandler, *The Tragedy of Cambodian History* (New Haven, CT: Yale University Press, 1993), 44–46, 87.

15. Daryl Collins and Helen Ross Grant, *Building Cambodia: New Khmer Architecture 1953–1970* (Bangkok, Thailand: Key Publisher, 2006), 36.

16. Anida Yoeu Ali, "The Legacy of Now" (unpublished document presented to Cambodian Living Arts Festival committee of curators, University of Chicago, 2011).

17. Cambodian Ministry of Agriculture, Forestry, and Fisheries, *Government Report 2006*.

18. John Paul Lederach, "Journey from Resolution to Transformative Peacebuilding" in *From the Ground Up: Mennonite Contributions to International Peacebuilding*, eds. Cynthia Sampson and John Paul Lederach (Oxford, UK: Oxford University Press, 2000).

19. Interview of Ieng Sithul by John Burt, Phnom Penh, 2011.

20. Ibid.

21. See Mike White, *Arts Development in Community Health: A Social Tonic* (Abingdon, UK: Radcliffe Publishing, 2009); Bowen Chung et al., "Using Community Arts Events to Enhance Collective Efficacy and Community Engagement to Address Depression in an African American Community" *American Journal of Public Health* 99, no. 2 (2009), 237.

22. UNICEF, *Basic Indicators: 2006*, accessed July 10, 2013, http://www.unicef.org/infoby country/cambodia.html.

23. Ibid.

24. Interview of Ieng Sithul by John Burt, Phnom Penh, 2011.

25. See e.g., Alison M. Rhodes and Rachel Schechter, "Fostering Resilience Among Youth in Inner City Community Arts Centers: The Case of the Artists Collective," *Education and Urban Society* (forthcoming).

26. See e.g., Sophie D. Walsh and Rivka Tuval-Mashiach, "Ethiopian Emerging Adult Immigrants in Israel Coping with Discrimination and Racism," *Youth and Society* 44, no. 1 (2011), 49.

27. See e.g., Julia Anwar McHenry, "Rural Empowerment through the Arts: The Role of Arts in Civic and Social Participation in the Mid West Region of Western Australia," *Journal of Rural Studies* 27, no. 3 (2011), 245.

28. See e.g., Jacqueline Siapno, "Dance and Martial Arts in Timor Leste: The Performance of Resilience in a Post conflict Environment," *Journal of Intercultural Studies* 33, no. 4 (2012), 427.

29. Interviews of students from Ieng Sithul's classes by John Burt, Phnom Penh, 2011.

30. Rama Mami, *Beyond Retribution: Seeking Justice in the Shadows of War* (Cambridge, UK: Polity Press, 2002).

31. David P. Chandler, *The Tragedy of Cambodian History: Politics, War, and Revolution since 1945* (New Haven, CT: Yale University Press, 1993), 138.

32. Interview with Teacher Vuthy by John Burt, Phnom Penh, 2011.

33. Sam-Ang Sam, "Religion and the Arts in Khmer Life: A Question of Continuity and Challenge," *Cambodian Visions & Paradigm Shifts* (blog), November 4, 2007, http://sophanse.blogspot.com/2007/11/religion-and-arts-in-khmer-life.html.

34. See notes 8, 9, 17, 21–24.

35. Interview with Ieng Sithul.

36. Interviews of Professor Michael Ungar, chair of the International Center for Resilience Research at Dalhousie University, Halifax, Canada, by John Burt, Phnom Penh, 2011.

37. Sophal Ear, *Cambodia: Negotiating the Peace Accords* (Princeton, NJ: Princeton University Press, 1994), 15.

15 / Cambodia *by* Carrie Herbert

1. Carrie Herbert, "Eye of a Storm" (unpublished song, 1997).

2. Robert J. Lifton and Eric Olson, "The Human Meaning of Total Disaster," *Psychiatry* 39 (1976), 1–17; Raija-LeenaPunamaki, "Factors Affecting the Mental Health of Palestinian Children Exposed to Political Violence," *International Journal of Mental Health* 18, no. 2 (1987), 63.

3. Robert J. Lifton, *Death in Life: Survivors of Hiroshima* (New York, NY: Random House, 1968); Mona Macksoud, "Assessing War Trauma in Children: A Case Study of Lebanese Children," *Journal of Refugee Studies* 5 (1992), 1–15.

4. Donald W. Winnicott, *Playing and Reality* (London, UK: Tavistiock Publications, 1971), 86–87.

5. Thomas S. Eliot, *Four Quartets* (New York, NY: Harcourt, Brace and Company, 1943), 119.

6. Ernesto Spinelli, *The Interpreted World: An Introduction to Phenomenological Psychology* (London, UK: Sage, 2005), 173.

7. Carl R. Rogers, *On Becoming a Person* (London, UK: Constable, 1961), 285.

8. Orah T. Krug, James Bugental, and Irvin Yalom, "Two Masters of Existential Therapy Cultivate Presence in the Therapeutic Encounter," *Journal of Humanistic Psychology* 49 (July 2009), 329–54.

9. Ernesto Spinelli, *The Interpreted World*, 124.

10. Anna Halprin, Tamalpa Institute, 2001, cited in Martha Eddy, "Somatic Practices and Dance: Global Influences," *Dance Research Journal* 34, no. 2 (2002), 46–62.

11. Bobby G. Bodenhamer and L. Michael Hall, "Embodying Negative Emotions: Guess Where a Stutterer Embodies His or Her Emotion?," Mastering Blocking & Stuttering: A Cognitive Approach to Achieving Fluency, accessed October 10, 2011, http://www.masteringstuttering.com/articles/embodying-negative-emotions-guess-where-a-stutterer-embodies-his-or-her-emotion/.

12. Susan Kleinman, *Use of Self as a Dance Movement Therapist: Our Greatest Therapeutic Tool.* Proceedings of the American Dance Therapy Association 39th Annual Conference, Columbia, Maryland, 2004.

13. Michael Shank and Lisa Schirch, "Strategic Arts-Based Peacebuilding," *Peace and Change* 33, no. 2 (April 2008), 235–36.

14. Julia Wood, *Spinning the Symbolic Web: Human Communication as Symbolic Interaction* (Norwood, NJ: Ablex Publishing Corporation, 1992), 86.

15. Stephen K. Levine, *Trauma, Tragedy, Therapy: The Arts and Human Suffering* (London, UK: Jessica Kingsley, 2009), 18.

16. LICADHO (Cambodian League for the Promotion and Defense of Human Rights), "Nightmare at Dey Krahorm: Forced Eviction in the Heart of Phnom Penh," LICADHO, February 8, 2009, accessed October 10, 2011, http://www.licadho-cambodia.org/articles/20090208/85/index.html.

17. Antoine D. Saint-Exupery, *Wind, Sand and Stars* (London, UK: Penguin, 1995), 110.

18. Virginia Satir, "The Therapist Story," *Journal of Psychotherapy & The Family* 3, no. 1 (1987), 25.

19. Carl G. Jung, *Modern Man in Search of a Soul* (London, UK: Routledge and Kegan Paul, 1961), 10.

16/Finding Coherence I *by* Mark McCrea

1. Ferne Caulker, "African Dance: Divine Motion," in *The Dance Experience*, eds. Myron Nadel and Mark Raymond Strauss (Hightstown, NJ: Princeton Book Company, 2003), 17–28

2. Ibid.

3. Sharon Chaiklin, "We Dance from the Moment Our Feet Touch the Earth," in *The Art and Science of Dance/Movement Therapy*, eds. Sharon Chaiklin and Hilda Wengrower (New York, NY: Routledge, 2009), 3–11.

4. Havelock Ellis, *The Dance of Life* (Cambridge, UK: Houghton Mifflin, 1923), 36.

5. Fran Levy, *Dance Movement Therapy, A Healing Art* (Reston, VA: National Dance Association, 2005), 1.

6. Brenda Allen, "Racial Harassment in the Workplace," in *Destructive Organizational Communication: Processes, Consequences, and Constructive Ways of Organizing*, eds. Pamela Lutgen-Sandvik and Beverly Davenport-Sypher (London, UK: Routledge, 2009), 164–84.

7. Workplace Bullying Institute, "Results of the 2010 and 2007 WBI U.S. Workplace Bullying Survey," Workplace Bullying Institute, accessed July 16, 2013, http://www.workplacebullying.org/wbiresearch/2010-wbi-national-survey.

8. Stale Einarsen, "The Nature and Causes of Bullying at Work," *International Journal of Manpower* 20 (1999), 22–24.

9. Ibid., 23.

10. Noreen Tehrani, "A Source of Chronic Post-traumatic Stress?," *British Journal of Guidance & Counselling* 32 (2004), 357–66.

11. Ragnar Olafsson and Hanna Johannsdottir, "Coping with Bullying in the Workplace: The Effect of Gender, Age and Type of Bullying," *British Journal of Guidance & Counselling* 32 (2004), 319–33.

12. Ronald Kessler, Kristin Mickelson, K. D. Williams, and David Williams, "The Prevalence, Distribution, and Mental Health Correlates of Perceived Discrimination in the United States," *Journal of Health and Social Behaviour* 40, no. 3 (1999), 208–30.

13. Janet Swim, Lauri Hyers, Melissa Ferguson, and Laurie Cohen, "Everyday Sexism: Evidence for Its Incidence, Nature and Psychological Impact from Three Diary Studies," *Journal of Social Issues* 57, no. 4 (2001), 31–53.

14. Peter Barnes and Owen Richard, "Perceived Racist Discrimination, Coping, Stress, and Life Satisfaction," *Journal of Multicultural Counseling and Development* 33 (2005), 48–61.

15. Milton Rokeach, *The Nature of Human Values* (New York, NY: Free Press, 1973), 6–7.

16. Michelle LeBaron, *Bridging Cultural Conflict* (San Francisco, CA: Jossey-Bass, 2003), 274–75.

17. Galen Bodenhausen, Andrew Todd, and Jennifer Richeson, "Controlling Prejudice and Stereotyping: Antecedents, Mechanisms and Contexts," in *Handbook of Prejudice, Stereotyping, and Discrimination*, ed. Todd Nelson (New York, NY: Psychology Press, 2009), 111–135.

18. Heesoon Jun, *Social Justice, Multicultural Counselling, and Practice* (Los Angeles, CA: Sage, 2010), 26–58.

19. Daniel Bar-Tal and Eran Halperin, "Socio-Psychological Barriers to Conflict Resolution," in *Intergroup Conflicts and Their Resolution: A Social Psychological Perspective*, ed. Daniel Bar-Tal (New York, NY: Psychology Press, 2011), 222–26.

20. Ibid.

21. Ziva Kunda, "The Case for Motivated Reasoning," *Psychological Bulletin* 108 (1990), 480–98.

22. Ho-Won Jeong, *Understanding Conflict and Conflict Analysis* (Los Angeles: Sage, 2008), 12.

23. John Lederach, *Building Peace: Sustainable Reconciliation in Divided Societies* (Washington, DC: United States Institute of Peace Press, 1997), 15.

24. Jon Kabat-Zinn, "Mindfulness-Based Interventions in Context: Past, Present, and Future," *Clinical Psychology: Science and Practice* 10 (2003), 144–56.

25. Ibid.

26. Ellen Langer, "Mindful Learning," *Current Directions in Psychological Science* 9, no. 6 (2000), 220–23.

27. Leonard Riskin, "Mindfulness: Foundational Training for Dispute Resolution," *Journal of Legal Education* 54, no. 1 (March 2004), 79–90.

28. Judith Hanna, *Dancing for Health* (New York, NY: Rowan & Littlefield, 2006), 35.

29. Anna Olvera, "Cultural Dance and Health: A Review of the Literature," *American Journal of Health Education* 39, no. 6 (2008), 353–59.

30. Ibid.

31. Wolfgang Jilek, "Therapeutic Use of Altered States of Consciousness in Contemporary North American Indian Dance Ceremonials," in *Altered States of Consciousness and Mental Health: A Cross-Cultural Perspective*, vol. 12, ed. Colleen Ward (Newbury Park, CA: Sage, 1989). 167–85. Howaida El Guindy and Claire Schmais, "The Zar: An Ancient Dance of Healing," *American Journal of Dance Therapy* 16 (1994), 111–17.

32. Ibid., 27, 31.

33. Richard Vetter, Susan Myllykangas, Laura Donoffio, and Alice Foose, "Creative Movement as a Stress Reduction Intervention for Caregivers," *Journal of Physical Education, Recreation & Dance* 82, no. 2 (2011), 35–38.

34. Ibid.

35. Kristina Stanton-Jones, *Dance Movement Therapy in Psychiatry* (London, UK: Tavistock and Routledge, 1992), 10.

36. Laurice Nemetz, "Moving with Meaning: The Historical Progression of Dance/Movement Therapy," in *Creative Arts Therapies Manual*, ed. Stephanie Brooke (Springfield, IL: Charles C. Thomas, 2006), 95–109.

37. Ibid., 27.

38. Ibid., 28.

39. Raymond Birdwhistell, *Kinesics and Context: Essays on Body Motion Communication* (Philadelphia, PA: University of Pennsylvania Press, 1970), 192.

40. Ibid.

41. Holly Kawakami, "Kinetic Facilitation Techniques for Promoting Relationships among Members of Diverse Groups," in *Facilitating Group Communication in Context: Innovations and Applications with Natural Groups*, ed. Lawrence Frey (Cresskill, NJ: Hampton Press, 2006), 93–121.

42. Ibid.

43. Ralph La Forge, "Aligning Mind and Body: Exploring the Disciplines of Mindful Exercise," *ACM's Health & Fitness Journal* 9, no. 5 (2005), 7–14.

44. Ralph La Forge, "Exercise-Associated Mood Alterations: A Review of Interactive Neurobiologic Mechanisms," *Medicine, Exercise, Nutrition, and Health* 4 (1995), 17–32.

45. Ronnie Lidor, "Learning Strategies and the Enhancement of Self-Paced Motor Tasks: Theoretical and Practical Implications," *Sports Psychology: Linking Theory and Practice*, eds. Ronnie Lidor and Michael Bar-Eli (Morgantown, WV: Fitness Information Technology, 1999), 109–32.

46. Ibid., 43.

47. Yael Netz and Ronnie Lidor, "Mood Alterations in Mindful Versus Aerobic Exercise Modes," *The Journal of Psychology* 137, no. 5 (2003), 405–19.

48. Ibid., 43.

49. Tahira Probst, David Gold, and Joannah Caborn, "A Preliminary Evaluation of SOLVE: Addressing Psychosocial Problems at Work," *Journal of Occupational Health Psychology* 13, no. 1 (2008), 32–42.

50. Jasper Smits and Michael Otto, *Exercise for Mood and Anxiety Disorders: Therapist Guide* (Oxford, UK: Oxford University Press, 2009), 13.

51. Ibid., 55–60.

52. Ibid.

53. Brad Walker, *The Anatomy of Stretching* (Berkeley, CA: North Atlantic Books, 2007), 33.

54. Ibid.

55. Ibid., 43–47.

56. Ibid., 43.

57. Ibid., 28.

58. Gail Elliot, *Cross-Cultural Awareness in an Aging Society: Effective Strategies for Communication and Caring*, 3rd ed. (Toronto, Canada: McMaster University, 2001), 4–5.

59. Paulina Ruf, "Understanding Elder Abuse in Minority Populations," in *Elder Abuse: A Public Health Perspective*, eds. Randal Summers and Allan Hoffman (Washington DC: American Public Health Association, 2006), 51–62.

60. Ruth Baer and Jennifer Krietemeyer, "Overview of Mindfulness and Acceptance-Based Treatment Approaches," in *Mindfulness-Based Treatment Approaches: Clinician's Guide to Evidence and Applications*, ed. Ruth Baer (New York, NY: Elsevier, 2006), 3–27.

61. Randall Epstein, "Mindful Practice," *Journal of the American Medical Association* 282, no. 9 (1999), 833–97.

62. Maureen Duffy and Len Sperry, "Workplace Mobbing: Individual and Family Health Consequences," *The Family Journal: Counseling and Therapy for Couples and Families* 15 (2007), 398–404.

63. David Jones, "Getting Even for Interpersonal Mistreatment in the Workplace: Triggers of Revenge Motives and Behavior," in *Insidious Workplace Behavior*, ed. Jerald Greenberg (New York, NY: Routledge. 2010), 101–47.

17 / Finding Coherence II *by* Clemens Lang

1. Richard D. Lewis, *When Cultures Collide: Managing Successfully across Cultures* (London, UK: Nicholas Brealey Publishing, 2000), 49.

2. Richard D. Lewis, *When Cultures Collide: Leading across Cultures* (Boston, MA: Nicholas Brealey, 1996).

3. Lewis, *When Cultures Collide: Managing Successfully across Cultures,* 15.

4. Susan Podziba, "The Human Side of Complex Public Policy Mediation," *Negotiation Journal* 19, no. 4 (Hoboken, NJ: Wiley, 2003), 289.

5. Michelle LeBaron, *Bridging Troubled Waters: Conflict Resolution from the Heart* (San Francisco, CA: Jossey-Bass, 2002), 52.

6. Ibid.

7. Podziba, "The Human Side of Complex Public Policy Mediation."

8. Lewis, *When Cultures Collide: Managing Successfully across Cultures,* 5.

9. P. Watzlawick, J. B. Beavin, and D. D. Jackson, *Menschliche Kommunikation* (Bern, Switzerland: Hans Huber, 1969), English: *Pragmatics of Human Communication* (New York, NY: W. W. Norton, 1967).

10. Michelle LeBaron, "Cross-Cultural Communication," Beyond Intractability, 2003, accessed October 15, 2011, http://www.beyondintractability.org/essay/cross-cultural _communication/?nid=1188.

11. Lewis, *When Cultures Collide: Managing Successfully across Cultures,* 37.

12. LeBaron, "Cross-Cultural Communication."

13. United Nations, "Culture of Peace" program, UNESCO, accessed October 16, 2011, http://www3.unesco.org/iycp > Information Exchange > Projects/Resources.

14. The Art Miles Mural Project, accessed October 16, 2011, http://www.artmiles.org/.

15. Edward T. Hall, *Beyond Culture* (Garden City, NY: Basic Books, 1976).

16. Joseph Luft, *Of Human Interaction* (Palo Alto, CA: National Press Books, 1969).

17. Michele Baldwin and Virginia Satir, *Familientherapie in Aktion. Die Konzepte von Virginia Satir in Theorie und Praxis* (Paderborn, Germany: Junfermann Verlag, 1999).

18. Regine Brick and Klaus-Peter Horn, *Organisationsaufstellung und systemisches Coaching* (Offenbach, Germany: Verlag, 2003).

19. Bert Hellinger, *Anerkennen, was ist* (Munich, Germany: Kösel-Verlag GmbH & Co., 1996).

20. LeBaron, *Bridging Troubled Waters,* 82–83.

21. Ibid., 88–89.

22. The film mentioned here is "Les Choristes" from Christophe Barratier, 2006.

23. See "The Heroic Journey of Social Change," adapted from Louise Diamond, by Mark Turpin, accessed July 1, 2013, http://www.kessels-smit.com/files/The_Heroic_Journey_of_Social _Change.pdf.

24. 5Rhythms website, www.gabrielleroth.com; and *Wikipedia,* s.v. "5Rhythms," last modified March 22, 2013, http://en.wikipedia.org/wiki/5Rhythms.

25. Noel Tshibangu, "Eine Richtschnur entlang der Beziehungsnähte zwischen Individuen und Gemeinschaft," *Perspektive Mediation* 3 (2008).

Conclusion—Carrie MacLeod

1. Paolo Knill, "Foundations for a Theory of Practice," in *Principles and Practice of Expressive Arts Therapy*, eds. Paolo J. Knill, Ellen G. Levine, and Stephen K. Levine (London, UK: Jessica Kingsley Publishers, 2005), 138.

2. Stephen K. Levine, "Art Opens to the World: Expressive Arts and Social Action," in *Art in Action*, eds. Ellen G. Levine and Stephen Levine (London, UK: Jessica Kingsley Publishers, 2011), 29.

Index